D0225889

THE ENGLISH IN WEST AFRICA
1681–1683

The Local Correspondence of the
Royal African Company of England, 1681–1699
Part 1

FONTES HISTORIAE AFRICANAE, NEW SERIES
SOURCES OF AFRICAN HISTORY
1

THE ENGLISH IN WEST AFRICA
1681–1683

The Local Correspondence of the
Royal African Company of England
1681–1699
Part 1

edited by
Robin Law

Published for THE BRITISH ACADEMY
by OXFORD UNIVERSITY PRESS

Oxford University Press, Great Clarendon Street, Oxford OX2 6DP

Oxford New York
Athens Auckland Bangkok Bogota Bombay
Buenos Aires Calcutta Cape Town Dar es Salaam
Delhi Florence Hong Kong Istanbul Karachi
Kuala Lumpar Madras Madrid Melbourne
Mexico City Nairobi Paris Singapore
Taipei Tokyo Toronto Warsaw

and associated companies in
Berlin Ibadan

British Library Cataloguing in Publication Data
Data available

ISBN 0–19–726176–0

Typeset by Books Unlimited (Nottm) NG19 7QZ
Printed in Great Britain
on acid-free paper by
Creative Print and Design (Wales),
Ebbw Vale

Contents

For S.O. Biobaku,
under whose guidance I was introduced to the study of African history, and to
the central importance of the critical study of source material

Introduction

The Royal African Company (RAC) of England was chartered in 1672, with a legal monopoly of English trade with West Africa.[1] Its local headquarters in West Africa was at Cape Coast (or, in the original form of the name, Cabo Corso) Castle on the Gold Coast (modern Ghana), and it maintained forts or factories not only on the Gold Coast itself, but also at the River Gambia and in Sierra Leone to the west, and on the 'Slave Coast' (the modern Republic of Bénin) and at Benin (in modern Nigeria) to the east. Its trade was mainly in gold and slaves, though other commodities such as ivory, wax and dyewoods were also purchased. The company lost its legal monopoly of the African trade in 1698, and thereafter went into decline, effectively ceasing to operate as a trading concern in the 1720s, although it continued to manage the English possessions on the coast of West Africa until it was replaced by a new regulated company (i.e. one open to all traders), the Company of Merchants Trading to Africa, in 1752.

The main body of the surviving records of the RAC is preserved in the Public Record Office (PRO) in London.[2] For the purposes of the Company's activities along the West African coast (and hence also of indigenous West African history), the most informative records of the Company are the series of Letter Books containing correspondence received from its agents in West Africa. Most of this correspondence, in fact, was received from the Company's West African headquarters at Cape Coast, since most of the other factories of the Company on the West African coast did not usually correspond directly with London. As preserved in the PRO, however, this correspondence is disappointing for the historian. The letters received were not recorded in their full original texts, but only in the form of extracts and summaries, often very brief. In consequence, as the RAC's principal historian has observed, these documents characteristically have a somewhat 'telegrammatic character', in which brevity often truncates the information and even obscures the meaning, and 'reduces considerably the value of the records'.[3]

The deficiencies of the PRO material, however, turn out to be offset by the existence of significant bodies of documentation of the RAC's activities which, having passed into private hands, are preserved in other archives. For the late

[1] See esp. Davies 1957.
[2] Classified in the series T70.
[3] Davies 1957, 374. For examples, see the correspondence relating to the RAC's Slave Coast factories published in Law 1990a.

seventeenth century, in particular, an important series of documents is preserved in the collection of Richard Rawlinson (1690–1755), held in the Bodleian Library at Oxford. The importance of these documents is such as to warrant publication in their entirety; and the British Academy has undertaken this project, of which the present volume represents the first instalment.

The Rawlinson corpus

The material in question comprises correspondence of the RAC relating to the last two decades of the seventeenth century.[4] It is preserved in three bound volumes (classified as Rawlinson C.745, 746 and 747), containing a total of around 1,300 folios or 2,600 pages (though several of these are blank). The material appears to comprise 34 separate letter books, each covering a brief period (usually, though not invariably, six months), and including a total of over 3,800 letters (the precise number depending upon whether particular documents are treated as separate items, or as inclosures in others). Some of the material, however, is reproduced twice — the transmission of letters and documents in duplicate being standard practice, as a hedge against the considerable danger of loss or delay in transit between Africa and England. Seven of the 34 letter books thus turn out to be duplicates. The total of original material is therefore 27 letter books, and rather more than 3,000 letters (though many of these are very short); the total length of text is estimated at around 450,000 words. The letter books have been bound together haphazardly, without much regard for chronological order; the three bound volumes, therefore, do not represent any logical grouping or sub-division of the material.

   The letter books extend from January 1681 to February 1699, but they do not cover this period altogether continuously; there are gaps between November 1683 and January 1686 and between April 1688 and April 1691; and a briefer hiatus from April 1696 to April 1697. Some of the letter books (including the first) carry the title 'Copies of Letters sent by the out-factors of the Royal African Company of England to the Chief Agents at Cape Coast Castle'. For the most part that is an accurate indication of their contents, consisting of letters received in Cape Coast from other factories on the West African coast. Overwhelmingly, these letters come from other RAC factories on the Gold Coast itself, but there are also a number from the factories of Offra and Whydah on the Slave Coast, and a few (three in 1686–7) from that at James Island on the Gambia. In addition to correspondence from the RAC's own factories, however, there are some letters received from English inter-lopers (i.e. individuals not connected with the RAC, and trading in breach of its legal monopoly) or foreigners established on the coast: in particular, around 49

---

[4] See further Law 1993.

letters from the headquarters of the Dutch West India Company at Elmina. There is also a considerable number of letters received from ships' captains (or RAC factors operating as supercargoes on ships). These include, of course, letters written from places other than those where the Company had factories, their geographical scope extending from Cape Mesurado (in Liberia) in the west to Cape Lopez (in Gabon) in the east, as well as some written from the offshore islands of São Tomé and Principe, by captains en route for the Americas. There is also a small group of letters in 1686–7, received from Barbados in the West Indies; some of these are from ships' captains, but others from the RAC's local resident agents on the island.

It should be stressed that this correspondence is entirely separate from the contemporary series of RAC letter books preserved in the PRO, which appear to record only letters received by the Company's parent office in London, whether from Cape Coast Castle or (less commonly) from other factories on the West African coast. There is only very occasional overlap, due to a letter sent to London being also copied to Cape Coast, and therefore registered in both places — though of course in several other cases letters sent to Cape Coast and London may cover similar ground. Even where there is some degree of overlap in contents, the value of the Rawlinson material is not thereby diminished, since the latter gives the full original texts of the letters, whereas that in the PRO, as already noted, offers normally only brief extracts and summaries. For most purposes the Rawlinson correspondence supersedes the PRO material, whose value is now principally to supplement — and in particular, to fill the chronological gaps in — the former.

Attention was first drawn to the Rawlinson material, and its potential value for the study of West African history, by David Henige in the early 1970s.[5] Henige compiled a 'Guide' to the contents of the corpus, identifying the dates, authors and places of writing of all the letters included, which although not formally published was deposited at major research libraries in the UK, USA, and Ghana in West Africa.[6] A partial transcription of some of the (relatively few) documents in the corpus which relate to the Slave Coast was prepared in the 1970s by Albert van Dantzig, although again not formally published;[7] and a fuller edition of the Slave Coast material was published more recently by myself.[8] The great bulk of the documents, however, has hitherto remained unpublished, and hence only partially within the public domain.[9]

---

[5] Esp. Henige 1972a.

[6] Henige 1972b.

[7] Van Dantzig 1976; cf. also Van Dantzig 1984, which summarizes the contents of these documents.

[8] Law 1992. For documents from 1681–3, this is now superseded by the transcription in the present volume.

[9] Microfilm copies of the documents have been supplied by the Bodleian Library to other libraries, as well as to individual scholars. The nature of the documents, however, including their reader-unfriendly arrangement (as explained later in this Introduction) as well as problems of legibility, make them ponderous to use even for specialist researchers, and effectively inaccessible to others.

The value of this material, especially by comparison with the longer-known RAC material preserved in the PRO, would be difficult to exaggerate. It is not too much to say that any work undertaken on English trade with West Africa, or on the history of African societies on the Gold and Slave Coasts, in the seventeenth century, which did not take account of it is thereby inadequate, and urgently due for supersession if not already superseded.[10] Although the period covered by the Rawlinson material is brief (under 20 years), it was a period of great historical significance, when the volume of European slave purchases was increasing rapidly and (arguably, in consequence) indigenous African societies were undergoing radical change, with a widespread disintegration of order and the rise of new military states, such as Akwamu.

Primarily, of course, the Rawlinson correspondence documents the activities of the RAC itself. By comparison with other contemporary material, its principal contribution, beyond a much greater density of detail, lies in its documentation of the local West African end of the trade, including in particular the lateral movement of gold, slaves and other commodities along the coast, to be bulked up at Cape Coast Castle or embarked on ships elsewhere. One particular aspect of this local feeder traffic is the supply of foodstuffs for the provisioning of slave ships — a subject which (since it offers a window on the links between overseas trade and the West African domestic economy) is overdue for detailed research, which might take as its basis the massive documentation which the Rawlinson corpus affords. Likewise, this correspondence reveals, perhaps more clearly than any other body of material, the dependence of European enterprise in West Africa, for coastwise communication as well as for trade, on African canoes and canoemen.[11] More generally, it illustrates the critical role in the activities of the RAC played by its African employees and associates — 'Captain Quow', 'Captain Hansico' etc. — in carrying messages, mediating in disputes, and by implication in determining policy.[12]

The RAC's factories also regularly reported on the operations of other traders operating competition with the Company. In particular, they offer considerable detailed information on the operations of English 'interlopers', trading in competition with the Company and in defiance of its monopoly rights. This 'interloping' trade is a recognised difficulty in any attempt to quantify English trade with Africa since, being illegal (until 1698), it did not generate records of its own comparable to those of the RAC;[13] it may be suggested that a close study of the Rawlinson

[10] The early studies of the RAC (Davies 1957) and of the history of the Gold Coast (Daaku 1970) and the Slave Coast (Akinjogbin 1967) made no use of the Rawlinson material. It has, however, been drawn upon in more recent studies of the Gold Coast (Kea 1982) and the Slave Coast (Law 1991a).

[11] For some discussion, cf. Law 1989.

[12] The role of such Africans in European enterprise was noted, on the basis of other evidence, by Daaku 1970, ch.5; but the Rawlinson corpus offers much more detailed, day-to-day documentation.

[13] For a recent discussion, cf. Inikori 1992, 681–4.

correspondence would provide a more secure basis for estimating its importance. The factories also reported on the trade of foreign competitors, and this correspondence thus constitutes a potential source for Dutch, Portuguese, French, Brandenburg and Danish, as well as English trade. This may be particularly valuable for the Portuguese and French trades, since relatively little documentation of these appears to be preserved in their own national archives for the decades before 1700.

The Rawlinson correspondence also provides information on, and sometimes identifies individually, the principal African traders and rulers who supplied goods to the RAC's factories and ships, and records their sometimes shifting policies towards the trade. Beyond this, it also contains incidental information on events and more general conditions within African societies, which were reported insofar as they materially affected the state of trade. Wars among African states, for example, might threaten the security of the Company's factories or disrupt the delivery of gold and slaves to the coast; but also might yield supplies of captives which were available for sale to Europeans. The Rawlinson corpus is thus an important source for indigenous West African history, as well as for African involvement in the European trade.

This is not to deny that the material in the Rawlinson corpus suffers from certain limitations — even beyond the obvious point that it represents the perspective of foreigners (albeit, in the case of locally resident factors, often relatively well-informed ones), whose understanding of the African societies upon which they reported must be presumed to have been in some degree distorted and partial. One self-evident limitation in its geographical coverage is that, since it comprises correspondence received in the RAC's headquarters at Cape Coast Castle, it does not include any reports emanating from Cape Coast itself; and this deficiency is only partly remedied by the correspondence from Cape Coast to London preserved in the PRO, given the limitations of the latter delineated earlier. There is also no correspondence from the RAC's establishments at the Gambia (with the minor exception noted above), in Sierra Leone (at Bunce Island and York Island), or Benin — though it should be remembered that these other areas were of much less importance in the Company's trade than the Gold and Slave Coasts. The documents themselves, although preserved in their full texts, present difficulties of understanding, arising not only from difficulties of transcription and obscurities of spelling and syntax, but also from the fact that they were often responding to enquiries in letters from Cape Coast which are themselves not preserved, so that particular matters are referred to in abbreviated terms which sometimes leave their precise nature unclear. Also, inclosures referred to in the letters are for the most part (though with some exceptions) not transcribed into the text.

The material in the Rawlinson corpus should, of course, be considered in combination with other available material, including most obviously other surviving correspondence of the RAC itself, preserved in the PRO; the RAC correspondence in the PRO relating specifically to its factories on the Slave Coast can be consulted in a published transcription.[14] In addition, there are the records of other European nations involved in the African trade. Most valuable are those of the Dutch West India Company, selections from which have been published in English translation.[15] Records of the Brandenburger African Company, a much less important participant in the African trade, have also been published, likewise in English translation.[16] Although there are no comparable publications of Danish, French or Portuguese documents, valuable monographs on the African trade of all these three nations are available.[17] There are also several published accounts by individual European traders who visited West Africa during this period, of which the most substantial are those of Jean Barbot, a French trader who made two voyages to West Africa between 1678–82;[18] and Willem Bosman, a factor of the Dutch West India Company in the 1690s.[19]

The present volume

The ultimate intention is to publish the entire Rawlinson corpus of documents, in three or possibly four volumes.[20] The present volume presents the material from the first continuous segment of time covered by the collection, which is included in eight separate successive letter books containing correspondence received in Cape Coast between 27 January 1681 and 11 November 1683. At the beginning of 1681, the RAC seems to have possessed a total of six establishments on the Gold and Slave Coasts: besides its headquarters at Cape Coast Castle, these were, on the Gold Coast itself (east of Cape Coast) at Anashan, Anomabu (Charles Fort), Egya, and Accra (James Fort); and at Offra on the Slave Coast. During the period 1681–3, additional factories were established at Sekondi and Komenda to the west of Cape Coast; at Winneba (briefly, in 1681), between Egya and Accra; and at Whydah on the Slave Coast. Besides correspondence from these nine factories (other than Cape Coast), there are a large number of letters received from ships trading along the coast. These serve to extend the geographical coverage of the corpus, since they include reports from places on the Gold Coast where the RAC did not currently maintain any factories — in particular, a number from the Adangme ('Allampo')

---

[14] Law 1990a.

[15] Van Dantzig 1978; cf. also Van Dantzig 1980.

[16] Jones 1985.

[17] See (respectively) Nørregård 1966; Ly 1958; Verger 1968.

[18] Barbot's account exists both in a French manuscript version (written in 1688) and an English version published posthumously in 1732; see the modern critical edition (Barbot 1992), which is cited in this work.

[19] Bosman 1705.

[20] In addition to the RAC correspondence of 1681-99, one of the Rawlinson volumes (C.747) also includes Minutes of the RAC Council at the Gambia for 1722-3 and 1729–30; since this material has no organic connexion with the rest of the corpus, it is not proposed to include it in the publication.

country east of Accra. The letters from the Gold and Slave Coasts also include occasional references to trade on the coast further east, reporting ships' arrivals from or departures for Benin, Calabar (or more vaguely, 'the Bight') and Angola. There is also one unique (and invaluable) account of a voyage to the River Gabon, and one letter from a ship bound for Madagascar (though it did not, in the event, get there).[21]

Besides the original texts, this edition also includes annotation, intended to clarify obscurities, and to direct attention to relevant published accounts and comparative material in other original sources, and (critically) to provide cross-references among documents within the Rawlinson corpus itself. A conscious decision has been made to keep such annotation within modest proportions, principally in order to avoid inflating the size of what is already a large book; but in addition, since the primary purpose of this publication is to make this material accessible to other scholars, it did not seem sensible to attempt to anticipate the detailed research for which they will hopefully utilize it. Among the other primary sources cited in the annotation, the most important for comparative purposes is Jean Barbot, whose second voyage to West Africa (in 1681/2) fell within this period; indeed, Barbot's passage along the coast is noted in the RAC correspondence.[22] A second (but less substantial) available contemporary account, by the Brandenburger Otto Friedrich von der Groeben, relates to a voyage to West Africa in 1682/3;[23] this Brandenburger expedition is also noted in the RAC correspondence, though Groeben is not mentioned by name.[24]

Beyond the evidence which it provides on European trade, including African involvement in it, the RAC correspondence of this period provides invaluable documentation of significant political developments among indigenous West African societies. In particular, the correspondence from Sekondi on the western Gold Coast documents the rise of the new power of Adom, which had lately established its control over this coastal port; while that from Accra in the east provides more detailed information on the conquests of the rising power of Akwamu. Correspondence from Anomabu, in the central Gold Coast, contains more fragmentary and tantalizing allusions to disturbances within and around the Fante state, including the military aggressions of Abora, apparently in the early stages of its rise to become the capital of Fante.

---

[21] Respectively nos 639 and 640 in this collection.
[22] Barbot is mentioned by name in two reports early in 1682: see nos 54 ('Monsieur Bardoe') and 425 ('Monsieur Barboate').
[23] Published in 1694; cited in this work from the English translation by Adam Jones (Groeben 1985).
[24] See esp. nos 549–50.

The treatment of the text

The presentation of these documents in this volume does not seek to reproduce exactly the original text from which they are taken. Most systematically, the sequence of documents has been radically rearranged. In the Rawlinson volumes, as noted earlier, the various letter books are bound together with little regard for their chronological order; but simply rearranging the letter books in their correct sequence did not seem an adequate means of rendering the corpus readily accessible and intelligible to potential users. The reason for this is that, in the original, within each letter book, the letters are entered simply according to the date of their receipt in Cape Coast Castle, without any regard to geographical provenance, so that letters received from the different 'outforts' are jumbled together without order. Moreover, owing to the vagaries of delivery (with some letters subject to delay in transit) the sequence in which letters even from any single place were received in Cape Coast did not necessarily correspond to that in which they were written or dispatched. For anybody interested in tracing conditions or events at one particular place on the African coast, therefore, the arrangement of the material in the original is evidently unhelpful, since it is impossible to predict precisely where in the sequence relevant documents may be found. To meet this need, the letters have been separated out according to provenance. For each of the RAC's factories, all the letters written from it over the whole period 1681–3 are grouped together, and in the order of their composition rather than of their receipt at Cape Coast; and the collected correspondence of the various factories is presented in geographical sequence, from west to east along the coast.

A different approach has evidently to be adopted in the cases of those correspondents who were mobile rather than static, namely the ships' captains (or RAC factors serving on board ships) moving along the coast. In these cases, it has seemed sensible to keep all the letters from any one ship together, rather than to break them up and allocate them to the geographical locations at which they were written. This has the disadvantage of sometimes separating letters by the local RAC factor and a visiting ship's captain which refer to the same events, and in some cases were even dispatched simultaneously, in a single mail packet; but cross-references have been included in the annotation, to facilitate the making of the relevant connections among documents.

As regards the actual texts, the strategy adopted represents a compromise between the contradictory demands of fidelity to the original, effective accessibility to potential readership, and minimizing overall length. The texts are reproduced in full, with the omission only of the purely formulaic beginnings and endings ('May it please your Worship', 'This is what offers', 'Your most humble servant' etc.) which add no substantive content. The spelling of the original, although often idiosyncratic and inconsistent as between different correspondents, has generally been retained; the only concession to the cause of more immediate intelligibility is the expansion of the conventional contractions commonly employed in the text (such as 'ye' for 'the', 'Compa.' for 'Company'). As a countervailing (albeit minor) contribution to reducing the length of the text, numbers are generally given as numerals rather than spelled out (usage in this matter in the original being inconsistent, sometimes even as between different transcriptions of the same document).

As regards punctuation and capitalization, it is admitted after some editorial soul-searching,[25] it has been decided not to attempt an exact reproduction. In the original text, it should be stressed, no consistent rules of punctuation or capitalization are applied; inconsistencies occurring, again, even between duplicate copies of a single document. As a guide to intended meaning, the usage of the original texts is often unhelpful and sometimes, by modern conventions, positively misleading. It has therefore been decided to ignore the punctuation and capitalization of the original, where it seemed likely to obstruct comprehension, and to revise these details in the direction of modern usage. While this is done without apology, in the interests of greater accessibility, its implications should be recognised. Although the sequence of words is (in intention, errors excepted) accurately reproduced from the original text, the grammatical structure is largely imputed to it, and in particular cases may be regarded as speculative or debatable. What is offered here, therefore, is a reading (in the sense of an interpretation) of the text, which at points may be capable of sustaining alternative readings. Readers should not feel constrained from envisaging other constructions of the grammar of these documents, if unhappy with those presented here; though, for the reasons already given, it should not be assumed that consultation of the original texts would necessarily resolve the issue.

All editorial matter inserted into the text is distinguished by being included within square brackets. This includes notes of occasional places where the reading of the text is uncertain, and also cases where the spelling of the original seemed likely to cause confusion, or where words necessary to the sense are omitted, and it seemed appropriate to supply the additional material required for easy comprehension. Variant readings, as between different versions of those documents which exist in duplicate, are noted only where they materially affect the sense.

It should be noted that the dates employed in these documents are according to the Julian (or Old Style) Calendar, which continued in official use in England until 1751. In the seventeenth century this was ten days behind the Gregorian (or Old Style) which most other Europeans involved in the African trade (including the Dutch) had already adopted.[26] In England in this period, the civil year also began officially on 25 March rather than 1 January; the ambiguity thus created was regularly resolved by citing the year for dates between 1 January and 24 March according to both conventions (as, for example, 1680/1). Readers should also note

---

[25] Cf. Law 1993, 180. Upon reflection, the imperative of comprehensibility has carried greater weight.
[26] Note the date given in 'Dutch style' in one of the RAC documents (no.47).

that the directions 'windward' and 'leeward' which appear frequently in these documents, correspond on the West African coast to west and east respectively.

Acknowledgements

The author thanks the Bodleian Library for permission to publish this material; the British Academy for their financial support of the research on which this publication is based; and the University of Stirling, which granted me two periods of sabbatical leave in the autumn semesters of 1991 and 1994 during which much of the work was undertaken. I also wish to place on record my appreciation of the assistance of many colleagues who have generously supplied advice and relevant information, including above all Paul Hair, David Henige, Adam Jones and Albert van Dantzig.

Glossary

Non-English words and titles used in the documents

ackie [Akan, *akye*]: greeting; commonly used with the verb 'frow', which has not been identified but from the context clearly means 'gives' or 'sends'

Braffoe [Akan, *obrafo*]: generally, the 'captain' or 'governor' of a village [cf. Barbot 1992, ii, 347]; but in Fante, in the absence of a 'king', the 'braffoe' was the military commander and head of government [Bosman 1705, 57].

bumboy [origin untraced]: slave foreman

Cabasheer [Portuguese, *cabeceira*, 'head']: chief, used of both officials of African kingdoms and senior employees of European establishments

cankey [Akan, *kankyew*]: maize bread; hence 'cankey money', subsistence allowance

Copeman [Dutch]: merchant, applied to chiefs of factories

consar [etymology uncertain: ?from Portuguese *casar*, 'marry']: to marry, or have sexual relations with

croome [Akan, *kurow*]: village. (Strictly, applied to dependent settlements, as opposed to capital cities [Kea 1982, 100–1].)

dashey [Portuguese, *dação*]: gift

Fetera [Portuguese, *feitor*, 'agent']: explained by Barbot [1992, ii, 593] as 'captain of the guard'

fetish [Portuguese, *feitiço*]: deity or magical charm; often in the phrase 'take (or drink) fetish', referring to the taking of a ritual oath

Fidalgo [Portuguese *fidalgo*, 'noble']: Governor [i.e. ruler subordinate to a king].

kickadevoo [etymology uncertain, ?from Portuguese *cadaver*, 'corpse'; cf. Atkins 1735, 60, giving 'kickatavoo' for 'killed, dead' in the 'Negrish' language of the Malagueta Coast]: used of canoes capsizing

Mareene [?Portuguese, *meirinho*, 'bailiff']: tax-collector

pallavora [Portuguese, *palavra*, 'word']: dispute, discussion

panyar [Portuguese, *penhorar*, 'distrain']: seize (goods or persons), usually as security to enforce payment.

prendee [Portuguese, *prender*, 'take']: fine

rowsawing/rowsaring [Portuguese *roçar*]: clearing ground for planting

Tetee [Akan, *tietie*]: herald

Quarrenteer/Curranteer: chief. Kea notes instances of this title, but without discussing its meaning or functions [1982, 128]. In the RAC correspondence it is used in the singular, when referring to particular towns such as Anomabu, but in the plural when referring to Fante as a whole; and there is also reference to a 'chief of the Quarranteers', who was presumably a federal officer. It may be inferred that the 'Quarranteers' were the rulers of towns (perhaps from *kurow*, 'croome', as above).

Weights, measures and values

angle (angel) [abbreviated as 'a']: $^1/_{16}$ ounce of gold (value 5 shillings sterling)
anker: liquid measure, 10½ gallons
bendy: 2 ounces of gold (value £8 sterling)
cask: as standard (liquid) measure, 32 gallons
chest: dry measure, of 8 bushels (= 32 gallons)
cracra: small piece of adulterated gold, of small value
                                       [Bosman 1705, 81–2]
fathom: 6 feet
firkin: liquid measure, 4½ gallons
gallon: at this period, the gallon was the 'old wine gallon'
                                       (3.785 litres), somewhat smaller than the modern
                                       'imperial' gallon (4.546 litres)
hogshead: liquid measure, of 63 gallons (= 6 ankers)
league   3 miles
mark ['mk', 'm']:   8 ounces of gold (= £32 sterling)
ounce ['oz', 'o']:   of gold, or equivalent value (= £4 sterling)
peaze (*peso*):   ¼ ounce of gold (= 4 angels)
tacco ['ta', 't']: $^1/_{12}$ of an angel

Trade goods

allejars   Indian cotton (or mixed silk and cotton) cloth
atlas   fine silk cloth
baftas   Indian coarse cotton cloth
bag   (as 'bag Holland') presumably, coarse cloth
booges   cowry shells
boysados   woollen cloth, made in England and the Netherlands
brawl   Indian coarse cotton cloth
calico   Indian striped or checked cloth (from Calicut)
carbine   short-barreled firearm
chercolees   Indian cotton cloth
chintz   Indian block-printed cotton cloth
commiters   not identified (probably Indian cloth)
cuttanees   Indian cloth of mixed silk and cotton
diaper   cloth with diamond or check pattern woven in relief
diglings   not identified (metal good, perhaps a form of basin)
dowlas   coarse linen cloth
firelock   early form of musket, with pyrites rather than flint ignition lock
fustian   coarse linen cloth
ginghams   Indian cotton cloth, woven with dyed thread
Guinea cloth   Indian cloth, specially made for the Guinea market
Holland   linen cloth made in the Netherlands
herba   (as 'herba longees') made of grass fibre

kettles	in seventeenth-century usage, pans
long cloth	Indian cotton cloth made in long pieces
longees	Indian cloth in small pieces, used e.g. as loin cloths or headscarves
malagueta	species of pepper
matchlock:	early form of musket, with match rather than lock ignition
manillas	bracelets (brass or copper)
mum	wheatmalt beer
muslin	fine cotton cloth (originally from Mosul in Iraq)
nicannees	Indian cotton cloth
paper	(as 'paper brawls') faced with paper
pautkaes	Indian cotton cloth
perpetuanos	hard-wearing serge (wool) cloth made in England
pintados	printed (batik) cloth from the East Indies
plains	(as 'Welsh plains') coarse woollen cloth
rangoes	sort of beads
salamporis	Indian cotton cloth (from Salem)
sayes	fine woollen cloth, made in the Netherlands and England
sletias	linen cloth, originally from Silesia but also made in England and the Netherlands
snap pans (more properly, snaphances):	early form of flintlock musket
tapsells	Indian cloth of mixed cotton and silk

I

SEKONDI

The westernmost factory of the RAC on the Gold Coast at this period was at Sekondi ('Succondee' in these documents). The Company had had a factory here in the late 1670s,[1] but this clearly no longer existed by the beginning of 1681.[2] As recorded elsewhere in the RAC correspondence (no.538), in February 1683 a vessel of the Company's, the *Cape Coast*, commanded by Hugh Shears, called at Sekondi to explore the possibility of re-settling the place, but received a discouraging response; but the attempt was evidently renewed soon afterwards. The first letter reproduced in this section relates to an abortive attempt to re-establish the Sekondi lodge, again supported by Shears in the *Cape Coast*, in April 1683. In the following month, Shears was back at Sekondi, and again negotiated for the re-establishment of the lodge there (nos 538–41); and in June 1683, as the correspondence in this section shows, it was finally established. The Sekondi lodge was clearly intended primarily for trade in gold, though in the latest correspondence preserved in this period, in October 1683, there was also some suggestion of purchasing slaves (nos 30–31).

The Dutch West India Company's principal lodge in this area was at Takoradi ('Tagarada'), west of Sekondi. In 1681, as reported elsewhere in the RAC correspondence (no.36), the Dutch Company had also taken advantage of the temporary absence of the English from Sekondi to establish a lodge of their own in Sekondi; and the first English attempt to re-settle Sekondi in April 1683 was frustrated by the opposition of the Dutch (no.1). The Dutch withdrew their factory from Sekondi (and also from Takoradi) in July 1683, when these places were threatened with attack in a local war (no.10). During this period of Dutch absence, the authorities at Takoradi invited the English to establish a factory there also, but nothing seems to have been done about this (nos 10–11, 16). In October 1683, however, the Dutch re-established their factories at both Sekondi and Takoradi (no.24).

[1] Cf. Van Dantzig 1978, no.3 (Herman Abramsz, 23 Nov. 1679). English trade at Sekondi dated back at least to 1668, though no permanently organized factory seems to have been established then (cf. no.635 in this collection).

[2] Barbot's allusion to an English factory at Sekondi (1992, ii, 346) must reflect the situation at the time of his first voyage in 1679, rather than his second in 1682.

Sekondi

Sekondi and Takoradi had earlier been regarded as belonging to the kingdom of Ahanta,[3] but the latter had come under attack from its northern neighbour, Adom ('Addoome' in these documents) during 1681–2.[4] In 1683, Sekondi was clearly dominated by Adom, and it was the 'king' of Adom, named here as 'Tickadoe',[5] with whom the English negotiated for the settlement of their factory and subsequent trade. It is implied, indeed, that it was the Adoms who wanted an English factory at Sekondi, while the local people (or at least a substantial section of them) were opposed to the English settlement and disposed to ally rather with the Dutch. The authority of Adom over the coastal area was evidently still fragile, with rumours of an impending second attack on Sekondi (which provoked the Dutch withdrawal in July 1683), though this did not in the event materialize.

The traders bringing gold for sale at Sekondi came not only from Adom itself, but also from Wassa, further north in the interior (nos 4, 16, 29, 31).

1. James Parris   Succondee, 25 Apr. 1683

These are to give you an account of our affaires here. Att our first comeing the Addoomes ordered us to bring our flagg and staff on shoare the which wee did, and on the sand the Dutch[6] sent all his people and slaves and tooke our staff from us and kept itt: soe I went on board the briganteen[7] and rideing att anchor here in the roade on the 23rd day being Monday att 11 of the clock att night the Addoomes came on board with two small canoes for to have us come on shoare againe with our flagg whereupon Coffee[8] and Thomas Hendrick went on shoare to see what all the people did say, whereupon Thomas Hendrick came on board againe and told us that all the business was ended and to bring the flagg on shoare againe and hoyst itt and all was well, but the Dutch was much troubled and carryed some of his goods downe to the waterside to begon, and this townes Cabosheers[9] haveing taken a fittish[10] to be true to the Dutch from the Generall of the Mina,[11] the Dutch factor fell out with them about hoysting our flagg here and sent for the Addoomes and

---

[3] Cf. e.g. Barbot 1992, ii 345.

[4] Barbot 1992, ii 346, 363 n.45 (saying the war ended in 1681). Cf. also reference to the devastation by the Adoms of the Cape Three Points area west of Ahanta, apparently in 1682, in Groeben 1985, 47. For the location and history of Adom, see Henige 1975.

[5] But cf. n.39 below, for the question of whether there was really a 'king' of Adom.

[6] i.e. the chief of the Dutch factory at Sekondi.

[7] i.e. the *Cape Coast*, commanded by Hugh Shears, who is mentioned later in this letter.

[8] Elsewhere, 'Captain Coffee', an African employee of the RAC.

[9] See Glossary.

[10] See Glossary.

[11] i.e. the Director-General of the Dutch West India Company, whose headquarters was at São Jorge da Mina (Elmina).

proffered them what they would demand to take our flagg downe, but the Adoomes would not hearken to them, for they would have the English to live here, whereupon the Adoomes demanded of us 3 perpettuanoes, 4 sheets, 1 carbine and 1 paper brawle, the which Mr Shears sent on shoare and I have them now in my custody. The Dutch fiscall[12] is comeing up hither to put us away and this townes Cabosheers are soe much affraid of the Dutch's displeasure that they have ordered us to begon. The Addoomes are goeing into the country and tells these Cabosheers that except the English lives here they will come immediatly and destroy them againe. Mr Shears hath been att a greate charge in liquors here in goeing to and fro and hoysting the flagg and now as I was wrighting they have pulled downe our flagg staff and I expect to goe aboard againe this day. They tell mee now they have orders from the Mina to pull downe our staff.[13]

*****

2. Mark Bedford Whiting   Succondee Factory, 12 June 1683

This is only to give your Worship an accompt that with the helpe of Mr Sheares[14] I was by the natives wellcom'd on shoare and have gotten free possession of the Royall Companys factory, but the Dutch [are] shamefully turn'd out of doores, being not lookt upon, all the Blacks promiseing to be true and honest to the English, hopeing they will build a fort with a few gunns and [saying] that wee shall not want trade. Here is a great man come from Tickadoe the King of the Addoomes, whoe is goeing tomorrow to him to give him an account of my settlement here, whoe was sent downe for that purpose. Wee are now in want of blew perpettuanoes, sheets, powder and carbines and severall other goods as brandy, wee haveing expended the most part of that I brought, in dashey's[15] and makeing pallavora's,[16] as Captain Shears and Coffee can give you an account, but some dashey's are yett wanting for the King of the Addoomes and Captain Asshume[17] which I hope your Worship will furnish them suddenly. As for goods I have according to order gotten some of Captain Sheares, as your Worship may see per receipt, and have disposed of some to the vallue of 6 ounces. I hope here will be a good trade, nothing shall be wanting by mee to increase the same.

---

[12] i.e. treasurer, the second-ranking official of the WIC at the Mina.

[13] For a Dutch account of this incident, cf. Van Dantzig 1978, no.42 (Resolutions of Council, Elmina, 1 May 1683).

[14] Still commanding the *Cape Coast*, and again assisting in the settlement of the Sekondi lodge (cf. no.542).

[15] See Glossary

[16] See Glossary.

[17] Apparently, a chief of Sekondi; cf. also no.635, for reference to a man of the same name there in the 1660s.

3. Mark Bedford Whiting   Succondee Factory, 20 June 1683

Since my last to your Worship here are come downe some of the Addoomes whoe are in want of goods as beads yallow, and corrall, perpettuanoes blew, knives, small basons and small brass panns, Welch plaines, blew and greene, but more especially narrow niccanees and tapsells, as alsoe powder which is a great commodity here and much inquired for by the said people, whoe hath promised to stay untill Munday for said goods and would faine speake with Captain Coffee from Tickadoe the King; I would that your Worship would send him up hither by all meanes. Here is money[18] come downe but noe goods as they want. Wee have now taken betwixt 4 and 5 marks, I doe not question a good trade. I must alsoe informe your Worship of our small house here and by noe means wee cannot with safety secure the Companys goods, but am forct to watch them night and day. I confess the houses are all alike, only [= except] the Dutch house, whoe still are here. Captain Sheares promis'd to speake to your Worship for a scarlett cloath for Captain Asshume whoe makes much enquiry for [it], as alsoe a hatt which you may send up with the goods. The Dutch att Tagarada sent their canoe this day to the Mina for sheets and beades which vends much att this place. I would wright your Worship oftener only am in want of a canoe and to hyre a canoe every time is chargable, the Dutch have them here for that purpose. Pray faile not to supply us that the Adooomes may have noe cause to complaine, I give them all the encouragement immaginable.

4. Mark Bedford Whiting   Succondee Factory, 26 June 1683

Your Worships of the 25th instant is come to hand by Captain Coffee, as alsoe the 9 hand canoe, by which I have received the goods mentioned in the said letter, there being 3 pieces of Welch plaines damnified, haveing 6 or 7 wholes apeece in them. Your Worship hath risen the prizes of all sorts of goods [so] that I can in noe wayes sell them att those rates, but as formerly sold by Mr Sheares as on the other side appeares. I could have taken 2 marks of gold more this day if not risen. Wee are in great want of powder and was in hopes to have been supply'd by this canoe, the people are soe greedy for itt that they have intrusted mee with 3 marks of gold for the same and would not lett me alone till I had dispatcht the canoe for the same. Here is money for 100 barrells in the towne I beleeve, therefore upon receipt hereof I would have your Worship dispatch the canoe up heither with the same for I understand that there is a ship at Dickiscove,[19] and I would not willingly lett slip soe good an oppertunity, for they will all be runing aboard, they have promised to stay untill Fryday morning and noe longer. Your Worship needs not question but that the powder will be safe here, for I feare itt will be taken all away att the

---

[18] i.e. gold (as often in these documents).

[19] Dixcove, further west along the coast from Takoradi (on the eastern point of Cape Three Points).

waterside, and what is not wee can safely secure itt from any danger. Your Worship may send halfe barrells and some whole barrells, as alsoe some sheets and Guyney clouts and alsoe pautkaes blew, and scarlett cloath and blew. The Dutch canoe passed by this place for Tagarada with goods for that place as beades, sheets, perpetuano's and brandy, but noe powder. They sell their green perpetuano's at 10a and blewes att 9a, brandy att 1½a per gallon.[20] Your Worships perpettuanoes that you sent will not hold up with the greens, there being as many more greens and [sic: = than?] blews.[21] Tickadoe the King hath sent some of his people to Coffee for a hatt and a chayre they desireing to have itt sent up heither that they may carry itt up with them in the country. Coffee tells mee that Griffin[22] att Cape Coast can supply him with a chayre, but where to gett a hatt I cannot tell. The Dutchman is still here, haveing noe goods only brandy and a few beades, as for brandy wee shall want for next Tuseday is the time of their danceing here[23] and according to contract made wee are to give the Cabasheers of this towne a perpetuanoe and one broad tapsell which wee have not here, as alsoe 2 halfe ankors of brandy. I beleeve that snap pans is a great commodyty here, for the people of this place runs as far as Accoda to the Brandenburgs[24] to buy them, whoe sells them att 5 angles a peece. I am glad your Worship will provide us a 5 hand canoe which wee want here much, there being scarcity of canoes att this place, I would have your Worship send her up alsoe by the canoe. I have according to order sent your Worship by David March what gold was in cash on account of the Royall Affrican Company and shall alsoe send itt by all safe conveyance; I now send you 7 marks, I hope to make itt 7 more before the month is out. Ile doe my endeavour, but powder is the thing which I would have your Worship send up by all meanes without delay and dispatch the canoe as soone as arrived unless others come and take all the money. Wee expect ships every day to trade here there being two to windward.

[inclosure]
Prizes of goods as Mr Sheares sold them here
sheets: 28 per bendy — wee want them
long cloaths att 10a
niccanees narrow att 3½a — wee want a hundred more
perpetuano's blew att 10a, greens att 9a and redds att 8a
Welch plaines blews att 10a, greens att 9a and redds att 8a

---

[20] 'a' = angles (cf. Glossary).

[21] The point seems to be that green perpetuanoes were less in demand than blue.

[22] Elsewhere, 'Doctor Griffin', another African employee of the RAC.

[23] Alluding to public ceremonies, celebrated with dancing.

[24] Akwida, west of Dixcove (on the middle point of Cape Three Points). Presumably this alludes to the fort of the Brandenburg African Company (Gross Friedrichsburg), established in 1682, though this was not in fact at Akwida, but further west again, on the westernmost point of Cape Three Points. The Brandenburgers did establish a second fort at Akwida, but not until 1684 (see Jones 1985, for details and documentation).

paper brawles att 2½a — will not sell att that rate but att 2a
Guyney clouts 24 per bendy — wee want them much
sletias course att 5a — will not sell att that rate
iron barrs 24 per bendy
2 lb basons att 1a — will not sell att that rate
4 lb basons att 2a — will not sell att that rate
3 lb ditto will not sell att that rate, [but will] att 1½a
sayes att 15 angles — doe not sell well here
firkins of tallow att 4a [per] halfe firkins — will not sell att that rate
powder att 1o 8a — wee want much.

[PS] Since my wrighting this letter the Addoomes and Wassaers mett together before the factory being about a hundred in company there, they made a greate pallavora, Coffee and I being sent for by them, saying that unless your Worship would abate the prizes of goods they would goe to Dickiscove or to the Dutch att Tagarada and lay out their money, wondering why the goods should be risen of a sudden and not sold att Mr Shears rates or as on board the Companys ships. Their prizes is this, they will give but 4a for tapsells narrow and 4a for niccanees, alsoe 9a for green perpetuano's and 10a for blews, 2 lb basons 9 for 8a and 4 lb ditto 1½a, Guyney clouts 7 for 8a, paper brawles att 2a each, sletias course 4a, tallow 3a the halfe firkin, powder 1 ounce and ½, sayes att 15 angles, blew pautkaes 1½a. As for beades I know not how to sell them haveing noe stilliards[25] to weight them, I have sent your Worship a sample of what beades is most vendible here. Pray faile not to send us word wheither your Worship pleases to alter the prizes, for they will not sell att those rates before mentioned, and this is all but what they urged mee to wright your Worship, alsoe not forgetting Tickado's hatt and chayre and powder allsoe. If your Worship could spare us a hammer and a saw wee could secure the house better for wee want some tooles.

5.   Mark Bedford Whiting   Succondee Factory, 27 June 1683

Just now arrived a canoe from Axim whoe informed us and the Dutch Copeman[26] here that yesterday night arrived att the said place a French pyrate whoe forct two ships under the protection of that fort.[27] This serves only to give your Worship advice [so] that Mr Sheares may not venture up heither. This is certainly true. The Dutch I beleeve will give your Worship noe advice therefore [I] could not trust to them, allthough they sent advice to the Mina. Pray faile not to send us more niccanees narrow but powder especially and dispatch this canoe up heither with the 9 hand canoe immediatly upon receipt hereof.

---

[25] steelyards, i.e. balances for weighing.
[26] See Glossary.
[27] i.e. the Dutch fort at Axim, west of Cape Three Points.

[PS] Pray fayle not to send us a chayre and a hatt for Tickadoe for the people are verry urgent to be gon, as alsoe Captain Assumes cloath and hatt not forgetting powder.

6.   Marke Bedford Whiting   Succondee Factory, 30 June 1683

Your Worships of the 28th instant I have per the 9 hand canoe with the goods mentioned in the letter, wherein your Worship wrights as to the prizes of goods. I shall observe your Worships orders as to that matter although I cannot sell them all, att the Castles rates,[28] here being an interloper one Captain Parris of Barbado's that undersells mee in some sorts of goods, as tallow att 3 angles the halfe firkin and other goods which hee sells att lower rates, which att present am not sencible of itt. I wrote your Worship per the 9 hand canoe for more sheets and niccanees, but received none, I have but one chest and halfe left and some of them are damnified and a parcell of sayes which came out of Mr Sheares his ship, which I feare [I] must sell by the fathom to the best advantage. The small tapsells will not vend at 5 angles, but att 4 angles as the niccanees, which goes well att that price, but the tapsells I have not sold one. Yours of [= by] John Downes is come to hand, I have accordingly sent a canoe to Dickiscove aboard of a Dutch interloper, one skeeper Johnson, whoe I am inform'd can give intelligence of the pyrate, att the returne of the canoe I shall according to order send her downe to your Worship. The said interloper sells abundance of sheets and snap pans. I inquired on board of Captain Parris whether hee saw any ships to windward, whoe tells mee noe, only spoke with the said interloper att Dickiscove whoe said nothing to him of any pyrate. Captain Parris informes mee that Captain Nurse was safe arrived att Barbado's when hee came thence which is about 5 months, alsoe Captain North whoe went thence to Jamaica. Captain Attwell run 40 slaves ashoare upon his own account att Barbado's and some of his men inform'd against him, and when hee was examined hee confessed the thing, soe they multed[29] him; his gunner is aboard of the said Parris whoe left the ship att Barbado's, [he] and severall others they lost all their wages. The scarlett cloath and hatt for Captain Asshume is delivered him whoe is well satisfied and thanks your Worship. Wee shall take care to send the carpett, chayre and hatt for Tickadoe when any of his people comes downe. I have disposed of the best part of the powder, itt will not be long before the other goes off. These interlopers have done mee a little injury, they being here before the canoe came up. I am glad your Worship will send us a 2 hand canoe itt being a thing necessary att this place.

---

[28] i.e. those current at Cape Coast Castle.
[29] mulcted, i.e. fined.

7. Marke Bedford Whiting   Succondee Factory, 2 July 1683

This is to acquaint your Worship that just now arrived the Dutch interloper from Dickiscove here and accordingly I sent a canoe on board to enquire of the pyrate, and hee writt mee word that there is one to windward of 40 gunns, whoe [he] beleeves itt is Van Horne, hee cannot justly tell. The said interloper was chased by him from Ashinee[30] to Axim, where hee left him, and went up to windward againe, and his intent is to stay a little to windward of Ashinee, and take ships as they come downe. Here is a Companys ship att Dickiscove, whoe I beleeve is Captain Phenney in a small ship, I am informed hee was never upon the coast before. The Dutch interloper spoke with him yesterday night, and desired him not to stay there, but to goe downe to Cabo Corsoe. Here the ships are ready for a fight. The Companys ship intends to wood and water att Dickiscove, shee past by Ashinee in the night and soe [I] beleeve escap'd the pyrate. This interloper hath been 7 months out of Holland. The other pyrate that went downe last, chased alsoe this man att Cestus.[31] Hee tells that Van Horns stearmen is aboard of that pyrate that went to leward and alsoe that Van Horne will take all nations. Here the Dutch interloper sells sheets 30 per bendy and snap pans 8 per bendy, tallow 3 angles per [half?] firkin.[32] I must expect to sell nothing as long as they lye here.

8. Marke Bedford Whiting   Succondee Factory, 9 July 1683

Your Worships letter per the 9 hand canoe is come to hand with 130 sheets, and 240 niccanees narrow, the niccanees are farr worse then those your Worship sent before, they being the same sort I had from Mr Sheares and doubt will not sell soe well; I have accordingly sent your Worship the tapsells narrow as per your order haveing sold but two att 5a, they will not give 5 for them, and severall other goods, which are now remaining here which alsoe will not vend att the Castles rate, as you shall perceive per accompt as soone as the month is out, then [I] doe intend to send James [Parris] that the docter may survey his legg, whoe will give your worship an accompt how affaires stands here. Captain Draper arrived here yesterday with another Dutch interloper whoe still affirmes of a pyrate to windward, but [I] beleeve [it] is a lye. Your Worship cannot expect any trade ashoare as long as they lye here. I am inform'd by the Blacks that before your Worship sent downe your letter to Captain Draper that hee sold his powder att 1o 4a per barrell, sheets att 1a per piece, boysado's att 18a, knives att 1a per douzen. I have according to your Worships order sent per David March 5 marks of gold.

---

[30] Assinie, west of Axim (in modern Ivory Coast).
[31] River Sestos (nowadays, Cess), in Liberia.
[32] Emendation required, by comparison with no.6.

9. Marke Bedford Whiting   Succondee Factory, 12 July 1683

This accompany's James [Parris] with my accompts in a 2 hand canoe, I shall not informe your Worship how affaires stand here att this place, James can give your Worship as good accompt and for that purpose I have sent him downe. Your Worship promised mee to send us a canoe which wee cannot have here some times for love nor money to goe to Cabo Corsoe, itt is one of the best things wee can have here to give your Worship advice of any thing that should happen. I received a letter yesterday from Captain Bell whoe desired mee to send him the prizes of goods as sould in the Castle which I did accordingly. Captain Phenney past by yesterday, Captain Draper is still here, I have not disposed of any goods since these ships arrivall. I now send your Worship 2 ounces, 7 angles and 9 tacco's of gold and 11 marks, 7 ounces, 7 angles and 6 tacco's sent before, makes 12 marks, 1 ounce, 15 angles and 3 tacco's which is the ballance of my accompt.

10. Mark Bedford Whiting   Succondee Factory, 27 July 1683

This accompany's Captain Coffee whoe is sent up by the Cabasheers of this place to informe your Worship that the Addooms and Ayampama the King of the Aquiffa's[33] will come downe to fight this people.[34] The Generall of the Mina I am inform'd hath sent a greate dashey to the said Ayampama to rout the English out here. Itt is the Cabasheers desire that your Worship would be pleased to send some body to this Ayampama and another to the King of Greate Commenda[35] to know the pallavora. The Dutch Copeman is goeing hence tomorrow, alsoe the other from Tagarada, the Generall haveing sent two greate canoes with their fiscall to take their goods away,[36] which I am glad of itt, itt will be the better for us. The Cabasheers desire your Worship that you'l be pleased now to keepe possession to yourselfe for they are resolv'd to entertaine noe more Dutch att this place. Here is arrived Captain Doegood a Companys ship, alsoe a Danes ship from St Thoma,[37] whoe hath a letter from Captain Waugh[38] who went from that place with the white woeman [var. woemen], two day's before this mans departure thence. Noe news of Captain Manlow. I have not taken one farthing since these ships arrivall. I now send your Worship per Captain Coffee 2 marks of gold on accompt of the Royall Company.

---

[33] Twifo, north-east of Wassa.

[34] Cf. rumours of an intended Adom attack on Sekondi and Dixcove reported a little earlier, in May 1683 (no.539); and of an attack on Dixcove later, in October 1683 (no.28).

35 The kingdom of Komenda (or Eguafo), Ahanta's eastern neighbour (cf. section II), 'Great Commenda' being its inland capital.

[36] Cf. Van Dantzig 1978, no.43 (Resolutions of Council, Elmina, 8 Aug. 1683), for the WIC's decision to withdraw its lodges from Takoradi and Akwida (Sekondi is not mentioned), in view of the impending attack by Adom.

[37] The island of São Tomé.

[38] = no.636.

The money for the brandy I shall send att the months end with my accompt. I hope now to have a better trade, for could not dispose of one sheet of late, the Dutch att Tagarada selling 32 per bendy, and beades 7 pounds for 4 angles. I have not sold any as yett but [they are] often enquired for. I want more powder, I have sold all only one barrell remaining. Pray dispatch Captain Coffee up hither as soone as possible.

11. Mark Bedford Whiting   Succondee Factory, 6 Aug. 1683

Your Worships of the 2nd of August is come to hand per Captain Coffee. This accompanys James Parris, whome I have sent downe to your Worship for some more goods now the country people being come downe, the goods they demand is powder and sheets, and boysado's, wee have none of those sort of goods to supply them. Your Worship needs not question the powder but safe, I doubt itt will not stay long in the factory. Here is now a good trade, and doe not question but that itt will continue soe if shiping doe not come here soe fast one after another. Yesterday came here the greate Cabasheer of Tagarada to desire your Worship to settle there, and that noe Dutch should ever be entertained att that place noe more. I now send your Worship 4 marks of gold. Pray faile not to supply us with the aforesaid goods as soone as possible alsoe with some silke longees.

12. Mark Bedford Whiting   Succondee Factory, 12 Aug. 1683

Your Worships of the 10th instant I have received per the 9 hand canoe, with the goods as per receipt inclosed appeares. As to powder I humbley begg, that your Worship would spare us a douzen barrells itt being for Tickadoe, hee haveing sent his man here 10 dayes agoe for that purpose and [the latter] is afraid to goe to his master without itt. Here is a good trade, I am in greate hopes itt will continue soe, now the Dutch being gon from both places. The Captain of Tagarada will be here tomorrow, I suppose is to desire your Worship the English might settle there hee haveing made a pallavora the other day to that purpose, they are resolved to enter-taine noe Dutch noe more att both places, but will stand to the English. The Ad-doomes have sent downe their people here to desire us to build a fort, but first [we] must buy the ground, the people of this place will assist in building of itt, they would faine have guns brought heither, then they would beleeve the English intended to build, their dayly pallavora's to mee is to write to your Worship of itt. I am inform'd that the Dutch have sent a dashey to the Cabasheers following vizt Quoteam-boushou, Nakaba, Obonie, and Aymbo, to come here and route the English out, they being halfe of the Adooms.[39] Tickadow desires that your Worship would send him

---

[39] As noted later by Bosman, Adom was 'governed by five or six principal men, there being here no King' (1705, 22). The Dutch were presumably attempting to exploit divisions within the Adom polity.

a dashey for them, and hee will see itt distributed amongst them they being not well pleased that Tickadoe should have a dashey and not them. My monthly account I shall send per first oppertunity. Here is a Portuguze att Dickiscove. I shall send your Worship the money for the empty caske alsoe with my account.

13. Mark Bedford Whiting   Succondee Factory, 18 Aug. 1683

This is to informe your Worship that Tickadoe hath sent here his people, to desire your Worship to buy the ground, as I wrote your Worship before. Then [I] did not know the price, they aske the same as Agent Bradley[40] proffered, which is 25 bendy's, I told them they must not expect soe much times now being not as formerly when the factory tooke 40 marks monthly. They desire halfe now, and halfe when the fort is built, they stay for your Worships answer, to know what your Worships willing to give, [they] alsoe desire your Worship to send some powder for Tickadoe, hee haveing sent downe money 10 dayes agoe for that purpose. I now send your Worship per James [Parris] with my accounts 4 marks and 4 angles and 5 marks, 7 ounces 13 angles sent before according to Mr Masters receipts makes just 10 marks, 1 angle. Tickado's people have sett their marke here underneath, I desire your Worship to send us some more Guyney clouts and some blew pautkaes.

× Cabesheere Obeen
× Tickado's sons marke

14. Mark Bedford Whiting   Succondee Factory, 21 Aug. 1683

Your Worships of the 20th instant I have received, being verry sorry to heare of Mr Stapletons death.[41] Alsoe to what your Worship mentions concerning takeing charge of the warehouse [i.e. at Cape Coast Castle], since your Worship was soe kind as to give mee my choyce which I humbley returne your Worship thanks, I had rather serve the Company here (I now being well settled) then remove, I hope itt will prove well as to the Companys interest and where ever I am I will ever doe my endeavour to increase the same.

15. Marke Bedford Whiting   Succondee Factory, 27 Aug. 1683

Your Worships of the 24th instant I have received with the goods as per receipt appeares. As to the pallavora made between Cabasheer Hansacoo[42] and the Ad-

---

[40] Nathaniel Bradley, Agent-General of the RAC at Cape Coast, 1678–81.

[41] Walter Stapleton, Member of Council at Cape Coast.

[42] For this man, cf. Daaku 1970, 104. He was a nephew of the King of Fetu, commonly employed by the RAC in the settlement of disputes with African rulers.

doomes I shall leave itt to him to give your Worship an account thereof,[43] the
Addooms being gon up to bring downe pawnes for the security of our goods here,
which wee have not att present, alsoe to acquaint Tickadoe what your Worship
sayes, a Thursday next [they] will be downe againe, then shall take care to send
downe Coffee with what gold will be in cash, alsoe to acquaint your Worship in full
of their demands. As concerning the Cabasheers belonging to Tickadoe itt will be
verry convenient to send them up some dashey they haveing had none as yett.

16.   Mark Bedford Whiting   Succondee Factory, 3 Sept. 1683

This is to acquaint your Worship that James Parris was taken verry ill last Sunday
morning with a voyolent paine in his head which continued till 12 a clock att night,
then lay speechless from that time untill Monday morning about 10, then spoake
but after a distracted manner, and doth continue soe. Hee was cupp'd by the Blacks
but recovered noe ease. I humbley begg of your Worship that if your Worship can
possibly spare, either the docter or his mate to send one of them up to give him ease,
for hee is in a verry bad condition and I feare will not recover. I now send downe
Captain Coffee, by whome you will receive a pawne for the security of the factory,
hee is one of Tickado's owne sonns. As concerning the ground the Addoomes will
not abate anything of the price, Coffee will informe your Worship in full of their
demands and pallavora's. Here is a greate many Addoomes and Wassa's in towne,
waiting for powder, hopeing to be supplyed when a ship comes. The Captain of
Taggarada was here yesterday, whoe proffered his own sonn for a pawne, provided
the English would settle there. I now send your Worship on accompt of the Royall
Affrican Company 8 marks of gold itt being all that is in cash att present. Here is a
good trade, I could wish wee had a biger house by ourselves on the topp of the hill
for wee cannot stow noe more goods with security the house being full, and if any
fire should happen, wee liveing amongst a parcell of houses itt would be impossible
for us to secure any. Wee want some blew pautka's, sheets and more perpettuanoes:
but where to stow them I know not.

17.   Marke Bedford Whiting   Succondee Factory, 8 Sept. 1683

Your Worships of the 5th instant is come to hand per Docter Meade, whoe arrived
here just as James Parris was dying, soe that Docter Meade could not assist him,
but [he] dyed presently after his arrivall, wee tooke care to see him buried decently.
As to what your Worship mentions concerning a brick house, I only desired your
Worship to furnish us with a new thatcht house on the top of the hill that if any fire
should happen in the towne, none could doe us any harme. Docter Meade can give
your Worship an account of this that I live in, haveing noe roome to stow the

---

[43] From a reference in a later letter (no.23), this 'palaver' was about the rate of payment for goods.

Companys goods I am forct to sett people to watch a nights, had itt not been don, the other night, I might have lost a parcell of goods, some of the Blacks in the night haveing lifted up the thatch for that purpose. I am in want for those goods which I wrote for in my last, but sheets and boysado's especially.

18. Marke Bedford Whiting   Succondee Factory, 9 Sept. 1683

I have according to your Worships order desired the Cabasheere from Tickadoe to goe to Cabo Corsoe but cannot perswade him soe to doe, unless Captain Coffee come [h]either before, being afraid that your Worship would detaine him. The Cabbasheers of this towne are willing that hee should goe downe, but cannot by noe meanes perswaide him unless leave be first granted from Tickadoe. As concerning James Parris I suppose your Worship hath an account of him per Docter Meade before this time, whoe [i.e. Parris] was dead before the said Docters arrivall. As to shiping to windward I heard of one yesterday being att Axim, I am inform'd by the Blacks that itt is a greate English ship. Wee are in want of boysado's and sheets, alsoe perpetuano's. I must informe you that here is one Cabasheer Yankey[44] that doth perswade Tickado's people not to goe downe. Captain Coffee knowes him verry well.

19. Marke Bedford Whiting   Succondee Factory, 15 Sept. 1683

Your Worships of the 10th and 11th I have received with 10 pieces of Welch plaines which I disposed of att their arrivall. This accompany's Tickado's Cabasheers whoe after many perswasions was willing to come downe to end the pallavora with your Worship. I now send downe alsoe Captain Coffee, with 3 marks of gold, itt being all that I have in cash att present. Here is a greate deale of gold in towne, but all for powder, which they could not be supplyed with by Captain Browse, hee haveing disposed of all to windward. I have not disposed of anything since the said ships arrivall, only the Welch plaines your Worship sent last, and if I had more, I could sell them all att their arrivall. The people wanting powder is a greate hinderance to mee, for they send all their gold aboard for powder, and when they come there, they buy other goods. Here in towne I beleeve [there is] above 20 marks for powder. I want more goods, as boysado's, sheets, perpetuano's, but our house is not fitt to put any goods in. I now send inclosed James Parris's inventory of what things hee left at his death. When the greate canoe comes I shall send them downe to your Worship, with my monthly accompts. Here is noe news to windward. As to what your Worship wrights concerning Samuell Chambers I undertake I shall follow itt.

---

[44] An African employee of the RAC.

20.   Mark Bedford Whiting   Succondee Factory, 18 Sept. 1683

Your Worships of the 15th instant I have received per the 9 hand canoe with the goods as per inclosed receipt appeares. As for the powder I shall keepe it till Tickado's Cabasheer comes up againe. I now send downe per the bearer hereof my accompt with the ballance of itt being 7 ounces, 9 angles and 3 tacco's of gold on accompt of the Royall Affrican Company. I must informe your Worship that 3 pieces of boysado's are verry much damnified, but I shall endeavour to dispose of them to the best advantage on account of said Company. As to news to windward I know of none, only I heare of a Dutch Companys ship being att Aboni [sic: = Abeni].[45] Here passed by the other day a small vessell, what shee was I know not. Per this canoe your Worship will alsoe receive James Parris his things.

21.   Mark Bedford Whiting   Succondee Factory, 22 Sept. 1683

Your Worships of the 17th and 20th instant I have received together with 10 pieces of green Welch plaines, on account of the Royall Affrican Company whereof I have enclosed receipt but for 8, haveing given your Worship a receipt before for 10 when I received but 8 which was my mistake, I humbley returning your Worship thanks for adviseing mee thereof. I have according to your Worships order sent a canoe to Axim, and another to Dickiscove to the Cabbasheers of that place to demand satisfaction of them for soe verry highly abuseing the English, which att the returne of the canoe I shall give your Worship an account thereof. As concerning the setlemen[t] of this place, the Addooms are come downe and are willing to comply with your Worships proffer, and here doe stay to know whether your Worship is willing to lett them have 10 bendy's worth of goods out of this factory; if your Worship is willing to comply with I shall follow your orders therein and furnish them accordingly.

22.   Mark Bedford Whiting   Succondee Factory, 24 Sept. 1683

This is to acquaint your Worship that the Cabosheer that made the pallavora with your Worship hath been with Tickadoe and is come downe againe whoe informes mee that his master is willing to accept of the proffer made by your Worship, soe that if your Worship is pleased, that hee should be furnished here, I can furnish him with a parcell of damaged goods whoe is willing to except of the same att the same price as if they were good, soe expecting an answer as to that matter.

---

[45] Albani (nowadays called Half Assini), between Assinie and Axim.

23.   Mark Bedford Whiting   Succondee Factory, 28 Sept. 1683

Your Worships of the 26th instant I have received together with the articles, which the Addoomes will not signe to unless your Worship will take 6 peaze for every bendy, being unwilling to take the same for every bendy's worth of goods.[46] Tickado's Cabasheere came downe yesterday with whome Hansacoe made the pallavora concerning that matter, but could not bring him to any reasonable terms, saying that if they had proffered any such thing to the Dutch, they would not make soe many words, Tickadoe being unwilling to entertaine them any more att this place. If your Worship is willing to lett them have 6 peaze for every bendy's worth of goods they will all signe the articles and take their fittish upon itt. As to the annuall charges they are all contented with [them]. Wee told them that the Company hath beene att a considerable charge in settleing the factory and with the annuall charges will amount to a greate sume of money. I shall take care to send up Captain Coffee, Atta[47] with Samuell Chambers to Tickadoe to signe the articles att the returne of your Worships answer. Here is enclosed a letter from Monsieur Scheffer at Axim.[48] As to Dickiscove people the Cabasheers hath promised to send a Cabasheere of that place up to Succondee that thereby wee may know what reason they have to abuse the English. Here arrived att this place two Dutch interlopers and an English one, whoe went hence for Shuma[49] yesterday. The Dutch interloper hath taken a considerable parcell of money att this place for powder, att 5 peaze and 2 angles per barrell, heare came ashoare yesterday att least 35 barrells.

24.   Marke Bedford Whiting   Succondee Factory, 1 Oct. 1683

This is to acquaint your Worship that the Dutch last Sunday came here on shoare with a quantity of goods as sheets, beades and ginghams att 4 a clock in the morning, unknowne to these townes people, in order to resettle their factory which they pretend they left for want of goods and now being furnished will settle all places againe.[50] Their arrivall here is unknowne to the Addooms whoe have often promised never to entertaine them noe more att this place. I have in order to this sent Captain Coffee, Samuell Chambers and Attah up to Tickadoe to acquaint him of itt, and to signe the articles of agreement, which if they signe they must either put the Dutch off or elce forfeite 100 marks according to the said agreement. Here is a greate disturbance att this place, some being for their staying and some for their

---

[46] The meaning is presumably that they wanted to pay only 6 pesos (1½ oz.) of gold for goods valued at 1 bendy (2 oz.), in effect a discount of 25%.

[47] Elsewhere, 'Attah', 'Atta Barba': like Coffee, an African employee of the RAC.

[48] Chief of the Dutch fort at Axim.

[49] Shama, east of Sekondi.

[50] Cf. Van Dantzig 1980, 53, for the re-establishment of the WIC factories at Sekondi and Takoradi at this time.

goeing off, and if they stay they will undersell us in beades and sheets, which they brought a considerable quantity. Sheets they sell 7 for 2 peaze and 8 for 2 peaze, that is 15 for an ounce. Here hath been dull trade with mee this month, but a good trade for those Dutch interlopers which sold a greate quantity of powder att 5 peaze per barrell, snap pans att 9 per bendy and those commodyty's swept up a considerable parcell of money. As to what your Worship writes concerning Captain Woolmans letter[51] your Worship is misinform'd for I received the same from Captain Smiths owne hand when the ship was under saile and past by Taggarada and before she anchored here, the said letter was sent by mee to Cabo Corsoe, which is a thing impossible that a ship should be att the Mina 6 dayes when shee never was there. As concerning Mr Scheffer's letter, here is noe secure passage for any Blacks to goe, there being a differance betwixt the people of this place and Dickiscove, neither can I send a canoe unless I hyre itt on purpose, itt is verry seldome that any of these cano's goe thither unless itt be canoes sent from the Mina and soe stop here for refreshment.

25.   Mark Bedford Whiting   Succondee Factory, 3 Oct. 1683

This accompany's Hansacoe by whome your Worship will understand how affaires stands att this place, alsoe this is to lett your Worship understand that Captain Coffee, Attah and Samuell Chambers, after foure dayes journey towards the Addooms was forct to come back againe, meeting some of the Addooms by the way whoe inform'd them that Tickadoe and rest of the Cabasheers of Mampone[52] are gon up to Wassa country which prevented their journey up, yett notwithstanding wee have taken care to send up a man to him to acquaint him of the Dutch landing here and of a White English man comeing up to Mampone, which if hee heares noe doubt but hee will come back. Here the Dutch doe undersell us both in sheets and beades, selling their sheets att 32 per bendy and wee 28 per bendy which is a greate deale of differance. I have not sold neither sheets nor beades since their arrivall. Sheets are the best commodyty that vends here. I shall take care to send downe the gold per Captain Coffee next weeke. I have taken care to send your Worships letter to Axim.

26.   Mark Bedford Whiting   Succondee Factory, 5 Oct. 1683

Since my last to your Worship per Hansacoe your Worships of the 4th instant I have

---

[51] = no.639, written from São Tomé, and evidently (like Captain Waugh's letter. cf. no.10 above) transmitted to Cape Coast via Sekondi.

[52] In other sources (e.g. Barbot 1992, ii, 345) this state ('Mompa' etc.) is treated as separate from Adom, which it bordered on the south-west; but here (and also in no.28) they seem to be identified: maybe Mampon had now been absorbed by Adom.

received wherein I shall observe your Worships order in lowering the sheets and greene perpetuano's. The Dutch have had this morning a fresh supply of goods as sayes, perpetuanoe's, broad tapsells, ginghams and beades; I understand that the Generall of the Mina is resolved to supply their factory here with all sorts of goods, and to sell them att low rates only to draw the country people in, and to gett us off of this place. The other day when I sent Coffee, Atta and Samuell Chambers to acquaint Tickadoe of the Dutch landing here, as soone as the Dutch Copeman heard of itt, hee presently sent for the Cabbasheers desireing them to goe and prevent us of our journey, which they came accordingly and would needs know what was the reason I sent a Whiteman to Tickadoe, and I would not informe them of itt, I asked them againe what was the reason they entertained the Dutch here after haveing made soe many promises never to entertaine them noe more, and for that verry reason I send a Whiteman to the Addoomes to acquaint them of itt, to knowe wheither they approve of it, then they desired mee to stay a weeke longer, I made answer that itt was your Worships order and I was not to observe theirs; then leave was granted, upon the condition that I had noe intent to doe any of this townes people any harme, yett notwithstanding they sent the Tetee[53] of this towne along with Samuell Chambers to heare what pallavora was made betwixt Tickadoe and us, whome they are in greate feare of, and soe are the Dutch. Here is one Cabasheer that is ordered by the Addooms to looke after the English whoe is a greate enemie of the Dutch and hath promised to doe his endeavour to gett the Dutch off, hee hath sent one of his men to Tickadoe to acquaint him of the Dutch landing here, hee told the Cabasheers of this place that if they would use noe means to gett them off, hee would; they tould him againe that they [= the Dutch] were here before and that they had noe reason to putt them off. The Dutch man heareing of the said Cabasheere standing up for the English, hee sent him word that one day hee hop'd to see him at the Mina without his head, hee sent him word againe that hee had not better speake too much, least Tickadoe make him carry his stoole after him. The Dutch sells their perpetuano's greene att 8 angles each, ours are farr before them, some of the Blacks loves their collor best itt being a deeper dye; they sell alsoe their sheets at 32 per bendy, hee haveing lowered his price two dayes agoe telling the Negro's that if they would bring their money to him, and not carry itt to the English hee would sell 32 per bendy. Hee alsoe sells ginghams att 5 angles each, being 9 for 2 peaze. Beades he sells great quantity's of. As to sayes and broad tapsells I know not how hee sells them, they comeing on shoare but this morning. Wee are in want of perpetuano's, greene Welch plaines and sheets. Sheets I have not sold any since this Dutch arrivall, only this morning att the receiveing of your letter I sold a bendy's worth att 32 per bendy according to your Worships order. As to my monthly ac-compts, I shall endeavour to send Coffee with itt next weeke, with the ballance of itt. I have according to your Worships orders sent Mynheer Schiffer[s] letter to

---

[53] See Glossary.

Axim, when I have an answer from thence itt shall be forwarded to your Worship with all expedition.

27. Marke Bedford Whiting   Succondee Factory, 8 Oct. 1683

This is to acquaint your Worship that last night the towne of Succondee was sett on fire in three severall places, by whome wee know not. The Cabasheers houses are all bur[n]t and if care had not been taken by the said Cabasheers our factory would have been bur[n]t too, but I thank God wee escaped the same and soe did the Dutch whoe escaped verry narrowly, one of the houses was blowne up with powder, haveing in one halfe barrell which burnt six severall people which I feare will not live. Here is a greate many Wassa's in towne which hath given mee in hand 9 marks of gold for powder att 6 pease per barrell which if your Worship can possibly supply them, they will take itt off my hands from the waterside and carry itt up to Wassa country least itt should come to any damage in the towne. Here the Dutch are lett alone in their wayes, noe body doth molest them, they sell abundance of beades and sheets alsoe ginghams and a few perpetuano's. If I had a better house on the top of the hill, where I could be out of danger of any fire and had a quantity of each sort of goods I should make a good hand of itt. The Dutch sells his sayes att 1 ounce, the Negro's loves their sayes better then ours, they esteeme their collour better. I am in want of green Welch plaines, perpetuano's, sheets (blew Welch plaines are noe commodity here, I have a parcell of them but will not sell). I have not yett had any news from the Addoomes, here is one of the said people in towne whoe informes mee that foure dayes hence Tickadoe will send downe one of his Cabasheers heither. As concerning Mr Scheffer I have noe answer as yett. Had not this fire happened last night I would have sent my accompts to your Worship according to your Worships order, but now I am takeing care to gett the thatch to cover the house againe which was taken downe last night for feare of the fire. As soone as itt is finished Coffee shall come downe with the said accompts and the gold.

28. Mark Bedford Whiting   Succondee Factory, 15 Oct. 1683

Your Worships of the 13th instant is come to hand together with the powder and the green Welch plaines per the 9 hand canoe. The powder I disposed according to promise which now I send downe the product of the same with my monthly accompts with the ballance thereof per this conveyance. I humbley begg your Worships pardon for not finishing my September accompt before. Had not this fire happened which caused us to pull downe the thatch off the house and made us take care for the covering of the same againe, I had finished them some dayes agoe, but for the future I shall observe your order per your last. I hope in a short time to be out of danger of any fire that shall happen in towne, when the Royall Companys factory is built, which is now put forwards, the people of this place being about itt, some are gon to cutt wood, some to make durt, others are rowsaing[54] the ground where your Worship ordered itt should be built. I shall be in this as spareing and in all other things as spareing as possible in order to the Royall Companys benefitt. I have according to your Worships order gott the articles of agreement signed by the Cabasheers of Mampone by order of Tickadoe,[55] they promiseing to putt the Dutch off and att the signing of the said articles, they made the Cabasheers of this towne take their fittish to be true and faithfull to the English. I delivered according to contract 10 green perpetuano's, whereof most of them being damaged and 10 green Welch plaines att the signing of the agreement. As to Dickiscove pallavora, I cannot come to speake with any of the Cabasheers of the said place, the people of this place haveing abused some of their wives which hath bred a differance betwixt them both soe that they panyar[56] one another. Tickadoe is comeing downe to fight that place, they haveing alsoe abused the Addooms severall times, and when hee doth come hee hath sent the Dutch here word that he will not show them a trick unless they remove. Wee are in great want for more powder alsoe brass basons which are a greate comodyty amongst the Wassa's, here being above 100 bendy's in towne att this time for those two sorts of comodyty's. If the Royall Companys factory was built and was but supplyed with powder, sheets and brass basons and green Welch plaines, the Dutch would take but little gold, and that as they would take would be for beades. If your Worship can possibly spare more powder I have ready money in hand for 30 barrells and here is also 10 bendy's for brass basons which I hope your Worship will be soe kind as to supply us with. I now send your Worship 7 marks, 7 ounces per the bearer hereof hopeing your Worship will supply us with the abovesaid goods. I must informe your Worship that the Wassa's are in great want of perpetuano's blew, the Dutch here have great quantity of them but the country people will not buy them being less then ours.

29. Mark Bedford Whiting Succondee Factory, 20 Oct. 1683

This is to acquaint your Worship that here is come to towne a greate many Wassa's and Addoomes whoe are want of sheets, perpetuano's, brass basons, powder. They might be supplyed here from the Dutch with some of these goods, but being ordered to the contrary by Tickadoe [not] to have any thing to doe with the said people. I have a few sheets but not enough, alsoe a few perpetuano's but noe blew ones to put the green off. The said country people are willing to stay soe many dayes, according to contract untill your Worship can possibley supply them. I must informe your Worship that Mr Scheffer of Axim was unwilling to put the 9 hand canoe in the 15 hand canoe least the 15 hand canoe should come to any harme

---

[54] See Glossary.
[55] Cf. n.52 above.
[56] See Glossary.

neither would hee suffer them to be lasht together, soe that hee was forst to hyre 5 men more to bring the 9 hand canoe downe which I discharg'd here and paid them 2 angles per man. Here came the other day a fresh supply of goods for the Dutch, as perpetuano's, sheets, and brandy. Perpetuano's, hee sells as we does, blews att 10a and green att 9a and reds att 8a. As to news I heare of none, neither doe I heare of any shiping to windward. If your Worship can possibly spare Coffee I humbly desire of your Worship to send him up, that hee may overlooke the people that are building the Royall Companys factory, hee knowing how itt was contrived before, hee then being here att the building of itt.

30. Mark Bedford Whiting   Succondee Factory, 22 Oct. 1683

Your Worships of the 20th instant I have received together with the 91 brass basons, which shall be disposd according to your Worships order, on accompt of the Royall Affrican Company. I wrote your Worship per the Axim canoes for some sheets, alsoe perpetuano's, powder, and if your Worship can spare us more basons of that size (if not bigger) I can dispose of them. But as for powder, sheets and perpetuano's blew, wee are in greate want which I humbly begg your Worship to supply us with that wee may keepe the money from the Dutch whoe are well supply'd with these two sorts of commodyty's, sheets and perpetuano's, and although their perpetuano's are most blew yett the country people chusing rather to stay for a fresh supply of ours, they being far better then the Dutch which are but small. Here is a greate quantity of gold in towne for powder and other goods. Tickadoe hath sent heither a lusty man slave and hath promised to send downe more if your Worship is willing to buy them, they aske for the said slave 7 peaze, but I proffer them but 6 and if your Worship is willing to comply with I humbly begg of your Worship to supply us with snap pans for the said slave, they being unwilling to take any other sort of goods. As to the Royall Companys factory itt goes forward and if your Worship can possibly spare Coffee I humbly begg of your Worship to send him up.

31. Mark Bedford Whiting   Succondee Factory, 27 Oct. 1683

Your Worships of the 24th instant I have received per Captain Coffee with the following goods vizt 2 bayles containing 50 perpetuano's, 92 brass basons containing 325 pounds, 5 chests containing 325 sheets, 10 barrells of gun powder, 50 pieces greene Welch plaines and 20 snap pans on accompt of the Royall Affrican Company of England. The powder I disposed att the waterside with other goods, I have alsoe disposed of most of the greene Welch plaines. If your Worship can possibly spare us more greens with redd and yallow but noe blews, they being not in demand here; I have a parcell here of blews, I could wish your Worship would be pleased to exchange them for redd and yallow, perhapps blews are better at Cabo Corsoe. As concerning the brass panns I cannot gett more then 7 taccoes per pound and hardly that, I have disposed of 3 bendy's worth of them after that rate, haveing used all possible meanes to gett 8 tacco's per pound but cannot prevaile. As to the snap pans your Worship sent for the procureing of slaves, the slave that I wrote your Worship about was redeemed by some of the Wassa's, whoe gave the Addooms a bendy for his redemption before the said snap pans came on shoare and with the said money [the latter] bought part of the snap pans att 8 per bendy, they being for Tickado's present occasion. Here is a good trade at present and as soone as the Royall Companys factory is finished I hope your Worship will be soe kind as to supply us with all sorts, then wee shall make a good hand of itt for some loves one sort of a thing and some loves other sorts. I shall send downe next weeke what money is in cash. Here is noe news to windward, some canoes came from Axim yesterday and noe shiping is to windward.

II

KOMENDA

The RAC had a factory at Komenda ('Commenda', 'Comenda'), east of Sekondi, from at least 1673;[1] but this had been abandoned in 1680, when it was thought to be under threat of atttack by an African force,[2] and was clearly still unoccupied at the beginning of 1681. Letters elsewhere in the RAC correspondence (nos 496–8) report that a vessel of the Company, the *African Merchant*, called at Komenda in August 1681, but found that 'no trade' could be done there. In November 1681, as the letters reproduced in this section show, the factory was re-established. Its subsequent history, however, was chequered, being again abandoned in September 1682, again re-established in January 1683, once more withdrawn in May, and then again re-established in October of that year. The Komenda factory served principally for the gold trade, though on at least some occasions it also supplied corn to Cape Coast Castle; there are only two allusions to the supply of slaves (nos 63, 71).

The Dutch WIC had also had a factory in Komenda earlier, but this too had been abandoned by 1679;[3] in 1681 the building was still unoccupied, and in ruins (cf. no.35). An attempt by the Dutch to re-settle in Komenda was thwarted by the English factor in January 1682 (no.53). In November 1682, however, during the temporary absence of the English, the WIC again decided to re-establish its Komenda lodge, and this time the project was carried out;[4] the English thus found a Dutch lodge in place at Komenda when they returned there in January 1683 (no.85). But this Dutch lodge was also abandoned in May 1683 (no.112). This pattern of discontinuous settlement partly reflected disappointing trade, but the withdrawal of both English and Dutch factories in May 1683 was further provoked by a local disturbance in Komenda.

Komenda was situated within the state of Eguafo ('Aguaffoe' in these documents), with whose king the English factory there periodically negotiated. The distinction between 'Great Commenda' and 'Small (or Little) Commenda' occa-

---

[1] Davies 1957, 249.
[2] PRO, T70/10, Nathaniel Bradley et al., Cape Coast Castle, 25 June 1680.
[3] Van Dantzig 1978, no.3 (Herman Abramsz, 23 Nov. 1679).
[4] Van Dantzig 1978, no.35 (Resolutions of Council, Elmina, 24 Nov. 1682).

sionally made in these letters alludes (respectively) to the royal capital inland and the coastal village where the factory was located. The principal local person with whom the English dealt during 1681–3 was 'Captain Bracon (or Abracon)', a substantial merchant of 'Little' Commenda, who did much business on commission for the RAC.[5] The most important hinterland merchants who brought trade to Komenda were the Akani ('Arcanies'),[6] though one letter (no.107) also names the Twifo ('Quiffers') alongside them. It appears that traders from the interior normally approached Komenda through the state of Abrem ('Abramboe'), immediately north-east of Eguafo, since early in 1683 unspecified disputes within Abrem reportedly interrupted their passage (nos 92, 102).

32. James Nightingale   Commenda, 8 Nov. 1681

I give your Honour humble and harty thankes for all your kindnesses especially for your fatherly advice when I came from Capo Corso. I hope by the blessing of God allmighty to follow the same. I am safe arrived here and pitcht upon a house for the Company's factory which with a little charge may be made very serviceable, it stands not far from the harber soe being better capable to see what canoes goes out and in to hinder their tradeing with interlopers. The King himselfe gave me this house. Captain Bracon and all the rest of Great and Small Commenda gives your honour harty thankes in sending me hither, they all say your comands or mine by your Honour shall be observed. The most goods at present here vendable are iron barrs which are good, narrow niccanees, and tapselles, blew perpettuanoes, sheets and brawles. If your Honour will send me 100 iron barrs they are sold, to be understood in a canoe. Pray send me such goods as the Castle affords as soon as possible you can and that good not damaged. Once I have the name to have good goods the traders will come the more to me

Pray send me two windows one for the warehouse with 3 iron barrs for a shutter the other plaine, a lock and staples for the warehouse doore, the other doors and windows I will see to gett them here my selfe. I heare of noe ships. When news presents shall informe in full. I begg pardon for not writing more, I am very lame both in hand and foot, the rest refer to Cabbisheers Hansico [var. Hansaco] and Agamaco [var. Agamacia][7] who are capable of all actions and transactions

[PS] Pray send also a hogshead or two of brandy.

---

[5] For a detailed account of Bracon and his commercial operations, see Kea 1982, 223–6.

[6] Akani may originally have been the name of a specific state (or confederation of states) in the interior, but seems also to have been used of gold traders generically: for a recent discussion, see Van Dantzig 1990.

[7] Like Hansico, an important African employee of the RAC.

33.   James Nightingale   Commenda, 9 Nov. 1681

Pray send mee one marke in iron barrs per first occasion of a canoe for they are
sould. Cabbisheer Hansico [var. Hansacoe] can give your Honour an account of all
proceedings. Hansico brings your Honours a pawne from Captain Bracon, his sonn
and Heckter [var. Hecter] being very sik.

    This ring Captain Bracon desires your Honour to lett Mr Downes cutt his name
Quacounou Abracon, his payment when hee knows it shall be complyed. In the
meane begg pardon, I not being well.

34.   James Nightingale   Commenda, 12 Nov. 1681

Your Honors much esteemed dated the 10th I have received; also 20 iron barrs for
which I shall acording [to] order give the Company creditt. Your Honour will be
pleased to send per bearer 40 iron barrs more, pray lett them be good barrs, or elce
for the future wee will have but little trade in them. I give your Honour hearty
thankes that you have pleased to consider to lett this factory have such goods as the
Castle affords. I doe pretend to nothing but will doe my endeavour for the creditt
and profitt of the Royall Company and your Honour.

    Pray send me as soone as possible the shipp and lett me desire your Honour to
send good goods not damaged. Pray send about 500 iron barrs, kettles of all sorts
and all sorts of goods elce your Honour thinks the most conveniant. I hope by the
blessing of God allmighty to procure a trade. In the meane time I leave the farther
reports to the bearer, I being troubled both with hand and foot with lamness I
humbley desire pardon. There is noe ships to windward only a Portugues at Butru.[8]

[PS] Captain Bracons ring wee have received. I would willingly know what he must
pay for the cutting of it. Ditto Bracon gives your Honour thankes.

35.   James Nightingale   Commenda, 16 Nov. 1681

Your Honours of the 14th instant came safe to my hands, also 40 iron barrs for
which shall give the Company creditt. If the ship be not gone pray send some brass
kettles, allso a halfe peece of red and a halfe peece of blew cloath. The Generall of
the Mine sent some dayes agone his Chief Cabbisheer Aban[9] to Chama,[10] Jabie[11]
and the Antha country[12] to agree with the natives not to bring theire gold to Commenda, he instigated them as much against the English as possible he can; but alas

[8] Butri, between Dixcove and Sekondi.
[9] For Aban, a prominent African employee of the Dutch WIC from the 1670s to the 1690s, cf. Daaku 1970, 104–5.
[10] Shama.
[11] Jabi (Yarbiw), Eguafo's western neighbour, to which Shama belonged (cf. Henige 1975).
[12] i.e. Ahanta, which included Sekondi.

the whole country hates him from Ashanee to Fanteen,[13] and as for this place they have broken downe the factory to the ground, and stolen away all the stones that was for the building theire fort. I could wish the ship was here to stop theire mouths.

36.   James Nightingale   Commenda, 18 Nov. 1681

Just now came a Commenda man from Axim who was aboard of a Dutch interloper: Ditto interloper tould the Blacke that he left at Ashanee and Abbene 3 English shipps, whereof 2 belong to the Royall Company and that they thought to be downe within 10 dayes. The Generall of the Minas Cabbisheer is mighty bussie, Aban by name, about resettling of a factory for the Dutch, also for turning us out. Ditto Aban has sent for a great many musketteers the which past by this place this day. They have also a difference with the natives at Chama. The factory they are settling is Succondee.[14] This being writ in hast begg pardon.

37.   James Nightingale   Commenda, 22 Nov. 1681

Just now Captain Samuell Starland[15] came ashoare and told me your Honour had not sent the 5 hand canoe. Wee having not one canoe at Commenda to bring the goods ashoare, therefore my humble desire is to send the 5 hand canoe heither, also one hogshead of brandy for I have had none this 6 dayes, and among the blacks there is nothing to be done without brandy. Pray send also halfe a peece of red and halfe a peece of blew cloath.

38.   James Nightingale   Commenda, 26 Nov. 1681

This serves to acquaint your Worship that the 2 halfe peeces of cloath and the 30 gallons of brandy which you were pleased to send for the supply of this factory, came safe ashoare. The 5 hand canoe has been imploy'd ever since in unloading the ship which wee hope to dispatch by Tuesday night. Be pleased to send us per this canoe halfe a peece of red cloath more, as likewise the price of it. This morning the blacks by the King of Aguaffos order tooke a Portugueze ship in this roade, and sent the people ashoare.

[PS] Wee must begg your Worship to excuse our not sealing this letter, for wee have neither wax nor wafers, which wee hope you will be pleased to supply us with, as likewise with some paper.

[13] Fante, which included the English factories of Anashan, Anomabu and Egya.
[14] Cf. section I above.
[15] Commander of the *African Merchant* (cf. no.39).

39.   James Nightingale & John Winder   Commenda, 29 Nov. 1681

Your Worships of the 28th instant with halfe a peece of red cloath wee have re-
ceived, and shall dispose of it at the rate you are pleased to mention (if possible).
Wee are sorry you should thinke wee would charge the Company with sending to
Capo Corso upon any frivolous account but it was Captain Bracons desire that you
should be informed of the Portugues being taken soe sent one of his owne canoes.
Wee have noe further account of the reason of it then that some time since a
Portugues in this roade paniard 5 of the Kings relations. Wee refer your Worship to
Captain Starland for a more perticular relacon of the busieness. Wee have received
out of the African Merchant according to your order, the following goods vizt 13 ¼
barrells of powder, 485 iron barrs, 96 blew baftas broad, 95 ditto narrow, 16 pieces
sayes, 50 musquetts, 8 ginghams, 44 barrs of lead, 20½ dozen knives of the best
sort, 27 dozen ordinary ditto, 10 pewter juggs, 20 fine sletias, 20 silke longees, 20
herba ditto, 20 stript silkes, 20 driven kettles, and 50 brass diglings for which shall
give the Company creditt according to order.

[PS] Wee received the wax for which shall give you hearty thanks.

40.   James Nightingale   Commenda, 2 Dec. 1681

Your honours dated the 29th November came safe to my hands and have punctually
observed the same. Cabisheer Agamaco has been with the King and told him your
honours commands, his answer is that about 4 yeares agoe he sent 5 men of his
relation to assist a Portuguese in selling his goods and buying his slaves, but ditto
Portuguese comeing to Wyamba[16] to leward carried them clearly away, and were
never heard of since. Ditto King has had no occasion since came in place to demand
satisfaction of any Portuguese, but this man hee suffering 4 of his men to lye
ashoare, which aforesaid men told the blacks that now was the time to have satisfaction, which one of them is by name Emanuell, a great rogue, for he has been in
service both of us and Danes. I have seen him whipt att the gunn att Capo Corsoe
severall times. Hee intends to serve your honour, I have turn'd him out of the factory
and broke his head. After the 4 men were ashoare ditto Captain came ashoare, and
afterwards his boate. I told the Capain pray goe aboard in your boate, the blacks
intend to take your ship, but hee being a low hearted man was afraid, and that time
his ship was not [sic?] taken. Ditto Portuguese Captain has been with the King, who
told him that hee should have his ship againe, and when satisfaction was made for
the 5 persons his relation, hee should have the remaynder now taken repaid either
in gold or slaves, and desired to know what he had lost because them that tooke itt
shall not steal any of the goods. Now as concerning our factory to sustayne any
damages or the looseing any of the Royall Company's goods, your honour will be

---

[16] Winneba, in Angona on the eastern Gold Coast (cf. section VI).

pleased to consider the contract between your honour and the King and alsoe their pawnes and our strength and commands upon the coast, alsoe the great charges the Company has been att in settleing itt. I doe assure your honour when the factory was last removed,[17] the King was the person that sent 300 men to our assistance, and brought Captain Seaman, Captain Hill, their mates, doctors, myselfe, Griffin [and] the Royall Companies goods safe off the shoare. I did not loose the worth of a cracra.[18] The King sends mee word that as long as Bracon is att the waterside and his relation and hee himselfe above att Great Commenda, that the haire of one of the Royall Companys servants shall not be touched, much less the loss of the Company goods. And as to my person pray rest assured your honours commands shall alwaies by mee be observed. According to orders [I] send my Accra accounts.[19] Your honour will find that Mr Hassell will give the Company creditt for the 1 ounce, 5 angles and 10 taccoes in his account; if not [I] will pay your honour and demand of Hassell the same. There is a Portuguese shipp att Axim.

[PS] Mr Wender presents his most humble service to your Honour.

41.   James Nightingale   Commenda, 3 Dec. 1681

This accompanies the Portuguese Captain, by name Emanuell Consalves, whoe left his smack in this roade. Ditto Captain reports that his ship is not serviceable to saile to St Thoma. Soe having noe more onely referr myselfe per letter to your honour by Cabisheer Agamaco.

42.   James Nightingale   Commenda, 4 Dec. 1681

I have received your letter and according to your order, have demanded of the blacks of this place whether they are willing to part with the Portuguese ship, whoe have freely consented that she shall be carried to Capo Corse. Tomorrow I shall give your worship a more particular answer to your letters.

43.   James Nightingale   Commenda, 9 Dec. 1681

According to your order I have been aboard the Dutch ship, whoe hath brought a cargoe of 10,000 pounds prime cost, from Middelborough, many sheets but few perpettuanoes. The news in Europe is that the King of France (alias French King) hath banished out of his Kingdome all Protestants.[20] The Prince of Orange hath

---

[17] i.e. in 1680.
[18] See Glossary.
[19] Nightingale had served in the RAC factory at Accra in August/September 1681 (cf. section VII).
[20] Evidently a false rumour: toleration of Protestants in France (under the Edict of Nantes) was not revoked until 1685.

been of late in England, and tis supposed uppon noe good intent.[21] One of the chiefest lords in England is put in the Tower, the relater not knowing his name.[22] The Duke of York is in England, and in great esteem both with King and people.[23] There is suppos'd to be a war between Sweden and Denmark, but not yett published.[24] This ship has brought two factors, three Assistants and 7 souldiers, sailed out of Zealand the last of October. There is a ship coming from Amsterdam, with a new Generall by name D. Peere, whoe was formerly one of the Lords of Zealand, and is dayley expected here.[25] Captain Balck tells mee that there is above 5,000 marks of gold in cash att the Mine and what the Generall intends to doe with it none knowes. The first ship that sailes from the Mine to Europe will be Captain Leendart Joosten van Dyck, with two of the small ships more. Itt will be the latter end of January before Captain Balk will depart. Both these Captains presents their humble servants to your worship, and will be glad to serve you in carrieing letters for Europe, or any thing elce that lies in their power but begg pardon that they cannot waite on you att Capo Corsoe. As for paints, linseed oyle, and the draughts of the coast I will procure for your worship if possible. Last night passed by two ships but know not what they were.

44.   James Nightingale   Commenda, 9 Dec. 1681

The 2 peeces of red cloath, and 20 silk longees came ashoare, for which shall give the Company creditt. Pray be pleased to send 20 sayes and as many herba longees for supply of the factory.

[PS] All the sayes are sold.

45.   James Nightingale   Commenda, 10 Dec. 1681

I am sorry that I must acquaint your Honour that Mr Wender has had these three dayes a feavour and ague, which continues upon him, and his desire is that you will be pleased to send Docter Meade here to know his opinion, and alsoe assist him. If Docter Mead cannot come pray send the docter of Captain Starland and alsoe halfe a douzen bottles of small beere, I haveing nothing to assist a sick man, onely brandy and mum which is not good in this distemper. Soe haveing nothing to inlarge onely

---

[21] Prince William (later King William III of England) visited England in July 1681.

[22] Probably alluding to Lord Shaftesbury, who was tried (but acquitted) in November 1681.

[23] James, Duke of York (later King James II) was at this time Royal Commissioner in Scotland.

[24] Another false rumour; although relations between Sweden and Denmark were tense at this time (following a war in 1675–9), there was no war in 1681.

[25] This seems to be a misunderstanding. The new Director-General of the WIC, who took office in 1682, was Thomas Ernsthuys; 'van den Pere' was the name of a family of prominent sugar-planters in Dutch Guiana, one of whom may possibly also have been on the ship.

your honour will be pleased to send 20 peeces of sayes and 20 herba longees per the first, all the sayes are sold.

PS. Mr Wender is not able to write himselfe. Pray send mee the man slave for the factories use. One of the ships past by last night came from the Beneen,[26] belongs to the Mine.

46. James Nightingale   Commenda, 20 Dec. 1681

Just now came a person from aboard of the ship John Bonadventure, John Woodfine Commander, whoe spoke with ditto Captain and tooke him by the hand. There is alsoe goods came from aboard with the Royall Companys marke. Ditto Woodfine intends to anchor att Tagarada tomorrow. Captain Brackon and other marchants here desires your honour to grant me the liberty to take out some goods which they want, which are consigned to the Castle for present payment, itt will alsoe save canoe hire. I expect your honours order,

PS. If I should gett any of those rogues aboard, which has abused the Companies trade here, also the canoe gentlemen, pray give me an order to the Companys Captains that they may keepe them and bring them to Capo Corsoe to your honour.

47. James Nightingale   Commenda, 20 Dec. 1681

According to your honours order [I] went aboard of the Dutch ships att the Mine, the skepers reports mee that they think to sett saile the 2nd January Dutch stile,[27] but they are not certaine either before or after, but my oppinion is that will goe very suddainly by reason the people that imbarks are aboard. The names of the skepers is as followeth, Leendart Joosten van Dick, Commander of the ship Roterdam bound for Roterdam; Marinues Willmess Commander of the ship the Armes of Zurch Zee, bound for Zeeland; Machiell Joosten Commander of the ship Minyder-bergh, bound for Amsterdam. Any of the aforesaid skepers will carry your honours letters safe. I am satisfied that there is arrived att Dickiscove an English ship pretty big and of good force, supposed to be a Company's ship. Wee may hope of Captain Woodfine being there.

PS. I would advise to wright your letters as soon as possible. I found Mr Wender pretty well, praised be God for itt.

---

[26] Benin, in modern Nigeria. For European trade with Benin at this period (mainly in ivory and cloth, the latter for re-sale on the Gold Coast), cf. Ryder 1969, 124–6.
[27] = 23 Dec. 1681, old style.

48.   John Wender   Commenda, 20 Dec. 1681

Although my weakness renders mee uncapable to write much, yett I should willingly in a few lines shew my gratitude to your worship for your kindness in sending the Docter to my assistance as likewise for the beere, for which I give you most humble and hearty thanks; I thank God I have not had any fitt since Saturedey night soe doe hope tis gon, only I continue still very weake, which is noe more then usuall after such distempers. Sir I have nothing elce to add, only desire your worship to remember mee if any imployment should present that may be better then what I have already.

49.   James Nightingale   Commenda, 22 Dec. 1681

Your honours dated 21 instant I have received, alsoe 20 pieces sayes, and 20 herba longees and halfe piece red cloath, for which shall give the Company creditt. There comes two gentlemen in Captain Woodfine both of the Councill supposed to [be] one your second the other warehousekeeper. Mr Kite is in this roade in an interloper, comes from Barbadoes.

50.   James Nightingale   Commenda, 28 Dec. 1681

According to order, I sent your honour 19 brass kettles, one being sold since I was att Capo Corsoe weighing 5 pound. The reason the canoe stay'd soe long the bearer can give your honour an account.

[PS] Pray send per this canoe, the man slave.

51.   James Nightingale   Commenda, 5 Jan. 1681/2

Your honours dated ultimo December came safe to my hands. As to an answer, that as soone I heard the slaves run away I sent immediatly to the King, Captain Bracon and the Mareene[28] to procure them for us according to contract, but they never came ashoare here, itt was above 6 miles from hence towards Jabin. As to the two slaves being paid [for] 11a apiece I never heard of itt. The Captain never came to mee, if [he] had [I] should have told him your honours contract, itt is his owne falt for he plainely told if the blacks had asked a bendy a head he would have paid itt, for he had a selfe interest in itt, which I beleeve he has for not one of the 12 slaves are bought for the Company marchandize, but [they were] absolutely panyard with all the teeth they had. I know 4 of them myselfe which are great traiders att Cestus, I have been ashoare with them both att Cestus and Basha.[29] I beleeve the next English

---

[28] See Glossary.
[29] (Grand) Bassam, in Ivory Coast.

ship will pay for itt. Docter Griffin and I have done our endeavour to gett the slaves, wee have gott 8, two are aboard before and two drownd. The king has had a great deale of trouble alsoe, wee heare, to gett the slaves, they being disperst in a great many places. As for your honour blameing my unjustice and Captain Bracon[s] ill conscience [it] is undeserved, as Docter Griffin will give your honour a particular account. Wee humbly begg your honour not to blame us for wee have committed noe fault, and as to abuse received att the factory, there has been none committed onely that the ships in the road have taken aboard above 160 marks in gold and wee to the contrary ashoare none at all, which may be very well supposed att the rates they sell their goods at and wee haveing none to supply them, but now I hope your honour will be pleased to send mee what supply your honour can spare mee per first occasion. In short, here is gold if wee had good currant goods and the rates accordingly, which I humbly begg your honour to consider, itt being the winder-most factory where shipping sells their goods soe abominable cheape. I send your honour my December account, you will be pleased to consider, that itt is the month of charges, being the first settleing, and I assure your honour itt has cost mee not little besides to gett the natives to bee friends with our masters the Royall Affrican Company, which will without doubt for the future be for their profitt if your honour continues this factory; if not am of opinion that the Dutch, French or other nations will soone inhabitt itt, which to the contrary in our possession noe other nations can doe itt, and wee once being removed itt will not easily be gott againe. The King of Commenda presents his service to your honour and understands by reports that the King of Fettue[30] intends to make war against him. Hee desires your honour to know what the reason may be, either if his person or people are abused or if hee or his country owes him any money, hee desires your honour to write mee an answer.[31] In the meanetime I take leave and referr the rest to the report of Docter Griffin whoe will give your honour an account in generall.

52. James Nightingale   Commenda, 24 Jan. 1681/2

This is onely to give your honour an account that I have received 4 peeces of boysados, 25 perpettuanoes, 6 3 lb and 30 4 lb pewter basons, 36 looking glasses, 30 brawles, 50 Guinie stuffs, 10 course sletias, 20 silk longees, 12 course blanketts, and 130 sheets, for which shall give the Royall Company credit

53. James Nightingale   Commenda, 19 Jan. 1681/2

Your honours dated the 17th instant per Mr John Smith came safe to my hands. As

---

[30] Fetu (Afutu), the eastern neighbour of Eguafo.

[31] Since the RAC headquarters Cape Coast Castle was situated within Fetu, the Eguafo king presumably assumed that the Agent-General could speak for or intercede with its ruler.

Komenda

to an answer of the fire itt is as followeth. On Monday being the 16th instant the fire began about 8 a clock at night about 50 paces to windward from us, which consumed within less than ¾ of an hours time above 200 houses, occasioned by one frieing of fish in palm oyle. The old Queene and Captain Bracon lost all they had, only saved their gold, and as to the Royall Company's concerns att the heate of the fire [I] was afraid that I should not save one cracra worth but the great mercy of God Almighty and assistance of my boys and Commenda people saved all only 1 chest of sheets, 21 lead barrs, 5 3lb pewter basons, 28 4lb ditto, 85 chests of corne, 10 pewter jugs. The remains [I] have with Mr Smith compared with my accounts and books and found that did agree. The lead barrs, juggs, basons, were in the roome with the iron [and?] are melted, I have saved of itt as much as possible could. The sheets were in my owne room which are consumed with most part of my owne goods. As to the corne [I] had bought and paid for 129 chests, whereof is remayning above 40 odd. I doe assure your honour if such an accident had befallen the Dutch, they would not have saved one penny's worth. The Dutch heareing that our factory was consumed with all the Royall Company's concerns, were very hott to settle their factory, but I have stopt their designe, and what is possible of the contract shall be observed. Here is in the road a great French ship between 30 or 40 guns, about 200 men.[32] I told the Capushers last night to remember your honours contract, and that none here should come ashoare for [I] intend absolutely with Captain Bracons assistance to hinder all them that should act anything prejudiciall to my masters the Royall Affrican Company. Here are likewise in the road two English interlopers, the one called Captain Young the other I doe not know. I desire your honour to send mee your order and Councill if any come ashoare to hinder their designe. I desire your honour be pleased to send some body here to see what is best to be done about the factory, either repairing this or to build where the factory was formerly, and what length and breadth your honour will be pleas'd to order it. I also desire your honour that you would be pleased to consider the loss and charge I am att, also to allow some gratuity to the people that soe trusty assisted mee in saveing the Company's goods, and especially Mr Harper for his care in the midst of the fire, for wee all were afraid the factory would blow up by reason of the powder. If my opinion may be excepted I could advise what is to be done, and att the least charge, about our factory. Soe haveing no more to inlarge only referr the rest to the report of Mr Smith whoe will give your honour a particular account. In the meane time am in a distressed condition as to my person but the Companys goods are secure.

[PS] The reason I have not writt before was for want of inke.

---

[32] Further information on the French is given in the following letters (nos 54–5), which make clear that this ship was part of the squadron on which Jean Barbot served.

54. James Nightingale   Commenda, 21 Jan. 1681/2

Last night understanding by the blacks that there was a differance between the
English interloper and the Frenchman in this road thought fitt to send this morning
aboard the French ship to understand the reason because I might give your honour
an account of it, which is as followeth. Mr Harper comeing from on board the
Frenchman reports mee that the French Captain sent his boate with his Leiuetenant
aboard of Captain Young an English interloper and demanded in the King of France
his name his pass and commission but ditto Captain replyed you French dogg gett
you gon with all your people out of my ship or else I will kill you, and said wee are
the King of Englands subjects and an interloper, and bid him come aboard to fight
him, whereupon hee made his guns ready but the French leiutenant comeing aboard
told his Captain all transactions, whereupon the French Captain with his marchant
Monsieur Bardoe [var. Bordoe][33] sent a civill answer in writing to the interloper
desireing not to be soe bold for hee would doe him noe harme here, but as soone
as the Frenchman had understood of your honour that the English man was an
interloper and noe Royall Company's ship, [he] would doe the Royall Company
that service as soone as once was to leward of Capo Corsoe, would take the interloper above mentioned; the which in Monsieur Bordoe [var. Berdoe] marchant
whose [= his] name and their companys seal I send your honour inclosed, [he]
reports that his ship came about 3 months agoe from Rusborg very neare Rochell,
their old company being broake, and haveing a new one[34] very desireous to settle
in these parts, and to that intent gives great encouragement to the Blacks, alsoe that
dayly here is expected two Frenchmen of war with a Generall and marchandize,
goods and materialls to settle the Gold Coast, especially to build a fort att Commenda,[35] which by contract has been agreed 10 yeares agoe, for these people here
sent a black to France whoe spoke with the King himselfe.[36] Therefore now is time
for us to looke after our masters the Royall Affrican Company's place and interests
upon the coast, and if once being gone itt will not be easie to gett them againe,
especially Commenda, Wyamba, Succonde, Lague[37] which are privilidged places
to the Royall Affrican Company of England.[38]

55. James Nightingale   Commenda, 24 Jan. 1681/2

Your honours dated the 21st instant came safe to my hands. [I] am glad to heare

---

[33] i.e. Jean Barbot ('Bardoe' being probably miscopied for 'Barboe').

[34] The Compagnie du Sénégal had been sold off to new owners in 1681.

[35] These abortive negotiations for a French fort at Komenda are recalled by Barbot 1992, ii, 348.

[36] For this embassy from Komenda to France in 1672, see Thilmans & de Moraes 1976, 295–6; also
recalled by Barbot 1992, ii, 348.

[37] Lagu, west of Winneba.

[38] The RAC claimed monopoly rights in the trade of these places on the basis of having having (or having
previously had) factories in them.

that your honour has been pleased to consider that I have done my endeavour as to the saveing the Royall Company's marchandise from burning and other damage. Itt was noe more but my duty, but doe assure your honour itt was difficult, but hope by the blessing of god almighty never to see such an accident att Commenda againe. Your honour has been pleased to command my small opinion about rebuilding the Royall Companys factory, which is as followeth. Att the first place in my opinion itt will be more profittable and secure for the Company to rebuild the factory where itt was formerly or there about, by reason itt is the only place to build a fort at, it being higher ground then any place att Commenda; alsoe [it is] the Royall Company's owne ground, itt is to windward of all the towne, to prevent fire, in short a small fort being built can command both sea and land. Secondly am advised by Captain Bracon and others here, that if your honour dus not resolve to sett both the people of Great and Small Commenda very speedily about building the old factory, that the raines will goe neare to prevent the finishing of itt, for I count but 3 months till the raines comes in. In the interim the people are willing to give mee their assistance in rebuilding this house for the security of the Companys goods and interest untill the other be built, and that att as little charge as may be. Therefore my desire is your honour will be pleased to keepe a good and faire corespondence with the King of Commenda and the people here soe that they and I may know your honours orders and designes, for I am confident they will doe what lies in their power for our advantages and assistance, both in the rebuilding and tradeing, as yesterday I have found, for haveing according to your honours orders notice of their tradeing with the French and other ships I sent my complaint to the King, whoe immediatly sent for the people of this place up to Aguaffo, whoe are not yett return'd but [I] have had advice from thence that the King made them take the fittish not to buy any goods aboard of ships provided wee had them in the factory or could procure them in 15 dayes time. Whatever your honour is pleased to conclude on for the rebuilding I desire your honour will send a fitt person who may survey the charge the Company will be att either for building or rebuilding, as likewise to contrive what may be done and att the least charge and best convenience for the Royall Companys interest, that in this case I may be blameless for any extravagancies of charge, for I am resolv'd not to extend the limitts of your honours order. As touching the French I have noe other information then what I have writt formerly, only that Monsieur Ducas comes Generall[39] with two men of warr of 45 gunns apeece, and one small frigat and two sloopes to settle upon this coast. Att present here noe transactions of any importance, only Captain Bracon with the rest of the marchants here and I thought fitt to send Captain Coffee to give your honour an account of all pasages and to know your honours commands. if your honour pleases to grant metigation of the prizes of your says, Guni stuffs, brawles, alsoe silk and

---

[39] This was a misunderstanding; although Ducasse was involved in the organization of the expedition (cf. Ly 1958, 178 n.15), he did not himself accompany it.

herba longees, itt is probable next month may take some gold. This month the Companys ships and others have sold soe cheape that I have had noe trade hitherto. The people who were soe trusty in assisting mee in the fire, dus dayly call out for some recompence according as I promis'd them in my extremity, to which I desire your honours order per next conveyance.

56. James Nightingale   Commenda, 28 Jan. 1681/2

Your Honours dated the 26th instant I have received and understand your Honour will be pleased to build a factory for the Royall Company at the old place it was formerly, but I begg your Honour to give me the liberty to build a little higher, to be understood the place where a fort may stand, it being hard by the old factory but better situated, also to inhedge soe much ground in for the Royall Company as possible can, for now is the time, and when I receive your Honours model and directions shall endeavour to carry on the affaires according to your Honours order.

The people here give your Honour humble thanks for the gratueity, and I have paid them in silke longees the worth of a peece of say, which does incourage them and upon all occasions [they] shall be at your Honours commands. Yesterday arrived here a small interloper bound for the Bite,[40] his name unknowne. Captain Young is still in the road. I here of noe ships to windward.

57. James Nightingale   Commenda, 1 Feb. 1681/2

Your Honours per Captain Coffie dated the 28th January came safe to hand, and shall according to your Honours resolution observe your order therein, soe in the building and prices of goods as have been formerly ordered, but if your Honour pleases to give 25 peeces of Guinea stuffs per benda I can dispose of 500 presently.

The reason I sent the rates of the goods to Capo Corsoe was that the Arcanies and others was informd that I vallued higher then Capo Corso rates, but now to the contrary they found their error.

I send your Honour my January account with the ballance of the same to Mr Spurvay[41] amounting to 7o 15a 2ta, also 2o 5a 9ta being the ballance of my Accra account[42] and 5o 9a 2ta being the ballance of December account of Comenda factory. The reason wee had noe more gold this month was because soe many ships of the Company, French and others have been in this road and undersold us, also the great disturbance of the fire. In the meane time am repairing this house for the safegard of the Company goods, till the other be build, which will come to some small charge. I will doe my endeavor to bring it soe lowe as possible can.

---

[40] Bight (i.e. of Guinea, or in later usage of Biafra).
[41] A member of the Council at Cape Coast Castle.
[42] Nightingale had served in the RAC factory at Accra in August/September 1681 (cf. section VII).

58.   James Nightingale   Commenda, 11 Feb. 1681/2

I having nothing of inportance to advise your Honour only that I heare of a great
English ship to windward, supose it may be the St George.

As to our building cannot possitive give your Honour an account, having a
palavera with the King and waterside people about it. Also a designe to turne some
of the great rogues out that hinders our trade and assist interlopers, therefore pray
send me downe one of your Cappusheers, that he may heare the palavero and give
your Honour an account.

It is not for our harme but profitt, for all is well heare.

[PS] Pray lett your Cappusheer be here in the morning.

59.   James Nightingale   Commenda, 15 Feb. 1681/2

Your Honours dated the 11th instant came safe to my hands. [I] answer that all the
powder remaining last month was sold the 5th instant, for as soon received your
Honours letter presently have shewed Hansico the warehouse as he can give your
Honour an account.

As to corne I have in all 85 chests. If your Honour pleases to order me to give
1½ angle per chest I am of oppinion can procure a good quantity, for course sletias,
green perpettuanes, or gold, for other ships give 2 angles per chest.

As to the reason I sent for one of your honours Cappusheers, was this, that I
would have these people know that your Honours comands in behalfe of the Royall
Affrican Company of England should absolutly be obteined, and would know
before wee build the factory the reason it was not on theire side accomplished, and
especially here being soe many rogues of other countrys that went aboard of ships
without leave, that I would panyare them. They not beleiving me sent of severall
canoes with musquetts to take them and put them all from aboard an interloper
comanded by Captain Been, which occasioned a long and strong palavora, but at
the end [I] made the merchants and Arcanies take this country fetish that none
should goe aboard of any ship to trade contrary to your Honours articles, and alsoe
prendee'd[43] them three sheep, whereof your Honour will receive two from the
transgressers, but it has been chargeable to me, besides [I] paid 12 angles in gold
and one anchor of brandy, the brandy was spent in the 5 dayes palavora, and the
12a was given to the fetishmakers and Cappusheers. The Comenda merchants and
Arcanies likewise paid to the Cappusheers and fetishmakers 1 ounce 8 angles of
gold besides the Kings Mareen. Your honour haveing formerly ordred me to incourage these people not to let any other nation come ashoare was the occasion, soe that
for the future wee may here order your Honours comands, which shall at all times
be observed in what lyes in my power.

---

[43] See Glossary.

As to the building of your Honours factory tomorrow the people intend to goe about it, they demand 10 anchors of brandy for the whole charge of building, halfe in hand the other halfe when it is build, and that according to the draught, for they will doe their endeavor to have it finished before the raines. Pray let me have one or two slaves that has expearence in building for assisting and directing the work-men.

There is at Axhim Captain Nicholas Van Horne in a ship of 36 gunns, his second with 24 ditto, and two Branderburgers of good force.[44] They are full of goods and lets noe trade be where they come to anchor.

I would have written more at large but am not well, therefore pray pardon me, the rest I leave to Cappusheer Hansico who will give your Honour a generall account.

60. James Nightingale   Commenda, 20 Feb. 1681/2

This accompanies Captain Daniell Gates, to whom I have delivered 103 chests of corne, 85 at 1a per chest and 18 at 1½a per ditto as per his receipt. As to the charge of giveing the people the fetish Hansico was wittness to the particular disburse-ments.

In referrence to the building of the house, upon receipt of your Honours order for giving of the 10 anchors of brandy, I called the Cappusheers together and gave them advice thereof and of your Honours pleasure for their provideing of doors and windows but they told me the brandy they desired was only for a dashey and that they expected besides that 3 marks in mony for the building, whereupon I disperst them in great anger, but Captain Bracon being loath [it] should goe soe brought the Cappusheers here this morning and by his perswasions in presents of Captain Gates did offer to take the fetish to have the house build before the raines providing your Honour would allow 5 bendaes vizt the one halfe in hand the other halfe at the finished of the worke and this for the whole charge of building without any dasheys except what I am willing to give of my selfe, which your Honour may consider will not be little, I being dayly among them when they are at worke. As to the doors, doorcases and windows it is unpossible for these people to gett, this country not affording wood for that use, wherefor I hope your Honour will be pleased to supply those necessaries from Capo Corso, also some pickaxes and iron crowes. As to preventing forreigners landing at this place, I hope my endeavor shall prove an-swerable to your Honours demands.

I desire your Honour to send me for the account of the Royall Company for the supply of this factory, some broad and narrow niccanees, tapseels ditto, white

---

[44] This does not refer to the Brandenburger expedition in which von der Groeben served, which did not arrive in West Africa until later in 1682. For earlier Brandenburger activity, cf. Jones 1985, 2–3.

long cloaths, course sletias, course blanketts, all sorts of pewter basons, likewise ¼ casque of brandy.

I have sent a merchant to Capo Corso with 6 bendaes of gold to be bestowed in copper barrs. I desire to know how many you give per benda, and if the rates be reasonable, it is like may prove heare a commodity vendible.

I begg your Honours speedy answer concerning the affaires of building by my boy Tom who brought your Honours pacquett from de Mina.

PS. As yet can give your Honour noe account about the Deanes [= Danes] slaves for had noe answer from Aguaffo.

61. James Nightingale   Commenda, 23 Feb. 1681/2

Your Honours of the 22nd of this instant came safe to my hand, per order thereof I have this day delivered to the Cappusheeres 5 ounces of gold according to agreement who are well satisfied, and doe faithfully promise the accomplishment of the factory before the raines.

I have sent this canoe cheifly aboard of the ship at the Mina for your Honours pacquett, whoe I doubt not but shall receive it, if ever comes to the Captains hands, for I did never heare any thing of your pacquett before which wayes I had writt for it with the last conveniencey.

I desire you would be pleased to send up one of the blacke bricklayers to oversee the building for whome wee now only waite, delaying the foundation for one fitt person to direct the same, likewise the crowes and pickaxes are much wanting for the worke. I also desire your Honour will be pleased to send me by this oppertunity upon account of the Royall Company 30 gallons of brandy, for the carrying whereof I have sent 5 anchors.

I am uncapable of writing at present by reason of a lameness both in hands and leggs, it is a very bad distemper in this country and hath keept me since Munday last. I take it to be the same desease that troubled Captain Seamans. I begg your Honour to acquaint Docter Mead with this my desease, that he may send up what he knowes convenient for preventing the same, and if Docter Asskin be in the Castle I begg your Honour to send him up for applying of Docter Meads directions.

In my last by Captain Gates I forgott to give you an account of the charges I was at in putting the corne aboard which was in all 8 angles.

62. James Nightingale   Commenda, 3 March 1681/2

Your honours dated the 24th February have received, alsoe 32 gallons of brandy for the which I have given the Company creditt for in my February accounts which I send per the bearer, alsoe the ballance thereof in gold amounting to Mk 1.4.5.4 ta to Mr Spurvay. I am sorry that our building does not goe on according to my desire, which is only occasioned by the wanting of crows, pickaxes and shovells, for the ground is soe hard it is unpossible for the people to worke itt without those necessaries, which I hope your Honour will send upon receipt hereof, as likewise a fitt person to direct the worke, for itt will not be without great trouble, labour and difficulty if this building be accomplished before the raines which I expect about the 25th of Aprille next. Here is in this roade an English interloper which sells his says att 14 angles per peece and other goods proportionable. There is likewise a Dutch interloper at Pompandee.[45] There are noe other English ships to windward that I know.

63. James Nightingale   Commenda, 3 March 1681/2

I send your honour by my boatswaine one good woeman slave for the Royall Company's account. Pray lett mee have a receipt, as alsoe a man that can direct the worke and the materialls which I writt for this day. All the people are working this day to breake clay.

64. James Nightingale   Commenda, 15 March 1681/2

Your honours of the 12th and 13th instant I have received, as likewise Yankey with his materialls,[46] but am sorry you term my charges extravagant seeing I have charged nothing but what was clearly disburst upon the Companys account. As to Mr Winders busieness I hope you will be pleased to allow of seeing I paid him his sallery in goods out of the warehouse haveing had noe order to the contrary. According to your honours order soe soone as haveing notice of the arrivall of any of the Companys ships [I] shall endeavour to acquaint them with your honours commands, I being very sencible of the Dutch their treachery to our nation if they can effect itt either by sea or land, therefore I humbly thank your honour for your kind advice thinking itt fitt if itt please your honour to send one to Dickiscove to prevent our peoples landing att Axim or any of the Dutch windward places. Just now is returned my boy from the Mina whoe brings mee an account of the pacquetts good dispatch as you may plainly see by the inclosed letters.

65. James Nightingale   Commenda, 5 Apr. 1682

I have sent your Honour by this canoe (being afraid to send by land) my March account with the ballance thereof to Mr Spurvay which is Mk 1: 7: 15: 2. Captain Shears arrived here upon Monday night[47] and I have done my endeavour to pur-

---

[45] Pompendi, between Butri and Takoradi.
[46] Yankey was a bricklayer (cf. no.211).
[47] Cf. no.521.

chase corne for him but can buy none cheaper then 2 angles per chest besides the charge for carrying itt aboard whereof I gave your honour advice in my last of the 29th March. Pray send with the first conveniency upon the account of the Royall Company for supply of this factory 100 niccanees narrow, 200 Guynea stuffs, 6 boysadoes, 4 chests of sheets, 20 sletias course, 20 course blanketts, pewter basons of all sorts. These are the goods wanting here att present and the marchants being come downe does keep their money for us, therefore I begg your honour to send up these goods with all speed, if delayed I feare they may buy their goods either of the Dutch or interlopers, there being two to windward. If your honour does not think itt safe to send the goods by the 15 hand canoe be pleased to order Captain Shears downe for the same and if the price of the corne be acceptable shall purchase what possibly I can against her returne. I beg your honour would order one man slave from aboard of Captain Shears for the use of the factory. Captain Bracon humbly thanks your honour for your kindess but the knives being alwayes sold att 1 angle per dozen [he] sendeth these back as too deare, therefore hee desires the Captain would send him his money or knives att the ordinary price of 1 angle per dozen. Soe soone as Captain Shears comes downe to Cabo Corsoe [I] shall send Yanky along with him I haveing noe more imployment for him here.

66.   James Nightingale   Commenda, 10 Apr. 1682

Your honours of the 6th of this instant I have received whereby I understand that my March accompts are allowed of, but stranges [strange is?] my canoe hyres are againe termed extravagant, seeing itt is your honours order I should give an account of what ships comes or passes att this place, which I hope your honour knowes I cannot doe without sending aboard and consequently charge itt to an account. I shall doe my endeavour to purchase what corne I can for Mr Shears at the rate of 2 angles per chest but the Blacks will not be att the charge of the canoe hyre for the interlopers pays 3 angles per chest now att this present both to windward and leward of this place. Pray send up the briganteen[48] with the first oppertunity with those goods mentioned in my last of the 5th of this instant and lett the iron barrs be of the best sort, especially those that are marked.

PS. If your honour will lower the price of the red and blew cloath there is a probabillity to dispose of itt but not att the former rates.

67.   James Nightingale   no date [May 1682]

Yours I have received and shall answer the particulars within this day or two, at present am not very well. I have desired all the sheets, Guyney stuffs and bassons,

---

[48] i.e. the *Cape Coast*, commanded by Charles Towgood.

only the 6 pounders and blanketts excepted, from Mr Towgood with a condition to pay him in gold att delivering according to your rates, but ditto Towgood will not doe it. It is for the creditt of the factory if you order itt, if not patience itt is a sad thing that a factor cannot keepe that respect among the natives as ought to be for the Companys creditt.

68. James Nightingale   Commenda, 1 June 1682

Your honours dated the 30th May I have this day received and am certaine your honour hath done the Royall Company good service in lowering the perpetuanoes 1 angle per piece and I question not but I shall be able to dispose of a good quantity thereof att this place soe soone as the natives knowes our rates. Wherefore I desire your honour will be pleased to send mee upon account of the Royall Company 3 bailes of perpetuanoes, 2 cases or 40 pieces sayes, 10 barrells of powder, alsoe the 29 pieces niccanees for which I have given receipt, and this with the first conveniency of faire weather. If your honour pleases to order mee to buy corne att 3 angles per chest I am in hopes to gett 20 or 30 chests in readyness to be sent downe by the canoe that brings up the above mentioned goods. I would have sent your honour my last two months account but must begg some few dayes delay, I being att present under physick. I am inform'd of two English ships to windward, not knowing whether Companys ships or interlopers.

69. James Nightingale   Commenda, 9 June 1682

By the oppertunity of this seasonable weather I have sent my boatswaine express to your honour with my last months accounts of Aprill and May, as alsoe the ballance of the same to Mr Spurvay being 4 markes 9 angles and 3 tacco's of good gold. I designed to have sent up sooner but hath been hitherto disappointed by the vehement raines which have fal'n for some dayes and have soe inraged the seas that noe canoes durst hazard off till now. I have by this conveyance alsoe sent up a good man slave for account of the Royall Company for whome I desire a receipt. This faire weather continuing I desire your honour will be pleased to send mee for account of the Royall Company by first conveniency the goods mentioned in my last to your honour of the 1st of this instant by the which I alsoe desire to know if you might be pleased to order the buying of corne att 3 angles per chest, whereto I begg your honours answer. If you might be pleased to order the selling the blew pottkeys att 24 per bendy I may dispose of them all this being the rate of the Guyney stuffs which the blacks esteems att equall vallue with the pottkeys. I desire your honour will be pleased to send mee a booke for keeping my accompts as alsoe two or three quires of paper I haveing but very little or none att all. Here is in this road a small ship bound to the Bite, Evan Leyes Commander.

70. James Nightingale   Commenda, 24 June 1682

Be pleased to know that I am this day safe arrived here as likewise the 15 hand
canoe whereout of I have received 6 pieces sayes, 75 pieces of perpetuano's, 10
barrells of powder, 50 iron barrs and 50 lead barrs and all for account of the Royall
Affrican Company. I desire your honour will be pleased to send mee by the said
canoe for account of the Royall Company soe many iron barrs marked and of the
best sort as the canoe conveniently can carry, as likewise 10 pewter juggs. I was
this morning aboard the Dutch ships bound for Europe whereof I understand that
there are two design'd to saile upon Monday next without faile, whereof one for
Zealand and the other for Amsterdam, but they are absolutely ordered by the Generall of the Mine not to carry any letters for the English nation without his especiall
order, but if your honour may be pleased to write under my covert I doubt not but
itt shall have a safe conveyance. I have the Commanders promise for the safe
conduct of my owne letters.

[PS] The St George is now in sight of this place.

71. James Nightingale   Commenda, 2 July 1682

Your honours of the 30th June by the 15 hand canoe I have received, as alsoe 225
iron barrs and 10 pewter juggs, for which I shall give the Company creditt. I have
sent your honour according to order 5 chests of corne per the 15 hand canoe, alsoe
a woeman slave for account of the Royall Company for which I desire a receipt. I
have alsoe sent up one barrell of powder being damnified, desireing one in leiw
thereof or a receipt for the same.

[PS] Tomorrow I shall send up my account with the ballance.

72. James Nightingale   Commenda, 3 July 1682

I have by this express sent your honour herein inclosed my June account with the
ballance of the same to Mr Henry Spurvay amounting to 8 marks, 4 angles and 3
tacco's, whereof paid ditto Spurvay the 23rd of June 6 marks, 7 ounces, 12 angles
and now per bearer 1 marke, 8 angles and 3 tacco's as per his receipts. Here is
arrived to windward of this place one small Barbarian [sic: = Barbadian] interloper
comeing from the Beneen and St Thoma, I suppose it may be Charles Langley. The
damaged barrill of powder whereof I writt yesterday was forgott by the canoemen
but shall be sent per first oppertunity.

73. James Nightingale   Commenda, 5 July 1682

Last night late I had advice from the Blacks of the arrivall of Captain Henry Nurse who lies now att Succondee. By the Blacks relation whoe hath been aboard, hee hath in his ship severall passingers, soe well factors as souldiers.

74. James Nightingale Commenda, 16 July 1682

Your honours dated of the 14th instant I have received whereby I understand my Aprill and May accounts are received and allowed of, but am sorry your honour is displeased with my putting both months into one account, which was occasioned by my being one month at Capo Corsoe in the which time there was little money taken and that which I have sent up was taken after my returne with goods, but in obediencye to your honours commands shall for the future take care to charge every months accounts by itt selfe. I begg your honour would be pleased to send up the 3 bales of perpetuano's, 40 pieces sayes, 10 barrells powder which I writt for last for account of the Royall Company, for these I brought downe last are almost sold and the mony in cash. I alsoe desire you would be pleased to send mee for account of the Royall Company 500 iron barrs of the best sort and marked for I have still upward of 80 per remaines but cannot put them off because not marked.

[PS] Pray send good goods, alsoe a booke to keepe my accounts in per first, want them much.

75. James Nightingale Commenda, 17 July 1682

Your honours of the 15 instant by the 15 hand canoe I have received, as alsoe 250 barrs of iron for which I shall give the Company creditt. According to order per returne of this canoe I send your honours 10 chests of corne. Charles Langley interloper lies to to windward of this place and is like to make but a bad markett of his Beneen cloaths[49] and is in a very weake condition haveing only 5 whitemen aboard. Here is a small interloper from the West Indias, his name unknowne only hee hath served the Company formerly and now intends to settle at Quida.[50] The Dutch interloper D Bruyne is alsoe here still.

[PS] I have alsoe sent per this canoe one man slave upon the Royall Company account for which I desire a receipt.

---

[49] Cloth from Benin was commonly sold on the Gold Coast, in exchange for gold: cf. Ryder 1969, 93–5.
[50] i.e. Whydah, on the Slave Coast (cf. section VIII). This does not allude to the notorious interloper Petley Wyburne, who had established his factory in Whydah earlier, in 1681 (cf. no.479). There is no other allusion in the RAC correspondence to this second interloping factory at Whydah, but in 1687 there is reference to a factory at Whydah which had formerly belonged to an English interloper called Thompson, which the King of Whydah then offered to the Dutch: Van Dantzig 1978, no.29 (Van Hoolwerff, Offra, 5 Sept. 1687).

76.   David Harper   Commenda, 2 Aug. 1682

Upon receipt of your honours dated ultimo July I sent for Mr Langley and delivered in his owne hands your honours letter, upon perusall whereof hee declared himselfe happy in being capable to doe your honour any service which hee sayes hee can and will very freely doe in this affaire of Mr Buckham, which I beleeve hee can well doe haveing transported the said Mr Buckham, his wife, children, slaves and estate from the Beneen[51] but complaines that hee dealt verry uncivilly by him after their comeing to St Thoma. I was very urgent with Mr Langley to have him come downe this day butt hee being troubled with a lameness and haveing some business to dispatch aboard humbly beggs your honours pardon for this dayes delay promiseing upon his faith and word to give his personall attendance tomorrow being the 3rd instant att Cabo Corsoe Castle.

[PS] Just now is arrived Mr Nightingale but soe ill disposed that hee could not write, yett hath spoke with Mr Langley about this affaire.

77.   James Nightingale   Commenda, 4 Aug. 1682

These are to acquaint your honour that since my returne hither I have still been verry ill disposed as to my health, wherefore begg some few dayes delay before I send up my monthly accompts, hopeing then to be in a better state of body then now and capable to write out my accompts which att present I cannot doe but hope in the mercy of God for a speedy recovery.

78.   James Nightingale   Commenda, 14 Aug. 1682

Itt haveing pleased God after a verry sore fitt of sickness to put mee in some way of recovery, although as yett I continue very weake and my health returns but slowly yett, I have endeavoured to draw up the last months accompt which I send your honour herein inclosed by this express of my boatswaine, as alsoe the ballance of the same to Mr Henry Spurvay being 4 marks, 7 ounces, 10 angles, 10 tacco's. Satureday night last came in this road Captain Andrews, Captain May and Captain Morphy, interlopers, they provided with all sorts of currant goods and takes a great deale of money and I to the contrary take not one cracra on shoare in the Companys factory.

79.   James Nightingale   Commenda, 17 Aug. 1682

Your honours of the 15th instant I have received. As to Agamaco's being sent to

---

[51] Presumably Buckham had been employed in the RAC's factory in Benin, which seems still to have existed in the 1680s, although abandoned soon thereafter: cf. Ryder 1969, 124.

Aguaffo I wish itt may tend to the Companys profitt for truely, although I have hitherto consealed what I could of the knavery of these people of Little Commenda upon expectation of their amendment, but finding them dayly to be worse and worse I am now forced to acquaint your honour that the Royall Companys interest in this place is very much abused for they now openly doe what they please in laying out their mony in all ships and I can sell nothing here but what I must trust for 2 or 3 months before I can gett my money and they only looke upon us here as pledges for their security that noe harme may come to them aboard ship. And they not only refraine buying the Companys goods but now attempts the stealing thereof, as I have severall times found by the chalks wherewith the iron barrs were marked and after counting the same in presence of Captain Brackon and the Kings Mareen have found 48 barrs wanting soe that except other meanes be used soe well for advance-ing the trade as secureing the Companys goods I shall grow scrupilous to take any longer charge of the Companys concerns here, feareing they may begin their old tricks in breaking open the warehouse and takeing the goods from thence. The bad money returned I have received and by this bearer have sent Mr Spurvay good money in leiu thereof, itt is my greate loss but occasioned by my sickness being unable to looke after itt my selfe.

80.   James Nightingale   Commenda, 19 Aug. 1682

After humbly begging your honours serious consideration of my last dated the 17th instant, these serves to acquaint your honour that last night about 9 of the clock there happened here some few houses to windward of the Royall Companys factory a most terrible and vehement fire which in the space of one halfe houre consumed above 60 houses but by the providence of God in calming the wind and our great industry in dethatching all the houses betwixt us and the fire which threatned any damage to our quarter [we] have, blessed be God, preserved the Royall Companys concerns from any damage of those threatning flames. The three interlopers are still in the roade corning and tradeing.

81.   James Nightingale   Commenda, 24 Aug. 1682

Your honours two letters of the 18th and 22nd instant I have received and according to order shall continue a good and faire correspondence with these people, the which hitherto I have done to my expences, although frustrate of my designe in advanceing the Royall Companys trade and interest, which they dayly more and more contemne by bringing all their goods from aboard ship and I have not taken one cracra since my last comeing from Cabo Corsoe and the money sent up last was for goods trusted out two months before and I truly beleeve soe long as there is a ship on this side Axim that they will buy none of the Companys goods, but I shall trust to your honours writting for redress of these wrongs by the first of the vessells that comes from leward. Whereas the King of Aguaffo's presence [pretence?] for conniveing with and assisting the rogues of Little Commenda in their villainy's only is my not duely paying his customes this I can prove to be a false untruth by Captain Brackon and the Mareen, whoe have received the customs off my hands and carryed them up to him att the time agreed upon by contract. The Feteras[52] custome I had hitherto detained upon account of the two slaves, but since the receipt of your Honours letter have sent him one peece of perpetuanoe with half an anchor of brandy, soe that they are wholly paid one years custome.

82.   James Nightingale   Commenda, 1 Sept. 1682

Your honours ultimo August I have received whereby I understand your honours order for removeing the Royall Companys factory from this place which shall in all points to the uttmost of my power punctually be obeyed soe soone as the briganteen is arrived here. The people here are soe refractory against our removing that they will give noe assistance in carrying the goods to the waterside, therefore desire your honour will be pleased to send up one of the big canoes with 5 or 6 slaves for carrying the goods to the waterside, otherwise itt will be impossible to gett the iron barrs off. Your honour has not been pleased to mention anything in the letter about David Harper or the flagg. If my small advice might be accepted I think itt fitt that the flagg may be left for the keeping the Royall Companys possession and that David Harper may come up with the goods, itt being impossible for a whiteman to stay here after the factory's removeall, but desire your honours answer therein which in this and all other things shall be obeyed. I desire your honour would send one of your Cabosheers whoe may see the removal and take notice of what pallavora either transactions may be occasioned by the natives soe well that your honour may understand rightly all the business. I desire a speedy answer.

83.   James Nightingale   Commenda, 8 Sept. 1682

Your honours of the 2d instant by Cabosheire Aggamaco with the 5 hand canoe, as alsoe one of this instant by Docter Griffins boy I have received. The reason I did not answer your Honours by Aggamaco before now was my dayly expecting Mr Towgoods arrivall here and soe after speedy imbarquing of the Royall Companys concerns att this factory in person to have given your honour a true and reale account of all affaires att this place. This accompany's Aggamaco whoe I have sent up by a 2 hand canoe to give your honour a full relation of what hath past here since his comeing to Commenda, and truly I have peremptoryly obeyed your orders in keeping a good correspondence with the natives, soe that there is noe pallavora here nor anything to be pretended in prejudice of the Royall Company's interest or my

---

[52] See Glossary.

own person, soe that I doubt not, the ship once arrived, but with creditt to my masters the Royall Affrican Company of England to bring of all the concerns att this factory, which in this and all others shall be obeyed by [James Nightingale].

PS. I heare noe news from the windward; Pray dispatch Aggamaco against the ships arrivall.

84. James Nightingale   Commenda, 10 Sept. 1682

Your honours of the 9th instant I have received and am sorry you are pleased to terme my letter frivilous, itt being soe full an answer to your honours of the 8th instant as I att that time could give. Whereas your honour takes itt ill my putting the Royall Company to the charge of the 2 hand canoe, my intention therein was for the best, for understanding your Honour was soe earnest to know how all affaires stood here I thought itt fitt besides my writting to send up Aggamaco whoe might give your honour a personall accompt how affaires stood here as to the Royall Companys concerns.

Last night came here the Kings man desireing Captain Bracon and mee up to Aguaffoe that hee might understand the reason of our removeing but I sent word that my business here was to looke after my masters concerns and if hee had any thing to say to the Royall Affrican Company that hee must have his recourse to Cabo Corsoe. I have formerly writt your honour my opinion about leaveing the fllagg for keeping the Royall Companys possession, concerning which I desire your pleasure as alsoe your honours order for bringing up David Harper, for as yett I have received noe particular order concerning either of them. To the 5 hand canoemen I have paid canky[53] money hitherto, I desire to know if your honour will allow of the continuance thereof while they are here.

I desire your honour to send mee for accompt of the Royall Affrican Company 10 gallons of brandy. I have sent a case to putt itt in and will be att the charge of canoe hyre myselfe. There is an interloper to windward att Dickiscove.

*****

85. David Harper   Commenda, 10 Jan. 1682/3

Immediatly after my arrivall here with Docter Griffin wee sent up your honours dasheys to the King and Fettera, and have alsoe disposed of the other two cases and anchor of brandy to the Cappusheers and merchants of Commenda, for which they all render your honour hearty thanks, as alsoe for your honours care in preserving the English's interest in this place. The Cappusheers promise with all care and

---

[53] See Glossary.

speed to goe about building the Royall Company's factory. The Dutch have here three whitemen besides the Cheife, and have been very large both in their brandy and customes, as Griffin can give your honour an account, which is the reason the people are somewhat urgent for their customes according to contract. Att settling Captain Bracon desires your honour would send up by his owne canoe 25 blew and 15 green perpettuanoes for account of the Royall Company and att the months end moneyes shall be sent downe for the goods that may be disposed of with an account of the remaines soe well of the goods formerly brought up by himselfe as of what may be consign'd to this place for the future.

86. David Harper   Commenda, 16 Jan. 1682/3

Your Honours of the 11th instant with the 40 pieces perpetuano's and brandy consigned to Captain Bracon came safe to hand. These may acquaint your honour that the Cabbisheers are very eager to goe about the building and have been two dayes att worke in breaking of earth for the worke, but they declare themselves unable to goe about the walls without the assistance of some better workeman than any att this place, which I understand by Captain Bracon to be the truth for although hee hath soe many slaves of his owne yett the building his house cost him one bendy to an Fanteener who he brought from Fanteen to direct and oversee his worke, wherefore if your honour be pleased that this building be brought to any perfection before the raines itt will be verry fitt that two or three men that have knowledge in building be provided and sent up with speed. The Fanteeners are said to be the best workemen, whereof there lives one with Captain Cooffy whoe knows his business verry well and may serve your honour in this affaire.

The Dutch Copeman is very busie in provideing for his building, hee hath gott a sloopes loading of timber from Shuma and hath here a carpenter a makeing of doors and windows. Hee expects to have his house up in six weeks for hee is to have 20 slaves from the Mina, hee will make his house two storyes high with only foure large roomes, two below and two above, the whole length 59 foot and 18 foot broad, the walls two foot thick. The goods the Dutch have here are sayes, iron barrs and perpetuano's which hee sells at 9a per piece, brandy, and Beneen cloaths. The Copeman tells mee hee hath found but small trade since his comeing, which hee does not much notice soe long as there are noe goods att the Mina to supply him with but soe soone as supplyes come, which are dayly expected by foure ships from Europe, hee expects to have a considerable trade though little to his masters profitt for hee says that by his brothers[54] order hee will undersell all ships that comes in the road, they selling soe cheape as they will. The trade is but little att present, which is the reason that the boysado's and perpettuanoes remaine unsold, but

---

[54] The Dutch factor at Komenda, Joris Ernsthuys, was the brother of the Director-General at Elmina, Thomas Ernsthuys.

Captain Bracon desires mee to acquaint your honour that there is some probabillity in selling the perpettuanoes as likewise a considerable quantity more before any ships come downe to hinder the trade, for he sayes that soe long as your honour will sell the Royall Companys goods att the same rates the Dutch does that they shall have but little trade in such goods as your Honour consignes to this place, which truely I verryly beleeve hee haveing the whole trade of the place in his hands. Upon Fryday last there was 4 interlopers in this roade, their names I can give your honour noe accoount of for the Blacks could only tell mee that they were English ships and interlopers, they are all gon to leward, soe that the roade is att present altogether without shipping though I doe not know how long for I am informed that Captain How with two more are to windward. I have alsoe had notice by a canoe that came from windward that upon Sunday last Captain Shears had gott no higher then Cape Trespointas.

87. David Harper   Commenda, 19 Jan. 1682/3

Your honours of the 17th instant I have received. In answer as to the building the factory [I] must acquaint your Honour that except people expert in building be sent up the worke will never be accomplished, for the people here will know noe pathern nor draught, but will make a house to their owne minds, which I see by their cutting of the halfe from the first draught, and what they build the walls does not exceed one foot thickness which I told them was but laboure in vaine, whereto they answered that if your honour sent up any here there should be noe want of earth to build with, but for themselves they know not to manage soe greate a worke as the draught of that factory is.

As to account of goods consigned to Captain Bracon be pleased to know that the 6 chests of sheets are only sold, which hee saies hee bought of your honour att 4a per chest, which comes to in all Mk 3, the which sume of 3 markes hee hath sent your honour per the bearer in good gold for account of the Royall Company desireing a receipt for the same.

The boysadoes and perpctuanoes remaine entire and not sold, neither can hee put off the perpettuanoes att 10a per piece, but saith if your honour will consider that this is the place where all goods are sold cheaper then to leward and abate 1 angle upon the perpettuanoes hee can immediatly dispose of what are here and doe the Company service in disposing of a considerable quantity more in a short time. Hee also desires your Honour to abate him 1 peaze upon each chest of sheets, if granted hee desires 10 chests may be sent up for account of the Royall Company. The marchants do not denie the payment of one piece of sletia and halfe an anchor of brandy, to which I myselfe was wittness at Mr Nightingals settleing, but they demand itt againe as due once a yeare.

88.   David Harper   Commenda, 24 Jan. 1682/3

This weeke merchants being come downe Captain Bracon hath disposed of 36
pieces of the Royall Companys perpettuanoes att 10 angles per piece, the 4 pieces
remaining being a little damaged will not goe off here. The 36 pieces perpettuanoes
sold att 10a per piece amounts to 2 marks, 6 ounces, 8 angles, which I have sent
your Honour in good gold for account of the Royall Company, alsoe 6 angles more
that Captain Bracon was owing upon account of the sheets, amounting in all to 2
marks, 6 ounces and 14 angles, for which I desire a receipt. Soe there remaines att
present in the hands of Captain Bracon only the 8 pieces boysado's, and if your
honour will soe order itt the 4 pieces perpettuanoes shall be return'd to Cabo Corsoe
per first conveniency. Captain Bracon desires your honour will be pleased to send
up per first oppertunity for account of the Royall Company 10 chests of sheets, with
30 blew and 30 green perpetuano's, which if sent up with speed will undoubtably
have some vent, there being noe ships here att present. Bracon desires to acquaint
your honour that hee is a looser in 5 angles which hee paid for canoe hyre for
bringing up the last sheets, but hopes your honour will prevent the same for the
future by sending the goods up in the Royall Companys canoes, alsoe by encour-
aging him according to desert for what service he may doe the Royall Company att
this place, especially now when the Dutch are labouring soe much to gett him to
their side but I hope shall not prevaile. I humbly begg your honour might be pleased
to allow some brandy to be spent, for the people does expect itt where the Company
goods are sold. In this and what else does concerne myselfe I trust wholy to your
honours goodness and pleasure. Since the receipt of your honours last letter I have
had two meeting with the Cabosheers of Commenda about the building of the
Companys factory and they absolutely declare themselves uncapable to undertake
the worke with fewer then three workmen from Cabo Corsoe for building the walls,
which if complyed with itt will be necessary they be sent up with speede soe the
raines may not againe prevent the worke

89.   David Harper   Commenda, 26 Jan. 1682/3

Your honours of the 25th instant I have received, alsoe the 60 pieces perpetuano's
and 10 chests of sheets consigned to Captain Bracon are come safe to hand. Here
are att present severall merchants from the country, soe Bracon expects that the
perpetuano's this day received may be disposed of by tomorrow night. Wherefore
Captain Bracon desires your honour would be pleased to send him with all possible
speede for account of the Royall Company 100 pieces green and blew perpetuano's,
40 pieces sayes, and 10 barrells powder. These goods Captain Bracon desires to be
here against tomorrow night or Sunday morning att farthest, for the merchants are
in great hast to be gon againe to the country. I humbly thank your honour in that
you have been pleased to allow us here 6 gallons brandy per month to be spent upon

the Royall Company's accompt, I have sent per this canoe one empty anchor containing 6 gallons which I hope your honour will cause to be filled and sent up for accompt of the ensueing month. Paper, pen and inke is very scarce with mee, which I hope your Honour will be pleased to supply. I desire the prizes of the sayes and powder.

90. David Harper   Commenda, 28 Jan. 1682/3

Your honours of the 27th instant I have received. The 100 pieces perpetuano's and 40 pieces sayes, with the 6 gallons brandy for the factory's use are all come safe to Captain Bracons hands. I have sent you per bearer for account of the Royall Company 4 marks, 5 ounces, and 8 angles, which is the just sume of the 60 perpettuanoes last received amounts to. The perpetuanoes this day received will immediatly be sold, wherefore Captain Bracon desires your honour would be pleased to send him more for account of the Royall Company 100 pieces blew and green perpetuano's with the 10 barrells powder last writt for with its price. Hee desires likewise if itt may please your Honour to lett him have 50 pieces of the now writt for perpetuanoes at 9a per piece, which hee intends to send up in the country upon his own account soe that hee may gett some profitt by them for himselfe. I see but little probabillity for building the factory this season, for the blacks sayes plainely they will not undertake such a building except your honour send people up to build itt, as alsoe the raines will goe neare to be a greate hinderance to itt. Captain Bracon humbly desires you would cause Oliver the blacksmith to make him a grapline of two iron barrs for a 9 hand canoe, the barrs hee desires may be placed to his account.

91. David Harper   Commenda, 30 Jan. 1682/3

Your honours of the 29th instant I have received. The 100 pieces of perpetuano's and 10 barrells powder consigned to Captain Bracon hee hath alsoe received. I would according to your honours commands have sent an account of the goods received, sold and remaines thereof per this conveniency but am resolved about the last of the weeke to come downe myselfe to Cabo Corsoe, to know your Honours mind about building the factory in some particulars, att which time I shall satisfie your honour as to that account and bring with mee what gold Captain Bracon hath gott in cash.

92. David Harper   Commenda, 8 Feb. 1682/3

Your honours of the 7th instant I have received, in answer whereof your honour may be pleased to know that I can by noe meanes perswade Captain Bracon to come downe to Cabo Corsoe at this time, his reasons are the great pallavoras that are up in the country att present, and that hee will not stir abroad before hee heares the effects thereof. Likewise hee complaines that hee cannot goe abroad without a greate charge in expences, as hee found by experience when hee was last at Cabo Corsoe. As to the particulars of agreeing with Bracon about commission of goods sold by him hee demands 1 peaze per marke soe well for the goods already sold as that may be sold for the future; I begg a line in answer whereby I may give him an account if your Worship does comply with his demands, alsoe if what you are pleased to allow him shall be deteyned here in his owne hands or sent up from Cabo Corsoe upon receipt of what moneys he sends downe. I have herewith sent your honour the Tanton Querrey account[55] which those people acknowledged to be owing in presence of the Quarranteer[56] and Captain Peeter. There is noe trade att present by reason of those outfallings in Abraboe,[57] however Captain Bracon hath some mony in cash which hee hath taken for sheets and shall send itt downe per next. Mr Towgood finds alsoe but small trade here.[58] As to account of shiping here or to windward I referr itt to Captain Shears.

93. David Harper   Commenda, 12 Feb. 1682/3

Your honours of the 8th instant by Docter Griffin I have received. As to the palavora with Abracon hee doe faithfully promise to advance the Royall Companys trade and maintaine their interest in this place. As to the commission money Captain Bracon stood hard upon 3 angles but by much perswasions have brought him to except of 2 angles per marke, which hee expects your honour will be pleas'd to send him from Cabo Corsoe for all the money that hath been taken since the goods were first consign'd to him and soe once a month for the future. Bracon hath sent downe by Docter Griffin 5 marks, 10 angles of good gold for account of the Royall Company, which payes for the 10 chests of sheets last sent up; Hee desires your honour would send him more for account of the Royall Company 10 chests of sheets with 1 anchor of brandy for this months allowance with one halfe anchor which Docter Griffin borrowed of him. The trade is but bad at present. Last night came in this roade a small ship with Companys jack and pendant but I have understood that hee is an interloper bound to the Bite.

94. David Harper   Commenda, 16 Feb. 1682/3

Your honours of the 14th instant with the brandy therein mentioned I have received. I am sorry your honour can spare Abracon noe more sheets, for the goods that are here yeilds noe money att present, they being soe much undersold aboard by

---

[55] Tantumkweri, in Fante. Harper had earlier been involved in evacuating RAC goods from this place (cf. no.207).
[56] See Glossary.
[57] Cf. no.102, which gives the more usual form 'Abramboe': i.e. Abrem, north-east of Eguafo.
[58] Cf. no.553.

Captain Price and Boles whoe sells their sayes att 13 and perpettuanoes att 9 angles per piece. Yesterday morning Captain Bracon with the rest of the merchants of this place went up to Aguaffoe being sitted [= cited] by the King upon account of a pallavora caused by the Arcanies of Little Commenda, whoe are alsoe there and threaten to leave the country because the merchants here will not suffer them to goe aboard and buy their goods themselves. It is said that the Dutch have complained of the small trade hee finds here, alsoe that the merchants slights his goods and have bought the Royall Companys goods out of Abracons hands, likewise [they complained] against them goeing aboard. What effects these pallavoras will take I can give your honour noe account before Captain Bracons return. Last night came in this road a small interloper whose Commander Bennitt dyed att Cape Trespointas, shee is now commanded by one Rolands who was Docter and part owner.

95. David Harper   Commenda, 23 Feb. 1682/3

This goes by Captain Bracons canoe by whome hee hath sent 1 marke, 4 ounces, 3 angles, good gold, for which hee desires your honour would please to send him 3 chests of sheets. Captain Bracon with the rest of the merchants of this place returned from Aguaffoe upon Wednesday night, by whome I understand the King hath given free leave to the three Cheife of the Arcanies to goe aboard ship and trade, which is a great signe of the little regard the King carry's to the factory's that are kept here. The Dutch Copeman hath left off his building a mud house and is now dayly with the King to suffer him to build a stone house, how his desire will be complyed with I know not, but am of opinion that hee shall hardly gett a house to live in this raines. Tradeing is soe dead that Bracon cannot put off any of the Royall Companys goods at present. There is noe news of any shiping to windward. Captain Price and Boles are still in this roade.

96. David Harper   Commenda, 24 Feb. 1682/3

Your honours two severall letters of the 23rd instant I have received. The 3 chests of sheets Captain Bracon hath received, acknowledging himselfe greatly bound to your honours favour in letting him have them att the former price, the which favour hee promised to recompence in his fidility in the Royall Company's concerns. As to a further account of the palavora att Aguaffoe be pleased to know that the Arcanies complaints have been very great against the people of Little Commenda, especially for pulling up their fittishes and throwing them in the sea, for which act the King hath prendeed the Commenda Cabosheers in 2 bendy's of gold. Captain Bracon was hard against their goeing aboard, alsoe Aban from the Mina told the King itt was the Generalls desire that none of the Arcanies should be tollerate to goe aboard, notwithstanding all this hee has given free leave to the three Cheife of the Arcany's to trade aboard ship. The Arcanies are all to returne hither tomorrow.

The Dutch is verry busie pulling downe all his former worke, for a little money gott leave of the King to build a stone house, which hee intends to goe about with all expedition.

97. David Harper   Commenda, 2 March 1682/3

Your Honours of the 26th February I have received and have made all possible enquirey after the sorts and quantities of goods brought over by the Dutch Company ship last arrived, yett can attain noe possitive account of the same, only the goods that are come are currant goods, but in quantity far short of expectation, the whole cargoe not exceeding 5000£ prime cost. The two ships that went downe yesterday are expected to have better cargoes then the first, the Copeman here received yesterday a fresh supply of sheets, sayes and perpettuanoes. Captain Bracon desires to acquaint your Honour that tradeing is soe very dead at this place that there is not the least enquirey made after the Royall Company goods now in his hands, but if your Honour will lett him have sheets at the former price of 32 per benda he desires 10 or 12 chests may be sent up by the first conveyance, not doubting but they may goe off by degrees in the intrime that other goods lyes dead.

98. David Harper   Commenda, 2 [var.22] March 1682/3

Your Honours of the 1st instant I have received, and have acquainted Captain Bracon, with the great supply of all sorts of goods brought to Cabo Corso by the Royall Company ship last arrived, of which goods he knows none to be a comodity here at present, only sheets excepted, which if your Honour will lett him have att 32 per benda as formerly, he will endeavour to dipose of 10 or 12 chests if sent up per the first conveyance, but at 28 per benda he will take none, the Dutch selling them also at the same rate of 32. Bracon desires to know how the broad and narrow niccanees and tapseels are sold in the Castle, and if he likes of their prices will take some quantity of each sort.

Since the sheets have been sold Bracon hath not taken one benda of gold for any of the Royall Companys goods that are in his hands, which proceeds from the deadness of trade, as also being dayly undersold by interlopers whoe sells their sayes att 12 and perpettuanoes att 08a each. Here is noe news of any ships to windward.

99. David Harper   Commenda, 5 March 1682/3

Your Honours of the 3rd instant I have received and have perused Captain Bracons account, which I find cleare and without mistake or error. The mony sent to Capo Corso by him comes in all Mk 23 3o 8a and just payes for the goods sold vizt 1040 sheets at 32 per benda and 196 perpettuanoes att 10a per peice. The goods remayning unsold are 104 perpettuanoes, 40 pieces sayes, 10 barrells powder and 8 pieces boysadoes. Captain Bracon desires your Honour will send him for account of the Royall Company 6 chests of sheets and 170 4 pound basons with their prices as they are sold in the Castle. Here waits a merchant for the basons therefore they are desired with hast. Bracon also desires the monthly allowance of brandy may be sent up, for which he hath sent a casque containing 6 gallons. I am informed by the merchants that sayes begins to goe well of in the country. Perpettuanoes are like to be noe such comodity as formerly. This morning Captain Boles departed this road. There is noe news of any shipping to windward.

100. David Harper   Commenda, 7 March 1682/3

Your Honours of the 6th instant I have received. The 6 chests of sheets and 199 [var. 169] 4lb basons with 6 gallons brandy factoryes use consigned to Captain Bracon he hath also received. I have acquainted Captain Bracon with your desire, and if the boysadoes and other goods [stay?] in his hands, whereto he answers that it is his none of his fault that merchants doe not buy the goods of him, also that the road hath not been cleare of shipping in a long time till now, whoe have very much undersold the Companys prices, but he desires your Honours patience till the end of this month, and if the boysadoes doe not goe off before, that he will pay for them himselfe and also give your Honour his advice what hopes may be for disposing of the rest of the goods, for he sayes the Dutch and blacks will looke upon as a great affront put upon him to withdraw the goods soe long as he thinkes himselfe capable to make them good upon all accounts and also to put them of when oppertunity offers. Bracon desires the prices of the narrow niccanees and tapseels, and if likes of their prices he thinkes they may yeald present mony.

101. David Harper   Commenda, 9 March 1682/3

By this express Captain Bracon hath sent downe for account of the Royall Company 3 marks 2 ounces good gold, whereof 1 marke 3 ounces payes for the 8 pieces of boysadoes, and 1 marke 7 ounces for the 10 barrells of powder, the boysadoes he hath paid with his owne mony. Bracon desires your Honour would please to send him for account of the Royall Company and with the first conveyance 12 barrells of powder, the halfe of the powder is desired in halfe barrells, also the prices of the narrow niccanees and tapseels as formerly desired.

[PS] Bracon desires your Honour would send him on account of the Royall Company a paire of scales and weights, for he finds himselfe a looser by his takeing mony on his small scales and weights.[59]

---

[59] Cf. also no.102. See Kea 1982, 225–6, who interprets this as alluding to the difference between the Portuguese and English systems of weights.

102. David Harper   Commenda, 11 March 1682/3

Your Honours of the 10th instant with 12 barrells powder consigned to Captain Bracon are well received. I have also received a line from Mr Spurvay complaining of the scarceness of the weight of the money sent downe, which Bracon takes to be very strange since there is not a parcell of mony sent downe but he puts 2 angles upon it to make it the better weight at Capo Corso, wherefore he desires your Honour againe to send him up a poyle[60] of scales and weights whereby he may both take and pay his mony. Otherwise he sayes his comission will not make the difference of the weight of the mony good betwixt what he receives and payes. The goods in the Dutch factory before the arrivall of the last ship where [= were] iron barrs, Beneen clouts, a few perpettuanoes and brandy, since he hath received 7 cases of sayes, 2 bales of perpettuanoes, 5 cases of fine sletias, 6 chests of sheets, 2 chests of carabines and firelocks with 4 halfe chests of beads, whereof he hath sold a good quantity of sayes (which is the reason those of the Royall Company goes of soe slowly, the blacks having alwayes a better opinion of the Dutch then English sayes). He hath also sold all his carbines and firelocks, with most of his beads, the rest of the goods doe not goe off but are like to lye upon his hands. Upon Fryday last came here Abraham [sic: = Aban] of the Mina in his returne from Abramboe when he had made an end of all palaveras, he had a palavera with the people of Little Commenda wherein he desired their care of the Generalls brother[61] with an advancing of his trade.

Since the writing of the above is the Dutch Copeman gone to the Mina being written by an express from his brother.

103. David Harper   Comenda, 18 March [1682/3]

Your Honours of the 16th instant with the box of scales and 4 ounces poyle of weights I have received. I have acquainted Captain Bracon with your Honours order for selling the sayes att 15 angles each, which he sayes will give the merchants more encouragement to buy the Royall Company goods. Upon Thursday last came to this road Captain Haywood from London, interloper, he reports that some 12 dayes agoe upon his departure from Abbeny that Captain Rickards arrived there. The Dutch fiscall went yesterday to windward, there being one of their Companys ships arrived at Axime.

Last night the Dutch Copeman received an express from the Generall ordering him to resigne his warehouse to his second and to repaire with all his own concernes to the Mina, in order to his goeing Copeman to Accra, the ship Affrica at the Mina waiting only for his transportation theither.[62]

---

[60] 'poyle' is a variant of 'pulley'; but 'payre' (i.e. pair) would make better sense.
[61] i.e. the Dutch chief factor at Komenda.
[62] Cf. Van Dantzig 1978, no.40 (Resolutions of Council, Elmina, 25 March 1683).

104. David Harper   Comenda, 27 March 1683

Your Honours of the 26th instant I have received. The reason of my not writing till now was I understood your Honour had advice of the Royall Companys ships being in this road, also there being noe trade on shoure since the ships arrivall soe there affords nothing elce worth the advising. Captain Low is still here and hath sent his pinke to windward with what goods he knew might be most vendible, he intends to fall downe to Capo Corso tomorrow. Captain Bracon hath betwixt 5 and 6 marks in cash, which he promises (after he hath made up his accounts) to send downe on Fryday or Saterday without faile. As to what goods may vend best here, can give your Honour noe certaine account till the merchants have disposed the goods they have upon hand from aboard ship, but afterwards shall not faile to acquaint your Honour what goods are most desired.

[PS] Captain Bracon sayes the narrow niccaness will yeald noe more then 3 angles here and narrow tapseels 4 angles per piece, at which prices if your Honour will send up 100 pieces of each he will endeavour to dispose of them.

105. David Harper   Comenda, 30 March 1683

By this express Captain Bracon hath sent your Honour for account of the Royall Company 6 marks, 8 angles good gold. The goods sold are as followeth vizt

169 4lb pewter basons att 2a per piece	M 2: 5: 2
195 sheets att 28 per benda	1: 5: 14
4 barrells powder att 1o 8a per barrell	0: 6: 0
8 pieces sayes att 15a per peice	0: 7: 8
	Mk 6: 0: 8

Captain Bracon desires your Honour might please to send him per bearer his comission mony for what mony he hath heitherto sent downe, which comes in all 32 marks 6 ounces, soe that his comission mony that is due to him at 2a per marke comes to 4 ounces, 1 angle and 6 taccoes. The King and Fetera, also the old and young Cappusheers[63] of Little Commenda doe demand their customes as due at putting the corne in the ground. Captain Bracon is very earnest it may be paid them, for he sayes if their brandy which is due be paid at this time they will not expect their other customes before the dancing times. There is now due in brandy to the King and Fetera each 1 anchor and to the old and young Cappusheers each 1 halfe anchor, in all 3 anchors. I desire if it might please your Honour to send up the brandy with the 6 gallons for next months factories use in a quarter casque and the caske shall be return'd by the canoe that brings it up, for I could gett noe anchors to send downe. The Kings man waites here for his portion of it. If your Honour will

---

[63] An allusion to the existence of chiefs of the youngmen (*asafo*), paralleling the senior chiefs, as described e.g. by Bosman (1705, 164–5).

lett Bracon have the narrow niccanees and tapseels the one at 3a and the other att 4a per piece he desires 100 pieces of each may be sent up. There lyes one Portugueze ship at Tacarada loaden with Brazeele tobaco, suger and rum, he hath a good markett for his tobaco and sells it at 4 lb per angle to the blacks.[64] There is also two English interlopers at Dickecove.

106.   David Harper   Commenda, 6 Apr. 1683

Your Honours of the 30th March I have received and have acquainted Captain Bracon with the bad weight of the money sent last downe, which seemes strange to him, however is well satisfied that the Royall Company is paid out of his commission money and renders your Honour hearty thanks for the remainder which hee hath received being 3 ounces, 10 angles, 7½ tacco's, which payes him for all the money hitherto sent to Cabo Corsoe by him. Bracon desires the grapling which your honour ordered to be made for him may be sent up for hee much wants itt and hath sent this canoe express for the same. I have sent downe 2 empty anchors desireing itt may please your Honour to order the brandy for the old and young Cabasheers customes and the 6 gallon's factory's allowance to be sent up in the same by this conveyance. Here is in this roade Captain Summervill interloper, alsoe the Portuguze. Tradeing is verry dead and but little money a stirring either ashoare or aboard. I humbly beg itt may please your honour to order the sending up my sallary now due per bearer for I verry much want itt, haveing been here the 8th of this instant 3 full yearly months, alsoe humbly entreating your Honour would consider that my liveing is farr more chargeable then att Cabo Corsoe and accordingly to grant some advancement of sallary, but in this as in all others I wholly trust to your honours goodness and pleasure.

107.   David Harper   Commenda, 12 Apr. 1683

Your Honours of the 11th instant with Abracons grapline and the 12 gallons brandy are well received. In answer to your honours concerning the trade here and shipping to windward be pleased to know that here hath been here no country merchants in 3 weeks either Arcanys or Quiffers soe that there are noe goods sold and all things verry dead as to tradeing. Yesterday came in the road Captain Thompson interloper, hee hath a verry great Gold Coast cargoe but hitherto hath had but a bad trade. Hee reports that Captain Pearson is to windward and may be expected here in a few dayes, hee hath a great ship of 46 guns and a cargoe of 12,000 pounds. There are alsoe three Dunkerkers to windward of 20 or 24 guns apeece.

---

[64] The only allusion to the importation of Brazilian tobacco in the 1681–3 correspondence, suggesting that this trade (for whose later importance cf. Verger 1968, 28–51) was as yet small in scale.

108. David Harper   Commenda, 18 Apr. 1683

Captain Bracon desires if itt may please your honour to send him for account of the Royall Affrican Company 10 chests sheets, for the 3 chests last remayning are sold and greater probabillity for selling some sheets then any other commodyty att this present dead time. Captain Sommevill is still in this roade and takes but verry little money's. There are two Dutch interlopers awatering att Cape Trespunctas. Itt is reported alsoe that there is an English ship att Axim but uncertain whether Companys ship or interloper.

109. David Harper   Commenda, 21 Apr. 1683

Your honours of the 18th instant I have received. The 10 chests sheets consign'd to Captain Bracon hee also received from aboard the sloope.[65] Abracon hath sent your honour by Mr Towgood for accompt of the Royall Company 2 marks, 5 ounces, 6 angles 10½ tacco's in good gold, the goods sold are these vizt 3 chests sheets containing 195 pieces att 28 per bendy, 1m 5o 14a 10½ta; 12 peeces perpettuano's att 10a per piece — -:7:8:- [making] 2: 5: 6: 10½. The reason why sayes and perpettuanoes lyes here upon hand is because there comes noe merrchants neither Arcany's nor any other to buy them and I doubt not but your Honour verry well knowes that is the cheife cause that tradeing is soe dead alongst the whole coast.

110. David Harper   Commenda, 26 Apr. 1683

Upon Monday last the slaves of this place being according to custome gon for water, news was brought that they were panyard by one of the Kings couzens whoe lives neareby, whereupon the Cabosheers went out to know the matter but found only the Arcany slaves carried away, whereupon they sent for this person but [he] refuseing to come in, some arm'd men went out and tooke him and sett his croome[66] on fire, alsoe wounded severall of his men whereof 2 freemen are dead. Upon this wrong the friends of this Kings couzen whoe are many and strong in Aguaffoe threatens to come down and be reveng'd of Commenda by setting itt on fire. The King for makeing up the pallavora hath sent for the Cabosheers and Arcany's, whoe went up last night, and Abracon is now departed thither whose desire is for the more security of the Royall Company's concerns that your honour would upon receipt hereof send a Cabasheer with the Companys caine to the King of Aguaffoe warning him that hee take great care noe harme be don to Little Commenda, but especially to the house of Captain Abracon, where now there is such a considerable quantity of the Royall Companys concerns, as also to dispatch Captain Bracon with hast to looke after the same in such a troublesome time, alsoe if the Royall Company

[65] i.e. the *Ann*, commanded by Charles Towgood.
[66] See Glossary.

sustaine any damage that itt will lye upon his head to make itt good according to contract. This in great hast.

111. David Harper   Commenda, 5 May 1683

Last night one of Aguaffoe Cabosheers with his souldiers being here, some of his people having taken a corrall necklace from Captain Coffee's boy our people reprehended him therefore, whereupon hee immediately discharg'd some shott and threatened to kill and plunder all, soe that Bracon put his men in armes but ere they were gott ready the rogue comes againe and fires a great many shott into Captain Bracons court, there stood amongst the rest of the people, soe that a great many were wounded whereof my boy the boatswaine was one, whoe I have sent downe by the canoe hopeing your honour will order his wounds to be cured, but after Bracons people were gott ready they fought a long time ere our people gott them driven out of the towne. Some hours afterwards our people went out and fought him againe soe that hee fled. There is 6 of our people kill'd and a great many wounded. How itt will goe still is uncertaine, there being noe people come from the King as yett. The Mareens croome is all burnt off. I shall waite your honours orders in this sad distress, for neither the Companys goods nor our lives are safe att present. The Generall of the Mina hath sent up Aban with some great canoes and Cabosheers here to looke after his factory, but hath as yett given noe orders to withdraw. Your honours immediat commands are expected.

112. David Harper   Commenda, 8 May 1683

Your honours of the 6th instant with the 9 and 3 hand canoes and boyes arrived here yesterday morning, and according to order (the Dutch haveing first removed all their concerns and Whitemen) [I] have shipt aboard the 9 hand canoe 79 per-petuano's, 17 pieces of sayes, and 4 barrells powder, which are the remaines of the Royall Company's concerns att Commenda factory. After the dispatch of the 9 hand canoe I went two severall times to the waterside with Captain Bracon thinking to have brought him with mee to Cabo Corsoe, but the Kings people would not suffer us to goe off, for they come downe hourly promiseing that this day people shall come to make pallavora's with him and give him all desired satisfaction for his staying and the factory's being continued, whereupon Captain Bracon hath per-swaded mee to waite for your honours answer of this one letter, wherein I desire your honours express order if I shall immediatly come downe to Cabo Corsoe, leaving Abracon here, or if I shall stay longer to heare the pallavora's, and if in case Bracon getts satisfaction soe that hee stayes if I shall put up the flagg againe and continue, for I find Bracon inclines to staying, although I doe what I can to per-swade him itt will be better to make his pallavora's at Cabo Corsoe then here, but hee tells mee that if hee leave the place the Cabosheers of Aguaffoe will turne the

King out, seeing the trouble came by one of his couzens. If your Honour inclines to keepe the place itt will not be amiss to send up to Aguaffoe desireing gold pawnes for the future security of the Royall Companys factory and Bracons person, or elce such men pawnes as shall be approven of by Captain Bracon, likewise to deliver Akasy in Bracons hands (for wee understand that the King of Fetue hath offered to deliver him for a little money),[67] alsoe to turne his couzen Taggee[68] out of the country. These are the conditions Bracon desires, otherwayes hee will leave the place, all the best of his things being gon and the great canoe lying here ready with the rest, for hee hath not left a doore nor window in his house. The goods for which Bracon remaines debter are 10 chests sheets, 4 barrells powder, 13 pieces perpetuanoes and 15 pieces sayes. If your honour shall please to order mee downe before Bracon can come along with mee to give satisfaction for the goods sold by him, hee proffers to send his cheife wife with mee to remayne till hee comes himselfe, whereunto I also desire your honours particular order; I only keepe the 3 hand canoe till I receive your Honours commands. Mr Towgood came in the roade today and waites for orders, the goods being already gon. I humbly begg your honours immediate particular answer to these concerns which shall be punctually obeyed.

*****

113. David March   3 Oct. 1683

Yours I received dated 5 instant by the Captain of the Arcany's[69] and [he?] doth advise for to have these goods following which will be convenient for this place, [they] will be sayes and perpetuano's, boysado's, Guyney stuffs, small tapsells, and greate tapsells, narrow niccanees, course sletias, sheets, tallow, and 2 douzen barrells of powder and iron barrs, new pewter tankards small and greate, with basons of first and seacond sort, blew lining, a sort of strip'd stuff that they call gingham, strip'd with white and redd, Captain Bracon hath 3 chests hee desires to have them sent. I would desire you not to forgett to send a caske of brandy, for hee will be verry much want of itt, and to send mee prizes of all goods and all necessary things belonging and necesssary for the factory, as both weights and scales, paper and what may be usefull. Here is a greate many men stayes here for goods, and there is

---

[67] Not identified: presumably somebody taken captive in the recent disturbance.

[68] This seems clearly to refer to the King's cousin, who had caused the disturbance (cf. 110 above), rather than Bracon's cousin (as suggested by Kea 1982, 227). This 'Taggee' may be identical with either of two brothers called 'Abe-Tecky' and 'Tecky-Ankan', who ruled successively as kings of Eguafo in the 1690s (Bosman 1705, 32–40).

[69] There are also references to a 'Captain of the Arcanies' at Anomabu (nos 219, 301), at Anashan (no.118) and at Cape Coast Castle (no.139). Akani traders resident in coastal towns seem to have been organized into communities with their own chiefs: for an analysis, cf. Kea 1982, esp. 261–8.

noe ship here but one interloper up to windward, and the sooner the better to have goods here. Soe desireing your pardon of my kind wrighting but honest endeavour.

114.   David March   Commenda, 11 Oct. 1683

I received yours of the 9th instant and understand that you have not conveniency to send the quantity of goods which wee did send for, these are therefore to desire you to send a small quantity of goods att the present which is for the present occasion, which is as followeth, 4 barrells powder, a small quantity of perpetuano's, boysado's and narrow tapsells, which small quantity of goods I would desire you to send with all speed that may be and more as you have conveniency, for I doe beleeve that wee shall have a verry considerable trade by meanes of the Captain of the Arcany's. The Captain of the Arcany's is att the charge of sending a canoe for some goods and would desire you to send what you can besides, as you find conveniency, for here is a greate many traiders come downe [so] that if wee had goods wee should have a greate trade. If you send powder if itt be 20 barrells wee need not house itt, and other goods may sell a greate deale, for the Captain of the Arcany's saith that hee will keepe all the money for mee to take if I can possible have goods for him, for hee professes greate kindness to mee.

115.   David March   17 Oct. 1683

I received yours dated the 16th, wherein I understand your reason in not sending of goods heither att present, for itt is verry dangerous especially for powder, and besides by reason there is a factory house to be built, which they say they will goe in hand with but as yett are not in hand with itt. I would desire you to lett mee know the proportion and all concerns as to the contract and I shall act accordingly. In the meane time I have lett them know, that in the meane time while the house is getting ready they shall be supplyed with goods according to your letter, and att the present by this bearer they have sent money for 10 barrells of powder, which they would desire to have tomorrow morning if possible, in one bulce[70] 5 marks and 7 peaze, the other bulce 5 ounces and 1 peaze. If you please to send by the canoe some small goods, as a few perpetuano's and a few sayes and course sletias and small tapsells and a few such small goods, they will be vendible and give them greate satisfaction att the present.

116.   David March   Commenda, 7 Nov. 1683

These are to lett you understand that on Satureday next the people of this towne doe goe in hand with building the factory, and when I see them in hand with itt you

---

[70] i.e. bulse (= purse).

shall heare from mee that you may send a carpenter and materialls for to make the doores and door cases and window cases. Captain Bracon remembers his service to you and would desire you to send him 4 barrells and halfe of powder and 2 pieces of sayes, for the which hee hath sent you money for them, soe desireing you would doe soe much as [will] pleasure Captain Brackon this time.

III

ANASHAN

The RAC's factory at Anashan ('Anishan'), east of Cape Coast Castle, had been established probably in the late 1670s.[1] It was still in existence at the beginning of 1681, and correspondence from it is continuous until November 1682; although this is not explicitly stated, it was presumably then abandoned.[2] The Anashan factory supplied relatively small quantities of gold, and occasional slaves; but the correspondence suggests that its principal function was to supply corn to provision slave-ships (and also timber, for building works at Cape Coast Castle).

There was also a Portuguese factory at Anishan, founded in 1680,[3] which is occasionally alluded to in the letters from the English factory.[4] As reported elsewhere in the RAC correspondence (no.322), this Portuguese factory was abandoned in 1683.

Anashan, together with the RAC factories at Anomabu and Egya and the Dutch fort at Kormantin further east along the coast, was situated within the state of Fante.[5] The Anashan factory correspondence contains little reference to its relations with the larger state; though when the chief of Anashan in 1682 'sent up to the Braffoe' for guidance in his dealings with the English (no.197), this presumably alludes to the Obrafo, or commander-in-chief, of the Fante state.[6] The hinterland merchants trading at Anashan are always referred to as the Akani ('Arcanies').

---

[1] It is documented in 1679, although then described as 'in a dilapidated state': Van Dantzig 1978, no.3 (Herman Abramsz, 23 Nov. 1679).

[2] An attempt had been made to abandon the factory in May 1682, but was prevented by the local chief (no.182).

[3] PRO, T70/10, Nathaniel Bradley et al., Cape Coast Castle, 24 Aug. 1680.

[4] See esp. no.143; and also allusions to the Portuguese 'Father' or 'Padre', i.e. the chaplain of the factory, in nos 173, 184. The existence of a Portuguese factory at Anashan was noted by Barbot (1992, ii, 416, 419); but there is no mention of it in Vogt 1979.

[5] e.g. Barbot 1992, ii, 416. It should be noted that Fante at this period was much smaller in extent than in the nineteenth century, when several previously separate states (including Fetu, Asebu and Kabestera) had been absorbed into it.

[6] Cf. also no.182, where it appears that a son of the Braffoe (as well as a son of the local chief of Anashan) was held as a pawn for the security of the factory.

117.   Arthur Richards   Anishan, 10 Feb. 1680/1

According to your order receaved per Mr Thelwall[7] [I] have made up all my accompts to the 29 January last past and by the bearers send you the ballance of said
accompts which amounts not to much by reason I have noe good goods here, which
if I had doe not much doubt of a quick saile and good money and slaves for them.
The goods wanting in this place is perpetuanoes reds greens and blewes, plaine
sayes, sheetes, sletias, long cloths and iron, which hope your Honour will please to
send a soone as possibly you cann, money and slaves goeing aboard shipps for want
of goods here. I have gott good warehouse roome here and that is all, [as] for othere
convenyences shall gett as fast as possibly can, it beinge rowsaringe tim cannot doe
soe well as I would.

Since the above mentioned order have receaved another from Mr Thelwall in
your Honours and Councells name forbiding corneing or dealeing with interloopers.[8] I acquainted the Curranter with this order, which hee likes itt well provided
you will send goods and buy his corne of him, which he sayes if you will nott he
must sell it where he can and not lett it spoile.

Inclosed goes my accompt to the 29 January last past with the ballance thereof
being 6 ounces 6 angles and 11 taccoes, itt goes by the bearers Mr Nightingale and
Mr Frankland, itt should have been sent before but sicknesse gave mee noe time to
write it.

[PS] By Mr Nightingale I have sent you the ballance of my accompts being 9
ounces 10 angles and 11 taccoes. By an error in casteing up before made it not so
much but since have corrected it.

118.   Arthur Richards   Anishan Factory, 20 Feb. 1680/1

Yours I receaved and have acquainted the Curranteer of your resolution, he confe-
ses 100 chestes of corne that he hath solled to the interlooper that laye here but does
promise now your Honour is pleased to buy his corne he will find a good roome for
it, noebody else shall have either corne, wood or watter more from this place.

He desires you will send some good goods downe heither vizt perpettuanoes,
sayes, course and fine slezias, sheetes, paper brawles, long clothes and irron. Here
is money in the towne, if I had good goods I could take itt. If you please to order
me to sell powder att 5 pease beleive I can sell a pretty good quantety, haveing this
month been proffered money att that price, lickewise broad tapseeles will not sell
for 7 angles but will for 6.

Pray send what good goods you can and the prices, and if you please send some
shorte irons to putt slaves in if buy any.

---

[7] Richard Thelwall, RAC chief factor at Anomabu, east of Anashan (cf. section IV).
[8] Cf. no.209.

James Paris shall goe for Cabo Corso a Teusday morneing, but hope you will bee pleased to send one Arda man and one Arda woeman[9] to assist the factory if buy slaves.

I hope you are sattisfied that the bad carrecter you heard of mee before was falce, I doe assure you that none shall be more obedient to your order then I will as fare as lyes in me to performe.

[PS] Pray bee pleased to send mee a little inck and wafers or wax for I have none nor inck but what is in my inck glasse.

Our Captain of the Arcanies and his second tells me you promised them a monthly sallary, if true or noe I know not, but you never orderd me to pay them anythinge.

119.   Arthur Richards   Anishan Factory, 22 Feb. 1680/1

Last night I receaved yours, wherein I finde your desires the Currunteer should provide a good roome for corne, which hath allready shewed me. I must gett a doure and wyndoe for it, and then shall beginn to take in corne. As to the allowance to the Arcanies I shall not tell them of it till the month is out, though they expect att this months end two months togethere, that is as much as the Curranteer hath and will receave. I have some money of the Arcanies in my hands for powder, which I cannot deliver without your order because they will give butt 5 peace for one barrill. If you will take that price pray send me down 10 or 20 barrills more for I beleive I can dispose of them at that price quickly. Pray send me the goods I write for as soone as possibly you can, here beinge people that are much in hast, as they pretend, to laye out ther money and I know they have money. Here is a great many of Arcanies in our towne.

Herewith goes James Parris. Lickewise have sent by this cannoe a bottle for incke, thankeing your Honour kindly for the stickes of wax you were pleased to send.

I begg you will be pleased to send downe in this canoe 2 men and 1 woeman Ardas, because I shall much want them att takeing in of the corne and the woeman to make cankey for slaves when gett any, which I doe not dispare of, and if I buy cankee and other neccessaryes for them it will be a great deal more chargeable. Lickwise pray send some shorte irons.[10]

I hope you receaved my last months account with the ballance which I sent by Mr Nightingale.

---

[9] Slaves from Allada ('Arda', 'Arder', 'Ardoe'), to the east, were commonly employed by the European factories on the Gold Coast.
[10] i.e. shackles, for slaves.

120. Arthur Richards   Anishan, 2 March 1680/1

This is to advise you that I have receaved the Arda man and woeman which you were pleased to send, and allsoe have receaved from Captain Bowler 100 iron barrs, 20 peeces of sayes and 10 of perpetuanoes, which shall endeavour to dispose of as soone as possible I can, but desier you to lett me know how I may sell the sayes and perpetuanoes.

Inclosed goes my last months account and by the bearer you will receive the ballance thereof which comes to 2 marks 1 ounce and 1 angles of gold.

Pray send downe some powder per first oppertunity and paire of dour hookes and hinges with nailes to naile one [= on] the hinges and some too naile on the lock, ours here being to small. Pray send downe some shorte irons.

121. Arthur Richards   Anishan, 10 March 1680/1

Inclosed goes the two accounts you ordred me to send you. Pray send me some more perpettuanoes, those you were pleased to send by Captain Bowler are all gon but one, and that beleve shall sell this night or in the morninge, it being bespoake. If you please to order me to sell knives at 12 dozen for 8 angles I belieive I can sell some soe, and I am informed here that you sell soe at Cape Corsoe. The Duch at Moree and Cormanteen[11] sell soe.

In your last you mentioned a paire of dore hookes and hinges but I receaved them not, pray lett them come with the bearer. I receaved the 6 pair of short irons. Pray lett your smith make me 20 or 30 large nails for to naile on hinges and a stock lock. Pray lett your smith make a key for the lock that goes by the bearer.

Pray send the goods as soone as you can vizt perpetuanoes and powder.

[PS] I have bought two slaves, hope for more this month.

122. Arthur Richards   Anishan, 12 March 1680/1

Yesterday received yours, and according to your order have inquired after the interloopers that are here, one is Richard Murphy in the Primrose from London and Mr John Belwood is an owner, is bound along the coast for Arda, the other is Roger Mathew in the Exeter Marchant and is bound to Calabar[12] if cannot gett slaves on the coast, he is a Devensheer man and came from Dartmouth and belongs to the Cornish Company.[13]

---

[11] i.e. the Dutch forts at Mouri, west of Anashan, and Kormantin, to the east.

[12] Probably New Calabar, in the Niger Delta; as distinct from Old Calabar (cf. no.600 below), further east along the coast.

[13] No other allusion to a 'Cornish company' engaged in the African trade at this time has been traced. Tattersfield 1991, 277–97, documents the involvement of Dartmouth and other West Country ports in trade to Africa after the ending of the RAC's monopoly in 1698, but does not mention any earlier ventures.

Just now receaved one from you concerning William Beard by Acabas daugh-ter. I have spoake to him, he sayes he never did paniar the boy but was ordered to paniar the man by Agent Bradley. The man understanding of it desiered him to the contrary, and gave him the boy himselfe for a pawne for some few days. As for goeing by the person that brought your Worships letter to me, they may have him if they please for he is not nor never was in my custody but has allwais been in the Curranteers, or his freinds keepeing. As to the man you say was paniard and brought to William Beard I never heard of it before. Here was a man and woemand brought to bee pawned to me for to paye the debt but the[y] would not consent to have them put in irons, neither would I at all meddle with such businesses.

[PS] As for William Beards wages he hath receaved 7 angles of me for last month and is to receave noe more per month here, 6 pounds sterling per annum being to be paid at home. The Curranter promises me assistance hindreing the interloopers from trade.

123.   Arthur Richards   Annishan, 5 April 1681

By the barer you will receive the balance of my last months account with the account, it amounting to 1 mark 1 ounce and 2 angles and 7 tackoes of gold the balance, which hope you will like.

Inclosed goes the inventory you ordered in your last. As for the gunns the blackes say theire is more, but I can find noe more in sight. If you please order me to serch for them I will indeavour to find them out and give your Worship an account of them when found.

Pray doe me the favour to cause to be sent per first opertunity as much beefe, porke or beacon, and pease as you can lett me have for 2 ounces, and will pay your Worship for it in gold and thankes, for provition is very scarse heere at present and will be more scarse quickly.

124.   Arthur Richards   Anishan, 7 April 1681

Yours of this date I just now received, being aboute 4 of the clocke in the evening. [I] am very sorry I should give you this trouble, for which I begg your pardon, there being noe other meaning then a mistake, it being in my book right 24 barrells of powder remaining the end of March, though at present there is but 22 remaining, having this month sould two barrells. On Monday next God willing shall send your Worshipp the two accounts you write for with the particular account you mentioned in your last, and shall take care for the future to make noe more mistakes in my accounts.

125. Arthur Richards   Anishan, 16 April 1681

Yours of yesterdaies date have received, and according to your order inclosed goes
the account you write for, and allso a particular account of the charges and dashes
in March, which hope you will approve of, being less I am shure then any one hath
paid in such accasions, though truly I have paid a great deal more then have sett
down to the Company[s] account, because I would indeavour to regaine my lost
creditt, hopeing to behave my selfe soe as to deserve your good word to the Royall
Company.

Pray be pleased to send downe as soone as you can 50 broad tapseeles, 50
narrow niccanees and the sorts of beads inclosed with the quantitys as write on
every parcell, vizt

No.1 10 pound — more if any smaller of the sort
No.2 20 pound
No.3 20 pound
No.4 10 pound

Pray be pleased to lett Captain Branfill take som corne heere, which if you doe
pray send some canvass before hand that wee may gitt some baggs made in time.

126. Arthur Richards   Anishan, 22 Apr. 1681

Last night receiving your verball order by a blacke, and considering the Companys
intrest and your Worships want of the canoe, I gaine [sic: gave?] creditt to the
Negroe, and the Curranteere and my selfe went off to sea with a 7 hand canoe and
some small canoes and were all last night upon the water. This day being about 3
of the clocke with the helpe of some old Cormanteen canoemen have brought the
15 hand canoe to this place with some sayes and niccanees, the cases being broke
much though not quite in peeces. The canoe must be brought a shore and burnt and
corked (which intended to doe as you shall order me) before shee can goe well to
Cape Corsoe or much from this place, at lowe watter intend to bring her ashore. Per
next shall advise you more particularly. If had not taken care last night as I did
beleeve had not had what goods I had. One whit man was seen in the cannoe at the
rod [= road] esseing [= essaying] of her but could not be taken up.

[PS] Your canoe lay about 2 leagues from the shore and as farr to leeward as the
oyster shell banke, rather lower.

127. Arthur Richards   Annishan, 3 May 1681

I am now about the accounts you write for and hope to send them up in two daies
more. Pray be pleased to send me the beads, broad tapseeles, and narrow niccanees
I formerly write for and some blew and greene perpettuanes, for which goods I have

had money brought me severall times but could not take itt, not having those goods, which desire your Worshipp will be pleased to send per first oppertunitye.

By the bearer goes a small turtle, if coulds but gott a bigger would have sent it but desire you will be pleased to except the will for the deed. If your Worshipp is desireous of such things pray advise and I beleeve in a few dayes mat [= might] gitt more and bigger.

128.   Arthur Richards   Anishan, 4 May 1681

Yours I just now received, wherin you are pleased to tell me that I may have some red perpettuanes, but I having 9 all ready by me which doth not sell, thinke not convenient to trouble you for any more till they are gone, it being greene and blews that I want, but am sorrey you cannot spare me any. [I] wish I had the tapseeles and niccanees. Pray when you send the beads, send me the prices. The niccannees that was saved in the canoe are all broads, being in all 41 pieces, as you will see per my monthly account when [I] send itt you, which shall be as soone as possible I can gett the other done to send you with it. When I can gett any larger shee turtles shall send them to your Worshipp.

[PS] I hope you have received the woemen slave that I sent your Worshipp by Mr Sterling [= Starland?], the Curranter desires you would not suffer her on any account to be redeemed, shee have much disobliged him he sayes, I can till [= tell] not otherwise but beleeve it is murder she hath committed.

129.   Arthur Richards   Anishan, 10 May 1681

Yours I received per Captain Branfill with 50 niccanees narrow much damaged and a box of beads, with a barell of brandy, a bagg of flower and a bagg of pease, hope they will proove good.

I should have answered your letter before but I was willing to see the things ashore first, and the weather being bad could not gitt them a shore before last night.

Inclosed goes duplicates of all my accounts and papers formerly sent you, with Aprill account and two coppys of itt, I hope itt will come in good time to your Worship, if otherwise pray pardon me, I being in a manner all alone, William Beard being sick of a feavour and ague this 6 or 8 days and I have noe body to helpe to doe any thing. I desire you will be pleased to order Dockter Mead to send him something, he being very ill.

[PS] By the bearer you will receive the ballance of Aprill account.

130.   Arthur Richards   Anishan, 21 May 1681

Yesterday Mr Thelwall and Captain Cope came here and told me you had ordered me to put corne aboard of Captain Cope, Mr Thelwall having none. I will put what quantity of corne I have aboard the Captain shall desire of me, and hope by the bearer you will send me an order for itt.

131.   Arthur Richards   Anishan, 30 May 1681

Pray be pleased to send me downe 100 pieces of broad niccanees and lett 50 of them be in halfe peices, pray send them quickly for I want them to pay for a man slave I bought yesterday of some Arcanyes people and they stay for the niccanees to goe up in the countrey. Pray send some green and blew perpetuanoes to help of with the redds I have here, and also 10 casses of speritts, some hole and some half cases.

132.   Arthur Richards   Anishan, 3 June 1681

In my last dated the 30th last past I desired your Worship to send me some broad niccanees, green and blew perpetuanoes and cases of speritts. The first and last I understand you have ordered mee, but of the niccanees you have ordered but 100 halfe peices which makes but 50 hole peices, pray make them up 100 all in halfe peices if noe hole ones, and the speritts pray lett some be hole and some be halfe casses, the most part halfe casses.

I have by me now about half a score scaines of twyne, am goeing to make a nett to catch turtle, if your Worships have any twine that you can spare mee some to add to the nett I shall be much obliged to you.

[PS] Pray be pleased to send the goods as soone as possible you cann, the Arcanies staying for some of them.

133.   Arthur Richards   Anishan, 7 June 1681

Yesterday by the 9 hand canoe I receaved your Worshipps letter of the 4 instant with 100 hundred halfe peices of broad niccanees and 10 cases of spirits, but much damnified, some bottles broake some but halfe full and some not so much as halfe full. I am sorry you have noe blew nor green perpetuanoes to spare me a few.

[PS] The sea being [omission?] I could send nothing in the canoe, else would have loaded her with corne.

134.   Arthur Richards   Anishan, 8 June 1681

By the bearer you will receave the ballance of the inclosed accounts, being 1 mark 5 ounces 3 angles, which hope you will like.

Pray if you have any allejars send down 20 and any ginghams.

[PS] By the next shall send two coppies of the inclosed account, which I supose you will desire as of others formerly.

135. Arthur Richards   Anishan, 18 June 1681

Yours I received yesterday with 10 allejars and 10 ginghams. As to the accounts you writ for, you shall have them as soone as possibly I can write them. I have put 200 chests of corne aboard of Rickard, I must goe for a receipt for itt. As to the charge of sending to Capo Corso I charges 1 angle for every time that I send by land.

136. Arthur Richards   Anishan, 22 June 1681

By this goes the two accounts you writ for. I am inform'd that you sell iron barrs 20 per bendy, at which pray if you please order mee to sell and I shall vend these I have by mee and a great many more, otherwise not, that is if you sell them at that price at Capo Corso. Pray be pleased to send mee the lowest price of the allejars. When I sent corne off aboard Captain Rickard the 7 hand canoe I borrowed of the blacks was staved a peeces and 15 chests of corne lost. I acquainted Captain Rickard of itt but hee sayes he will make noe satisfaction, though his men have confessed they could have saved the canoe and some of the corne but feared to pay damage for wet corne. I must refer myselfe to your worshipp, knowing you will doe what is just on both sides, soe if you please to give mee leave I will wait on you at Capo Corsoe and meete Captain Rickard there.

[PS] Just as my boy was goeing your boy came in with yours. As to the corne here goes a baskitt of it. Besides Captain Rickard had 1 chest off first in his yatt as hee desired, if hee had not liked it he might not have sent his long boate imediatly ashoare with his mate for more. His mate saw all and said it was good, and I beleeve your worshipp will say nothing to the contrary when you see this baskitt, which I will sweare was the same as hee had.

137. Arthur Richards   Anishan, 13 July 1681

Herewith goes the last months account with two coppies and the ballance thereof, being 4 ounces 12 angles and 5 tackoos. I pray be pleased to order me what I shall give for bringing mee anyone of the slaves run away, I haveing offered the Captain of Anamaboe[14] 3 angles each head, but he will not deliver me any if I will not give him 6 angles for each. I have this day given the Curranteer mony in part for two that he says he will fetch back, saying he knowes where they be, soe hope in few dayes to gett them all againe, there shall be no endeavour of mine wanting.

---

[14] Anomabu, to the east (cf. section IV).

[PS] I understand by Mr Hassell that you cannot spare mee noe beere [but] are pleased to spare mum, I desire to know the price of itt, which if not too great shall begg the favour of a caske of you.

138.   Arthur Richards   Anishan, 4 Aug. 1681

Herewith goes July account and two coppies with the ballance thereof. I received your worshipps dated the 2nd instant and shall returne the sletias according to your order if [I] doe not sell them att your price in few dayes, which hope shall as soone as the country pallavers is over.

139.   Arthur Richards   Anishan, 6 Aug. 1681

Yours I received last night, wherein I find you are not well satisfied with my accounts, which I am very sorry for but doe not question I shall (God willing) give you full satisfaction a Monday next.

[PS] Your Captain of Arcanees and his second came here last night and will be finely prendeed this day for carrying somebody out of this towne without leave.

140.   Arthur Richards   Anishan, 13 Aug. 1681

This goes by one of Mr Thelwalls men and serves to advise you that upon Hansacoes demanding satisfaction for the cutting downe of the flagg staffe the people here are gone to cutt a new one and this day twill be brought; they beg your worships pardon, and promise they will serve you in what they can for the future. If your worshipp demands further satisfaction, as far as they are able they will give itt, but plead much poverty. Ansacoe staies to see the flagg put up againe and I for farther order concerning the flagg.

[PS] By the bearer send 24 hens, which hope they will deliver safe.

141.   Arthur Richards   Anishan, 17 Aug. 1681

This goes by Hanscoe, whoe will give you an account how things stand efected here. Pray be pleased to send as soone as you can 20 barrells powder, most in halves and quarter barrells, 10 cases of spirits, 10 ginghams, 20 red perpettuanoes, and as many broad and narrow niccanees as you can spare. I thought I had something to put oyle in but have not, if your worshipp can find any things to put 4 gallons of oyle and as much vinegar, and send itt by the canoe you will much oblege.

142.   Arthur Richards   Anishan, 24 Aug. 1681

Pray be pleased to send mee as many red perpettuanoes as you can spare, 200 iron barrs. The caske of oyle you sent for 4 gallons houlds but 8 3 pint case bottles and about halfe a pint more. Pray send the goods this night if possible you can, if not early in the morning.

[PS] Pray send my boy that is in irons downe loose in the canoe with some more sletias if you can.

143.   Arthur Richards   Anishan, 2 Sept. 1681

This is to desire your worship to send downe what red, green and blew perpettuanoes you can, and [what] sheets and sletias and narrow and broad niccanees you can, as you promised mee you would, I very much want them. Yesterday came a letter from Jullian de Campos at Accra[15] to the Captain of the Portuguese here and I understand that Ahenesa[16] intends to fight the English and Dutch Castles.[17] Jullian de Campos has sent here for succor, that's for timber and what elce can be sent from the Captain here, fearing they may when their hands are in medle with him likewise.

[PS] This news I had from the Frier here, the Captain telling mee but by halfes.

144.   Arthur Richards   Anishan, 3 Sept. 1681

Two notes I received from you this night, and have sent them forward for Annamaboe but before I had received the 2nd I spoake to the Curranteere and have sent to Sabboe,[18] and severall people to the brooke and towards Sinquay's.[19] I am sorry for the loss and there shall be noe endeavours of mine wanting for the recovery. Oliver the smith and Henry the brickmaker came hither from Cabo Corsoe a Satureday with one Arda (as they call them) slave more, and went for Capo Corsoe yesterday about 2 of the clock in the afternoone.

145.   Arthur Richards   Anishan, 6 Sept. 1681

Yours I have received yesterday, with 20 redd perpettuanoes, but beleeve I shall not put them off without some others with them. I want broad and narrow niccanees,

---

[15] Julião de Campos Barreto, Commander of the Portuguese fort at Accra.

[16] Ansa Sasraku, King of Akwamu, at this time overlord of Accra (cf. section VII).

[17] Cf. no.406.

[18] Asebu, a small kingdom on the coast between Fetu and Fante, which included the coastal town of Mouri.

[19] Not identified, but cf. 'Sonquaij' on a map of 1629, shown north-east of Fante (Daaku 1970, 199); the 'brook' mentioned is perhaps the Amisa River.

sheets and sletias and herba longees redds. I am very sorry your Worshipp disappointed mee in these goods, having promised them to our Arcanies.

The Curranteer sayes if you have occation for any timber you may have what you please and he will not differ with you for wood. He has 20 or 30 great trees at a croome of his hard by, soe if you please to have any you may.

146. Arthur Richards   Anishan, 7 Sept. 1681

Yours of this date I have received, and by the 5 hand canoe 20 herba longees, 40 narrow and 20 broad niccanees, 10 sletias and 65 sheets, which sheets are all gone. Pray be pleased to send downe some more sheets and some brass basonns and kettles, the basons of all sorts small and greate. I have sent by Mr Harper 5 marks and 4 ounces of good gold, by reason when my accounts are all made up I doe not think itt convenient to send soe much money by a boy by land. I will send my accounts as soone as possible I can. Pray send alsoe some screw'd juggs.

[PS] I hope you received the henns I sent you the other day.

147. Arthur Richards   Anishan, 11 Sept. 1681

This is to desire you to send the canoe downe with the goods I writt for the other day, and what white longe cloaths you can, though damaged, putting a reasonable price [var. rate] on them. Pray if possible you can lett the canoe be here in the morning.

148. Arthur Richards   Anishan, 12 Sept. 1681

Herewith goes August accompts and the ballance, being 1 angle and 7 taccoes. Being not well and besides have been busied with our Arcanes (who have bought most of the powder you sent last) is the reason I sent you not now two copies of the account, but shall send them as soon as possibly I can. Pray send 20 or 30 barrells of powder in whole and halfe and quarter barrells.

[PS] Since the above written is arrived here the 7 hand canoe with 20 perpettuanoes, 4 chests of sheets, 106 brass pans, 11 brass kettles, which shall endeavour to dispose of according to your order. Pray send the above mentioned powder and some small pewter basons as soone in the morning as you can, tomorrow being markett day.

[PPS] You forgott to send the long cloaths, which be pleased to send tomorrow with other goods. Pray be pleased to send me a little paper and a few wafers.

149.   Arthur Richards   Anishan, 13 Sept. 1681

Yours I received per the 7 hand canoe and the 20 barrells of powder, but much want
the pewter basons, course and fine sletias and more powder and sheets, and more
perpetuanoes greens and blews. As to the timber John Wise can informe you what
it is better then I, he haveing seen it, only as I am inform'd by the Curranteere itt is
a sort of wood that the wormes will not take itt. As to the price of the timber every
joist will cost you 3 taccoes to bring downe, and when you have enough if you
please to give the Curranteere a small dashey hee will thank you for itt but will not
make a price with you for timber. I have sent one woman slave aboard Captain
Rickard this month and have two more in the house and beleeve can buy more
slaves if you please to send me some course sletias.

[PS] Goods wanting here
20 or 30 barrills of powder
small and great pewter basons
course and fine sletias, sheets
green and blew perpetuanoes
Guiney stuffs and paper brawles
boysadoes

150.   Arthur Richards   Anishan, 13 Sept. 1681

Pray doe mee the favour to send mee the powder and other goods I writt for
yesterday, for our Arcanies are ready to pull me in peeces for powder and pewter
basons, great and small.

151.   Arthur Richards   Anishan, 17 Sept. 1681

This serves for covert to the duplicates of last months accounts and goes by Mr
Wendover, whoe is now goeing for Capo Corsoe. Pray be pleased to send my boy
with the goods I writt for, I want them much.

[PS] Pray send mee some paper and wafers.

152.   Arthur Richards   Anishan, 17 Sept. 1681

Yours I received yesterday with 40 barrells of powder, but much want the other
goods I writt for.

153.   Arthur Richards   Anishan, 20 Sept. 1681

This goes in company with the canoemen that came downe yesterday in the 7 hand canoe with goods for this place, which goods I received all but 5 4 pound basons and one piece of white longcloth which was lost when the canoe was broke, and the rest very wett, which am now a drying as well as I can. When wee came off this place I would have had the canoe acame ashoare as she used to doe, the canoemen would not but would come to a graplin and forced Mr Hassell and my selfe to goe ashoare in a small canoe. Wee both came ashoare very well and I ordered the canoe to ly off and I would send for the goods. Before Mr Hassell and my selfe was gott up into the factory and satt downe, news was brought us that the canoe was come ashoare and oversett, she is broke all to peeces, her graplin and rope mast and saile [we] have saved. Truly I beleeve the men were either drunk or bewitched, for the canoe was ashoare and the sletias and perpetuanoes out before this happened.

[PS] John Wise hath cutt downe some trees and is gone this day to cutt downe more.

154. Arthur Richards   Anishan, 25 Sept. 1681

This goes by the Curranteers man and is to desire you will be pleased to order Captain Rickard to deliver to the bearer one man slave that hee hath on board his ship of the Curranteers, and take the man slave in his roome, that the Curranteer sent up the other day.

[PS] One of the pewter basons is found and am promised the rest.

155. Arthur Richards   Anishan, 27 Sept. 1681

Yours I received yesterday, and according to your order have spoake to the Curranteere, whoe will goe downe in the shipp tomorrow, where they will agree on the price of the oyster shells.[20]

156. Arthur Richards   Anishan, 3 Oct. 1681

Pray be pleased to send tomorrow some greene and blew perpettuanoes, large sletias, sheets, 4 pound 3 pound and 2 pound pewter basons, broad and narrow niccanees. I cannot sell the fine sletias at 9 angles but if you please to take 8 angles, if you send 20 or 30 more I can sell them.

20 green and blew perpettuanoes
20 large sletia
20 4lb
20 3   } pewter basons
20 2

---

[20] Oyster shells were burned to make lime for building (cf. section IV, passim).

20 broad $\Big\}$ niccanees
40 narrow

157. Arthur Richards   Anishan, 15 Oct. 1681

This goes with September accounts and ballance, being 3 marks 6 ounces, 13 angles and 9 tacoes of gold (have been troubled with a feavour and ague, elce should have sent up before).

   I humbley thanke you for the spice you sent me. Herewith goes 3 dozen of fowles, as soone as I can gett more and small shoates[21] shall send them up to you. I have received your order concerning Captain Lawrance and Captain Woodfine, which shall obey. I shall also hasten the Curranteere as much as I can to bring timber downe to the waterside, but his people are all in armes against Saboe about one of his wives they have panyard, what itt will end in I know not but he threatens hard.

158. Arthur Richards   Anishan, 19 Oct. 1681

This is to acquaint you that last night, passed by this place (at about 12 a clock at night) two of your runaway slaves. I immediately gave notice to Mr Thelwall of itt and went out myselfe with the Curranteer and his people, but could not take them. Their names is Baffo and Booba, I beleeve they are gone to one Ashams croome, a Cabasheere of Agga,[22] who hath consared[23] Boobas sister. I have sent to the said Ashams croome, not to demand them but to see if they be there or thereaboutes. If can find or here of them shall acquaint your worshipp of it.[24]

159. Arthur Richards   Anishan, 23 Oct. 1681

This goes [by] one of your Arders whose wife by your order lives here at this place, he having stayed Sunday with his wife, intending to have been at Cape Corso this day morning, but by mistake William Beard sent him for wood this morning, and prayed me to write to your Worship the reason of his stay for fear of being punished. I have but two men and one woman that are the Company's that lives with me.

160. Arthur Richards   Anishan, 7 Nov. 1681

This goes by the 15 hand canoe, per which I received yours with 20 barrells of

---

[21] shoats, i.e. young pigs.
[22] Egya, east of Anomabu (cf. section V).
[23] See Glossary.
[24] Cf. no.242.

powder, 20 longees, 20 ginghams, 10 chercolees, 10 broad niccanees and 50 blew baftas broad and 2 caske of brandy.

[PS] As soone as you can pray send the canoe downe againe with more powder, for I hope to have sold tomorrow most of what I have here by me. Pray send me a little paper. Herewith goe 35 peeces of timber.

161.   Arthur Richards   Anishan, 11 Nov. 1681

This goes by a Portuguese seaman who is discharged of this place and is desireous to serve the English in one of your Worships ships on the coast if you thinke fitt to entertaine him. Yours I received yesterday, and desire you will be pleased to send the canoe downe as soon as possible you can with more powder and niccanees. I shall doe what I can to gett the canoes loading of timber, here is allready some peeces of timber downe at the waterside, the Curranteer desires you will order him a peece of say for his timber.

[PS] Pray be pleased to send me some paper and a few wafers if you have any to spare.

162.   Arthur Richards   Anishan, 21 Nov. 1681

Yours I received last night and shall obey your orders as much as possible I can, though doe not know of any interlopers being soe nigh our parts as Amersa.[25] The Curranteer is gone this day to fetch timber and tomorrow morning God willing I will goe with him.

163.   Arthur Richards   Anishan, 23 Nov. 1681

Pray be pleased to send 40 barrells of powder as soon as possible you can, I being just now agoeing with the Curranteer to fetch some of the girders downe.

164.   Arthur Richards   Anishan, 27 Nov. 1681

Yours I received yesterday per the 15 hand canoe, with 30 barrells of powder. Per this canoe goes one girder and 4 other peeces of timber, which is all is downe and at the water side and all I beleeve I shall be able to gett except you send your slaves to fetch it, for the Curranteers people would have me give them cankey money besides their pay, which I have not order to doe. John Wise will give you a farther account of it.

---

[25] Amisa, east of Kormantin.

165.   Arthur Richards   Anishan, 23 Dec. 1681

Yours I received of the 21 instant per the 15 hand canoe, with 10 fine sletias, 10 blew long cloaths, 5 cases of spirritts and 199 iron barrs. How the other barr comes to be wanting I doe not know, there can be noe mistake here for they were all told out of the great canoe upon the sand and after told in the warehouse. By this canoe goes 2 girders and 4 smaller peeces of timber, which is all I can gett except I should detayne the canoe longer, which doe not doe not being ordered soe to doe.

166.   Arthur Richards   Anishan, 28 Dec. 1681

Yours I received yesterday and shall obey your orders, as much as possibly I can, but beleive I cannot gett soe much corne for sayes and perpettuanoes as you order, I will doe what I can. I hope you have ordered Captain Woodfine to deliver the Curranteers boy.

167.   Arthur Richards   Anishan, 2 Jan. 1681/2

Yesterday I received a letter for Captain Woodfine concerning the delivering the Curranteers boy, but hee was gon before the letter came, soe shall give itt to Mr Shears to give him, and if you please to order that the boy may come up in the canoe that Mr Wendover goes in, itt will save the Curranteer some money, Captain Wood-fine being at Wyamba.

168.   Arthur Richards   Anishan, 4 Jan. 1681/2

Yours I received in which you desire to know what I have done about purchaseing of corne. As yett I have not bought one chest and feare I shall not buy any att your price, there being but little to be had and our people here will not agree on any price till they have agreed at Annamaboe first, which as yett I doe not heare they have. I will doe what I can. I desire you will be pleased to send some boards to flower the corne roome.

169.   Arthur Richards   Anishan, 13 Jan. 1681/2

Yours I received by John Comma. As to corne I shall this day begin to take in, but att what price I know not, only I must pay as Mr Thelwall payes at Annamaboe. The Curranteers people are gone this day for wood. I wonder you have no news from the Mina. The Cheife of Moree[26] hath released all the Curranteers people he had panyard.[27] When I came last from Capo Corsoe, as I came ashoare the boyes

---

[26] i.e. the Dutch chief agent at Mouri, not the indigenous ruler.

[27] This incident is not explained; but for the subsequent development of the dispute, cf. no.177 below.

in the canoe fired some musketts, but in halfe an hour I beleeve there came no less than 400 or 500 men from Anamaboe in arms, they thinking the Morees had been come here.

170.   Arthur Richards   Anishan, 22 Jan. 1681/2

Your worships I received yesterday. I have done what possible I could to gett timber, and have sent in the 15 hand canoe 4 girders and one small piece of timber, which is all I could gett. As to corne I have not much by mee, but the bearer will informe you that I shall have some in few dayes and that very good. Inclosed goes December account and the ballance. I wish you had sent mee some tapsells, musketts and allejars.

[PS] The ballance of December account is 7 ounces 6 angles and 2 taccoes.

171.   Arthur Richards   Anishan, 1 Feb. 1681/2

Yours I received by the boy yesterday. Captain Gates hath now 135 chests of corne aboard and wee are getting off more as fast as wee can and hope in a few dayes between Mr Thelwall and myselfe to procure what corne you have ordered for him, but corne is very scarce.[28] As to timber here is 2 girders downe, which is all I know off. There is some small peeces in the woods which I will doe what I can to gett it downe with speed. For fouls I can hardly gett (at present) for our own spending, there being great mortallity of them at this time a yeare, but I will send you some as soon as I can gett them.

[PS] Captain Woodfine carried a longboats load of wood away of the Curranteers and did not pay him for it, the wood and canoe hire to carry it off to his boat comes to 11 angles, I must pay but hope you lett me putt it to the Royall Company account, it is John Woodfine I speake of.

172.   Arthur Richards   .   Anishan, 2 Feb. 1681/2

Yours of the first instant I just now received by the small canoe bound for Captain Hills ship,[29] and give your Worship and the rest of the Gentlemen in Councill many thanks for your kindness in Captain Woodfines concerne, and shall doe in my account as you have ordered me. As to the timber I know there is a girder more in the wood and I know of noe more, and that one John Wise tould me was not for your Worship, I haveing desired him to cut one downe for me, but since your Worship desires it you shall have it and tomorrow God willing I will goe with the

[28] Cf. no.611.
[29] In Anomabu road, to the east (cf. nos 605–6).

townes people and the Curranteer and see what timber is left, but I beleive John Wise is a little mistaken.

[PS] I am sorry your Worship hath forbid me to panyar any whites (I meane Dutch men) since they threaten me if ever I goe to Capo Corso.[30]

173.   Arthur Richards   Anishan, 8 Feb. 1681/2

Yesterday I writt to your Worship by the Portuguese Father here, the Father told me he was to goe to Capo Corso Castle, soe I give him the letter I had writt to your Worship, but they are all alike, soe brought me the letter againe. Pray be pleased to send as soon as you can some powder, blew and green perpettuanoes, blew long cloathes in halves, and some blew and green Welch plaines, and some tappseels broad. I hope to load your great canoe up againe with timber and also intend to come up in her to Cape Corso to waite on your Worship with my accounts and ballance of them.

40 barrells of powder
25 blew and green perpettuanoes
20 blew long cloaths
10 blew and green Welch plaines
50 tapseels broad.

174.   Arthur Richards   Anishan, 10 Feb. 1681/2

This is only to desire your Worship will be pleased to send the goods writt for (two dayes agoe) as soon as possible you can, vizt powder, blew and green perpettuanos, blew long cloathes and broad tapseeles, blew and green Welch plaines. If you please to send the canoe with these goods shee shall be return'd with timber and my accounts and ballance.

175.   Arthur Richards   Anishan, 12 Feb. 1681/2

Yours I received last with one for Mr Thelwall, which have sent to him. As to the price of the powder, if you sell it at a benda per barrell at Capo Corso wee must doe soe here, heitherto have not undersould the price in any goods. As to the mixing red with the blew and green perpettuanoes it will cost me some trouble but if you doe it I may doe it likewise. As to corne I have put 214 chests aboard Captain Gates and

---

[30] Not explained; but probably connected with the earlier panyarring of people from Anashan by the Dutch agent at Mouri (no.169); although forbidden to take action against the Dutch, Richards subsequently organized the panyarring of some of the Mouri people, presumably in retaliation (no.177).

am doeing what I can to procure more, but it is very scarce. Foules if I can gett any shall send you up some per returne of your canoe.

176. Arthur Richards   Anishan, 17 Feb. 1682

This goes by the 15 hand canoe, in which goes 3 girders, which is all the timber could gett, for the people of this towne asked me 2 angles to drink besides their pay for bringing that peece they brought this day, soe know not when I shall gett any more downe, it being rowsaring time. I received the 15th instant 20 pintadoes, 10 barrells of powder, 10 perpettuanos, 10 blew long cloathes, 10 silke longees, 10 stript silkes for account of the Royall Affrican Company of England. One [= on] Sunday next God willing William Beard shall wait on your Worship with my accounts.

177. Arthur Richards   Anishan, 2 March 1681/2

Yours I received yesterday by your boy. As to the corne you order for Captain Starland, shall doe my endeavour to put itt on board, as I doe not doubt but I shall. This with a letter from Mr Thelwall goes by an Arcany boy, I not being willing before [I] have order from your worship to venture your boy up by land. [I] have last night fitted out some canoes from this place and panyard some Morea people,[31] to whome I will be as they intend to be to mee if the Curranteer continues to stand by mee as hee doth now.

[PS] Pray be pleased to spare mee halfe a douzen fire lock musketts for I shall want them much. Pray dispatch the bearer as soon you can.

178. Arthur Richards   Anishan, 10 March 1681/2

Yours I received yesterday concerning a man that Captain Affada sayes is his slave. I beleeve itt not to be soe for the Mareen of Agga pretends that all three are his. Hee is aboard Captain Hill, whoe suppose will be with your worship shortly. As to Captain Starland hee will sayle this day, I haveing put what corne I could gett that was good aboard, and will wright my last months accounts as soone as hee is gon and send them up.

179. Arthur Richards   Anishan, 13 March 1681/2

Your order I received being directed to Mr Thelwall and my selfe,[32] and shall

---

[31] Cf. n.30 above; cf. also no.262 below, for an attack by the Mouri people on an English ship a few days later, probably in counter-retaliation.

[32] i.e. to panyar canoes belonging to the Dutch (cf. no.264 below).

endeavour to performe your command, but would willingly know when you would have the Curranteer meete your people, hee being a getting ready.

180.   Arthur Richards   Anishan, 8 Apr. 1682

Yours I received last night, and am now about complying with your orders, and will gett done as soone as possible I can. The Curranteer tells mee the Morea people threatens this towne very hard,[33] but beleeves they are set on by the Mina people.

181.   Arthur Richards   Anishan, 9 Apr. 1682

According to your order have inclosed sent you February and March accounts distinctly. I wish your Worship would bee pleased to send downe some broad tapsells, broad niccanees, course sletias, sheets, allejars, blew and green perpettuanos, blew and green Welch plaines, 1: 2: 3: and 4 pound pewter basons. I hope your Worship will be pleased to think on mee when you make up your pallavora with the Dutch.

182.   Arthur Richards   Anishan, 5 May 1682

This is to acquaint you that the faire hopes wee had of removeing the goods from Anishan factory is now quite frustrated, for the Curranteer will lett now noe more goods come off but would have mee goe ashoare[34] and come to another pallavora with the Arcanies, and hee will make them make satisfaction as hee sent off word, but for severall reasons I cannot yett goe ashoare. First, if I goe hee will demand the Braffo's[35] and his sonn ashoare which are now on board and cannot be delivered till satisfaction be given or an order from your Worship; Secondly, I know not what satisfaction your Worship will have; Thirdly, if they gett mee ashoare they will have two Whitemen for two Blacks and soe doe what they please, which now they cannot, for as the Curranteer himselfe brought the Whitemen to Anishan I will not lett any voiolence be offered to their goods, but will demand his sonn of the Arcanies etc. I hope your Worship will be pleased to pardon my over freedome in writing, it is but my duty to write and my weake opinion as to what I have writt, I leaveing all to your Worship whose orders I shall endeavour to follow as long as I live.

[PS] The Arcanies threatned to goe all to live att Anamaboe and have declared that what they have done was but to force mee to comply with them, but finding that I

---

[33] Presumably in reaction to Richards' panyarring of their people, reported in no. 177.

[34] Richards had gone on board the *African Merchant*, apparently intending to abandon the factory if he could not obtain satisfaction for a dispute with the local traders (cf. no.508).

[35] See Glossary.

was in earnest in removeing the goods they are not yett gon soe [I] desire to know what satisfaction you will be pleased to have of them.

183. Arthur Richards   Anishan, 20 May 1682

Yours I received this morning, wherein I find your Worship desires to know what I have done in the palavora. I have not done nor cannot myselfe doe anything more then what I wrote you last, yett have done my endeavour, only have in your worships name perswaided the Curranteer to goe to Capo Corso to make up all differences himselfe, and to him I referr your Worship, he sayes he will goe up on Wednesday next. I desire noe goods yett, haveing noe trade here, and the Arcanies say they will not trade here if I give them not the goods seized on againe.

[PS] I have been since Fryday every night endeavouring to goe up to Capo Corso but the weather would not permitt.

184. Arthur Richards   Anishan, 1 June 1682

This is cheifly to accompany the inclosed, which I received this morning from Accra, and allsoe to acquaint you that God be thanked I gott well with goods ashoare but splitt the 11 hand canoe from starne on the starboard side about 10 yards long fault of the canoemen, hope to mend her pretty well againe but as shee went up with the Curranteere and brought the Company's goods downe, the Curranteer desires that when hee goes about to mend her, that if hee has occasion for iron worke that he cannot gett done here you will be pleased to lett your smiths at Capo Corsoe make itt for him.

[PS] The Portugueze Padre desires that the inclosed be sent for St Thoma, it is for the Governour.

185. Arthur Richards   Anishan, 20 June 1682

Yours of the 17th instant received on Monday night last, with a staple which goes by the bearer that the smith make the rest accordingly. Inclosed goes May account and by the bearer alsoe goes the ballance which is 7 angles and 3 tacco's. As to the Portugueze boards[36] hee will not abate any thing of 6 peaze a douzen.

186. Arthur Richards   Anishan, 27 June 1682

Yours I received this day concerning 9 or 11 hand canoes. In answer to your Worships first letter about canoes, I wrote you that I had one 9 hand canoe but she

---

[36] Presumably, boards to be purchased from the Portuguese factory in Anashan.

was not come downe to the waterside, as shee is not yett, when shee comes shall give you an account of itt, before I cannot give you any account att all concerning the price, haveing not as yett seen her, though have given earnest for her and have secured her from being sold to any body but myselfe or your order. [I] wish I may gett her downe time enough for Captain Norths service, I will use my endeavour to doe itt.

187. Arthur Richards   Anishan, 14 July 1682

Herewith goes June accounts and the ballance being 2 marks, 2 ounces, 1 angle and 6 tacco's. Pray be pleased to lett me know what price you will now give for corne if any old corne should offer, your last order to mee was 2a½ or 3 angles per chest but I know not if you will continue to give that price still or noe.

188. Arthur Richards   Anishan, 15 July 1682

This is to acquaint you that the Arcanies here have been with mee for their months pay as you ordered them, but notwithstanding that order I have not paid but proffered to give them a letter to your Worship, not knowing how you would approve itt if I should pay them, they haveing not brought mee above halfe that little money I now send you. Soe if you please to order mee to pay them I shall doe itt.

189. Arthur Richards   Anishan, 6 Aug. 1682

Yours I received last night but I was gone to hasten the canoe I told your worship of, soe could not answer you before now. I doe not doubt the canoe butt as for corne I beleeve I shall not gett any att 1 angle per chest but shall use my uttmost endeavour to gett the quantity you mention as cheape as I can.

190. Arthur Richards   Anishan, 14 Aug. 1682

This is to desire your Worship will be pleased to send Samuell Bostick downe in William Beards place, William Beard not being well satisfied with his liveing here, something about his pay troubles him which I shall answer to God willing in two or three day's, as I have told Mr Spurvay expect to be up with a canoe for Captain Ware in that time.[37] Pray be pleased to lett Samuell Bostick come downe in this canoe for William is gott a little hott headed and I know not what time hee will goe and I will not force him to any thin, leaving all to your Worship.

[PS] William Beard's gon out of the house, where I know not and I am alone. If I

---

[37] Cf. no.625.

have not some body to leave in the house I feare I shall not comply with my word in procureing the canoe, because I cannot leave the house alone though the canoe be ready.

191. William Beard   Anishan, 18 Aug. 1682

My love and respects to your Worship and Mr Spurvay and this is to acquaint your Worship that I have sent to Mr Richards for him to come up, for there is Mr Wallis come to take an account of the goods and your letter will goe this night, I would have sent itt sooner but could not gett any canoemen before night. I pray doe not think itt ill of mee for I have done to the utermost of my power, for Mr Richards is gon to Tantonquerry to buy some canoes for your Worship to bring to Capo Corsoe.

193. Arthur Richards   Anishan, 25 Aug. 1682

This morning I have told over all the Companys concerns att Anishan, and as inordered have delivered the keys to Benjamin Cantrill. This comes by William Beard, alsoe an account of what goods remaines.

193. Arthur Richards   Anishan, 2 Sept. 1682

Yours I received dated the 28th of August past, and had sent the canoe up before but I doe assure you I have had as many croses about her as could be wished to any man, first being beaten off by the Accrongs and the Anguynas,[38] then canoemen run away and leave mee, and last forc'd to send to Cormanteen for canoemen and they had bad luck, and I now understand your Worship has been pleased to be verry secure [sic: severe?] upon mee in my absence. In your last you wrote mee I should come up and take charge of the factory againe, that charge is taken already by Benjamin Cantrill, whoe of his owne accord told mee hee was not to deliver any thing to mee. I am inform'd that in my absence late att night William Beard went into the warehouse and tooke severall goods out and putt them into a chest hee has in thet towne, upon what account I know not. I am now come to follow up your Worships orders. About 3 a clock in the afternoone yesterday (as Benjamin Cantrill informes mee) run away two woemen slaves of the Companys and I am since inform'd they were stole by some Arcanies and that they are att Morea. The Quarrenteer hath promised mee I shall have them againe verry suddenly.

194. Benjamin Cantrill   Anishan, 7 Sept. 1682

Yours I received the 4th of this instant, and as concerning Mr Richards he shewed

---

[38] Akron and Angona, two kingdoms on the coast immediately east of Fante.

mee a letter that come from your Worship last Saturdeay night, wherein you please to order him up to Cabo Corsoe, something wanting to his canoe which is now a fitting and hee said hee would come up this night, but the occasion hee did not come up is because his canoe wanted mending, and as concerning what hee does here att present is nothing att all but hee is troubled att William Beard goeing away and hee not here but hee said hee is a great rogue. And all is well att the factory.

195.   Benjamin Cantrill   Anishan, 7 Sept. 1682

Since the last I have had some discourse with Mr Richards concerning his goeing to Cabo Corsoe but hee tells mee hee wont goe up without hee has a copie of the order that your Worship ordered Mr Thelwall to come here and I and to order William Beard to Cabo Corsoe, and when hee has a copie of that order hee will come and not before except your Worship take him by force. All is well att the factory.

196.   Benjamin Cantrill   Anishan, 16 Sept. 1682

Since Mr Richards his departure from Anishan I have had some discourse with his boyes [about] what hee carryed along with him to Tanton Querry,[39] they say the first time hee went hee carryed 30 blew pottkeys, 10 Guyney clouts, 6 long cloaths, 16 perpettuanoes and the seacond time hee carried 20 niccanees broad, 10 tapsells 5 broad and 5 narrow, and 50 iron barrs, 6 lead barrs, 30 pottkeys, 2 long cloaths and 4 perpetuano's, and there remaines at Tanton Querry 43 pottkeys, 5 narrow tapsells, 2 lead barrs, 35 iron barrs, and 13 perpettuanoes, and the rest Mr Richards disposed of and his boy Ampa will take his fitish upon itt.

197.   Benjamin Cantrill   Anishan, 18 Sept. 1682

Since Mr Pley's departure from Anishan I have not had a slave to fetch any water or wood but what I faint to buy, for Mr Pley ordered Mr Thelwall to keepe them till further order and the Quarranteer fro's your Worship ackie[40] and hee saies hee would willingly come up to justifie himselfe before your Worship and Mr Richards but his people wont lett him goe up yett but hee has sent up to the Braffoe to know if hee may goe up or noe, and the Quarranteer saies the reason is because there is a differance between the Fettuers and them, and hee sayes if hee should come up without their leave they would prendee him a great deale when hee comes downe againe, but the Quarranteer has sent his man up to the Braffoe this day in the

---

[39] In the previous month Richards had gone to Tantumkweri to purchase a canoe (no.191); but the details given here suggest a larger-scale venture, perhaps the establishment of a subordinate factory.
[40] See Glossary.

morning if should come up to waite on your Worship or noe, but the Quarranteer saies hee durst not come up to waite on your Worship before hee acquaint the Braffoe of itt because they think hee goes up to make a pallavora upon their heads with the Fetuers. And all things are well.

198.   Benjamin Cantrill   Anishan, 22 Sept. 1682

According to your Worships order that came with Captain Quow's[41] boy have sent the names of those boyes, that broke open the Quarranteers sons house, there was Prince and Yacon, Hance and Coffee, and what goods they stole away are these following, 2 perpettuanoes 9 Guyney clouts, 10 pottkeys, 14 Beneen cloaths, 4 musketts, 1 carbine, 2 angles of gold, 2 other cloaths, 3 douzen and 4 pipes. And the names of the other boy's that had noe hand in itt is Ampa, John Jack, Aque, Afadan [var. Affoaden], Abando [var. Bando] and Accoree.

199.   Benjamin Cantrill   Anishan, 5 Oct. 1682

I have spoke to the Quarranteer about the goods at Tanton Querry and hee saies hee will fetch them up for your Worship if your Worship please to order him canoemen, but the 11 hand canoe that is att Tanton Querry is none of Mr Richards's hee says, for hee never paid for itt but only gave the people a niccanee to them to haule itt downe to the waterside, and itt is there now. Here is but one slave here of Mr Richards's and the Quarranteer sayes lett Mr Richards make up his account to what hee owes him and hee will pay him, hee has sent up his son along with Captain Coffee to know of Mr Richards whatt hee has to say to him, hee would have come up himselfe but hee is lame.

200.   Benjamin Cantrill   Anishan, 7 Oct. 1682

I have made up the Quarranteers accompts and I have sent itt up by his son, and the Quarranteer sayes that is all that ever hee had of Mr Richards but hee paid him, for there wants to ballance his accompt 6 ounces, 7 angles, and 4 tacco's, which hee sayes hee will pay your Worship in slaves, corne or in gold, which your Worship pleases. The Quarranteer fro's your Worship ackie and any thing hee can serve your Worship in hee will serve you.

201.   Benjamin Cantrill   Anishan, 11 Oct. 1682

I have spoke to the Quarranteer about what Mr Richards wrote about but the Quarranteer sayes hee cant say nothing to itt before hee speake to him his selfe, but

---

[41] A prominent African employee of the RAC.

hee is lame att present in his hip, but hee sayes within this 4 or 5 dayes hee will come up to Cabo Corsoe his selfe to justifie his selfe before your Worship, and hee now desires your Worship to excuse him till then. Hee will keep Bassa and Aggo till hee has made up his accompts with Mr Richards and when hee has made itt up what is due to him hee will pay to your Worship.

202.   Benjamin Cantrill   Anishan, 16 Oct. 1682

I have acquainted the Quarranteer about the goods att Tanton Querry and hee sayes if your Worship please to order the canoe downe there itt may bring up what goods that are left, for last Fryday there come up from Tanton Que[r]ey some men to speake to the Quarranteer about what goods that are left there, they say some are sold and what are remaining they shall be sent by the canoe and what goods they have sold they will send up the money for, but they say that Mr Richards owes for a 5 hand canoe 10 angles of gold and for 12 chests of corne. The Quarranteer fro's your Worship ackie and hee has promised faithfully that on Thursday next hee will come up to Cabo Corsoe if your Worship will promise that hee shall come downe againe on Fryday, if not hee wont come before Satureday.

203.   Benjamin Cantrill   Anishan, 17 Oct. 1682

I have acquainted the Quarranteer about what your Worship wrote and the Quarranteer has promised mee faithfully hee will be att Cabo Corsoe on Thursday in the morning, and about the goods att Tanton Querry hee will send Cuttaba the old Braffoes son to fetch the goods off, hee would have sent his son Quacoone but hee would not goe because of his fathers goeing up to Capo Corsoe.

204.   Benjamin Cantrill   Anishan, 19 Oct. 1682

This morning I went to the Quarranteer to know of him if hee would goe up to Cabo Corsoe according to his promise, but hee tould mee hee was taken in the night with a vomitting and hee could gett noe rest but he saies if he be any better, if the 15 hand canoe goe by this day hee will come up in her, if not if hee be well tomorrow he saies he will waite on your Worship. The Quarranteer sayes he would not have your Worship think ill of him because Mr Richards sayes hee owes him 3m 0o 0a 1ta. He tells mee if hee owed him 20m, if your Worship sends for him, if hee be well hee would come up to your Worship. I would desire your Worship to send me a sheet or two of paper.

205.   Benjamin Cantrill   Anishan, 24 Oct. 1682

I have acquainted the Quarranteer with what your Worship wrote about but hee would desire your Worship to excuse him, but as for withdrawing the factory[42] hee would say nothing but hee tells Captain Coffee and mee hee will come up to Cabo Corsoe this day and hee saies hee will satisfie your Worship, hee would have gon up along with Coffee but itt is his Sunday. The Quarranteer has put his marke to this letter.

206. Benjamin Cantrill   Anishan, 6 Nov. 1682

The Quarranteer fro's your Worship ackie and he desires your Worship to send downe a canoe for to goe to Tanton Querry for within this 8 dayes hee goes up into the country and sayes itt will be 6 or 7 day's before hee comes downe againe, soe if your worship pleases to send downe the canoe before, hee will goe and fetch off all the goods at Tanton Querry.

207. David Harper   Anishan, 8 Nov. 1682

Being arrived here with the 9 hand canoe I acquainted the Quarranteer with your Honours pleasure about his goeing to Tanton Querry to bring off the Royall Companys concerns from that place according to his promise, but he saies that he cannot goe downe himselfe but will send his boy downe, hee haveing sent up to the country before and made all pallavoras up soe that the goods will be delivered to us soe well as if hee were there himselfe. I very much doubting that our goeing downe without the Quarranteer may prove to as little effect as when the greate canoe was there last, which I well understood from the people of that place, wherefore I thought fitt to acquaint your Honour herewith, expecting an answer whether wee shall goe downe to Tanton Querry or only take the goods that are remaining here and soe returne to Cabo Corsoe.

208. Benjamin Cantrill   Anishan, 12 Nov. 1682

I humbly begg your Honour to exuse mee for I have disposed of 7 firkins of tallow and will satisfie your Honour for them. I had not disposed of any but I was forc'd to buy me victualls. I will pay your Honour this pay day 1oz 2a, which is for 3 the other 4 the next. I am owing for 2 yett, if could gett the money for them I would have sent your Honour by the bearer. I hope your Honour will excuse.

---

[42] It is not clear whether this alludes to the evacuation of the RAC's goods from Tantumkweri (as discussed in the immediately preceding letters), or to the possible withdrawal of the Anashan factory itself.

IV

ANOMABU

The RAC factory at Anomabu ('Annamaboe') had been established in 1679.[1] It was occupied continuously through the period 1681–3; the same man, Richard Thelwall, serving as chief factor there throughout. As is alluded to in this correspondence (no.242) the factory in 1681 was in the process of being fortified (with 'flankers', or defensive earthworks). It was already known as Charles Fort; although Thelwall's letters never use this name, it does appear in a letter written from Anomabu by a visiting ship in 1682 (no.529). The factory supplied mainly gold, but also some slaves; it was also important for the provision of corn to slave-ships, and served as a base for fishing for oyster shells (burned to produce lime for building), at the sandbank off Amisa ('Amersa', 'Amessa') to the east.

Anomabu, like Anashan to the west (and Egya to the east) belonged to the state of Fante ('Fanteene'); hence the factory sent representatives to negotiate with 'the Quantrees and Braffo' at Fante (nos 215, 247–8), and the town's own chiefs went to Fante to attend the celebration of 'their Christmas day' (no. 277). The hinterland traders, as at Anashan, were the Akani ('Arcanies'). Recurrently trade from the interior to Anomabu was interrupted by Kabestera and other states in the immediate interior associated with it (nos 268–9, 325, 358).

209. Richard Thelwall   Annamaboe, 7 Feb. 1680/1

Last night I received yours, whereby I understand that one Allen an England interlooper passed by Cape Corso. He is att an anchour att Agga, but shall have noe corne their but what the Blackes send of, that I cante helpe theire. I have writte to Mr Richardes to Annishan and shall take care that they shall bee secured till further order if [they] come ashoare.[2] By Mr Hassell I write your Honour what I had sent for Annamaboe and thought itt not convenient for to take all att once because the people should not take any notice of itt.

[1] Davies 1957, 246.
[2] Cf. no.117.

210.   Richard Thelwall   Annamaboe, 11 Feb. 1680/1

This services cheifely for coverte to the inclosed accompt to the 29 January past, and allso a noate of what whitte men and Blackes, which hope will finde right and make noate accordingley. Captain Bowler hath 106 buttes shells, suppose may arrive Cape Corso this day. Captain Clarke will have all his corne in this day.

211.   Richard Thelwall   Annamaboe, 13 Feb. 1680/1

Last night received yours and as to Gallantia,[3] indeed every body knowes hee is a great rogue, he left mee when I was robbed when I beleeive might have told me of itt if [he] would. Hee owes Mr Belwood[4] 3 slaves, which said would pay me but wonte. Itt was said [he] owede Captain Archer a greate deale of money, butt howe to prove itt I cante tell. He owes me one woeman and 8 angles, and Ottadadiqueene owes mee 4 ounces and Captain Peter 1 ounce and 2 angles. Butt truely I beleive itt is better nott for too meddle with him, for if should would not lett the white man that is at Wyamba come away nor any of the goods their. Nay they wonte lett a cannoe passe by for Accra or too Accra butt they will pannayer itt, and the cannoes must staye thiere goeing and commeing, soe of two evills a man ought for to chose the least. This morning Mr Franckland and Mr Winder went for Accra, Mr Winder beinge verry ill haveing a violent feavour. Last night came a shippe in to Annishan road, I suppose an interlooper, and their is two more shippes comeing downe, [I] shall take care that none come ashoare. This morning Captain Clarke sett saile for Cape Corso. By the 15 hands cannoe have sent 35 chestes of corne.

212.   Richard Thelwall   Annamaboe, 18 Feb. 1680/1

Last night I received yours, and according as in ordred have sent the two bricklayers Yankey and Coeampa. As too wood, I have none but what is to burne. What wood was att Aga is aboard Captain Clarke, I suppose may arrive Cape Corso this day. By first conveniency of cannoe shall send such wood as this place affords. As too the interloopers, theire is none in this roade butt two at Amessa and one att Annishan, yett I cannot heare of any goeing ashoare. They give 7 pease 2 angles for a man slaves.

[PS] I shall want 2 hogsheads of tarrise[5] now, soe may please for to send it by first conveniency.

---

[3] Apparently an African, employed in the RAC factory at Winneba (cf. nos 385–6, 579).
[4] From later references (e.g. no.213), evidently a former RAC chief agent at Anomabu.
[5] tarras, a form of cement.

213.   Richard Thelwall   Annamaboe, 20 Feb. 1680/1

Last night I received yours just as I came from Agga,[6] but Mr Hassell said nothing
to mee. [I] had writte but that Captain Yankey[7] was gone to Cape Corso. Yankey Mr
Belwood made Captain, a man not worth 2 pence and of noe repute. The Quarranteers man was with mee and asked mee if that Aga factory was to bee removed, and
I told him no, but a white man or two for to bee theire as in Mr Belwoodes tyme.
He said no more to me, he said nothinge of stoppinge a trade. Besides I told them
just before Mr Carter went away they brooke oppen the warehouse and tooke about
a marks worth of longes and plaid the rogue when they pleased.[8] I have been here
allmost 2 yeares and indeed all the gold comes by the way of Aga first, and ever
since I have been att Annamaboe itt has been as much as I can doe to pay whitte
men and Blacks. The charge is great and the other place gettes all the moneye.

214.   Richard Thelwall   Annamaboe, 25 Feb. 1680/1

This day Captain Bowler arrived here,[9] and according as in ordered shall deliver
what corne he wants and what sheetes [you] have orderd to Mr Nightingale. Butt
Captain Bowler sayeth your Honour hath ordred some canvis for bagges, as yet see
none so desiers some a soone as possible for the expeditione of his shippe away
from hence. Lickwise shall deliver him what slaves I have.

215.   Richard Thelwall   Annamaboe, 28 Feb. 1680/1

This night I received your[s] per Captaine Yankey and according as in ordred shall
send a white man to the Quantrees and Braffo. Itt will bee expiences, though shall
goe as neare as possible. Tomorrowe I hope Captain Bowler will have all his corne
a board. I take notice [you] will send a supply for Agga, I hope will not forgett
Annamaboe. I have 27 sayes whitte, nay they are brooken and noe body will buy
them, if you please Mr Franckland cann informe you what they are. This comes by
the 15 hand and 4 hand cannoe, which bringes in all 15 buttes [i.e. of shells], they
goe from hence when the winde is downe in the night.

216.   Richard Thelwall   Annamaboa, 4 March 1680/1

This morninge earley Mr Franckland wente for Accra, the day before being verry
raine. I take notice should not send aney [person] to Fanteene, indeed it would have

[6] Thelwall had been to Egya to reorganize the factory there: cf. no.376.
[7] It is not entirely clear whether this man (who appears elsewhere as an important employee of the RAC)
is the same as the bricklayer Yankey just mentioned.
[8] As is clear from no.247, Carter was formerly RAC factor at Egya.
[9] Cf. no.574.

lost a great deale money. Incloosed is myne and Mr Hassells accompts, which hope will finde right and make noate accordingley This comes by the gunners mate in the 15 hand cannoe with 15 buttes of oyster shelles more, and allsoe the ballance of the accompts beinge in all 4oz 00a 4ta.

[PS] I receeived per the 15 hand cannoe one ball of sayes and 2 hogsheads tarrise. Incloosed is the receipts from Captain Bowler.

217. Richard Thelwall   Annamaboa, 10 March 1680/1

Yesterday I received yours by the 15 hand cannoe, with 10 barrills of powder, 19 broad tapp[s]ell[s] and 1 narrowe, 17 broad nicconees and 23 narrowe, and 50 blew pottkies. As to the over charged oyster shelles, some came to Annamaboa so their is no mistake as per Mr Hilliards inclosed noate appeares, which I paid and his charges, and thought he had acquainted your Honour before he went away. And as to the 4oz 5a for puttinge 700 and odde chestes of corne a board shippes, I shall aske the white men for their tallies of each shippe and shall give you a more perticular accompt. As for the 35 chestes of corne, itt was putt into the 15 hand cannoe, and if any be lost by the way I cante helpe itt.

[Inclosed] An accompt att Amersa February the 4 1680/1

	oz	a	t
The 4 hand cannoe 27 turns	0	7	3
The 5 hand cannoe 29 turns	–	10	4
The canoe men cankee money	0	6	0
For charges	0	11	6
ffor 106 casks of shels	6	10	0
	8	13	01

218. Richard Thelwall   Annamaboe, 16 March 1680/1

Yours I received of the 14 instant by Mr Richardes. Inclosed is all the accompts writte for, and as to the blew baftas I never se[e] any such before, for they used to be as stiffe as a board. They sell att Succonde and to windward, I have sold them, shall use my endeavour to sell them. Inclosed is a noate of what gunns is here, I have but 10 great shott and they not halfe fittinge for these gunns but hope your Honour will spare me some, and allsoe some spunges and ladles for the gunns. I allso shall want some paper and incke.

219. Richard Thellwall   Annamaboe, 25 March 1681

This comes by the 15 hand canoe, by which [you] have but 7 butts of oyster shells, the wather being very bad, and they lost 10 in 15. Yesterday the Captain of the

Arcanies brought me a pound of good gold for perpetuanoes, but I told him had none, soe [he] desired for to write to Cape Corsoe if had any. Per first good convenience be pleased for to send some tapseeles, nicconees. Just now is come in this road a shipp, I suppose an interloper.

220.   Richard Thelwall   Annamaboe, 2 April 1681

Last night by the 15 hand canoe I received the goods mentioned, being safe ashore but a little wette. As to the canoe going for oyster shells, the mans sone was here, and sayeth he would be paid for all the shells that should bee lost, and said it would better stay till after the raines and then send a shipp. Indeed they lost 10 in 15 buttes the last tyme, when sent but 7 in the great canoe, soe are unwilling to send any more till better weather. By the 15 hand canoe have sent a bull, the best I have, which is att your Honnours service. As concerning the buying of 11, 9, 7 and five hand canoes I shall doe my indeavoure, but the cheapest and best canoes are to be bought up to windward at Axhim, and as to any canoes going to Alampo,[10] theire will none goe till the raines be over.

[PS] I wish your honnour a merry Easter; and many thanks for all favours, but understand the small poxe is verry much att Cape Corsoe, and I never had them, soe desire your pardon for not comeing this Easter.

221.   Richard Thelwall   Annamaboe, 6 April 1681

Yours of the 4th instant I received by Frances Nixson, and as for those people they will neither send not sell their canoes. As to Captain Hoocomey [var. Hookeme], indeed he promised me to pay me the first time I came to Cape Corso, soe I was contented. By Captain Peeter I nowe send Marches account, and alsoe the ballance being 11oz 14a 7ta, which hope will find right and make noate accordingly, and in few daies shall send the copyes. As to the bull I hope your Honnour will be pleased to except of.

[PS] I desire to know the price of perpettuanes and sayes, for these people sayeth the price is something abated.

222.   Richard Thelwall   Annamaboe, 16 April 1681

Last night I received yours, and as concerning the charges paid the canoemen the gunners mate that came with them see me pay them, and they say they had but one dayes cankey when they came here. Inclosed is two months accompts more. I desire to know the prices of the red perpettuanoes and sayes. I want also ink and paper.

---

[10] Adangme, east of Accra.

[PS] Please to send by first good conveniance, som[e] broad tapseels.

223.   Richard Thelwall   Annamaboe, 19 April 1681

This comes by one George Taylor, one that served the Company formerly. He came ashore at Aga; he is desirous to serve the Company againe if your honour pleaseth, he is a civill man and not given to drinking. Heere lyeth three interlopers, one Dutch and two English; and George Taylor sayeth that Mr Edlin and Mr Harvey is at Commenda, and one Richard Lumley, hee canne informe better.

[PS] Please to send per first convenience some broad tapseels and 4 or 5 bushells of sea coales for the smith to mend the [h]inges and bolts about the fort, for all is gone.

224.   Richard Thelwall   Annamaboe, 24 April 1681

This morning is come the bad news of the 15 hand canoe being lost off Amessa [at] the oyster shell banke at sea; and I doe not heere of any white men saved, the canoe broken all in peeces and but few blackes saved. I have sent to Amessa and per next shall know further. As to the gitting of anything there is noe hopes, for when our sloope run ashore theire their was moneys spent but the blackes would restore nothing againe. I pray God the white men be alive.

225.   Richard Thelwall   Annamaboe, 12 May 1681

Yesterday wee received yours, and according as in ordered, when the 9 hand canoe appeareth [I] shall put what slaves I have for Wyamba for Captain Bowler.[11] I have received the 20 sayes and 100 blew pottkeys out of Captain Branfill, I supose he may be going from hence the beginning of next weeke.

226.   Richard Thelwall   Annamaboe, 21 May 1681

This serves cheifely for coverte to inclosed Aprill accounts, which hope will find right and make noate accordingly. As concerning Captain Peeters buisness, it see-mes one of the Companyes pawnes that was in the canoe that was going for Wyamba had layen with one of Aquas souldiers wifes; and had I not gone downe to the water side I believe they had pulled the man in peeces; they panyard Captain Peeter and one of the canoemen, and it cost me 12a before I could redeeme Captain Peeter and the man with him, and I was forced for to pass my word for them, but since I have gott the Capposheers, and they have pulled there houses downe to the

[11] Cf. no.589.

ground; Captain Peeter can tell the canoemans name, he must pay the 12a. Inclosed is the ballance of Aprill account being 1o 13a 10ta.

227.   Richard Thelwall   Anamaboe, 12 June 1681

Yesterday I received yours, and as concerning corne for Captain Rickard it is ready when he pleaseth to come for itt. Inclosed also is the May accounts with the ballance being 6oz, which hope will find right and make note accordingly. Indeede I have been troubled with the gripping of the gutts for this four in five dayes, soe hope your honour will excuse my not sending them sooner.

[PS] The weight very bare and the gold bad.

228.   Richard Thelwall   Anamaboe, 22 June 1681

Yesterday I received yours, and as to the corne Captain Rickard received at An-ishan, if it was bad it was his fault, for hee might have had corne at Anamaboe or Agga, but it is not the time for the best corne; and as to Mr Harvey or if any interlopers goe ashore at Agga, Ile assure your Honour I cannot helpe it; but none shall come ashoare att Anamaboe. Last night came into this road an interloper and Captain Rickard supposeth it may be Captain Poorteene; and as in ordred for Captain Rickard 30 chests of corne more [he] shall have.

229.   Richard Thelwall   Anamaboe, 9 July 1681

This serves chiefly for coverte to the inclosed June accompts and the ballance being 4o 10a 1ta, all which hope will find right and make note accordingly; and desire your honour per first good conveyniance for to send some goods: perpetuanoes, sayes, sheets, sletias, broad tapsells and niccanees, or what your honour can spare.

230.   Richard Thelwall   Annamaboe, 15 July 1681

This day I have one of yours of the 12 ditto; and shall give your honour creditt for what goods sent for this place and Agga: vizt 20 sayes, 60 shott, 30 saker and 30 minion[12] for Annamaboe; for Agga: 50 narrow niccanees, 15 allejaars and 59 gal-lons brandy; and if I can gett any wood shall send itt by the 15 hand canoe. I also received 6 spunge staves, and 100 iron barrs by Captain Rickards boate for Agga.

---

[12] saker, minion: types of small cannon.

231. Richard Thelwall   Annamaboe, 12 Aug. 1681

This comes by John Ratliffe as in ordred, and allso July accounts with the ballance being 5o 13a 9ta, which hope will find right and make note accordingly. Evan Price is very sick of a feavour, but hope in God the worst is past.

[PS] Awina Quida the black is gone by land. Pray by the returne of the canoe for to send some coales for the smith which wee want much.

232. Richard Thelwall   Annamaboe, 10 Sept. 1681

Last night I received yours with the citation, which this morning early was nailed on the gate, as inordered. At present I am not well neither have been since left Capo Corsoe Castle, but on Monday at farthest God willing I will come or send Augusts accompts with the ballance. I pray per first good conveniency to send vizt imprimis perpetuanoes blew and greene, sletias fine and course, tapsells broad and narrow, niccanees broad and narrow, sayes, and allejars and powder for they say that the Dankeries[13] and our people and Ahenesa[14] are to fight the Ackims and Anguinas.[15] If soe powder may goe off here.

[PS] George King had 6 weekes pay due, thought will not pay all his debts; but I shall pay as farr as itt will goe. He died the first of this month.

233. Richard Thelwall   Annamaboe, 12 Sept. 1681

This serves chiefly for covert to the inclosed August accompts and the ballance being 4m 1o 9a 6ta, which hope will find right and make note accordingly. I pray send per first good conveyance vizt imprimis perpettuanoes blew and greene, sletias course and fine, niccanees broad and narrow, tapsells broad and narrow, sayes, and allejars, and powder, for if wars be as they say, powder will goe off.

234. Richard Thelwall   Annamaboe, 14 Sept. 1681

Last night by the 15 hand canoe I received 30 pieces narrow niccanees, 30 broad

---

[13] Denkyira, in the hinterland to the north-west. This must be one of the earliest references (if not the earliest) to Denkyira in contemporary sources: Bosman, writing in 1704, said that its name had become known to Europeans only 'in the past 15 or 16 years' (Daaku 1970, 73). It appears (as 'Danckreijs') in the accompanying map, though not in the text, of Barbot's 1688 manuscript, but possibly as a later interpolation: cf. Barbot 1992, 336, n.2.

[14] King of Akwamu, currently in control of Accra (see section VIII).

[15] Akyem, in the hinterland north-west of Akwamu, and Angona, on the coast between Fante and Accra. Cf. later references to a conflict between Akwamu and Akyem (in 1682), though these do not mention any involvement by Denkyira, Anomabu or Angona (nos.423, 425, 439).

niccanees in halves, 20 sayes, 25 pieces perpettuanoes, 20 barrells of powder and 2 chests of sheets.

[PS] I suppose sletias, allejars and coales were forgott, which are much wanted.

235.   Richard Thelwall   Annamaboe, 17 Sept. 1681

Last night by the 15 hand canoe I received 40 sletias whereof 20 are finer then ordinary; and have made noate of the price.

[PS] Pray send some coales by first good conveniencie.

236.   Ralph Hassell   Annamaboe, 22 Sept. 1681

These are to acquaint you that all things, the corne excepted, are removed from Agga though with much difficulty, for there were more than 300 people in armes to stop the goods from being carried away: for they are very loath the factory should be broake up, and Mr Thelwall and myselfe hired souldiers of Annamaboe to bring the goods per force, and gave them an anchor of brandy soe all is here well; and the Agga people desired a white man there, and are very much incenced against mee and say that Mr Thelwall and myselfe have sold the place. I have lost some things belonging to myselfe.

I waite your Honours orders and commands in order to my goeing downe, and alsoe that Captain Rickard may take all my things into his ship with a canoe to bring them ashoare. I will pay halfe hyre and she may bring what is att Accra up that your Honour shall order; Soe desire your honours ample commands.

237.   Ralph Hassell   Annamaboe, 26 Sept. 1681

These are onely to acquaint your honour that since Captain Sheares[16] and the souldiers arrivall here hath not been any pallavora with the blacks, but one Satureday about 4 or 5 hundred people were in armes for most part of the afternoone: they say it was onely to settle a new Mareene. I have had noe more news from the Agga people, they are at present contented that a white man is there and are in expectation of more goods: they have been informed per James [Cunduitt][17] that after some time they shall have another factor and goods, soe are at quiet for the present. All here are in good health.

---

[16] Commanding the *John* (cf. no.238).
[17] RAC factor at Egya: cf. no.383.

238. Richard Thelwall   Annamaboe, 27 Sept. 1681

Last night I received yours; and by the John of Barbados came ashoare a serjant and 5 souldiers. This morning is come into this road Captain Rickard; soe hope shall gett all Mr Hassells things aboard. This day Captain Starland is gone to Anishan to see what Mr Richards and the Curranteer can doe, but I beleeve it is onely an idle pallavora.[18] If I send a white man to Amersa it must be one of those that came from Capo Corsoe last, but shall send a black for to show them the way. When your honour would have the whitemen for Capo Corsoe must send a canoe, but I have but few here if they all goe, for Jeremy Michell is at Agga, George King dead, John Ratlif at Capo Corsoe, and two lame. Mr Hassell this morning went for Capo Corsoe Castle.

239. Richard Thelwall   Annamaboe, 30 Sept. 1681

This day I received two of yours; and as in ordered, by the yaule goes the people writt for, and tomorrow morning early shall write Mr Starland the needfull. I have made note concerning what writt about the canoemen.

240. Richard Thelwall   Annamaboe, 30 Sept. 1681

This morning came the 5 hand canoe from Amersa, they say they will have 1 angle per butt as formerly in Mr Bellwood and Mr Pysings time, and that the Curranteere hath nothing to doe with their shells. Inclosed is Mr Starlands note alsoe.[19] I pray a word what I shall doe; and whether must pay the canoe men their cankey and their turnes goeing off.

241. Richard Thelwall   Anamaboe, 13 Oct. 1681

Last night I received a letter per your order. Indeed I have not been well ever since I was at Cabo Corso. By the bearer Francis Nixson I send September accompts and alsoe the ballance being 4m 4o 12a 7ta, which hope will find right and make note accordingly. There is 2 marks of gold, pure Arcanie gold.[20] Inclosed is a coppye for what slaves and corne Captain Rickard had here. The Arcanies wantes more sheets and of the largest sort of sletias; they will give but 6a for the smallest sorte. If your Honour will send some good sheets, large sletias, green and blew perpettuanes, broad tapseeles, narrow niccanees, or what your Honour will please to spare.

[PS] Two dayes since I received a noate from Captain Starland and he sayeth hopeth

---

[18] Cf. no.501.
[19] = no.502.
[20] Cf. Bosman 1705, 37: 'the best gold is called Acanni sika, or Accani gold'.

to gett all his shells in this weeke, but sayeth that one of the canoemen was run away but he hath gott another there. There is an Arda missing, one Quonnu, the people saye he is at Fetue.

242. Richard Thelwall   Anamaboe, 21 Oct. 1681

Yesterday I received two of yours, and as to the slaves being at Ashams croome[21] I have sent twice, at night and in the day; and if should heare where they were would get them secured, but every one thinks if in any of these parts, they are at Abbra, which entertaines all vaggabones and runnawayes for souldiers.[22] If Mr Richards per thee Curranteer have any interest with them, if in these parts [they] must be theire. As concerning the fort at Anamaboe I beleeve there be 4 peeces of sayes dew, when the other 2 flankers are built, and as yet their is but one built, and that was the reason Agent Bradley put them off; they need not aske for the old Braffoes debts for he owes the Company 16 slaves he gott of Mr Pysing at once beside others things, and there was severall writings drawne in Mr Belwood and Mr Pysings time which come to little effect, and when they gett goods in theire hands I am afraid [they] will play the rogue as all of their collour will doe.

[PS] To morrow God willing I intend to send the Arders by land, for if should send them by sea, they would thinke I send them aboard of ship.

243. Richard Thelwall   Anamaboe, 22 Oct. 1681

This comes by the Arda slaves which came from Capo Corsoe formerly thought [= though] can be very ill spared; but hope your Honour will send John Rattlife and Awinna Quidda per first conveniency, for have here but few hands both of whites and blackes. Inclosed is a noat of what slaves sent now, I have paid them all a monthe's pay because they should leave no debts here. This morning about breake of day was brought heare the two slaves your Honour writt to me of, I have put them in irons; and shall take care of them till further order, they asked me a peece of saye for takeing of them, but I told them I would give them the custome of the country; but they said that was to little, soe I told them I would give them an angle more, that is 9 angles, soe they are gone to consider of it.

[PS] Per the slaves have sent three dozen of henns.

---

[21] Cf. no.158.

[22] Abora, in the north of Fante. Cf. also the later reference to an attack by Abora on Kormantin, in 1682 (nos 287–8). Abora was later the capital of Fante, but is thought not to have attained this status until the 1690s (cf. Kea 1982, 30); note, however, the implication in no.257 below that Abora in some sense exercised authority over Anomabu; and cf. also no.339, where the Anomabu chiefs attend the installation ceremonies of a chief at Abora.

244. Richard Thelwall   Anamaboe, 24 Oct. 1681

This day the Arcanies came and bought 7 barrells of powder, and in the opening of the powder it proves small powder, which they doe not like, they love great cannon powder. They also bought a halfe bendy of iron barrs, but they would have barrs all marked; they say they will be with me to tomorrow or next day, so desire your honour tomorrow to send great powder, iron barrs marked and what goods elce can be sparred.

[PS] I beleeve a warr will come on this country soe powder will not doe amiss here. On Satureday last I sent 12 Arder men and one woman, but as yett doe heare noe word of their arrivall.

245. Richard Thelwall   Anamaboe, 25 Oct. 1681

Yesterday by a boy that came from Mr Nightingale I sent a letter for powder and iron barrs; but it must be great powder and marked iron barrs, which letter I hope came safe to hands, soe that the goods may come in Captain Starland and the canoe that comes with Captain Starland may helpe gett them on shoare, and what goods elce your Honour can spare. If ship should goe without must gett your Honour for to send some this day per canoe or tomorrow morning at farthest, for the Arcanies some of them haveing promised for to be with me this day and some tomorrow, and I think its better I should take their good money then lett the Dutch have it, soe must desire your Honours excuse for not comeing to Cabo Corsoe.

Inclosed is a noate of what I paid for the oyster shells and the canoemen. I understand the slaves were all arrived but one I suppose he was lame.

[PS] I sent a coppy of all the receipts Captain Rickards gave me but I and Francis Nixson can take our othes the two boxes of letters went of with Captain Rickards.

246. Richard Thelwall   Anamaboe, 27 Oct. 1681

Yesterday morning per Captain Lawrances boate I received 20 barrells of powder, but I opened some and found 3 fine powder. I also per the 15 hand canoe received 200 iron barrs. Captain Coffe and wee had a palavera about the woman but Asham is at Fanteen, soe must stay till his returne home. There was 4 sletias and a little hogg paid on the womens freedome, but them men in irons paid but 2 sletias; and his owne sonn which went from hence in Captain Seaman paid the 2 sletias and the little hogg. Captain Coffe hear'd all.

247. Richard Thelwall   Anamaboe, 29 Oct. 1681

Yesterday by Dominee of Agga I received yours, and as to dashies given att Cristmas etc. I suppose Mr Carter gave as much as was given att Anamaboe, though indeed there is not a quarter of the Cabbisheers, soe must gett them for to take the less: imprimis to the Quantrees and Braffo 1 saye and 2 perpettuanes and 2 anchors brandy; to the Cabbisheers of Anamaboe 1 saye, 2 perpettuanes and 1 anchor of brandy; to the people for openinge the way 1 broad niccanee and 1 bottle of brandy; for the people when they put the small corne in the ground 1 case of spiritts; and to the dancing people sometimes 1 case of spiritts, 1 dozen of knives and some one [sic] paper brawle and 2 sheets, they come 4 or 5 times in a yeare. This comes by James Cunditt, who can informe your Honour how things went att Agga formerly.[23]

248.   Richard Thelwall   Anamaboe, 11 Nov. 1681

This day I received yours and God willing on Munday shall waite on your Honour; and what John Rattlife hath had shall repay Mr Lewin for he had order to lett him have what he wanted as far as his pay went; I have put [this] in the month's accounts but Awinna Quidda I have not put downe, this month will be 4 months this day he came from Anishan verry ill. Just now Griffen is come from Fanteen, and the Quarranteeres and Braffo; and they would have custome for every ship that comes here. They demand 1 say and 1 anchor of brandy and say the Dutch at Cormanteen pay soe for every ship that comes to the Mina, and Griffen told them if they had not sold Cormanteen to the Dutch they might had had theire customes still; but as far as the 2 iron barrs and 2 dozen of knives itt used to be paid formerly. Doctor Griffen frowes your Honour acckie, and desires an answer tomorrow morning by his boy, which goes with the boye that brought the letter heither

[PS] James Cunditte sayeth he write to Mr Swindall. All the great powder is gone, soe if please to send some tomorrow and sayes or allejarrs, and narrow niccanees or what your honour can spaire.

249.   Richard Thelwall   Anamaboe, 21 Nov. 1681

Last night I received yours, and as to Captain Hows being at Amersa as yett [there are] noe shipps theire, but the blacks sayeth there is two shipps at Lague and Crowces;[24] one of them supposed to be Mr Shears. If How cometh, shall use my utmost endeavour to paniare men or boates.[25]

[PS] I pray send the canoe as soone as possible, here is some Arcanies newly come with good gold.

---

[23] Cunduitt had been briefly agent at Egya: cf. no.383.

[24] Not identified.

[25] How had panyarred three chiefs at Alampo, and the RAC had been requested to assist in securing redress: cf. no.420.

250. Richard Thelwall   Anamaboe, 23 Nov. 1681

Yesterday by the 15 hand canoe I received yours with the goods vizt: 20 sayes, 20 chercolees, 20 herba longees, 20 silke longees, 40 broad blew baftas, 10 striped silks, 20 peeces blew long cloathes in halves, 20 barrells powder, and 20 printed perpettuanes.

[PS] The canoe goes to Anishan this evening for wood.

251. Richard Thelwall   Annamaboe, 10 Dec. 1681

Just now I have received yours and have made note of whatt writt concerning Moree people. On Sunday last the Anguinas and supposed Cabesa Tera[26] people fell on the Accrongs; these people say the Accrongs have gott the best, but as yett not knowne because the Accrongs and these [Annamaboe] people are all one country people,[27] though severall heads doe appeare, and some slaves. Captain Woodfine presents his service to your honour and intends for Capo Corsoe in 2 or 3 dayes; but will see whether slaves will present or noe; in few dayes God willing shall send November accounts and the ballance.

252. Richard Thelwall   Annamaboe, 15 Dec. 1681

This serves chiefely for a covert to the inclosed November accompt with the ballance being 8m 13a 8ta, which with the 3m 1o 8a I paid Mr Henry Spurvay on the 15 ditto as per accompt, all which hope will find right and make noate accordingly; itt goes by Francis Nixon.

As to Agga factory itt must all be pulled downe, and new built or elce it will fall the next raines, thought [= though] the windows and doors and some of the thatch may serve againe. I beleive itt may cost 3 or 4 ounces. I gave James Cunduitt a forme how Wyamba house was built, which is in a better forme than ever Agga was built; and itt will be all one charge.

[PS] There is 7 marks of very good Arcanie gold.

253. Richard Thelwall   Annamaboe, 28 Dec. 1681

Last night I received yours, and have made noat of whatt writt about corne, which shall be effected as soon as possible. I shall want about 30 or 40 deale boards, for

---

[26] Kabestera, inland from Fante.

[27] Presumably the implication is that the Anomabu people were therefore unreliable witnesses. This seems to suggest that Akron, to the east, was already in some sense confederated with Fante; in the 1690s it was described as 'protected' by Fante (Bosman 1705, 61).

to keepe the corne dry att the bottom. The chercolees [I] shall deliver to Captain Thomas Woodfine as inordered.

254. Richard Thelwall   Annamaboe, 4 Jan. 1681/2

Yesterday I received yours, and as to the unkind usage to Mr Shears, they took him for to be Mr Starland, hee fireing att the canoes had like for to doe these people some harm, soe they sweare if could gett him or his people would beate them soundly; I told them that the Braffo and Quantrees [var. Quarranteers] if they did soe would forfeit 400 bendies; but they say they must gett cracras to buy their wives cloaths and to eate. Indeed I told them they were all Braffoes;[28] they are the worst rogues on all the coast of Guynie, and I must have patience, perforce. As to getting of corne they wont take under 1 angle and half for they say the interlopers give soe. Captain Thomas Woodfine had the 10 chercolees and 50 chests of corne as in ordered him; hee sett saile from hence on Sunday noone last past.

[PS] I shall see and gett some good fowls and send per first oppertunity.

255. Richard Thelwall   Annamaboe, 12 Jan. 1681/2

Last night I received yours; and as to corne these people will not sell any under 1 angle and 6 taccoes; Docter Griffin can informe your honour. Indeed I am afraid itt will be very deare, they say itt is 6 angles a chest at Axim; and if ships come itt will raise the price here, soe cannot gett any att the prices mentioned. May please to send per first good conveyance, tapsells, sheets, perpettuanoes blew and green, narrow niccanees, sayes, sletias, and what elce your honour can spare. I have sent for Yabboyes about the canoe, so if comes before sealing shall write what he saith.

[PS] Per the canoe have sent 2 dozen of hens, all could gett att present.

256. Richard Thelwall   Anamaboe, 13 Jan. 1681/2

Last night I spoke with Yabboys about the canoe, and hee saith there is 11 hand canoe att Laggue and they will have for it, 6 sayes; soe if Captain Woodfine likes the canoe and the price [he] may have itt. As concerning the corne they will not lett itt goe under 1 angle and halfe. When Captain Hill was here last I paid 3 angles a chest, and buy itt by the taccoe callibash. I am promised by some of the Cabisheers about a 100 chests tomorrow, soe doe not doubt but in few dayes to gett what your honour hath orderd mee. Docter Griffin is att Fanteen; when he returneth shall send Decembers accompt and the ballance. I hope your honour will not altogether forgett

---

[28] sic: meaning unclear.

Anamaboe but lett mee have a few goods as tapsells, sheets, blew and greene perpettuanoes, sletias, paper brawles, sayes and what other goods can spare.

257. Richard Thelwall   Annamaboe, 16 Jan. 1681/2

Last night Docter Griffin came from Fanteen. The reason of his long stay there was because these Capusheers not goeing to Fanteen, soe if they doe not goe before this and Wensday, all the Quantrees and Abbraers will be on these people for their abuses to the English and their tradeing with interlopers.[29] Docter Griffin desires an answer by this canoe this night.

[PS] Docter Griffin intends to stay here till Wensday till all the pallavora is over unless your honour sends for him before.

258. Richard Thelwall   Annamaboe, 20 Jan. 1681/2

Last night by the 15 hand canoe I received 30 broad tapsells, 25 perpettuanoes, 20 sayes, 20 course sletias, 4 chests of sheets, 50 paper brawles, and 50 Guinie stuffs, for which have given creditt. By Docter Griffin I send December accompts and the ballance being 8 ounces of good Arcanie gold, all which hope will find right and make noate accordingly. Yesterday the Quantres and Docter Griffin made an end of the pallavora and they have prendeed these people, and promised that noe such thing shall be done any more; they have put Captain Quashee with Captain Dick to looke after the white men here, soe desire your honour will be pleased to adde something more to their months sallary. Docter Griffin will acquaint your honour of all. Indeed hee hath been att a great deale of trouble and charge to doe what hath been done.

PS. Per the returne of the canoe may please to send some coales.

259. Richard Thelwall   Anamaboe, 1 Feb. 1681/2

Last night I received yours, and as to corne Captain Hill hath aboard 270 chests, he wantes but 2 boates loads.[30] As for slaves your Honour knows they sell goods cheaper and give more for slaves then the Company price is, soe cannot buy any if any ships here. Last night came into Anishan roade 2 French ships[31] for corne, so am afraid will raise the price of corne, being very scarce. I must begg your Honours

---

[29] The wording seems to imply that Abora, in the interior, exercised authority over Anomabu: cf. n.22 above.

[30] Cf. no.605.

[31] This is again Barbot's squadron; although Barbot does not explicitly refer to calling at Anashan in 1682, he does provide some original information on it (1992, ii, 416, 419).

pardon for not inlarging at present, being very lame, having three wormes in one legg, being in a great paine, soe that am hardly able to write.

260.   Richard Thelwall   Anamaboe, 16 Feb. 1681/2

Last night by the 15 hand canoe I received 150 iron barrs, 200 blew long cloathes in halves, and 50 Guinea stuffs, for which I shall give creditt. The 100 broad blew baftas went to Anishan by James Cunduitt. I now send Januaryes account with balance being 3m 1o 8a, which hope will find right and make noat accordingly. The gold is good Arcanie gold. I hope your Honour will spare me some blew and green perpettuanoes, sheets, course sletias, tapseels, niccanees broad and narrow, allejars, paper brawles.

261.   Richard Thelwall   Anamaboe, 2 March 1681/2

Last night I received yours with an order for 30 or 40 chests of corne. Indeed I have not halfe so much, nor none can gett, for the interlopers lye in Agga and Corman-teen road and buy up all the corne, nay they give 2 angles and 2 angles 6 taccoes a chest in good gold; soe that I cannot gett any without a larger price. I think Captain Starland must pick out some of the best of the corne at Agga factory.

   The Arcanies come to mee every day and say if your honour will not send mee some blew and green perpetuanos, sheets, course sletias, tapsells, niccannees etc. that they will goe aboard the interlopers, and buy goods there.

262.   Richard Thelwall   Anamaboe, 10 March 1681/2

Last night I received yours with a mould for to cutt some timber, but doe not mention how many peeces. Itt will bee difficult to gett, and if should find any if itt be their fetish trees they will not suffer any body to cutt them. John Rattlife shall see if any possible to be gott. As to slaves it is impossible I should gett any as long as any ships in these parts; for they give more than I can and sell goods for less then I can; neither have I the goods they would have. Per Captain Hill God willing I intend to send my February accompts. Yesterday Captain Hill's boate was going for water to Cabo Corsoe and the Morea people hath most barbarously abused them, foure very bad and they think will dye; they tooke away their maine saile, 1 blunderbuss, 2 cuttlaces, and 2 musketts.[32] Captain Hill will be at Cabo Corsoe in 2 or 3 dayes.

---

[32] No explanation is offered of this attack, but it may have been in retaliation against the panyarring of Mouri people by Arthur Richards, the RAC factor at Anashan, a few days earlier (cf. no.177).

263.   Richard Thelwall   Anamaboe, 13 March 1681/2

This serves cheifly for covert to the inclosed February months accompts, which goes with Captain Hill, and alsoe the ballance being 1 ounce 3 angles, all which hope will find right and make note accordingly. As to the timber according to the mould, I have sent John Ratttlife and one white man more and two Blacks, they have been 2 dayes out and could find but one, and that the Blacks would not lett them cutt, for they say it is their fetish; if any of that sort be gott it must be where few or none inhabbitts, or by the rivers or brooks. I suppose if to be gott any where on this coast, is att Wyamba.

264.   Richard Thelwall   Anamaboe, 14 March 1681/2

Just now I received yours with an order to panyar all Dutch canoes etc.[33] This morning Captain Hill sett saile for Cabo Corsoe, hee panyard a Mine canoe one Udrae, bound for Allampo, hee has 13 men and 1 women and some goods, but panyard them on the Morea mens heads for the abuse done to his men.[34] I desire may heare from your honour as soon as possible, for Captain Hill said when he was here, that hee would not medle with any white men but blacks; soe desire to know whether should panyar white men or noe. May please to send mee some iron barrs and blew and greene perpettuanoes, when Captain Hill comes for Annamaboe.

[PS] May please to send a good quantity of iron barrs, but they must be all marked, otherwise they will not take them if they be never soe bigg.

265.   Richard Thelwall   Anamaboe, 18 March 1681/2

Yours I have received dated the 15th instant and have made noate accordingly to take Dutchmen and blacks that belong to them, and to use them more civilly then Captain Hills men were. As to the timber to be gott here, I feare it is impossible, it grows by the rivers and brookes, and must be gott where few or non inhabbitters are, for tis their fetish; and [they] will not lett any one cut them; if to be gott any where on this coast I suppose att Wyamba. May please if not sent already [send] a good quantity of iron barrs, and some blew and green perpettuanoes, the barrs must be marked.

266.   Richard Thelwall   Annamaboe, 30 March 1682

Last night I received yours, and have made noate to seize both Whites and Blacks

---

[33] Probably in retaliation for the attack on Captain Hill's crew by the Mouri people (no.262); the RAC presumably held the Dutch, who had a fort at Mouri, responsible for the latter's actions.
[34] The Mina people were closely allied to the Dutch, who had their headquarters in their territory.

all possible I can. I received of Mr Shears 600 iron barrs, 20 red and 20 blew and green perpettuanoes, and have given creditt for them.

267. Richard Thelwall   Anamaboe, 7 Apr. 1682

Yesterday I received yours with an order for to purchase 30 or 40 good slaves with the goods I have in the factory, but doe not mention the prices, the men here are 7 pezos 2 angles and the women 6 pezos 2 angles in good gold, Captain Hill can informe your honour, and they will not give but 9 or 10 angles att the most for red perpettuanos, soe if your honour will order mee for to give money or goods as others give, it is probable I may gett some, otherwise they carry their slaves aboard ships. I have made noate to purchase 5 or 600 chests of corne, and shall gett it as cheap as possible I can, but not to exceed 2 angles per chest, but fear itt will be very difficult to gett soe much, itt being very scarce att present.

268. Richard Thelwall   Anamaboe, 8 Apr. 1682

Last night I received yours and have made noate of what writt about purchaseing slaves and getting corne, I shall gett as cheape as is[?] possible. The Cabessa Terra people last weeke, would not lett the Arcanies come downe,[35] but on Monday God willing, if any slaves come, shall gett them as cheape as any one, they want tapsells and sheets, but tapsells most.

[PS] May please to send mee some paper and inke, per first oppertunity, which I much want.

269. Richard Thelwall   Anamaboe, 13 Apr. 1682

Yesterday I received yours by the 15 hand canoe with 3 chests of sheetes, 50 broad tapsells, 14 fine sletias and 30 course sletias, for which have given creditt for the same, and have made noate that they are for the purchasing of slaves for Captain Hills quick dispatch. I assure your honour I shall use my utmost endeavour to gett what slaves possible I can. Inclosed I send Marchs monthly account by James Cunduitt with the ballance being 3 ounces, 1 angle, which hope will find right and make noate accordingly. As I wrote in my former the Cabessa Terra, Quomong,[36] Angan[37] and these people have stoped the way, soe that noe slaves nor any trade att present.

---

[35] Cf. nos 325, 358, for subsequent references to disputes with Kabestera.

[36] Cf. also no.287, where the 'Quomongs' join Abora in a raid on Kormantin. The allusion is evidently to Kwaman, north of Kormantin. This is to be distinguished from another Kwaman mentioned elsewhere in the RAC correspondence (nos 431, 435, 'Coma', 'Commongs'), which was in the area of later Asante.

[37] Not identified (but cf. 'Annian' in no.281).

270.   Richard Thelwall   Anamaboe, 20 Apr. 1682

Just now I received yours whereby I understand [you] admire [you] have not heard from mee. In my two former I advised your honour the ways are stopped soe that there are few slaves and little trade. I have in irons but 6 men slaves and I beleeve shall gett but 5 of them, but I am promised if any slaves come I shall have them. As to corne it is very scarce, I have but 26 in 28 chests. I will assure your honour I will doe what possible I can for to gett slaves and corne, being boathe scarce att present.

271.   Richard Thelwall   Anamaboe, 4 May 1682

Last night I received yours whereby [you] doe wonder have not heard from mee. Indeede I have not had an oppertunity till now, only by Mr Pley whoe departed the same night Captain Hill sett saile; and I desired him to informe your honour what was past, soe hope will please to pardon my neglect in not writting. I put aboard Captain Hill 16 slaves, 8 men and 8 woemen, and 44 chests of corne, all I could gett. And since I cannot hardly gett corne to eate, these people as yett have not done sowing their small corne, soe that att present I cannot gett any great corne,[38] and now they aske more for their corne, Captain Attwell can informe your honour.[39] As to the Company's concerns att Anamaboe I thank God all is very well and God willing I doe not doubt but for to give a good accompt thereof. As concerning the Arcanies tradeing with interlopers, att this place they doe not, but what they doe att other places I cannot tell, yett they carry slaves aboard the Company ships and they sell them goods as cheape as any interloper, indeed I think they [i.e. Company ships] are the greatest, and spoyle the factory's. I have made inquiry after Aboun-shee, hee liveth att Anishan but if I can get him here I shall secure him till further order.

272.   Richard Thelwall   Annamaboe, 23 May 1682

Yours of the 20th instant I have received, and had sent James Cunduitt up sooner, but the weather was very bad, and now hee goes in Captain Shepheards boate with him; and have sent John Rattliffe for to looke after Agga factory. Per James Cunduitt I alsoe sent Aprills months accompt with the ballance, being 2 marks, 1 ounce and 10 tacco's, which hope will find right and make noate accordingly; I had sent them sooner but could not gett any safe Conveyance before now. As concerning corne, this day I putt aboard Captain Shepheard 50 chests of corne, att 2 angles per chest, and since his ship is come hither it is risen to 2 angles and 6 tacco's per chest. Indeed corne is very scarce att present and if any more ships come hither I am afraid

---

[38] i.e. millet and maize, respectively.
[39] Cf. no.617.

itt will raise corne to 3a or 4a per chest. Captain Shepheard God willing this evening intends for Cabo Corsoe, I suppose hee may have gott of the Blacks 15 in 20 chests of corne. I am promised some more corne. I assure your honour I doe what lieth in my power, and would send oftener but am loath to put the Company to 2 angles charge for every letter.

[PS] May please to send per first good conveyance some broad tapsells, lead barrs, sheets, Guyney clouts, large sletias and blew and green perpetuano's. I alsoe want some match, carteridge paper and minion shott.

273.   Richard Thelwall   Anamaboe, 27 May 1682

Last night I received yours whereby [you] desire to know how Captain Shepheard proceeds in getting of corne, I suppose hee may have about 100 chests aboard. Yesterday writt your honour by James Cunduitt, which hope is arrived safe. I have large promises of corne, though little performance, itt being very scarce.

[PS] Just now I received 30 minion shott, one quire of carteridge paper and one scane of match. Indeed if the ships had stayed att Capo Corsoe I belieeve that corne might have been att a cheaper rate then it is now.

274.   [receipts]

Richard Shepheard   Anamaboe, 28 May 1682

I doe acknowledge to have received from Mr Thelwall one 11 hand canoe, for which he paid 1 mark and 4 ounces of gold, itt being on account of the Royall Affrican Company at Arda.[40]

Richard Shepheard   Anamaboe, 29 May 1682

I doe acknowledge to have received 100 chests of corne from Mr Richard Thelwall on accompt of the Royall Affrican Company of England for the use of their slaves on board the St George.

275.   Richard Thelwall   Anamaboe, 3 June 1682

I have received two of yours, one by Mr Shears and one by Captain Shepheard, and hee hath seen thee corne att Agga but doth not like itt, and [I] have alsoe bought a 11 hand canoe, a verry good strong canoe, but must give 6 bendy's. I hope in a few dayes to gett the 10 slaves for Mr Shears, but cannot gett them under 7 peze 2 angles and 6 peze 2 angles. May please to send per Mr Shears or per first conveyniency

---

[40] i.e. intended for use in the RAC factory there, which had earlier requested the sending of a canoe (nos 477–9).

some blew and green perpetuanoes, broad tapsells, lead barrs, sheets, Guyney clouts, large sletias.

276.   Richard Thelwall   Annamaboe, 20 June 1682

This morning came one of the Quantrees from Cabo Corsoe but never a letter, and they want something towards their danceing which begins to morrow or next day, and they wont lett mee alone till had writt your honour about itt. Indeed I want a copie of the agreement, or else a line or two what I must give them, they send a man on purpose.

277.   Richard Thelwall   Annamaboe, 23 June 1682

Last night I received yours whereby would know how corne sells here. Itt is att 2 angles 6 tacco's per chest in good gold, besides what dashey's in brandy and cloaths. Last night most of the Cabisheers went for Fanteen, this day being their Christmas day, as they call it, soe till they returne will be little corne gott, and will stay there 9 in 10 dayes, and new corne will not be good here this 6 weeks; the corne att Cabo Corsoe will be ripe a month or three weekes before this; but if your honour will order mee to buy old corne and give gold and dashies, as others did and doe, I suppose may gett some as well as others, but what quantity I cannot tell, till our people returne. Inclosed is the two May accompts.

278.   Richard Thelwall   Annamaboe, 24 June 1682

Yesterday I received yours, with an order for the bricklayer to be sent on board Mr Shears for Accra, which shall be effected and in the evening Mr Shears will sett saile, and with this letter goes Huckamee one of the brickmakers, the other I sent yesterday to Cabo Corsoe, with May accompts. When [he] returnes shall be sent also.

279.   Richard Thelwall   Anamaboe, 27 June 1682

This comes by Francis Nixon by whome I have sent 6 marks of good Arcanie gold on acccompt of June monthly accompt, and desire your honour will be pleased for to send mee some more iron barrs; but they must be all marked, for indeed I have a great many barrs here, but they are very small and most of them not marked; and [send] some perpettuano's, for I have 12 perpetuanoes that came downe last, a little broken, and they wont take them without some abatements. I want some powder but itt must be all greate else they wont buy itt, all the powder I have is small and they wont buy itt. May please to send me some brandy, for itt draws neare the bottom, and some paper for itt almost gon.

[PS] I have bought Captain Starlands canoe man as in ordered but could not gett him under a bendy,[41] soe when your honour pleases to order mee I shall send him for Cabo Corsoe Castle.

280.   Richard Thelwall   Anamaboe, 29 June 1682

Yesterday by the 15 hand canoe I received 150 iron barrs, 2 bailes of perpetuano's, and 20 barrells of powder, and very speedily would send one hogshead of brandy. I have per Captain Peeter sent the canoeman that was panyard att Wyamba but was forced to give a bendy and much adoe to gett him.

281.   Richard Thelwall   Anamaboe, 4 July 1682

Last night I received yours, whereby [you] desire for to gett 450 or 500 chests of corne for Captain North. This morning I spake with our Cabisheers, and hee that hath most hath but 5 chests; but they say if I would give as others did, they would send to Annian[42] and gett some; I told them all the ships were gon, and the other ships would take new corne, but att last when they went away, they said if your honour will give 2 angles they will send up into the country for to gett some, soe if please to send present advice, what [you] will give, I shall use my utmost endeavour, but [you] must send word before the ship comes downe, otherwise they will raise the price. Yesterday and this day I sold 43 perpetuano's and most of the iron that came downe in the canoes, I have 6 in 7 marks of good gold which shall send per first good oppertunity. May please to send some more perpetuano's per first good oppertunity, for great many of these are broken and wormeaten. The Arcanies like these last iron barrs, and would have mee write for some more of the same, and some good perpetuano's.

283.   Richard Thelwall   Annamaboe, 6 July 1682

Yesterday I received yours, and as in ordered have made bargaine with the Cabisheers for 500 chests of corne att 2 angles per chest, and their canoes to carry itt aboard, but itt is their custome they will have something, they will not make a dry bargaine; they tell me I shall have itt all in a few dayes. This morning they have brought in 20 in 30 chests, and have sent their people into the country for to gett the rest. I have made noate of the brandy, iron and perpetuanoes that comes by Captain North, for which I returne your honour many thanks. In 2 or 3 dayes shall send June account with the ballance.

---

[41] Starland's canoeman had been captured in an attack on Winneba by the Akrons in March 1682 (no.506); 'bought' here clearly means 'redeemed'.
[42] Cf. 'Angan' in no.269.

283. Richard Thelwall   Annamaboe, 7 July 1682

This serves cheifly for covert to the inclosed June accompt which goes with Francis Nixon, and the ballance being 7 marks, 4 ounces, 3 angles, and 6 tacco's, which with the 6 marks formerly sent, makes the full ballance in all 13 marks, 4 ounces, 3 angles, and 6 taccoes, which hope will find right and make noate accordingly.

284. Richard Thelwall   Annamaboe, 16 July 1682

Yesterday I received yours. And as to the corne I shall putt aboard 76 chests of old corne, all that I have att present, though they promise every day more, butt itt comes but slowly; and new corne they will have 1 angle and 6 taccoes per chest, and I am afraid that there is not old corne enough in the country for this ship. Captain North is very weake.[43]

[PS] I spake to Yaboyes about the cow and hee wont take under a bendy and 12 angles, which I think is very deare.

285. Richard Thelwall   Annamaboe, 19 July 1682

Yesterday I received yours, and as to old corne, as I wrote in my former it comes in but slowly, I have but 15 chests, since the other putt aboard, I have spoke to the Cabisheers and this day suppose may have about 100 chests of new corne, but they wont take under 1 angle 6 taccoes per chest and itt will be 6 in 7 dayes adrying before itt will be fitting to put aboard ship, I put itt on the top of the house and on the flankers adrying every day. I assure your honour I doe what possible I can for Captain Norths speedie dispatch, hee is very weake but the Docter saith hee is on the mending hand.

286. Richard Thelwall   no date [July 1682]

This serves chiefely for covert to the inclosed accompt with the ballance being 2 markes, 3 ounces, 3 angles and 4 tacco's, which goes by Mr John Smith, which hope will find right and make noate accordingly. I received of Captain Sheppard 8 sayes whereof 3 broken, 5 perpetuano's and 3 broken and 2 of them redds, 9 fine sletias and 30 Guyney clouts, for which shall give creditt for in June account with the other goods received from Cabo Corsoe Castle.

287. Richard Thelwall   Anamaboe, 6 Aug. 1682

Yesterday I received yours whereby understand on Monday the 15 hand canoe will

---

[43] Cf. no.621.

come hither with goods, for which I give your honour many thanks. As concerning buying 1,000 chests of corne, itt may be gott in a shorte time, but the people here wont take under 1 angle and a halfe. I told them your honour paid but 1 angle, but they told mee that all Fetue had not corne enough for 2 shipps and then must be forced for to give a larger price, these people are cunning rogues; soe if please to in order to gett itt at 1 angle and halfe itt may be done.

[PS] Yesterday the Abbraers and Quomong people fell on Cormanteen people and killed 6, and panyard 33, burnt halfe the great towne, some came hither but they are all run away.

288.   Richard Thelwall   Annamaboe, 9 Aug. 1682

Yesterday I received yours by the 15 hand canoe, as alsoe 2 bailes of sayes, 10 piecess white longcloath and 99 pieces of blew longcloaths, there wanting 2 halfe pieces, they were told 3 times. And haveing this good oppertunity of the 15 hand canoe I have by Benjamin Cantrill sent 4 marks of good Arcanie gold on July months accompt, and as to the corne shall gett as soone as possible; as concerning slaves, though the Abbraers panyard the Cormanteen people, yett they dare not sell them for they are all of one country,[44] and itt is thought that that man [who] was the occasion of Cormanteen being burnt, will be ruined and all his generation. Indeed I beleeve slaves will be very deare, and these people will not sell now under 7 pease 2 angles for a man and 6 pease 2 angles for a woeman; and if please to in order to give as others give I may gett some.

[PS] John Wise desires that Tom True may come downe to him, Awina Quidda being lame and ill.

289.   Richard Wallis   Annamaboe, 19 Aug. 1682

This goes by the canoe that brought mee hither and serves chiefely to give your honour advice that I haveing made an end Thirsday night in Mr Thelwalls business my stay hath been here ever since for Mr Richards, whoe the same day I came hither [I] heard was abroad, soe immediatly wrote William Beard to dispatch some one to him for his quick returne, he wrote mee back hee had done itt and that in all probabillity hee might be att home on Fryday. This morning a small noate came to Mr Thelwall from Mr Richards that hee was getting of canoes and should not be att home in 3 dayes time, I shall waite for his comeing if your honour order mee not to the contrary, and intend back in a hammack, for yesterday morning I was voiolently attacqu'd with an ague and feavour and vomitting, which I judge pro-

---

[44] Abora and Kormantin both belonged to the Fante confederacy. According to normal conventions, only foreigners could be sold into overseas slavery.

ceeded from cold that I had taken in the canoe. Captain Ware is come ashoare but brings noe order what quantity of corne hee is to take in, which Mr Thelwall desires your honour would be pleased to send. Hee hath 700 chests or thereabouts and more dayly is brought in.[45]

290.   Richard Thelwall   Anamaboe, 23 Aug. 1682

Yesterday Captain Ware had aboard ship 310 chests and this day hope will gett most of his corne. I have made noate for the 50 chests as inordered. Captain Ware God willing on Fryday intends for Capo Corsoe. Mr Wallis is very ill and the Docter saith past all recovery, hee had an ague and a feavour the first day hee came ashoare here, hee saith hee gott cold in the canoe.

291.   Richard Thelwall   Anamaboe, 23 Aug. 1682

This morning I wrote your honour that Mr Wallis was very ill, in 3 or 4 hours after hee departed this life and desired mee to send his body to Cabo Corsoe for to be buryed, soe for to fulfill the desire of the dead I have sent itt, hee desireth that Mr Stapleton should looke after his concerns as by the papers in his small trunk which comes by his boy, as alsoe desires Mr Stapleton for to see him decently buryed.

292.   Richard Thelwall   Anamaboe, 30 Aug. 1682

Yours of the 28th ditto I received and immediatly as inordered sent the inclosed to Mr Richards but hee would not write, saying to the man that hee had neither pen, inke nor paper, itt was all att Anishan; and as to gett the goods I beleeve itt is the best way for to lett them alone a little while till the Curranteer comes, for his son Quacoone told mee nothing should be medled withall, and Benjamin Cantrill hath the keys. Yesterday Captain Nurse sett saile, I put aboard him 200 chests of corne and hee saith must have more. This day Captain Ware will saile, hee hath gott a canoe. Captain Nurse his letter arrived him att Lague, hee presents his service to your honour. Inclosed is July accompt, which hope will find right and make noate accordingly. May please to send per first good oppertunity some Guyney clouts and some paper bralls.

293.   Richard Thelwall   Annamaboe, 13 Sept. 1682

This day I received the goods put aboard Captain Starland vizt 6 boysado's, 30 peeces of blew longcloaths in halves, 100 Guyney clouts, 100 paper brawls and 50 narrow niccanees, and for what wood and corne Captain Starland shall want I shall

[45] Cf. no.625.

furnish him with. Captain Ambrose tomorrow about noone I suppose will have all his corne aboard.[46] I shall take care for to send a white man to Amersa about the oystershells but am afraid there will not be anything abated. As soone as these ships are gon I shall gett the timber downe to the waterside, and shall send the slave per first oppertunity. The other slave that Bonishee hath, hee saith hee paid a bendy; but as I understand him, is desirous for to change for a slave Mr Shears hath. I shall make further enquiry after and shall acquaint your honour.

294.   Richard Thelwall   Annamaboe, 14 Sept. 1682

Just now I received yours and if your honour think fitting I beleeve itt would be better taken that William Pley and William Beard goe by your order, but if any thing that they should want any of my assistance, I can be there in one houre; besides these people are great rogues and will say that I am the occasion of that factory's being remov'd, and may breed a differance between these people and mee, soe if possible I desire your honour I may be excused; else these people will lay all the fault on mee and I shall never live in quiett.

295.   [receipt]   Annamaboe, 16 Sept. 1682

Then received from Mr Richard Thelwall 316 chests of corne whereof 6 was lost in the sea comeing off, for use of the Royall Affrican Company of England on board the Goulden Fortune, I say received perLott Ambrose

296.   Richard Thelwall   Annamaboe, 18 Sept. 1682

Just now I received yours as Captain Ambrose was goeing off, and I tould him what your honour wrote; and hee protesteth that hee desired Mr Richards for to come into the fort and resigne up himselfe unto mee,[47] but Mr Richards answered what, will you betray mee, that was all hee said, in the time they were discourseing I went and gave our people powder and bulletts for feare of any trouble, soe Mr Richards went to one of our Cabosheers houses in towne, but I tould him they must not protect him, soe I beleeve his boyes telling him hee thought for to make an escape and run away, soe our Bendyfoo's[48] quickly fought him back againe, they say hee fired att them 6 times, that was the reason they tooke away all his cloaths, but his gun would not goe off. They will have 8 gallons of brandy and some powder for takeing of him. I think your honour would doe well for to send Docter Meade

[46] Cf. no.626.

[47] Arthur Richards, lately displaced as RAC factor at Anashan, had been ordered to go to Cape Coast Castle (cf. nos 194–5); presumably, he was travelling in Ambrose's ship.

[48] Cf. Kea 1982, 136–7, for discussion of this and other references to 'bendyfoos', concluding that they were a form of urban militia.

downe this night, itt being his sick night,[49] and the other Docter is gon and hee being verry weake, soe for feare of a relapse and noe body for to helpe him itt is better that hee comes as soon as possible.

297.   Ambrose Meade   [Annamaboe], 18 Sept. 1682

Yesterday a little after sunsett I arrived at Anamaboe where I found Mr Starland in his paroxisme and very delireous, whereupon I immediatly cupped him and tooke a considerable quantity of blood from his temples, whereupon hee quickly fell asleep and rested all the whole night, this is the third fitt which hee hath had. This morning have given him a doce of physick because hee hath not been purged since hee hath been taken ill, for the chirurgeon of Captain Ambrose only lett him blood and gave him one or two glysters His fitt comes every other day towards evening. I doe intend to draw blisters but if I can possibly be spared from Cabo Corsoe itt will be more proper to apply one 8 or 10 hours before his fitt comes, which I hope in god may prevent itt. If your worship cannot spare mee soe long I will apply them this night and come up according to your first order, although they will not be soe proper.

298.   Richard Thelwall   Annamaboe, 22 Sept. 1682

This comes with the corpes of Mr Starland, whoe departed this life, this day a quarter of an houre past 11; hee had in gold about him 1 ounce, 3 angles, three gold rings, three silver buttons for his shirt, one gowne and one coate, which God willing shall send tomorrow by John, Docter Meads mate, whoe can informe your honour how hee was after Docter Mead left him.

[PS] Here is a pockett book which shall goe by John, but his key's and everything are left with his mate aboard ship, as the Docters mate can informe your Honour.

299.   Richard Thelwall   Annamaboe, 28 Sept. 1682

This serves cheifly for covert to the inclosed August accompt with the ballance being 2 ounces, 10 angles, and 8 taccoes, which with the 2 markes of gold I gave Mr Spurvay when I was last att Cabo Corsoe Castle makes even that accompt, which hope will find right and make noate accordingly. This comes by Francis Nixon, by whome I have sent 10 markes of good Arcanie gold on September months accompt, soe there is in all 10 markes, 2 ounces, 10 angles and 8 taccoes. May please to send per first good oppertunity some good perpettuano's, white long cloaths, sayes, pewter basons great and small, Guyney clouts and some great pow-

---

[49] From the following letters (nos 297–8), this clearly refers to Captain Starland.

der. I expect the Arcanies downe here on Monday next, I have sold them some of the perpettuanoes that were broken and wormeaten att 10a, the good att 11a one with another, but if your honour would order the red perpettuano's for to be sold att 9a and 10a they would goe off, better then to lett the wormes and cockroaches eate them.

[PS] Since Mr Starlands death Oystershell Quashee is dayly with mee about the slave to desire [he] may have an order to pay him.

300.   Richard Thelwall   Annamaboe, 30 Sept. 1682

Yesterday by the 15 hand canoe I received 5 bailes of perpettuano's, 3 bailes of say's, 200 Guyney clouts, and 25 pieces of white long cloaths, which have given creditt for accordingly; by the same canoe I have sent one Arda slave and 24 sticks of wood which John Wise cutt att Anishan, the rest shall get downe as soon as possible, for itt is a greate way off this place.

301.   Richard Thelwall   Annamaboe, 4 Oct. 1682

Last night I received yours, and concerning the Captain of the Arcanies I have spoke to him and told him if [he] gave your honour encouragement you would consider him something, hee saith hee would looke out for to gett some, Indeed hee hath brought mee already above 3 marks. I beleive the Dutch have but little goods, that is one reason, but the Captain saith Anishan Arcanies have above 2 pease a month, soe hee saith hee may deserve itt as well as others. Here is one slave in towne of the Ardas but they would change for one Fanteen man that is aboard Captain Nurse. Last night I paid Oystershell Quashee for 109 butts. The canoemen made 38 [var. 39] turns aboard ship. Quashee is still att mee about the slave.

302.   Richard Thelwall   Annamaboe, 12 Oct. 1682

This serves cheifly for covert to the inclosed September accompt with the ballance being 1 marke, 1 ounce, 1 angle and 10 tacco's, which with the 10 markes I sent up the 18th September past makes even that accompt, which hope will find right and make noate accordingly. This comes by Francis Nixon by whome I have sent 10 markes of good Arcanie gold on October months accompt, soe there is in all 11 marks, 1 ounce, 1 angle and 10 taccoes.

May please to send per first good oppertunity some perpetuano's and good iron barrs, but they must be all marked else they wont take them. As concerning the red slave[50] I bought him of an Arcanie but as yett hee is not come out of the country,

---

[50] an albino?

but Boneshee saith hee bought his slave of a Fanteen man, but will not tell his name without a greate dashey and if [he] should give itt I question whether [it?] should be ever the better, nay hee saith there hath been 5 slaves sold aboard interlopers. Indeed these people are the greatest rogues in all these country's. As to the custome of the country, if they had been taken in Fettue country then but a pease, but if in another Kings country they sell them; soe they say is the custome.[51] I cannot heare of any slaves at Quobinas croome.

303. Richard Thelwall   Annamaboe, 16 Oct. 1682

Last night I received yours. When Captain Nurse was here hee saith hee writt to your Honour by his boate which was gon for Cabo Corsoe; on Monday God willing hee begins to take in his corne, soe about the latter end of the weeke hee will be ready to saile.

304. [receipts]

Annamaboe, 15 Sept. 1682
Received then of Richard Thellwall 35 chests of corne on board the Cape Coast Briganteen for the use of the Royall Affrican Company of England, I say received per mee   Hugh Shears

Annamaboe, 17 Sept. 1682
Received of Mr Thelwall 3 chests of Corne and 200 of wood, I say received per mee   William Triming

Annamaboe, 19 Oct. 1682
Received of Mr Richard Thelwall 500 chests of corne, there being an order from the Agent and Councill for 400, the other 100 I shall desire the Agent to give an order for; likewise 2 men and 4 woemen received for accompt of the Royall Affrican Company, I say received per mee   Henry Nurse

305. Richard Thelwall   Anamaboe [var. Anishan], 22 Oct. 1682

Yesterday I received yours and by the 15 hand canoe I received 200 iron barrs, and 2 bailes of perpetuanoes and I sent all the poles were left, being 21. As to the gold I sent your Honour all I had by Francis Nixon, and the Arcanies doe not come every

[51] From no.309, it appears that this relates to slaves of the Company, who had presumably been kidnapped or captured, and whom Thelwall was trying to redeem. Again (cf. no.288) the 'custom of the country' forbade the selling of fellow-citizens into slavery, although a ransom (of 1 peso) could be demanded.

weeke, some they stay as they call itt for their boone day, I have spoke to them and if any comes I shall send itt as soone as possible.

306. Richard Thelwall   Annamaboe, 24 Oct. 1682

Last night I received yours and immediatly as inordered I sent a Whiteman to Amersa for to take care and see they make good measure.

307. Richard Thelwall   Annamaboe, 8 Nov. 1682

Yesterday I received yours, and as inordered I have by Evan Price sent all the gold I have being 9 markes of good Arcanie gold. May please to send per first good oppertunity a good quantity of perpettuano's and iron barrs, but the barrs must be marked, and some sayes.

308. Richard Thelwall   Annamaboe, 15 Nov. 1682

Yesterday by the 9 hand canoe I received yours with 170 iron barrs, and before by the small canoe 30, which makes in all 200, and 4 bailes of perpetuano's and 1 baile of sayes, which have given creditt for accordingly, and as inordered I have sent Charles Roberts up, soe hope when the powder is don your Honour will send Charles Roberts downe againe, for I have but few people here and most of them lame. Inclosed is October accompt, which hope will find right and make noate accordingly, the ballance I sent up by Evan Price and 2 marks, 4 ounces, and 1 angle on November accompt as per accompt appears. On the 12 October I sent 11m 1o 1a 10ta, whereof 10m was on October accompt, and by Evan 9m, whereof 6m 3o 15a is on October accompt and 2m 4o 1a on November accompt. This day our towne Arcanies come and to morrow the Arcanies from Cormanteen, soe I beleeve in a few day's these goods will be gon, and as yett the pallavora is not ended soe hope your Honour will excuse my goeing up to Cabo Corsoe. Indeed I cannot tell but these people may play the rogue in my absence, for I know these people are great rogues.

309. Richard Thelwall   Annamaboe, 16 Nov. 1682

Just now I received yours, and as to the slave that was profered mee that was one of the Companys, it was rogue Bonishee's, but hee would not sell him under a bendy, which I did acquaint your Honour, but your answer was itt was unreasonable, and itt was mentioned when Griffin was att Fanteen. I know of noe other, neither was any other proffered mee, if should I would have given the price of a man slave. As to corne, if Captain Churchey comes in 3 or 4 day's itt is ready. And as to a 9 hand canoe, here is one here, but they aske 5 bendy's.

310.   Richard Thelwall   Annamaboe, 22 Nov. 1682

This comes by Francis Nixon by whome I have sent 10 marks of good Arcanie gold on November accompt. May please to send per first good oppertunity some perpetuano's, sheets, and sletias, and if Captain Churchey be not gon before this arrives may send some iron.

311.   Richard Thelwall   Annamaboe, 1 Dec. 1682

I owe answer to two for want of conveniency of sending. By James Bayly in the Busse I received 200 iron barrs, 4 cases of say's and 8 bailes of perpetuano's; per the Heron, Captain George Churchey 2 cases of say's, 2 bales of perpetuano's, 2 cases of course sletias, and 1 of fine sletias, 10 chests of sheets and 200 iron barrs, for which have given creditt for accordingly and doe not doubt but in a small time for to give a a good accompt thereof, as the Arcanies come downe. Att present sayes is a drug, for the Dutch have lowered their say's to 17 angles and the people say theirs is of a better couller (Patience). Two or three day's agoe the Dutch Copeman of Cormanteen was shott with a peece of iron in his left eye and one through his hatt by one of Annamaboe.[52] All these Cabasheers are att Fanteen as yett, soe I know not anything of their pallavora. Tomorrow I suppose Captain Churchey will have all his corne aboard.

312.   Richard Thelwall   Annamaboe, 7 Dec. 1682

Yesterday I received yours, and as to the Company's affaires I thank God all is well, though att present a small trade by reason the Dutch had lowered the prizes of goods. I have made note of what your Honour writt concerning the lowering the prizes of goods, and doe not doubt but shall take money as well as they. On Monday last Captain Churchey sett saile for Arda. In few dayes God willing shall send November accompt.

313.   Richard Thelwall   Annamaboe, 17 Dec. 1682

This morning I received yours, and as to the Companys affaires here I thank God all is verry well, though but little trade att present, for I find the Dutch are a kind of cunning sort of underminding people; they have sent a bendy to our Arcanies here to gett them send mony's to them; soe I have sent some to theirs; and have had them here twice or thrice, and tould them would sell them goods as cheape as they; and they have promised to come to mee; I expect some of them this weeke, they come some times but once in a fortnight and they say the Dutch sells sheets for 1

---

[52] Subsequently, in April 1683, the Fante were reported to be 'at war' with the Dutch at Kormantin (no.330).

angle apeece. Inclosed is November accompt, which hope will find right and make note accordingly; there wants 5 ounces 15 angles for the ballance, which shall send with more money as itt comes in per first good oppertunity. In the 9m sent per Evan Price was 2m 4o 1a on November accompt, and by Francis Nixon 10 arkes, soe 5 ounces, 15 angles makes the ballance of that accompt.

314.   Richard Thelwall   Annamaboe, 2 Jan. 1682/3

Yesterday I received yours, and have spoken to the Cabasheers about the two slaves that ran away, they tell mee they will doe what they can if [they] should come in these parts. And as soone as the ships appears shall send a whiteman to Amersa to see the shells measured. Captain Branfill hath the letter for Thorne,[53] hee presents his service to your honour, hee saith will saile tomorrow in the evening.

315.   Richard Thelwall   Annamaboe, 4 Jan. 1682/3

Yesterday I received yours by Mr Lewin, and as in ordered I have made inquiry about the powder and I cannot heare of any more then 2 barrells that was bought out of an interloper; and for to search their houses I have not force enough, and if hee hath any I suppose itt must be to windward, for I cannot understand hath sold any here, but what Cormanteen or Agga people doe I cannot understand, as yett. I sent one aboard with Mr Lewin to wittness what was don. I have received all the goods by the Busse, James Bayley [Commander] and have given creditt for accordingly, but as long as these ships undersell mee I cannot take any money.

316.   Richard Thelwall   Annamaboe, 7 Jan. 1682/3

Yesterday I received two of yours and have made inquiry after Captain Maples slaves and boat but as yett I cannot heare any thing of them. I shall alsoe gett what green birds I can and as soon as possible.

317.   Richard Thelwall   Annamaboe, 17 Jan. 1682/3

Last night I received yours, and when Captain Cope comes hee shall have what corne your Honour have ordered him. Likewise have made noate to take a larger quantity for store. Yesterday Captain Maples sett saile for Angola.

318.   Richard Thelwall   Annamaboe, 18 Jan. 1682/3

This comes by Captain Cope whoe can informe your Honour. As concerning of

---

[53] John Thorne, RAC factor at Offra in Allada (cf. section VIII).

trade, as long as these interlopers stay here I cannot take any money for they undersell mee, they sell perpetuano's at 6 and 7 angles, sayes att 12 and 13 angles Fanteen money,[54] and other goods accordingly. Indeed since I came here from Cabo Corsoe att Christmas I can hardly take money to pay the Whitemen and blacks this month. There hath been 10 interlopers since Christmas. This day two sett saile, and I beleeve the Dutch furnish themselves with goods out of them, but I hope they are all gon and then I dont doubt but shall have a good trade againe. Tomorrow God willing Captain Cope will have all his corne aboard, the 5 hand canoe kickade-voo'd[55] with 8 chests corne and was all lost. I have been troubled with vommitting this 4 or 5 dayes or else had sent December account, but shall send itt by first oppertunity.

319. Richard Thelwall   Annamaboe, 23 Jan. 1682/3

Yesterday I received yours with a pacquett for Captain Cope but hee was gone above 4 houres before, soe I have returned itt againe, hee stayed till betwixt 12 and 1 for the letters. As to James Mills, for a certaine hee is drownded att Allampo and two of the canoemen, the goods all lost, and the canoe broken all to peeces. Here is come one or two of rogue Bonishee's men here; itt seemes James Mills was to have been factor for rogue Bonishee att Allampo. The canoe and one Whiteman is gon to Amersa. I have the two canoemen from Captain Cope. Yesterday the Dutch Copeman of Cormanteen sent to mee two Whitemen and desired mee for to keepe the men here and in a small time they will send mee two for them. The canoe was an old canoe and broken all to peeces, itt is left aboard ship. Yesterday appeared a ship off Amersa, his boate was aboard Captain Cope, itt seems one Captain Davis, [he] is bound for the Bite. As to trade att present itt is glutted for here hath been soe many interlopers that hath spoyl'd itt, butt hope in a small time itt will come againe (Patience). Inclosed is December account, which hope will find right and make noate accordingly. Indeed I had sent it sooner but I have not been well this 10 day's; yesterday was my ill day, but I hope when gott something from Docter Meade itt will remove the distemper. This morning all our Capasheers came here about Ampeteens pallavora, they brought 3 sheepe but I told them that would not doe, I bid them goe to Capo Corsoe, soe then they desired mee for to give them Ampeteens chests, but I told them they should not have them till the pallavora was over, soe they went away angry.

320. Richard Thelwall   Annamaboe, 8 Feb. 1682/3

Yesterday I received yours, and this morning I sent up Francis Nixon to Cabo

---

[54] No explanation of this term has been traced; but probably, in contrast to 'Akani gold' (cf. n.20 above), it refers to gold of inferior quality.

[55] See Glossary.

Corsoe in a canoe with the ballance of Decembers accompt and January, alsoe 5 marks on February accompt, which hope will arrive before this. I sent 10 marks, 5 angles and 7 tacco's in all. As to trade I have but little, only last Monday and Tuseday I tooke 4 in 5 marks, which was most for sheets. As money comes in I shall send itt to your honour, but the Arcanies doe not come every weeke. In a little time I shall want sheets and marked iron barrs, they will be the first I shall want, which may please to send per first good oppertunity. The other day I opened a bale of perpetuano's and they were all rotten with salt water, all but 5 or 6, Francis Nixon can informe your honour. As to any thing elce here all is well.

321.   Richard Thelwall   Annamaboe, 9 Feb. 1682/3

This serves chiefely for covert to the inclosed Januarys accompt, which hope will find right and make note accordingly. By Francis Nixon I have sent to your honour 10 marks, 5 angles and 7 taccoes of good Arcanie gold, whereof 1 mark 2 ounces 1 angle and 9 tacco's being the ballance of Decembers accompt and 3 marks, 6 ounces, 3 angles and 10 tacco's on January's accompt, and 5 marks on Februarys accompt, makes in all 10m 0a 5a 7ta. I must begg your honours pardon that I have not writt oftener nor sent the accompt, for I am not as yett throughly well. May please per first good oppertunity for to send a good quantity of sheets and marked iron barrs, for them I shall first want, and 3 pound basons.

322.   Richard Thelwall   Annamaboe, 12 Feb. 1682/3

Just now I received yours whereby I understand you desire to know what quantity of iron barrs I wanted. I spoke to the Arcanies; they say 1,000 will be gone in a little time if marked barrs, and noe flawes in them, and 20 chests of sheets, or what your honour can spare. I have but halfe a chest of sheets left, and some 3 pound basons, the other will not goe off. As to the news of the country the Captain of the Portugueze of Anishan and the Quarranteer can not agree, and hee would remove from Anishan and take his people and his things; some say hath gott most part of his best things aboard the ship. The ship for this 2 dayes hath panyard Annamaboe and Anishan canoes, and att Accra they have panyard a 11 hand canoe of Annamaboe peoples full of cowes; and they say when they deliver up their whitemen and things they will deliver up their men and things.[56] Indeed these Fanteeners are all great rogues and there is noe doeing with them unless [you] sett other nations and them by land. They want warrs.[57]

---

[56] The Portuguese factory at Accra was evacuated at the same time (no.448).

[57] The proposal to incite other nations to attack Fante is elaborated in the following letters (nos 324–7), in one of which (no.326) this practice is described as being 'as the Dutch doe'. For the ability of European nations on the Gold Coast to recruit African armies to fight in their interests, cf. generally Daaku 1970, ch.4. On this particular occasion, however, it does not seem that anything came of the idea.

323. Richard Thelwall   Annamaboe, 28 Feb. 1682/3

Last night I received yours, whereby I understand there was a Company's ship arrived and that [you] desired to know what goods I most wanted. Att present I only want sheets and 3 pound basons. As to corne per former order to keepe a store, I have above 900 chests, and when this ship hath taken her corne I shall fill the corne room againe, but shall not lett them know any thing, if should they would quickly raise the price, for these people are all greate rogues.

324. Richard Thelwall   Annamaboe, 10 March 1682/3

Last night I received yours, whereby I understood what goods I wanted I should be supplied by Captain Woolliford, for which give your Honour many thankes, and as inordred this morning I send Millington for Capo Corsoe Castle. The last ship that came downe here was a Frenchman as the Blacks sayes, he sett saile last night. As to Aga palavera they would not lett John Ratclifte have any thing to eat or drinke there for this 2 dayes, and last night they sent Arda Jack and his wife hither, I left them to helpe John Ratclifte there, and this morning John Ratclifte hath been heere to fetch his chest and other things there, soe they lett him take his things but would not lett him take the key of the doore, soe I bid him take an account of the benches and windows that was there etc., and when he asked for the key they thrust him away and bid him begon. I sent them word last night if any bench etc. was missing, one day will come when they must pay for it. Indeed these people may very well say their Braffoe is a foole, for they all doe what they please. They want warrs here to make them poore, and untill then I feare they will never be at quiett.

325. Richard Thelwall   Anamaboe, 12 March 1682/3

On the 10th instant I received yours, and as to hazard a fight with these Fanteen rogues I beleive I could, for I have wood water and corne enough, but I want granadoe shells and firelocks, bandileirs and swords for the people. Nay I veryly beleive it will not be long ere they play the rogue againe, when they must be sure to have some mischeife come to them. But if your Worship could gett some other nation to come by land and burne their houses and sell their wives and children for slaves, take their corne and all they have, [that] will make them humble. Inclosed is February account, which hope will find right and make noat accordingly. By Francis Nixon I now send 7 marks, 1 ounce, 15 angles of good Arcanie gold, which with 5 marks sent the 9th ditto makes the ballance of February account.

[PS] In few dayes it is hoped the palavera with Cabesa Terra will be over and then trade will be open.[58]

---

[58] Cf. nos 268–9.

326.   Richard Thelwall   Anamaboe, 20 March 1682/3

Last night I received yours, and to my opinion I beleive it is the best way for to send
to the Braffo to acquaint him of all these people[s] roguery, and if they dont give
satisfaction to sett some other neighbouring nation on them, for to bring them to,
as the Dutch doe, and then they will be glad to come to the English for help, and
[ourselves] not to be seen, but as friends to their friends. The goods in Captain
Woolliford are coming on shoare, and the corne agoeing off, but at present little
trade by reason of the interlopers continually coming.

327.   Richard Thelwall   Anamaboe, 22 March 1682/3

Last night I received yours whereby I understand Captain Rickard and Captain Low
is on the coast, and that Captain Waugh is at Capo Corso. I have acquainted Captain
Woollifords two mates, to tell him that your Honour desires him to stay until
Saterday; and then he should not faile of his dispatches. This day Captain Woollifords corne will be all aboard. As to the Fanteens they are as great rogues as ever
they was. Yesterday they beat John Ratclift as he was looking for to see the corne
goe downe to the waterside. I sent to the Captain of the towne and Mareene and
they have put the man in irons and they say they will punish him. Indeed I beleive
veryly they will never be quiett unless they have war to bring them low, which must
be done by some neighbouring nation and they not know who it is that setts them
on; and then they would be glad to come to the English for help.

[PS] I am forct at present not to take much notice, for if should would not let the
corne nor anything come in or goe out here.

328.   Richard Thelwall   Annamaboe, 31 March 1683

Last night I received yours, and as inordred God willing on Sunday I shall goe for
Cabo Corso Castle and shall bring what gold I have. Just now I received another of
yours with an order to gett about 1500 chests of corne, which shall be effected as
soone as possible; but must desire your Honour to keep the shipps there as long as
may be, and not for to come all togeather, for if they doe they will raise the price,
and now corne growes scarce, and these people are cunning rogues. I shall see if
there be a 9 hand canoe to be sold and the lowest price.

329.   [receipts]

Anamaboe 23 March 1682/3
Received on board the Lisbon Merchant from Mr Richard Thelwall for the use of
the Royall Affrican Company 450 chests of corne, I say received per me
                                                    William Woolliford

Anamaboe 11 April 1683
Received then of Mr Richard Thelwall 500 chests of corne for account of the Royall
Affrican Company of England and use on board the ship Blessing by

Samuell Rickard

Anamaboe 17 April (83)
Received of Mr Richard Thelwall 260 chests of corne for account of the Royall
Affrican Company of England and for the use of the ship Eaglett of London by me

John Waugh

330. Richard Thelwall   Annamaboe, 19 Apr. 1683

Last night I received yours and as inordered have had the accompt of Captain
Lowes corrected, which inclosed I now send per the bearer, and the ounce of gold
hee will pay to mee, which by first good oppertunity shall send with what gold I
have of the Companys and March accompt as soone as the corne is all aboard,
which I hope will be in few dayes. These Fanteen people for these 4 or 5 dayes have
been att warr with the Dutch att Cormanteen and have panyard 20 in 30 of their
slaves as they went for water and wood and have sent them to Fanteen, and yesterday the Dutch shutt up their Castle gates, for these people will not lett them have
any thing to eate or drink. I see I am not alone, but these people play the rogue with
all people. The Dutch have 25 Whitemen and more Blacks, 4 flankers and 16 guns,
but for ought I see dont care for to meddle with these people. These people say they
will have custome for all Dutch ships that goes to the Mina.

331. Richard Thelwall   Annamaboe, 20 Apr. 1683

Just now I received yours, and as to the settling of Agga factory, Mr Burrowes may
goe for Agga when hee pleaseth and shall have what goods I have here as inordered,
but if any thing should prove otherwise then, well, I must not be responsable, but
only for my selfe, if all be in one accompt, though Mr Burrow's is a verry good
husband, yett Mr Hassell gave security in England. Captain Lowe hath 570 chests
corne measur'd, which is all I have att present.

332. Thomas Burrowes   Annamaboe, 20 Apr. 1683

Mr Thelwall shewed mee your order and the rest of the Gentlemen of the Councill
for my goeing to Agga, for which I give your Honour thanks. The house att present
is out of repaire for want of thatch, but suppose Mr Thelwall will in a short time
take care to repaire itt. I hope your honour and the Councill have taken into consideration that I cannot live there for the same sallary that I have here, and although

I eate now at Mr Thelwalls table I doe not expect to put up a penney of my sallary, but be thankfull to him to except of the same for my dyett. I find that the custome of the place is to give the Cabosheers of the place both morning and evening drams and that they dayly expect itt, therefore hope there will be an allowance for itt. I thought fitt to give your honour an accompt of itt, for although I have given but my owne security I will not make soe bold with the Companys goods as to give a bitt of them in dashey's to the Blacks, which I know will be expected of mee, till such time as I know whether my sallary will bear itt. Your Honour is sencible that my stock is but small, therefore am unwilling to run beyond itt; therefore humbly begg your pardon for what I have writt.

333.   [receipts]

Annamaboe, 24 April 1683
Then received of Mr Richard Thelwall 550 chests corne aboard the Merchants Bonadventure for the use of the Royall Companys slaves   per mee John Lowe

More received 1 man and 4 woemen for the Royall Company's accompt.

per mee John Lowe

Annamaboe, 24 April 1683
Received aboard the Jacob Pinke of Mr Richard Thelwall 30 chests corne for the use of the Royall Company   per mee Thomas Woolman

Annamaboe, 24 April 1683
Received of Mr Richard Thelwall Cheife factor for the Royall Affrican Company of England att Annamaboe 1 woemen slave and a child on board of the Merchants Bonadventure Captain Lowe Commander   per mee William Jumper

334.   Richard Thelwall   Annamaboe, 1 May 1683

Just now I received [yours], whereby I understand Captain Richard Lumley was arrived in one of the Companys ships, and verry shortly were more expected. As inordered I have made note for to gett what corne possible I can, but att present itt growes scarce and if these Fanteen rogues should know there is a want of corne they would quickly raise the price, but I never lett them know till the ships come into this roade for itt. As to slaves here they are scarce and good slaves, men are 7 pease 2 angles and woemen 6 pease 2 angles, nay some people give a bendy for a man. Inclosed is March accompts and the receipts for corne and slaves, which hope will find right and make noate accordingly; And God willing in few dayes shall send Aprill months accompt with their ballance. When I was att Cabo Corsoe last I paid Mr Walter Stapleton 6 marks of gold on March months accompt, soe there remaines on that accompt 2 marks, 1 ounce, 13 angles and 10 tacco's, and as soone as possible shall send that and the ballance of Aprill accompt altogether. This morning the Quantrees Tetee was here and I have sent all Whiteman and some Blacks with him for to take possession of Agga factory, for the house wants a greate deale of repairing and thatching, but would desire your honour when the house is fitting to put goods in you would send what goods your honour thinks fitting from Cabo Corsoe, for if should come from mee they would never be att peace with mee nor I should never bee att quiett here. I suppose Mr Burrowes expects an answer from your honour of the letter hee sent. Last night came in Agga roade Captain How an interloper, hee comes from Allampo.

335. Thomas Burrow's   Annamaboe, 3 May 1683

I have yours of the 1st instant, for which I give your honour thanks and shall observe the contents of and repaire myselfe to Agga as soone as the house is fitted, which I suppose will be don by Satureday next, where I shall endeavour to advance the Royall Companys interest as much as in mee ly's.

336. Richard Thelwall   Annamaboe, 4 May 1683

Yesterday I received yours, and as to Agga Factory itt will be ready on Monday next for to goe thither. Soe if your honour sends the sloope with goods they shall be landed as inordered and suppose Mr Burrowes will goe but hee will want brandy and I have but 30 gallons left, which will not last both places but a little, while Mr Burrowes desires mee for to have Michaell Millington for to goe with him to Agga, I tould him hee should, soe thought fitt to acquaint your honour. The corne roome att Agga must be all new built, which shall be don as soone as possible, for the thatch is almost all off, and the poles are all rotton. I shall send some Ardars and a woeman to Agga to helpe Mr Burrowes in any thing hee shall want. I have about 100 chests corne and have sent up in the country for the people to bring their corne downe, but itt doth not come as formerly by reason itt grows scarce. I shall gett what possible I can.

337. Richard Thelwall   Annamaboe, 6 May 1683

Last night I received yours. As to corne I have 100 and odd chests but I cannot tell whether I shall gett enough corne betwixt this and Wensday for Captain Lumley, but desire your honour for to keepe him till this day sennitt[59] for now they are forct to send up in the country a great way for their corne, I shall seeke for to gett itt as soone as possible may be. As to goods proper for Agga, iron barrs, lead barrs, sayes, perpetuano's, sheets, paper brawles, and Guyney clouts etc., what your Honour

---

[59] sennight, i.e. a week (seven nights).

thinks fitting, but itt would be convenient the sloope be here 2 or 3 dayes before the ship comes here, for itt will be a great trouble for to land the goods here and send them afterwards a mile by land to Agga. Mr Burrowes hath been troubled with a paine in his head and bones, I suppose gott cold. Francis Nixon hath been ill this 10 day's. Old Harrey, old Charles, John Ratlife, they have been all ill, but thanks be to God they are all on the mending hand. As to a canoe, here is none to be gott for love nor money. I and Mr Burrows wants wrighting paper and inke and some brandy for Mr Burrow's, for I have but little left.

338.   Richard Thelwall   Annamaboe, 7 May 1683

This is by the request of Mr Burrow's that your honour would be pleased to lett Docter Meade come to see him this night, for the last night hee had a voyolent feavour and noe ague, which is soe much the worse, hee expects his feavour this night, hee is alsoe verry drye and nothing will stay with him but water, and hath a great paine in all his bones, hee hath sweated for this 3 dayes and saith is verry weake. Indeed I never knew a lustie young man soe faint hearted as hee is, soe desires if possible that Docter Meade may come, if not that hee would send him something that may abate his feavour.

339.   Richard Thelwall   Annamaboe, 10 May 1683

Just now I received [yours], and as to Mr Burrows, since the Docters mate hath blooded him and gave him two glisters his feavour hath something abated but hee is verry weake, and as the people that looke after him say they never see a man soe faint hearted as hee is, and in grace of God hee may doe well againe if his faint heartedness dont cast him downe againe. Mr Burrow's likewise desires your honour would be pleased that the Docters mate may stay with him till the ship comes downe here. Our Cabasheers have been in the country att Abbra this 5 dayes amakeing a new Captain there,[60] soe this week I have gott but little corne. I beleeve I may have upwards of 200 chests, but tomorrow expect our Cabasheers here and for once must take in corne of a Sunday. I have gave some of them goods beforehand to buy corne and doe not doubt before Captain Lumley hath taken what corne I have that I shall gett enough for him, though the interloprs att present hinder mee, for they give 2 angles per chest. Tomorrow morning God willing if wind and weather doth permitt I shall send Francis Nixon with Aprill account and allsoe the ballance, and alsoe what hens possible I can gett.

---

[60] Cf. n.22 above.

340.   Richard Thelwall   Annamaboe, 11 May 1683

This serves cheifly for covert to the inclosed Aprill months accompt, which hope will find right and make noate accordingly. By Francis Nixon I now send 2 marks, 1 ounce, 13 angles and 10 tacco's being the ballance of March accompt. And alsoe 4 marks, 2 ounces 11 angles and 10 tacco's being the ballance of Aprills months accompt; in all 6 marks, 4 ounces, 9 angles and 8 tacco's. Att present two interlopers in these roads, one in Anishan roade and the other in Agga roade, soe but little trade. The first goods I shall want will be sheets, which may please to send per first good oppertunity.

341.   Richard Thelwall   Annamaboe, 11 May 1683

Since I writt this morning I have received a letter from Charles Towgood that two Frenchmen that came downe last night have taken Captain Lumley and one interloper,[61] and itt will not be long ere the other is taken and I am getting all the canoes I can for to gett the goods out of Captain Charles, soe in hast att present.

342.   Richard Thelwall   Annamaboe, 14 May 1683

Last night I received yours, and as to a chirurgeon of an interloper being att Agga, there is one Richard Pearse, but I assure your honour there is none here, and indeed Mr Burrowes though unknowne to mee did send for him, or else noe interloper will come to this place. I suppose the blacks of Agga doe protect him, but if hee comes here I shall send him for Cabo Corsoe Castle. Truly itt was Mr Burrow's his fault, hee is verry weake and verry faint hearted, yesterday hee had his feavour verry voyolent. This morning I sold all the sheets I have, except about 6 old broken ones, and 48 blew and green perpetuano's, one with the other.

343.   Richard Thelwall   Annamaboe, 15 May 1683

Last night arrived in Anishan roade one of the interlopers that the Frenchmen taken, most barbarously used, they told the canoemen that Captain Lumley lay att Lague, most desperatly wounded and his ship disabled. They have taken out all the goods, water etc., they lett only Captain Lumley and Captain Summervills ships goe. Agent Pearsons attendant and Captain Thompsons ships they tooke with them, they are resolved for to have a bout with the Companys ships att Arda, for they think they have gold chests, and they are resolved for to have them,[62] soe thought fitt to acquaint your honour [so] that Captain Lumley may have some helpe sent him.

---

[61] Cf. no.556; the two French ships were pirates.
[62] As, indeed, they did: cf. nos 494, 632, 637.

344.   Richard Thelwall   Annamaboe, 17 May 1683

Last night came on shoare here Captain Thompson and his docter, that their ship
was taken by the Frenchmen and they kept their ship. They most barbarously
abused them, such punishments noe one never heard of, they put their yards[63] in a
vice and their thumbs, they say Captain Summervills mate wont live, they will
informe your Honour of all passages. As per your former order I have sent them up
to Cabo Corsoe Castle. The Arcany's have been att mee for more sheets.

345.   Richard Thelwall   Annamaboe, 23 May 1683

Yesterday I received yours, whereby I understand [you] did wonder that Agga
factory was not repaired. In answer, ever since I had your honours order, the next
day I sent a white man and Blacks with thatch from hence and they had mended all
the dwelling house, but the corne roome will aske a greate time for to fetch poules
and thatch; besides itt must be ready to putt on before the old thatch be taken off,
for feare the raines should wash the walls downe. I am sure there is never an English
man here will say or write soe, but whomesoever did, did itt undeserving. Yesterday
Mr Burrow's and Michael Millington went to Agga with their things. Mr Burrow's
expects fresh goods from Cabo Corsoe, the goods proper for that place, iron barrs,
and lead barrs, sayes, perpetuanoe's, sheets, course sletias, and what your honour
thinke fitting. The Arcany's wants sheets and blew perpetuano's, for all the blew
perpetuanoes I have are gon, for there is more green in a baile then blew, I have
green, redd and printed perpetuanoes enough but they wont goe off here. There will
want brandy for Mr Burrowes for I have but little, as alsoe paper and inke.

346.   [receipts]

Annamaboe, 11 April 1683
Then received from Mr Richard Thelwall on board the Ann Sloope for account of
the Royall Affrican Company of England 100 billitts of firewood for the use of the
said sloope with 1 chest of corne, per   Charles Towgood

Annamaboe, 29 May 1683
Received from Mr Richard Thelwall aboard the Adventure Ketch upon the Royall
Company's accompt 25 chests corne   per mee John Groome

Annamaboe, 29 May 1683
Received on board the Hopewell 320 chests corne for the use of the Royall Affrican
Company from Mr Richard Thelwall Cheife of Annamaboe Castle
                                                    per mee Richard Lumley

[63] i.e. penises.

Annamaboe, 30 May 1683
Then received from Mr Richard Thelwall on board the Ann Sloope for accompt of the Royall Affrican Company of England 100 billitts of firewood and 2 chests of corne for the use of the said sloope   per mee Charles Towgood

347.   Richard Thelwall   Annamaboe, 1 June 1683

As to Mr Groome, hee sett saile on Wensday morning as soone as hee had got all his corne aboard, and Captain Lumley had sett saile last night but hee hath broke a new cable and is forct for to stay for to sweepe for his anchor. I have made noate as in ordered aboute corne and slaves, I hope before Saturdey night for to have 8 in 900 chests corne. As to tradeing, here they aske for nothing but blew perpetuano's and sheets and I have noe blew, I have a great many perpetuano's, greens, redds and printed, but they wont goe off unless have blews with them, for in any bale there is more green then blews. As to Agga all is well, but Mr Burrowes hee wants blew perpetuano's and writes for 8 deale boards for the warehouse, penns, inke and paper, and as for brandy I have but little which wont last both factory's not passing a month.

348.   Richard Thelwall   Annamaboe, 7 June 1683

This comes by Francis Nixon by whome I have sent your honour 10 marks of good Arcany gold, on May and June accompt, and God willing in few dayes shall send May accompt. May please to send per first good oppertunity some perpetuano's, sayes, sheets, and course sletias, for in sending goods to Agga and buying corne makes the warehouse looke thin. Though I have green and redd and printed perpetuano's, yett they wont goe off without blews, and I never sold any but one with another, but there is more green in every bale then blew, besides redds.

349.   Richard Thelwall   Annamaboe, 10 June 1683

Last night I received yours by the sloope, and God willing tomorrow morning shall gett all the goods ashoare, there being 4 bailes of perpetuano's, 4 cases of sayes, 4 cases of course sletias and 10 chests of sheets, for which shall give creditt for, and sell them for the Companys best advantage and remitt the gold as soone as in cash.

350.   Richard Thelwall   Annamaboe, 20 June 1683

Inclosed is May months account and alsoe the receipts for corne, which hope will find right and make noate accordingly. On the 7th instant I sent 10 marks of gold, whereof 8 marks 3 ounces and 6 angles being the ballance of May account and 1 marke, 4 ounces, 10 angles on June account, and now I send by Francis Nixon 12 marks, 3 ounces and 6 angles, which make with the 1 marke, 4 ounces and 10 angles, just 14 marks on this months June account. May please to send per first good oppertunity a good quantity of sheets and sayes, for att present they are in request. And the people of Agga say I dont write for goods such as they would have, but I tell them when your honour has gold for what has been sent, they shall have fresh goods, but I gett the ill will of the whites and Blacks because the goods are landed here before they goe to Agga.

351.   Richard Thelwall   Annamaboe, 29 June 1683

Yesterday I received yours, and immediately delivered the letter to Mr Sheares. I am afraid the coast will never be cleare unless men of warr stay here to cleare these places of those pyrates rogues. As to the pallavora about [var. att] Annamaboe itt is almost ended, yett the Capasheers has not taken away their trunks and boxes, my chamber being almost full of them.

352.   Richard Thelwall   Annamaboe, 7 July 1683

Last night I received yours, and God willing by Captain Young I shall send what gold I have in cash. Last night came a white man from Captain Groome, I suppose hee hath some gold, but the seas runs soe bad that the canoes cannot gett corne off, soe I thought itt fitting for to send your Honours letters by land, and as soone as the weather permitts the canoe shall goe.

353.   Richard Thelwall   Annamaboe, 8 July 1683

Last night I received yours, and as inordered I have sent all the money I have in cash. This day by Captain Young, which is in all 11 marke of good Arcany gold on June and July accompt. As to Michaell Millington I have spoke to him and he saith hee was a miller by trade, but att present hee is infirme in his legg, being troubled with nocternall paines.

354.   Richard Thelwall   Annamaboe, 11 July 1683

Yours of the 9th instant I received, and as inordered I have taken accompt of the Royall Affrican Companys concerns att Agga and sent Francis Nixon there, and as soone as the corne is measured and I have Mr Burrows's accompt, I shall send him for Cabo Corsoe. Last night departed this world Captain Clarks docter.

355.   Richard Thelwall   Annamaboe, 17 July 1683

This comes by Mr Thomas Burrow's, and have adjusted with him the Companys concernes and measured all his corne, there being 255 chests. I could not dispatch him before Captain Clarke and Mr Sheares were gon. May please for to send a good quantity of iron barrs marked, sheets and perpetuano's for the supply of this place and Agga. These people begin for to aske for iron barrs and I have a greate many but they doe not like them, for they must be all marked and noe flau's in them.

356. Richard Thelwall   Annamaboe, 18 July 1683

Last night I received yours, and suppose Mr Burrows was not arrived att Cabo Corsoe when [you] writt but I beleeve in a little time after, for hee went in my 3 hand canoe. As yett I cannot heare any news of the sloope, when doe as in ordered shall send them up immediatly, if stop here. May please per first good oppertunity to send a good quantity of iron barrs marked, sheets and perpetuano's. Indeed I have a greate many of iron barrs but they dont like them, some small and some not marked and some flawes and they wont goe off here nor att Agga.

357. Richard Thelwall   Annamaboe, 24 July 1683

This serves cheiefly for covert to the inclosed June monthly accompt, which hope will find right and make noate accordingly. On my letter dated the 20th June past will see there was 14m on June accompt and on the 8th July 11m sent, soe there is on July months accompt 21m 40 14a 3ta. Yesterday morning arrived att Agga a great canoe to Yaboyes with cowes, as Francis Nixon writes mee, whoe saith Mr Groome was att Accra with slaves.

358. Richard Thelwall   Annamaboe, 26 July 1683

Yesterday I received yours, and as inordered this day I have sent Andrea the Black bricklayer up to Cabo Corsoe Castle, and hope when your honour hath don with him will send him heither againe. I shall want one hundred or two of Bricks, and some lyme to repair some small breaches before the latter raines come. As to the Royall Companys affaires I thank God all is well here and att Agga, but Cabessa Terra people hath panyard severall of the Arcany's and their gold.[64] Last night our Captain and severall Arcany's went to Cabessa Terra about the pallavora. Here is in towne now, 3 marks, 2 ounces for sheets and iron, and att Agga 4 marks. A good quantity of marked iron barres will goe off in a little time.

359. Richard Thelwall   Annamaboe, 29 July 1683

Yesterday I received yours, and I have spoke to our Cabasheers about Quomina and

[64] Cf. the earlier reference to Kabestera (along with others) having 'stoped the way' down to the coast (nos 268–9).

Epheba, if should come into these parts, that they may be seized on and brought to mee. Andrea the Black bricklayer is also come, for which I give your honour many thanks, but I want one hundred or two of bricks and some lyme. Last night came a ship into the roade, I suppose Captain Phenney, as yett noe body come ashoare and they lye a great way off.

360.   Richard Thelwall   Annamaboe, 3 Aug. 1683

This morning I received yours, and I have received of Captain Phenney 5 bailes of perpetuano's, 200 iron barrs and 20 chests of sheets. Hee sett saile from hence the first of this month in the evening. As to trade here, the Arcany's as yett are not come from Cabessa Terra, but sheets and iron barrs are att present most in request. The sloope[65] is neare Amersa.

361.   Richard Thelwall   Annamaboe, 11 Aug. 1683

Just now I received yours, and I understand that Captain Draper hath aboard, 1300 sheets, 300 iron barrs, and 120 broad blew baftas, the goods are a comeing ashoare, and for which said goods shall give the Royall Company creditt for.

362.   Richard Thelwall   Annamaboe, 26 Aug. 1683

This morning I received yours, and as to purchase two 7 hand canoes, I beleeve itt is impossible, but I beleeve they may gett a 11 and 9 hand canoe, but they are verry deare. When they come downe here they may make the bargaine themselves, for I bought once a 11 hand canoe for Captain Shepheard and hee left itt on my hands. I shall assist them what I can and see for to gett men to goe to Lague with them, if I dont gett cano's here. May please for to send some perpetuano's with the sheets and sayes. On Monday morning God willing I shall goe for Cabo Corsoe Castle and shall bring with mee what gold I have in cash.

363.   Richard Thelwall   Annamaboe, 10 Sept. 1683

This morning the Arcany's was here and now they buy only perpetuano's and sayes and they wont lett mee alone till I write for more fresh sayes and perpetuano's from Cabo Corsoe Castle, they tell mee they have a greate deale of gold, but they wont buy one sheete since the price is raised, soe thought fitting to acquaint your honour that [you] may send by the first ship a good quantity of perpetuano's and sayes.

---

[65] i.e. the *Ann*, commanded by Charles Towgood.

364. Richard Thelwall   Annamaboe, 18 Sept. 1683

Last night I received yours, and as to my opinion concerning Mr Hassell I beleeve itt will doe well for to make him bookkeeper, hee being bred up a merchant. As to the 10 ounces itt had been sent before now, but I had not oppertunity, but God willing I shall send itt to morrow, and alsoe what gold I have of the Company's. Here is a greate deale of gold for fresh sayes and perpetuanoes, but they desire a larger quantity against Monday next.

365. Richard Thelwall   Annamaboe, 20 Sept. 1683

This serves cheifly for covert to the enclosed August monthly account and alsoe the receipts for corne, all which I hope will find right and make note accordingly. This comes by Evan Price, by whome I have sent 32 marks, 1 ounce, 1 angle and 5 tacco's of good Arcany gold, whereof 10 marks, 1 ounce, 1 angle and 5 tacco's is on August accompt and 22 marks on September months accompt as per Mr Master's receipts will appeare. May please to send a good quantity of fresh sayes and perpetuano's per first good oppertunity, for here is a greate deale of gold in towne, and they are att mee every day to write for a larger quantity then came last, and would have them be here before Monday next which is their day of tradeing here.

366. Richard Thelwall   Annamaboe, 21 Sept. 1683

Yours I have received, and doe understand that the 32 marks, 1 ounce, 1 angle and 5 tacco's was safe arrived att Cabo Corsoe. I have received per the two 9 hand canoes, 10 bailes of perpetuano's and 5 bailes of sayes, and as soone as the breeze is over, the canoes shall goe for Cabo Corsoe this evening. I understand that there is arrived at the Mine a greate Dutch ship, and the Copeman of Cormanteen this day is gon to the Mine, soe would willingly have some more sayes and perpetuano's, as soone as possible, for they are only in request att present, that [I] may gett what gold I can before the Dutch goods come, the Blacks reckoning them the better dye and collours.

367. Richard Thelwall   Annamaboe, 22 Sept. 1683

This day I have received yours, and alsoe by the two 9 hand canoes, 12 cases of sayes. I have taken here this day 8 marks odd ounces and att Agga 2 marks odd ounces, att both places in all this day 11 marks of good Arcany gold. I hope on Monday for to gett all the Arcany's good gold before the Dutch goods arrive here, I meane in these part. There is I beleeve a cheate with the packers att home, or elce the Captains of ships, for I opened in 4 of perpetuano's, and there was not one blew perpetuano in itt, I meane one in the 4 bailes, but 18 greens and 7 redds, and att Agga Francis Nixon had but 9 blews in two bayles, therefore I feare shall want some blew perpetuano's for to helpe off with these sayes, for I make them take one with the other. The Arcany's have promis'd to be here on Monday next. I doe what I can to advance the Company's interest.

368.   Richard Thelwall   Annamaboe, 25 Sept. 1683

Last night I received yours, and as to the greene perpetuano's I said there was two bailes opened, one here and one att Agga, that had only greene and redds in them, noe blews. On Satureday and yesterday I have taken here and att Agga in all upwards of 20 marks of good Arcany gold, soe that all the gold is gon till more comes out of the country, which I suppose may be on Monday next. This morning is gon by to Cormanteene a greate canoe loaden with goods and the Blacks saith the Dutch sayes are of a better dye then ours. If [sic] my opinion is that if the green perpetuano's were lowered to 9 angles, they would goe off and helpe to putt off our sayes and wee might bauke the Dutch, and itt would be better then they should lye for the cockroaches and moaths to eate them, they being a commodity that will not goe off att present. As to corne I have spoake to the Cabasheers and told them that att Commenda, Cabo Corsoe and other places, they sold for 1 [angle] a chest, but their answer is that wee have had but little raine this yeare and that they shall have but on[e] cropp this yeare and that Corne will be verry deare and they wont sell soe, not under 1 angle and halfe per chest. I desire to know how damnified goods goes off att Cabo Corsoe for gold or corne, that I may not make any error.

369.   Richard Thelwall   Annamaboe, 25 Sept. 1683

Last night I received yours, and I have made noate about the sheets. Yesterday I writt my opinion concerning greene perpetuano's and what our people said about corne. I understand the Dutch have most sayes come into these parts, soe if the greene perpetuano's be not lowered for to helpe off our sayes, I feare they will lye on hand, the Dutch sayes being of a better dye then ours. I desire to know how damnified goods goes off for gold or corne, but I dare not trust goods for corne here, if I should I never should see goods nor corne, for I have severall gold pawnes, I cannot gett them for to redeeme them and they are of a long standing.

370.   Richard Thelwall   Annamaboe, 26 Sept. 1683

Last night I received yours, and have made noate about lowering the prizes of goods, as soone as the Arcany's come downe, and doe not doubt but shall take money as well as the Dutch. I understand how goods were bartered for corne, but I dare not trust any goods, if should I never should see goods nor corne and they wont take 1 angle per chest. Yesterday all our Cabbasheers were att Anishan and they say that an Anishan canoeman was att Cape Tres Punctas, where is now two greate ships a takeing in wood and water, they say Portuguze and that there is English and French men aboard, they say will take the Dutch ships. I feare they are the pyrates come on the coast againe.

371. Richard Thelwall   Annamaboe, 2 Oct. 1683

Yesterday I received yours, and as to old corne there is 225 chests at Agga. Captain Cole had all mine but 20 odd chests I keepe for my own spending. As I w[r]itt in my former letters, I cannot buy corne here under 1 angle and a halfe per chest, and our Capasheers will not sell under and I beleeve they buy up all the corne themselves. Last night came into this roade Captain Draper, hee saith hee will sett saile when the breaze comes in. This day thought lett him gett what corne hee can off, his boate is gon to Agga for his corne, for hee wont loose the windward currant. The ship that came downe the other day ly's in Anishan roade is an interloper, hee wont tell his ships name nor his owne, but the Blacks say they call him Captain James and hee snuffles in the nose, that is all I can learne of the Blacks. As to trade itt is verry small att present, for I have taken but one bendy this two dayes of trade and that was for iron barrs, but I hope when the interloper is gon and the Dutch sayes, I shall have a trade againe.

[PS] Captain Drapers 50 chests corne is all on board.

372. Richard Thelwall   Annamaboe, 5 Oct. 1683

This morning I received yours, and as inordered, when Mr Sheares or Mr Groome comes shall put what slaves in [I] have in irons aboard. As to trade this weeke, has been verry small for I have taken but one bendy and that was in iron barrs. On Monday and Tuseday next, which is the dayes of trade with the Arcany's, I shall see what may be don. The Dutch sayes and sheets, the blacks like better then ours, but for corne here the Blacks will have one angle and halfe per chest, and if [you] will give mee an order for to give soe I may gett new corne, but otherwise I cannot, There is 205 chests of old corne att Agga, which is all is left.

373. Richard Thelwall   Annamaboe, 27 Oct. 1683

Yesterday I received yours and imediatly I delivered Captain Browse his letters; hee sett sayle yesterday after dinner. As to the Royall Companys affaires, I thank God all is well but little gold stirring att present. Captain James the interloper for this fortnight hath spoyled the trade here, now the ships are gon I hope tradeing may be good againe.

374.   Richard Thelwall   Annamaboe, 11 Nov. 1683

This morning I received yours, and as inordered I have sent a Whiteman to Amersa
to see they make good measure and good shells. There is in Agga roade the old
interloper Captain James. This is the fifth or sixth Monday hee hath beene here and
if any money should come out of the country I feare [he] will spoyle the trade here.

V

EGYA

The RAC factory at Egya ('Agga'), east of Anomabu, had been established by 1674.[1] Its history during the period 1681–3 is not altogether clear. The initial series of correspondence from it terminates in March 1681, though without any explicit indication that the factory was about to be abandoned.[2] It seems, in fact, that the factory was either continued or quickly re-established, since it appears from the Anomabu correspondence (nos 236–7) that it was in existence in September, when most of the goods were removed, though the Egya people were assured that more goods would be sent and one white man was left there. This sole white man was James Cunduitt, who wrote one letter from Egya in October 1681 (no.384). Although Cunduitt returned to Anomabu shortly afterward (cf. no.247), it does not appear that the Egya factory was wholly abandoned, since its rebuilding was under discussion in December 1681 (no.252), and in May 1682 John Ratclif was sent to look after it (no.272). In March 1683 Ratcliff was still at Egya, and involved in a 'palaver' with the local people (no.324), and he may have been obliged to withdraw, since in April 1683 another man, Thomas Burrows, was appointed to take charge of the Egya factory (no 332). After delays due to ill health. Burrows finally left Anomabu for Egya in May (no.345). Only a single letter from Burrows at Egya survives, in July 1683; but it seems clear, from subsequent references in the Anomabu correspondence (nos 367, 368, 373) that the factory continued to be occupied. The fragmentary character character of the Egya correspondence may mean only that after March 1681 the factory normally reported to the fort at Anomabu, rather than directly to Cape Coast Castle. The Egya factory took some gold, but was probably principally important for the supply of corn to slave-ships.

Like Anashan and Anomabu, Egya lay within the state of Fante; hence, early in 1681, the chief of Egya was sent to negotiate with the RAC at Cape Coast by 'the King and Quantrees of Fanteene' (no.379).

[1] Davies 1957, 224.
[2] Though there were local apprehensions that the factory was to be abandoned, in February 1681 (reported in no.379).

375.   Ralph Hassell   Agga, 28 Jan. 1680/1

I had not been guilty of silence had I not this misfortune befallen mee which by the loss of upwards of 200 ounces of blood has soe weakened me that I have not been in a capacity to write to your Honour before now, which I hope will not be imputed as a crime to me. A soone as I am able shall by your order pay my due respects to you and bring up with me an exact accompt of all things belonging to my masters the Royall Affrican Company which I inventoryed at the takein charge of this factory, not being able to inlarge now.

376.   Richard Thelwall   Agga, 6 Feb. 1680/1

This morning I received yours, and according as in order[ed] have taken care this night for to send all the goods of most importe for Annamaboe, imprimis 17 sayes, 4 chestes of sheetes, 39 ginghames, 10 halfe firkines of tallowe, and Mr Hassell hath Captain Coffee here and his people, which will have a care of what remaines, being ordinary goods, and if any occation shall send helpe from Annamaboe. This comes by Mr Hassell.

377.   Ralph Hassell   Agga, 13 Feb. 1680/1

According to order have putt on board the Prosperous, Captain Henry Clarke Commander 9 woemen slaves and 140 musquetts, 300 chestes of corne which are the Company['s], allso 2 peices firr and 60 peices of timber. I paid 2 ounces and 4 angles for them all and hope your Honour will allowe mee the same, which I begg your Honourr will signifie to mee by first oppertunity. What other goods are here are convenient for buying of corne, soe Mr Thelwall thinkes meete they remayne here. For what othere slaves are here four Arda men, one woeman, two boyes, which are requessett to bee here for to turne and shift the corne, nevertheless if you please to have two men up they shall come up by land, for they will not runn away. If you please to send a baile of tapseeles which will vend here for corne or money att 6a per peice, allsoe nicconees, wich goods doe not vend at Cape Corse. Here is left u[w]pards of 300 chestes of corne. I had a great deale of trouble in sending of the musquetts of[f], the people would not suffer for them to goe out of the factory and say nothing more shall goe, soe beleive within 2 or 3 dayes some of the Capusheires will be up with you.

378.   Ralph Hassell   Agga, 13 Feb. 1680/1

This comes per Captain Cophes people, who hath been here ever since I began to remove away goods for feare any molestation, which I mett with but little till the 140 musquetts went aboard. I advised your Honour this morninge of what corne slaves &ca are aboard Captain Clarke, which letter I deliverd to Captain Clarke. Here is now onely some iron barres, lead barrs, 12 narrow dammagged nicconnees, 4 red playnes, 7 verry corse sletias, 10 diglins and 5 brass panns old, and upwards of 300 chests corne, with 4 Arda men, 1 woeman and 2 boyes. The 4 men watch a nights, the woeman makes them cankey, the 1 boy is a cooke, the othere if occation serves to send on messages to Cape Coste. Findeing all things right pray signifie your Honours minde therein.

379.   Ralph Hassell   Agga, 19 Feb. 1680/1

These comes to your hands per Captain Yankey, the Captain of Agga,[3] who is sent to you on purpose per the King and Quontrees of Fanteene.[4] They have been severall times with mee to buy goods, which I have not, and would know the reason why they cannot bee supplyd as formerly, butt that I sent the goods to Annamaboe, to which queries I made answer I followed my Generalls order, and reason'd with them as much as could and used as many forcible arguments to induce them to beleive theire was not any goods att Cape Corso to supply this place and other out factoryes, so they have sent the bearer to your Worship to dispute the buisness that they may be the better satisfyed.

   The Cheife of thee Quontrees (which Griffin knowes what hee is) told me that if thee factory was not continued that there should bee noe trade at Annamaboe, for hee would stop the passage to Annamaboe, and that all boors[5] should come and bring corne to this factory, and that they would take it in theire own hands and sell it to interloopers and purchase goods for themselves, soe that noe English ship for the future should have any corne and by that meanes theire voyages would be ruined. What their intentions are I leave it to your judicious consideratioons, this being the verrity of what was said to mee. Read it verbatem and lett Griffin interpritt it to the bearer, and he will verrifie the same. They binde me to stay as a pawne till the bearers returne.

380.   Ralph Hassell   Agga, 23 Feb. 1680/1

Yours I received per via Annamaboe from Mr Thelwall and understand what he wrote that the Quantrees man had said nothing to him about what I wrote you, which per adventure might cause a suspition in you that I should write the thinges that were erronious, butt in the future you will find the verrity confirmed. In Mr Belwoods time there were noe factor that had given security, which was the reason,

---

[3] Presumably, this is a different person from the 'Captain Yankey' mentioned elsewhere (e.g. no.213) as in the employment of the RAC.
[4] There was not, strictly, a 'king' of Fante, the head of the state being the Obrafo or commander-in-chief (cf. e.g. Bosman 1705, 57).
[5] i.e. country people.

nor Mr Belwood himselfe, and I quaere if it be not soe now. It will be noe discharge to mee to render an account to any one butt your selfe and the Royall Company, with whome I have contracted to that purpose. If I write not reason pray lett me begg the favour to know what I err in and it shall be rectifyed. Had I the goods that has been sent to Annamaboe I could remitt more money than ever has been remitted from thence, which if you had the accounts would appeare. Your Worship writes me not a woard aboute the slaves I sent per Captain Clarke, the musquettes and timber liekwise.

I could vend 10 or 12 barrells of powder for corne, allsoe tapseeles is required here. if your Worship please to send the great canoe with neccessaryes, as powder, tapseeles, nicconees etc., I will load here [= her] up with woode, which suppose may be wanted att Cape Corso for bricke, lyme etc., and if have your order can furnish you with what wood you shall want. I pray your candid construction of this for it is nothing butt verrity.

[PS] I begg an answer per messenger if you please to favour mee with one.

381.   Ralph Hassell   [undated]

In pursuance to your order with Councells of yesterdays dayte I have here inclosed sent an inventory of all the co[n]cerns of my masters the Royall Affrican Company of England at this place, which hope may be sattisfactory.

Your Honour allsoe requires an account what goods sold till the 29 last past, which was onely 6 barrs iron and 1 corse sletia, which being soe small I transmitt it to this month account and remaine debitor till further order, and shall be as carefull for my masters intrest and my owne creditt as may render myselfe boath to theirs and yours good likeing. Here hath been these two dayes all the Capusheeres of this place, who dunns me much for the useuall custome of a new factors comeing to a factory, which they say and indeed hath been ever heretofore allowed. Theire demands are 1 anchor brandy, 1 perpetuanoe, 1 greene Welch playne or othere couler but red, and 3 yards blew broad cloth. I would not give any thing till I had your order, butt they are soe obstinate they will have that or as much, soe begg your answer and then I may govern myselfe as you shall perscribe. If your Honour can spare some course sletias, a bale of tapseeles amd perpetuanoes, with 200 barrs iron that are all markt, I question not but in a months time to take 20m of gold, for theise things are much inquired for per the Arcanyes that are now come downe.

382.   Ralph Hassell   Agga, 3 March 1680/1

This comes per Coophe, who hath been rousawing his ground for corne and desired to be the bearer of a letter to your Worship, though have onely to informe you that yesterday I delivered my months account to Mr Thelwall and yesterday Captain Bowler sayld, aboard whome I putt 2 boyes and furnished him with what wood he wanted, which was 670 sticks. When I demanded a receipt he would give it lieu of timber put ashoar at Cape Corso, which I was unwilling to take till I had Mr Thelwalls approbation. I have rumiged and found the othere musquett, which sent per the bearer. I could wish a supply of goods such as you can best spare, for now I have nothing butt lead, iron, playnes 2½ ps, and 10 diglins. I bought a considerable quantity of corne last month, it begins to be scarce, that quantity is good. I want some powder, tapseeles broad, and nicconees, blew bafts, if you please to send them to Annamaboe, and what other sort of goods you please.

*****

383. James Cunduitt   Agga, 4 Oct. 1681

The Cabisheers came to mee to demand the reason why the factory was with-drawne.[6] I declared I did not know but did beleeve the unkindness was the cause. I did declare the covenant was broke that they made with Agent Mellish[7] at the settlement of the same, which covenant I did declare in regard I was present at the same time, and some other wrongs which the Company have received, soe Braffo and Quantrees and Cabisheers of Abbra and Cabisheers of Agga and Mareens doe declare they will make good the covenant they made with Agent Mellish, which covenant is this, that noe slaves shall be carryed aboard any interloper whatsoever but first brought into the factory, and they shall have the refusall of them, and that noe money shall be carryed aboard any interloper, and if any one doe the goods shall be seazed by the Marens for the Braffo and Company, which covenant was in force since I came to Agga to live, and I can give an account how it was broke, that noe interlopers men shall be suffered to come to Agga ashoare but be panyard. They desire that Mr Thelwall be chiefe and I may remayne with him. The Braffo will imploy some to looke after the factory that shall pay for what goods are stole and what slaves brake away, if not taken shall be paid for, and what lost in old Braffo's time this Braffo will not concerne himselfe with. The Cabisheers would not be satisfied unless I would write to your honour about this, for which I hope your honour will pardone my boldness in soe doeing. This new Braffo hath been a trader with the English in my time, I doe know him. They desire your answer and will further waite uppon your honour as you will appoint. There was severall present att the writting hereof, and they have been with Mr Thelwall about this business.

******

[6] Referring to the removal of most of the goods from Egya (cf. no.236); as noted above, it does not appear that the factory was wholly abandoned.

[7] Thomas Mellish, Chief Agent of the RAC at Cape Coast in the 1670s.

384.   Thomas Burrowes   Agga, 8 July 1683

I have yours of the 7th instant, and am sorry to heare that my practices or behaviour amongst the Blacks, now I have given them almost halfe I have in the country, should be soe ill as to cause any of them to give your honour falce reports of mee. I can safely say I have not a word of differance with any black since I came to this place, which your Honour may be better inform'd by the Whitemen that has lived with mee. You are pleased to tax mee with entertaining the master of an interloper. Its true that since I came here that one Hudson, whoe was master of an interloper from Barbado's, came ashoare here and being my verry entimate freind told mee hee made bold to come up to the house to see mee, haveing a letter for mee from Barbado's. I desired him to goe from hence, which accordingly hee did, and I am sure was not halfe an houre ashoare. I was not att that time capeable to entertaine him or to seize him, haveing the feavour and ague. Upon the next day hee writt mee a noate ashoare per a black that [being] formerly acquaintance and seeing mee to be a new beginer to house keeping, hee had sent mee a sow pigg and 3 Muscoval ducks. Mr Sheares comeing here since told mee the ducks belonged to your Honour, and that Captain Clarke heard Hudson say they were sent you from Barbado's, which has ever since been a trouble to mee that hee should give mee your present, although att first I designed to present them to you, but when Mr Sheares told mee the ducks was your honours I was resolved to know the truth of itt and spake with Captain Clarke before I sent them. I hope you will not any wayes take this amiss of mee, for I protest had there been the least word of sending them to you as a present from Barbado's spoken to mee, I would not have kept them 12 houres. I have per bearer sent the 3 ducks and a douzen of good fowles with them, which I hope you will please to except of, and hope your honour will harbour noe ill thought of mee for that action, haveing writt the whole truth of itt, and as for the selling of slaves itt was more then could doe for I have not bought any since I came here. Itts true a boy that I had before I came to Cabo Corsoe, att my first comeing here had stolen severall things from mee and haveing whipt him, [he] run away from mee for two dayes, and rashly and foolishly I sent him aboard ship and sold him for rum, which I have often since repented, and hope your Honours pardon, haveing writt you the whole truth to every passage, but suppose the informer might make an addition to them. I doe not expect to doe the least thing that hold can be taken of, but itt will be immediatly carryed to your Honour, for I am much envyed by comeing here, but not by the Blacks but whites. Mr Thelwall taxes mee much with informing your honour against him, and that particularly I writt that hee had cursed you and spoken verry ill words of you; I begg your Honour to favoure mee soe farr with a line or two for to cleare mee of itt, for without hee will not be satisfied. If should wrighte any such thing I should be a verry greate rogue, for I never heard him say ill of you. His man Francis [i.e. Nixon?] justifies itt, and sayes hee had itt from credible people att Cabo Corsoe. I have delivered in my last months accompt, and tooke upwards of 15 marks of gold besides the corne. I hope this month will prove noe worse.

VI

WINNEBA

Winneba ('Wyamba', 'Wimba'), in the state of Angona ('Anguyna'), east of Fante, was always primarily important as a source of slaves, rather than gold. The RAC had had a factory here in the mid-1670s,[1] but this had been destroyed in an attack by local people in 1679.[2] It appears from the Anomabu correspondence (no. 211) that there was still (or again) a white man and some goods there in April 1681, though it was hoped to get them away.[3] In May 1681 an RAC ship traded at Winneba, and received proposals for the settlement of a factory there (nos 584, 585). The four letters preserved here relate to an attempt to re-establish the factory, in August 1681. Unfortunately, this coincided with an attack on Angona by Akron ('Accrong'), its western neighbour, which provoked a flight of the inhabitants from Winneba. Presumably, the attempt was then abandoned. In March 1682, another RAC vessel tried to trade at Winneba, but this coincided with a further attack from Akron, which again dispersed the Winneba people (no.506).

385. Hugh Sheares   Wyamba, 15 Aug. 1681

This is to give an account of our proceedings. Satureday being the 13, at 10 of the clock wee came to Wyamba and went to the towne and found noe person in it, for they were run to Sanya but 15 miles distance from Wyamba,[4] soe wee went by land and there found James Mills and the Wyamba people, and wee stayed there all Sonday, and Monday morning departed and came to Wyamba with part of the Wyamba men, and the next day they are all intended to come to Wyamba. The cause of their runing away was the reason that the Anguinnas had kild and taken of

---

[1] Davies 1957, 224 (referring to a list of 1674).
[2] Barbot 1992, ii, 426.
[3] Cf. also no.577, referring to James Mills, together with an African called Galansa, as being at Winneba in April 1681. James Mills was again at Winneba in August 1681 (no.385), but it is not clear whether he had been there continuously since April.
[4] Senya Beraku, east of Winneba.

Momford people 183 and they are affraid of the Accrongs.[5] I would not have your worshipp send any goods till I heare further, for to morrow I will send a man to Accrong and another to both Anguinnas,[6] and if they have done their pallavora I shall acquaint your worshipp with itt. As for expence here will be some hereafter, for haveing noe time I cannot acquaint better, and by relation of the Wyamba Cabasheers Mr Nightingalle had the Anguinna Cabashers and the Accrong and the Lague Cabasheers here at Wyamba, and gave them dasheys and spent largly on them and made the said Cabasheers all take their fittish to be true and trusty to thee Royall Affrican Company of England and their concerns before hee brought any goods ashoare or settled the factory.[7] As concerning the house itt is in a bad condition, for there is noe doores nor windows in it, but Gallansa and John Grandy will make itt serve till there be a better made.

386. Hugh Shears   Wyamba, 18 Aug. 1681

This is to give your worshipp an account [that] this morning about 3 of the clock came here Captain Phipps and Mr Wendover and Mr Nightingale and James Mills and Nicholas Battrell but came not on shoare.[8] I spake with them but they went straite for Accra. This day is come Atta Barba[9] from Anguinna and hee tells mee that within 3 or 4 dayes to the most all will be well, and that the Accrongs will give them pawnes and they likewise to the Accrongs for to be true one to the other. As for the man sent for Accrong I heare nothing of him as yett but expect him every houre. As for the townes people there is none but Gallansa and his people and some of John Grandy's, soe haveing nothing to trouble your worshipp but by the next conveniency you shall heare better.

387. Hugh Shears   Wyamba, 22 Aug. 1681

This is to trouble your worshipp [that] as for the man that I sent to Accrong he came Satureday last and give mee an account that the Accrong Cabasheers will come to Momfort to meet the Wyamba and Anguinna Cabasheers any day that they will appoint, and take their fittish together and give pawnes, which I will see and gett them into my hand and send them to your worshipp, but doe what I can I cannot get them to come to make their pallavora till their fittish tell them, as they say or fancy as I suppose, but will hasten them all as possible may. This morning came into this road an interloper.

[5] Mumford (Amanforo), west of Winneba, which belonged to the kingdom of Akron.
[6] Not explained: perhaps referring to the Winneba people (now at Senya) and the capital inland.
[7] Cf. Nightingale's account, no.516.
[8] George Phipps (a member of the Council at Cape Coast Castle) was on his way to reorganize the RAC factory at Accra (cf. section VII).
[9] An African employee of the RAC.

388.   Hugh Sheares   Wyamba, 28 Aug. 1681

This is to give your worshipp an account of Wyamba people that they would not like to come together, for the Accrongs give them onely faire words and promise them pawnes for nothing but for them to come together, and then doe by them as the Anguinnas did by the Momford people. Thursday last the Queens[10] people were here and brought some slaves for powder and lead, and other people with some slaves but all woemen for powder likewise, and money for other goods. Soe they told mee the Queen would have mee goe and live to Sanya and write to your worshipp for goods, and there should be as good a trade as if wee were here till the trouble be over. I told them that I could not goe, for my orders was for Wyamba, and told them that your worshipp would be angry with mee and punish mee for goeing there without your knowledge. They told mee that if I came to damage your worshipp would be angry with them, and they should gett noe whiteman to live with them againe, and told mee that I must goe, and soe they went away for Sanya and there ordred canoemen to come this day to carry my things by watter and bring mee by land, which I expect every moment, and soe I hope your worshipp will not be angry with mee, but as for the place if you please to send goods itt is more secure, for the people that belong to itt now can defend againe ten thousand that shall oppose them, for itt is naterally strong, and but two waies to come to the towne and but two a breast att most and three or four gates each way before you gett in, soe I hope your worshipp will send goods to Sanya. Your two hand canoe came here Fryday about 3 of the clock but itt was broke. I beleeve they gott to Accra this last night about midnight.

[PS] Just now people are come for mee. I would have sent your worshipp a canoe this night from Sanya but mett with this oppertunity.

---

[10] As Bosman later noted, Angona had been ruled by a Queen 'for some time past' (1705, 63).

VII

JAMES FORT, ACCRA

James Fort, Accra, was the easternmost of the RAC's Gold Coast establishments; a factory here had been established by 1674, and was raised to the status of a fort in 1679.[1] There was also a Dutch fort (Fort Crevecour) and a Danish fort (Christiansborg) in Accra. The latter had fallen into Portuguese hands in 1680;[2] however, as is reported in this correspondence (no.448), the Portuguese abandoned the fort to the Danes again in 1683. Accra was important for trade in both gold and slaves.

Accra had been conquered by the hinterland power of Akwamu ('Quomboe', 'Comboe' in these documents) in 1680.[3] The king of Akwamu, Ansa Sasraku ('Ahenesa', 'Ahenesah') figures prominently in these letters. Early in 1681, there were apprehensions that Ansa might launch a further attack on Accra, including the European forts there (nos 405–6). But in the end, the English fort negotiated an agreement with him (no.409). The Accra correspondence provides important information on Ansa's continuing conquests thereafter, including a war against Akyem ('Achim', 'Akim') early in 1682 (nos 423, 425); the conquest of Tafo ('Taffo') in the interior in 1682 (no.425); a victory against Kwaman ('Coma', 'Commong') in 1682 (nos 431, 435); and campaigns against the Adangme ('Allampo'), east of Accra, in both 1682 (no.431) and 1683 (nos 451–2).

The hinterland merchants who had previously traded to Accra are named as the Akani ('Arcanies') and the Akyems ('Ackims') (nos 425, 458). However, it is made clear in this correspondence that the Akwamu conquest had had the effect of cutting off these hinterland traders from free access to the coast, King Ansa seeking to interpose himself as a monopolizing middleman, to the great detriment of the trade.

---

389. Arthur Wendover   James Fort, Accra, 27 Jan. 1680/1

Understanding that your Honour hath brought over sundrey neccesarys, fitting and

---

[1] Davies 1957, 224, 246.

[2] Cf. Nørregård 1966, 45–6; Vogt 1979, 203–4; also Barbot 1992, ii, 433–4; Groeben 1985, 55.

[3] Daaku 1970, 154–5; also Barbot 1992, ii, 430–1. For the rise of Akwamu power in this period, see also Wilks 1959.

useful for the factory, vid: as beef, porke, pease, flower, beere, etc. I desire that if your Honour would dispose of any of them that I may have a sheare with otheres. I had before this advised your Honour of my wants in this particular, but it hath pleased God to visit me with this cuntry distemper, which is lingring, soe I hope your Honours goodness will parden a man just risen as it were from the grave.

Itt is very needfull that I should give you to understand the greate neccessity that there is of the goods following, which hath often been sent for, but never cold receive any, nor noe or satisfaction or ahnswer of late to what I have write.

The goods most wanted att present are vid.
course sletias a many as cann bee spared
sheets if any to bee had but good
allijars ditto
long cloths 3, 4, or 5 bails and more

[PS]   2 punctions[4] of beef with the pease[?]
1 of pork
1 caske of flower
and 1 of beer with the pried[?]
an anker of vinegar
1 caske of palme oyle

390.   Arthur Wendover   James Fort, Accra, 10 Feb. 1680/1

Your Honours of primo February came to my hands on Sunday last the 6 instant, and according to your orders I have made up all my accounts to January the 29 last past with the account of all whites men, Negroes slaves and allso negroes freemen, as in the schedule doth appeare.

[PS] I hope your Honour hath perused my last as to the want of goods in this factory of all sorts, but espetially course sletias, which if not supplyed speedyly may prove very prejuditiall. Fine sletias, sheets, allejars, carpetts, blankets, long cloths etc. have been ofteen write for but could not get any answere.

[PS] This cannoe I send on purpose will cost 8 oz 8a.

391.   Arthur Wendover   James Fort, Accra, 20 Feb. 1680/1

Both your Honourrs I received from Captain Low, Comander of the Marchant Boonadventure, one being dated the 7 and the other the 8, the former of which being an order for the delivering of 33¾ cask of coureyes [= cowries] and that of the 8 to

---

[4] puncheons, i.e. barrels.

receive from on board him one hogghead of beef and alsoe one ankor of vinegar, which I had.

What booges were remaining in January account last past I deliver'd, which were 5,091 pound as per stilliards, for we were forced to weigh them all, the cask being soe brooken, and alsoe per his request did lett him have 8 verry good slaves vid: 2 men and 6 woemen as per his reicept, and soe dispatched him Satterday the 12 instant too his great contentment, as I hope he may sattisfy your Honour per his 1st from Arder.

In obedience to your order and Counsells I shall bee verry dilligent in apprehending such persons as are interloopers and readily send them to Cape Corso per the first oppertunity.

And alsoe in my answer to your last per Mr Franckland shall give your Honour the sattisfaction required as to the slaves Captain Robert Norsworthy carryed away unpaid for in March last [16]79/80, which was a most unchristianly action and never will be forgot by the natives of this place, and lickwise the accompt of what goods doth not belong to the Royall Company.

392. Arthur Wendover   James Fort, Accra, 20 Feb. 16801/1

Your Honours of the 12 from Mr Frances Franckland I received, with whom came one Mr John Wender [as] second, and accordinge too orders [I] did order Mr John Kyte to give him all the assistance possibly, I then being not able of myselfe to performe your Honours commands by reason of an extream vomitting and loseness which had ceised mee that day and continued untill evening, butt notwithstanding nothing was neglected and ere this your Honour hath sattisfaction from Mr Franckland, with whome came Mr John Kyte according to your orders.

The slaves that were taken unpaid and putt on board Captain John Woodfine per Captain Robert Norsworthy were 12 men, 27 woemen, 4 boyes and 7 girles, alsoe about 17 or 18 other pritty chilldren not looked upon or any notice in the least taken of them. These I am certaine of and did enter them, they were 50 persons besides the 17 chilldren, which in all will make 67.

Goods not belonging to the Royall Company are
10 pieces tapseells
20 pieces nicconees
450 iron barrs

Mr Maccabeus Hollis   } both
Mr Edwardd Penn   } deceased

I thank God I am gott on my legg againe and att present in indifferent good health.

393. Arthur Wendover   James Fort, Accra, 14 March 1680/1

Your Honours of the 26 of the last month was per Mr John Kyte, which came safe
to my hand, and I returne your Honour many thankes for your good wish of my
health, which I thank God att present is indifferent. As for them slaves delivered
Captain Lowe as per his receipt [it] was to help make up his complement, by reason
I had sould 1720 lbs weight of booges before your Honours letter came to my
hands, as per January accompt, which were for 33¾ caske of booges, them 8 slaves
amounting to 504 pounds, soe that there are still wanting to compleat your orderes
1216 pound, an accompt of which he promised to give your Honour per his first
from Ardoe.

I have accordinge to your orders made William Pew Sarjant, and Nicolas
Battrell intends for England per the first opperunitye. There shall nouthing be
wantinge of my endeavours to procure slaves for Captain Bowler.

The goods not belonging to the Royall Company shall be sold as fast as
possible.

Your last was of the 2nd instant per Mr Franckland, from whome I received
one of the 28 of February being ane order for Mr James Nightingale to reiceive 200
bralls and 20 white long cloths to be shippt on board Captain Bowler.

And in answewer to them I have sent to him at Wyamba 20 white long cloths
and lickwise what bralls were remaining, which were 120[5] as my February accompt
will manifest, which your Honour will reeceive from the bearer Richard Griffith,
the Company apprentice, with whome comes one Anthony Meadows [a] maison, a
refractory person who threatens that upon a misdemeanor tis but runing to the
Portugueze forte. Here are some otheres, but for them I shall not trouble your
Honour with untill the time comes that I shall have the happiness of kissing your
hand, which shall not be long.

I have marked your prices of provisions and desier that I shall have a supply
of them according to my noat of perticulars.

[PS] By February accompt your Honour will find thee great want that here are of
goods, for what were vendable are all gone, as course sletias, bralls, Ginny clouts
and alsoe long cloths, soe that what remaines will not maintaine the factory without a supply, for the whole dependance that we have relyes uppon iron and
tappseels, which sell but sloly. If there be any goods that can be spared for God sake
lett us have them, as sayes, perpetuanoes blews [and] greens, bralls, carpetts,
blanketts, pewter baisons, allijars, sletias course or fine, sheets, or any sorts of
linnens, as long cloths good ones.

---

[5] Cf. nos 575–6. Nightingale was on board Bowler's ship (the *Edgar*), but later (cf. no.396) came to take
over command of the Accra fort.

394.   Arthur Wendover   James Fort, Accra, 29 March 1681

Your Honours of the 5th instant I have received, and understand I made noe mention, in mine of the 20 of February as concerning the powder belonging to Agent
Bradley, which is 11 barrells and one halfe, but of the other tonn which my account
per Mr Frankland makes mention of I doe not know to whome they belong, but I
suppose they are the Companys and ought soe to be charged.

I have alsoe received one of the 19 instant with one for Mr James Nightingale,
who is at Alampa, wherein your honour orders what gold is remaining in my hands,
to be sent home per Captain Bowler to bee consigned to the Companys factors
Edwin Steed and Stephen Gascoyne Esquires at Barbadoes,[6] which shall be done,
but then the people must remaine unpaid for a considerable time, by reason of the
great want wee have of goods, the whole dependenace being only in tapseels and
iron barrs, which are very dull comoditys in this place.

As for your canoe that came with Mr Wender, it was as cheape as possible I
can gitt one here, but he told me that he would be at the charge himself; and alsoe
the medecines for the forts use cost (bona fides) 5 ounces on board Captain Bell,
and had I not had them I myself or others might have perrished, but I have charged
but 3 oz and there is enough for two 12 months.

Mr Kyte was gone from hence before your last came to my hands, with the
New England man, Captain Bowler refusing to carry him unless he would deposite
6 pees, which he was not able to doe.[7]

This canoe which is the bearer one [= on] Saterday last came from Alampa,
per order of Mr James Nightingale, with 5 peices of sayes and 24 blew pottkeys,
they being for Gallanca at Wyamba.[8] Coming ashore at the Dutch landing per the
Accra people [they] were all paniard, but upon what account wee know not. Wee
sent to them to know the reason, a base daring answer was returned, that we should
provide ourselves with watter and doe our worst. Imediatly wee sent two shott into
the towne, and left of firing, it being night; all Sunday wee fought them, and killed
one man and wounded some others, and likewise part of Monday, the Quamboo
people being very helpful, for as God would have it they ware downe, but at last
wee forced them to bring in all to our great contentment.

The time we were ingaged, wee ware forced to send the 5 hand canoe to the
Portuguize for watter, for want of that necessary in this factory by reason our tank
is not finished, the want of which wee desire may be seriously considered of, for
these base rascalls will alwayes be doing one mischeife or other, they knowing the
want wee have of watter, our dayly send 8 miles for every drop wee drink; also [we
need] some shott and match.

---

[6] The RAC's agents on Barbados.
[7] Cf. no.583.
[8] Cf. no.579.

395.   Arthur Wendover to James Nightingale   James Fort, Accra, 25 April 1681

Yours at 4 this morning came safe, your boye from Wyamba is heere with a letter for you, who hath informed me of the loss of the 15 hand canoe, 3 white men and what other lost I cannot tell as yett.[9] Heere are noe slaves, but what you left are still remaining.

396.   James Nightingale   James Fort, Accra, 25 May 1681

Your Honours and Councells much estemed dated the 25th instant came safe to my hands, wherein I perceeve your Honour and Councells order to take in my possession the fort and merchandise and all other goods belonging to Mr Wendover or any parson else into my charge.

Where upon imediately comeing from on bord Captain Bowler after haveing dispatched him, [I] called up every man, to be understood both Blacks and whits, belonging to the Royal African Company of England and read before [them] your Honour and Councells order. They all tould mee they would observe it and they acknowledged mee to be their Cheif tell further order from your Honour and Councell, where upon wee hysed up the flagge, fiered 5 guns and drank your Honour and Councells good health.

Your Honour and Councell will find per this inclosed invoice what goods are in the Castle belonging to the Royall African Company and other persons, but I doe ashure your Honour and Councell that I cannot find out those perticular to whome th[e]y belong, I have examined every person in the fort.

I give your Honour and Councell most humble and hearty thanks that you have bine pleased to intrust me with this charge. Your Honour and Councll may rest assured that neither Dutch, Portugues or Blacks shall take any advantage of us, I will give noe afront nor take any, and as for the trade will doe my uytmoost indeavor for the profitt and creditt of your Honour and Counsell.

The Docter Samuell Stone shall have command according your Honours order both for lodging and dyett.

Just now the Blacks hearing I was hear came with some gould for our goods. I ordered Mr Frankland to take itt to avoid all suspition. By the blessing of God Almighty I hope toe procure a trade here again.

Ahenessa sent to me this day and desired a good correspondence. His people be about 50 in number. They also tould mee the Dutch Copeman Van der Lypfe[10] hinder them from comeing to our fort for trading, not onely that, but orders his Blacks being a great number to stale our hodges [= hogs], sheep or what they can lay their hands upon. Nay he is soe convident that he rights to Mr Sheers at Alampo

---

[9] Cf. no.582.
[10] Sebastiaan van der Liffe, chief of the Dutch fort at Accra.

that some white men of our fort, nay the Copeman himself shall suffer the death of a certain person which was killed. I have his own letter.

My small opinion is that you right to his master the Gennerall of the Minna of his unhandsome action, to prevent for the future.

[PS] I also send your honour an account signed by Mr Hollings and my selfe of the goods wee had from Cape Cors. In the remains you will find wanting 2 pieces of sayes, 4 perpetiaens, 25 pieces tapseels and 45 pottkeys, which aforesaid goods has since the aforesaid account was signed, since I bought slaves at Wimba, deduktes 3 months canky mony for 7 canoe men [and] my owne dyett, as I shall give your Honour an account per the next. I had a great deal of trouble with Bowler. Pray take it not unkindly that I doe it not now.

[PS] Here being noe brandy in the Castle, desire your Honour to send a hogshead. Whatt wee had here was put on bord of Captain Bowler according order.

397. Francis Franckland   James Fort, Accra, 25 May 1681

Yours under 12 instant I have received and am sorry that you should beleeve I should be concern'd with Mr Wendover in acting anything contrary to the interest of our masters the Royall Affrican Company. What I know touching Mr Wendover is as followeth, and the reason of my not acquainting you with it sooner was the want of an oppertunity and I thought it not worth while to send a canoe on purpose. Mr Wendover did sell unto Captain Mathews 4 woemen slaves for sayes [and] perpetuanoes, and did also buy more for gold, the woemen was the same you take notice of was denied Captain Bowler and I must doe Mr Wendover the justice to say they were not denyed by him but mee (he being at that time very sick) and I will if required take my oath that at that time they were not slaves but pawnes, as was then told to Captain Bowler, and that when Ahenesa sent downe his son to sell them he also sent that Mr Wendover should send them a board the first ship, and if hee refused to take them away and sell them to the Dutch or Portuguese. Captain Mathews being then in the roade, Ahenesas son would have them sent a board before he went.

As to Mr Wendovers sending a letter to Captain Mathews at Mingo,[11] hee to my knowledge never did, and for helping him to the slaves out of the Portuguese he nor I knew nothing of nor was concern'd in any way with the buying or selling them. Mr Wendover did further buy out of Captain Mathews 2 great guns for the defence of the fort, because the Accras dayley play the rogue with us, and there being never a gun in the fort that will carry far enough to command them. Hee also bought out of the New England man (whoe was in the roade when wee fought the Accraers and without whose helpe wee could not have got water) some pork and

---

[11] sic: more correctly Ningo, i.e. Nungoa, on the coast east of Accra.

pease. As to what you take notice of concerning the powder that was hiding in the souldiers roomes when I tooke an account of the goods att this place, that was noe fault of mine, for I went as far as my orders gave me leave and gave an exact account of what I found, and had any one told mee of them I should have put them in my account with the rest.

398.   Francis Franckland   James Fort, Accra, 25 May 1681

Yours under 19th and 21st instant have received and am sorry for Mr Wendovers sake that soe ill a business should happen. I acquainted the Agent in my letter to him per Mr Wendover of what I knew touching the slaves etc., as also the reason of my not writting of it sooner, which I hope will satisfie him, for I doe assure you it is true and that for the future I will never be guilty of the like, for if noe opportunity presents I will send a canoe on purpose. I cannot be so large to you as I would, being much importuned by Mr Nightingale (nay commanded) to goe aboard an interloper now in the roade, aboard whom he hath bought severall things, as a watch, wine, beare etc. of one Mr Harvey and one Mr Edlin. I doe beleeve he hath noe good meaning to mee in being soe earnest to have mee goe a board, whether itt be to informe the Agent of it or to make mee as culpable as himself I know not, but be it how it will I care not, for shall by you give the Agent an acount of it, being the best way to keepe pease and quietness here, and therefore I desire if you think convenient to show the Agent this and hee may act as hee sees cause.

I take notice what you writt touching Captain Phipps and Mr Stone (who is safe arrived here) and shall doe what lies in my power to serve the Captain.

[PS] Here inclosed I have sent you Mr Nightingales note which hee would have had mee carry aboard, but with much adoe I excused it by writting a note by his command which you have also inclosed, and I can prove that I was commanded to doe itt by him. I beleeve in a day or twos time I shall trouble you with another by a canoe on purpose, for Mr Harvey is now ashoare by his invitation, though att the Dutch fort, and hee hath been with him att the Portuguese fort and commanded mee to stay with him at the Dutch fort and in the mean time would have sent away the canoe had not the canoemen accidentally staid till I come.

[inclosure 1]
James Nightingale [to Mr Harvey]   James Fort, Accra, 25 May 1681
The bearer hereof is Mr Francis Franckland, the Companies factor. I desire you to be pleased to send mee some sack ashoare, alsoe a cask of beere, and what you it cost will send payment.

[inclosure 2]
Francis Franckland to Mr Harvey   James Fort, Accra, 26 May 1681
Mr Nightingale desires you to send him by the bearer 12 bottles of sack, 2 ankors

of brandy, 1 halfe houre glass, one barrill of beare, some cavieare, anchoveys, olives, and capers, and oynions, and if you please to come ashoare at the Dutch fort hee will meet you there and be very glad to see you there. The bearer will pay you for the things above mentioned.

399.　Francis Franckland　　　　　　　　James Fort, Accra, 6 June 1681

Yours under the 31 May past received per Mr Wendover, and take notice what you write as to shewing my letter to the Agent, for which and all other kindnesses I give you many hearty thanks. I received a letter from the Agent per said Mr Wendover and desire you to doe mee the kindness to give my hearty thanks for his kindness and asshure him that for the future I will not be guiltie of the like misdemeanor and shall be shure to observe his command in all things, and also further acquaint him that I made a further inquiry after what I write you in my last touching the bearer hereof Mr Nightingalle, and that I find that hee gave for a watch to Mr Harvey 1 man slave and to one Turner, a Dutch interloper, a boy for a caske of wine. He also told mee that hee gave for women slaves at Allampo 4 tapsells, 1 sheet, which is good [for] 1 bendie, 1 angle and a halfe, for a tapsell is never sold under 6 angles at Allampa, and at the same time the Dutch bought for 5 pease. There was also the other day in the roade one Doegood, an interloper, who sent his mate ashoare to him to know what hee wanted. He treated the mate very civilly and sent the docter off with him to buy a quarter cask of wine, which he did. I should have writ this to the Agent himselfe had I had another conveyance, but he carrying it himselfe [I] fear'd least he should suspect the truth and not deliver it. Pray give my service to Mr Spurvay, Mr Stapleton Captain Phipps and the rest of the Gentlemen with you and tell Captain Phipps I will write to him per Mr Wendover, and answer his desire.

[PS] I have sent you by the bearer a boy. He is not so handsome as I could wish he were but is the best I could gett, therefor hope you will accept the will for the deede.

400.　Francis Franckland　　　　　　　　James Fort, Accra, 8 July 1681

Your worshipp and Councells letter under the 2nd instant received per Mr Pley, and give you my hearty thanks for your kindness in makeing mee chiefe of this place and doe asshure you I will take all the care imaginable to advance the interest of the Royall Company my masters, and doe not question (if can gett goods) but to take as much gold as any factory upon the coast. I take notice of what your worshipp writes touching Mr Pleys being second etc. and shall observe your orders in every particular. I shall also take care to use my endeavour to regaine the affection of the blacks in this place (who I can asshure you are a company of great rogues from whome comes noe trade, and whosoever lives here must keepe them in feare of himself or elce hee must keepe nothing here) but more especially of Ahenesa (from whome all the trade comes), who I intend to goe see, as soone as Mr Wendover is well to goe up with mee, whoe hath been extreamly ill of a voiolent feavour in soe much that wee looked every day for his death but praised be God he is something better, when he is in a condition shall observe your order to send him up, Ahenesa haveing sent severall times for he that was made Chiefe, and for Mr Wendover. Here inclosed I send your worshipp an account of what goods remained in my warehouse when Mr Wendover was made incapable of his imployment, also what slaves etc. belongs to the fort, with last months account, which you will find to be very small (the Quomboers not comeing downe), and your worshipp will find by the account of goods what goods was received from aboard Captain Bowler, also what slaves delivered said Captain. (I have seen a great many goods come out of shipps but doe asshure your worshipp never see any come out in such a condition, being most of them spoyl'd by carelessness.) In my account I have given the Company creditt for the goods etc. received from aboard Captain Bramfill (but know noe price of the provisions) and shall in my next give them creditt for the corne received from the 15 hand canoe, haveing scarce enough corne in the castle to last 4 dayes. Before she came I had sent a 5 hand canoe to Wyamba to fetch corne but there was none to be had.

I have according to your order sent what damnified goods is in the warehouse, but for the potkeys they are all sold, and had I more could have sold them. The price of them I knew not onely as Mr Nightingale told mee that I should sell them at an angle per peece, but you will find by my account I have got more for them. When Mr Wendover is in a condition shall observe your worshipps order about his goods, an account of which you receive with the rest. I writt your worshipp about 5 dayes since per a 2 hand canoe on purpose for to acquaint you in what distress wee were in for corne, but the canoe was unfortunately cast away. The men saved their lives and got to Wyamba where they got another canoe, but the weather proving very bad was forc't to put in at Momford neare Dague [var. Tague],[12] where they panyard the men and kept them severall dayes, but at last they sent one of them downe to tell mee that except I sent them 10a I should not have the man againe. I sent the mony by the 5 hand canoe when she went to Wyamba to corne and sent for the man but could heare nothing of him, he was one of the pawnes of the fort. If any canoe comes from your worshipp they had best have a care of touching there for they will serve them in the same manner. I doe not question but in a few dayes to have some of them in the fort, and if have will make them pay severly.

[PS] I have sent per this conveyance 25 long cloths damnified and 2 tapsells.

---

[12] i.e. Lague (Lagu).

401.   Francis Franckland   James Fort, Accra, 9 July 1681

I have received your worshipps under the 4 instant and returne your worshipp my most humble and hearty thanks for your severall kindnesses, but more especially for the last, and doe asshure your worshipp that I will take all care possible to shew you my gratefullness by doeing nothing that may be against the Royall Company interest, that thereby you shall see that what formerly was guiltie of I am very sorry for, but one thing I humbly beg of your worship (which I am confident your goodness will not denie) that is what reports soever you have of me, that you would be pleased to judge favourablely of me till I can come to justify myselfe, for your worship will perceive by the inclosed note there is one that endeavours to doe mee all the diskindness he can, by faire promises to them that will impeach mee though falsly. I am hearty sorry that I should give your worship the trouble of a second time remembring me of the money I had att Cape Corsoe, but doe asshure your worship I sent per Mr Wendover when he was last with you, but his troubles made him forget to give it you. I have sent it per Peter the canoeman, as also a hee and shee goate with a black boy which I would beg of your worship to accept. The boy is the best I can gett at present, when goe up to Ahenesa shall endeavour to gett you another.

    This fort is very much out of repair, one flanker being falen in and two more is proped up, and also severall things wanting which is too long to give an account in writting per this conveyance. If I thought your worship would not take it ill I would come up to Cape Corsoe and acquaint your worship in what a condition the place is in per word of mouth, and also acquaint your worship which way it might be made good at a small charge, to last for severall years whereas now it is repairing every day. If your worship think convenient of my comeing up I can come in the canoe with Mr Wendover.

[PS] One thing I had almost forgot to acquaint your worship with, that is when Mr Nightingalle was here cheife that he ordered me to give the Docter 2o 2a -ta to goe aboard Doogood to buy wine, which I could not denie. I would not charge itt in the Company account without your worships leave but hope your worship will not let me loose itt, itt not being in my power to withstand his order.

[Inclosure]
Samuel Stone   James Fort, Accra, 10 July 1681
Mr Nightingale did desire mee that I would say that Mr Franckland was in as much fault as Mr Wendover, and did desire that I would aske and inquire of John Clarke of all the transactions in itt, [he] being an acquaintance of mine formerly, that hee would tell mee and that I should send to him about itt, for hee did not question but hee should be chiefe here and it should be the better for me. I do know nothing of this concerning Mr Franckland with Mr Wendover in the least.[13]

[13] Stone later retracted this statement: cf. no.410.

402.   William Pley   14 July 1681

Haveing received a letter per the Dutch canoe from Captain Bramfill from Allampo, and not knowing what importance the contence might be (Mr Franckland being gon up to Comboe to Ahenesa, being sent for by one of his sons), I humbly thought itt my duty to dispatch a canoe with itt, not doubting of your worships approbation therein. Mr Franckland hath not yett overhal'd the warehouse since my arrivall here, but hath promised to doe itt when hee returnes, however just at his departure hee left me the key of the warehouse, which I was forst to take, there being none elce to doe it, hopeing Mr Franckland will prove as honest to mee in that respect, as I will be always true and faithfull to my charge, and the Company and your worships interest. Hee likwise tells mee he hath noe gold chest (only a small trunk), soe that I can have noe key to that corespondent to your worships and Councells order. As Mr Wendover hath for some time past been almost at the point of death but is now much better, yet so extreame weake that Mr Franckland durst not venture on the consideration to send him up to Cape Corsoe as yet. When Captain Rickards comes downe here, I will use my utmost endeavour with the boatswayne, and others, to heare of Mr Spurvays brandy, and will send an attestation (witnessed) about itt.

403.   William Pley   James Fort, Accra, 18 July 1681

Your worships packett to Mr Franckland arrived here yesterday morning by the 2 hand canoe, and at his returne from Quomboe (which wee hourly expect) shall be delivered him, in whose absence I take the greatest care possible of the forts wellfare, he having three whitemen with him. I wrote your worship Fryday last, to which I shall refer.

404.   William Pley   James Fort, Accra, 13 Aug. 1681

Understanding by a canoe which came to this place from Cape Corsoe the indisposition of Mr Franckland, I humbly presume to trouble your worshipp with this letter, in which I have sent a true list of the goods that were in the warehouse when overhall'd by Mr Franckland at his departure (fearing through sickness hee may omitt itt). For the muskets, powder etc. I have as yet noe account of them, neither have I as yet (nor I beleeve I shall not) sell any till Mr Francklands returne, for till then wee shall have noe trade with the Quomboers (on whome almost our whole trade depends), of which I suppose your worshipp understands the reason ere this. I should make itt my business to be exact carefull and honest in the account expected from mee since Mr Francklands departure, which (the promises[?] considered and the great want of vendable goods) your worshipp cannot expect very considerable. However I am resolv'd my care both in that particular [and] the forts wellfare, and all my other actions shall declare how great my resentment is of the infinit favours your worshipp hath been pleas'd to heap on me. Wee have had very sickly season here since Mr Francklands departure, the Docter and most of the men in the fort have been very ill, but I bless God all upon their leggs againe except one (John Clarke) of whose recovery we dispaire, and hourly expect his death by the flux. The Accraers att the Dutch Towne and the Dutch themselves (whoe are it seems threatned too) expect Ahenesas comeing upon them, the blacks lying in the Dutch fort, and makeing great fiers in the night. Whether this may be a falce allarme or not wee are ignorant, and though wee are assured from all hands, that Ahenesa hath noe thoughts (but of amity) concerning this fort, yet I humbly hope our utmost care, both in good watching and putting our selves in the best posture of defence we can, will not be amiss.

405. Samuell Stone   [James Fort, Accra], 17 Aug. 1681

I presume to send this canoe to acquaint your worshipp that Mr Pley is taken dangerous sick of a feavour and a voiolent vomiting, which I thought to acquaint your worshipp of itt, this being the 3rd day of his sickness. I would desire the Docter might send mee these medicines that I shall write him for by this canoe. I would desire your worshipp might dispatch the canoe with all speede. The reason of my wanting medicines is wee have had all the men in the castle sick with myselfe alsoe, but now praised be God wee are all in pretty good health againe except Mr Pley. This day wee have buried one John Clarke who dyed of a voiolent feavour.

406. James Nightingale & George Phipps   James Fort, Accra, 27 Aug. 1681

This is to give your honour an account of our arrivall here being the 18th instant, where wee found Mr Pley and most of our whitemen very sick. The first wee undertooke was with all speed to gett the fort in good order. We have mended both our flankers [and] gott in the fort wood, water and stones. Afterward being the 21 instant wee send a person to Ahenesa to know his demands against Mr Wendover, and if ditto Ahenesa send his son Boebie or any other person here to make his pallavora should by us come and goe free back againe, but as yett wee received noe answer. Here is a generall report by both Dutch and the Governour of the Por- tugueese that Ahenesa has divided his army in 3 parts and intends in person with his party for our forte, the two other generalls the one for the Dutch the other for the Portuguese. Wee will doe our indeavour if they come, if not will if itt is possible to put by all differance to procure a trade againe, but we doe assure your honour itt will not be easily done, for this factory has been abominably abused by our Com- pany servants, as your honour will assurly find. Your honour will be pleased to send us for the use of the fort one hogshead brandy [and] some beefe, wee have not a dram of brandy in the fort and drink nothing but stinking water. I send your honour the accounts of remaines found here. Pray send the canoe with all speede back againe. Our canoemen are all quartered on the foure flankers.

407.   James Nightingale   James Fort, Accra, 27 Aug. 1681

This onely to give you an account as that Mr Wendover demands from Ahenesa 9m 7o 5a, soe that I beleeve his beloved girl will balance the accounts,[14] for I heare Ahenesa demands 40 bendys. This factory has been abominably abused, and further I can assure your honour itt will be not a little trouble to resettle it againe. Ahenesa is our enemy on the one side and the Accra people on the other. Your honour will find likewise per the account of remaines that Mr Franckland has sold a great deale of goods, with what hee received of Captain Bramfill, but here is noe gold in cash only 2 or 3 ounces.

Mr Wendover demands from Ahenesa, March 16 1679/80

	m	o	a
100 musketts[15]	2	4	–
7½ barrells powder att 4 ounces p.	3	6	–
40 musketts more	1	–	–
to sundry accounts of Mr Wendover	2	2	–
to Dabo	–	3	4
Comes in all	9	7	4

I will doe my endeavour to reconcile differance, to be understood as far as itt is for the profitt and creditt of our masters the Royall Company. Wee doe expect news from Ahenesa every houre. When I know his demands and wee come to a pallavora, shall per the 2 hand canoe give your honour an account. I am very lame and one of my feet allmost spoyl'd with thee journy to Barracoe.[16] Your honour be pleased to assist us what you can, for ther is here nothing to be gott, onely stinking durty water. Wee all expect Ahenesa with his armye every houre but wee keepe a good watch with our whitmen, slaves and canoemen.

408.   William Pley   James Fort, Accra, 8 Sept. 1681

I bless God I have overcome a desperate and dangerous feavour (under which I hav a long time linguished) soe far as I am againe uppon my leggs, though soe weake I am scarce able to stand.

---

[14] Presumably an allusion to 'Boque', one of Ansa's wives held as pawn in the English fort, with whom Wendover had had sexual relations (cf. nos 409, 414).

[15] Ansa had borrowed 100 muskets and 14 barrels of gunpowder from the English fort in 1680: Daaku 1970, 154.

[16] Beraku, west of Accra: probably not Senya Beraku, which is referred to elsewhere in this correspondence (nos 385, 388) as 'Sanya'; but perhaps 'Little' Beraku, further east (cf. Barbot 1992, ii, 426).

Though Mr Frankland is dead yet must needs complaine of a very grosse abuse he has put on mee in two or three particulars of the invoice of goods he gave mee at his departure, for haveing severall times desireing him to overhall the warehouse hee still put mee off till the very instant of his departure to Capo Corsoe, and then he went into the warehouse with a penn and ink, and in an hurry, would not suffer mee to overhall all the goods, especially the pottkeys, but made mee sett them downe as hee dictated, and hee being my supperiour I could not helpp itt, but hee protested the truth of itt. I confess I was much dissatisfied, but was induct to beleeve him, not knowing his actions then as I have heard since, for which I am sorry. I feared the pottkeys at first, because hee made and gave soe many of them away, soe that upon the tale of them since I find 24 less then hee assured mee there was. That this is true I call the God of truth to witness and I hope your Worshipp will beleeve mee, for in the presence of God I wish I may forfeit my eternall happyness if any goods hath gone out of the warehouse more than my enclosed account makes out since Mr Franklands departure. I must confess the thoughts of being so overcatcht by one I thought my friend, was a great trouble to mee in my sickness, but God that knowes the secreets of my soule knows my inocence too, and I hope your worshipp will not suffer mee to come to any damage where I am guiltless, through the unequall dealings of my superiour, since I never yett did wrong to any man, but will still make itt my great endeavour to answer your worshipps goodness to mee, in my dilligence and fidellity as long as I live. Another mistake he made was, hee gave me an account but of 10 Guynie clouts, when (under other goods) there was 82. And in his account 19 paper brawles, when there was but 7½. This is the errors and God knows (and others here) occationed by Mr Frankland, the rest is right, onlely divers goods cutt by him for cloaths etc. Besides of the 39 peeces of tapsele 3 (that were on the shelfe, and reckoned to mee) were owned, and prooved, to be due to a black for cows Mr Frankland had bought and delivered per order since Mr Nightingalls arrivall. I was sent hither by your worshipp in a time of very intricate and clandestine dealeings (as appears since), though I was kept ignorant, and I thank God inocent of all, but I hope for the future wee shall have noe more such base transactions here, which wee'll use all imaginable care to prevent. Enclosed is my account since Mr Frankland departure, and Mr Nightigalls receipt for the money what goods were sold while Mr Frankland was there. I constantly gave him the money, as I received itt, and hee tooke an account of the goods delivered (as I suppose Mr Wendover can informe your worshpp) and told mee hee would make itt up in his account. If hee hath not done it and your worshipp require itt I can doe it out of my booke. Two slaves bought by Mr Frankland hath died in his absence.

I most humbly begg your worshipps pardone for my tediousness and bad writting, which is occasioned by my sickness, and doe most humbly and heartyly thank your worshipp for your great goodness to mee.

[PS] I doe assure your honour all this above I have heard reported by severall to be true.

James Nightingale

409. James Nightingale   James Fort, Accra, undated [Sept. 1681]

Your Honours much esteemed dated the 25th August and the other the 31st ditto have received, wherein I was very sorry to heare the death of my friend Mr Frankland, and since your Honour and Councill have been pleased to make mee Chiefe of this fort, wherefore I give your Honour and Councill most humble and hearty thanks, worthy Gentlemen you may rest assured that I shall doe the utmost of my endeavour to procure a trade againe, but itt can not be done without trouble and some small charges, wherein I will be as spaireing as possible I can, and as for my accounts your Honour will find them at all times to agree with the warehouse, for I doe not intend to trust the blacks nor run out the Company's goods or trade with interlopers.

Captain George Phipps and I have according to order sold Mr Franklands goods at publique outcry, as per account will appeare, wee have found noe money then 5a in gold in his chest or elcewhere. What provisions out of Captain Bramfild I found here, according the account shall give the Company creditt. Docter Stone I have displac't according to order and have paid him 4 months pay at 9a 1ta per month

Mr Wendover hath with mee and Captain Phipps overhall'd the warehouse two times, wherein wee found no more goods as have given your Honour account the 27th August last, only 60 iron barrs more belonging to Mr Frankland, whereof 10 is paid for the debts he owes as per ballance of account will appeare. Mr Wendover will give your Honour an account of all actions and transactions, alsoe the account of the wanting of goods which comes to M 12.5 gold, besides provisions.

In answer of 31 August: Wee were informed Ahenesa would be downe with us with 3 armies, but wee hope it is but a lying report, however if it be or not wee are provided for them as much as possible wee can. I have received 59 gallons of brandy and shall give the Company creditt.

Mr Wendover hath had all the freedome imaginable to make up his pallavora with Ahenesa, as will appeare.

I send your Honour an inventory of Mr Franklands goods, which [we] found here, the account at what rates they were sold att, the account of paying the garrison 2 months pay beginning the 22nd July and ending the 16 September, an inventory of Mr Wendovers goods and chattles, and the pallavora with Ahenesa of our proceedings.

Goods wanting here: sheets, brawles, carpetts, and blanketts of all sorts, perpettuanes, tapsells, allejars, ginghams, pewter juggs, longees, red ground pintadoes, yellow beads, brandy, some bright musketts and good powder, for almost here is much damnified, fine and course sletias, cowryes, and longcloath. Pray let Captain Phipps send mee my goods in the 5 hand canoe, for I want them. My desire is that your Honour and Councill will be pleased to send mee the rates and prizes of the disposall of the Company's goods in this place, that soe I may follow order, also if I shall give the Company creditt for the goods found here per remaynes in my booke or any other persons, the quantity and quallity, for the account is strangely to mee, therefore expect order. Your honour will be pleased to send a booke to keep my accounts in, some wax and paper. I desire your Honour to be pleased to lett mee have for a time James Mills, I being not able to come downe staires for lameness in my foot, and Mr Pley not yet well, have noe body to looke after the Companys concernes. Pray do not faile to give Ahenesa a gift, to be understood firelocks and spirrits, alsoe send some good powder and bright musketts. Ahenesa desires the same, in soe doeing wee may procure a traid and to hinder our neighbours. Now is the time according to my small oppinion. At the months end shall give my accounts, soe haveing noe more att present onely referr the remainder to Captain Phipps.

[PS] Mr Wendover nor Mr Frankland has paid Ahenesa monthly this 10 months.

[inclosure]
Nota
August 21st 1681
Wee sent up to Ahenesa Ba: Conton a black with these following orders:
1st to desire Ahenesa to send his sonn Bobie or any other to know his demands against Mr Wendover as soone as possible hee could.
2ndly That whome Ahenesa should send to our fort should goe free back againe.

28th ditto
Ahenesa sent to us 3 of his men with a message that the person wee sent to him the 21st was there safely arrived, but would not send his sonn Bobie or any other person to make a pallavora with us before wee tooke our oath upon the Bible and James Mills [took his oath on] their fittish that whome Ahenesa should send, should by us goe free back againe, where uppon Captain George Phipps and I tooke our oath upon the Bible, and James Mills their fettish, as aforesaid, all to regaine the creditt of the Royall Affrican Company, which is abominabley abused, and to procure a trade againe if itt be possible.

The 3 persons Ahenesa sent down to us tould us he designed noe harme against us, onely demanded his owne, of which at present wee are unsensible, and besides bid us beware of the Dutch, for they were all rogues and lyers.

September the 2nd
Ahenesas sonn Bobie came hither and made his palavora with us to say as followeth:

That Ahenesa hath noe demands against Mr Wendover for lying with Boque his wife, neither did hee take any great notice of itt when wee tould his sonn Bobie of itt, onely ditto Bobie tould us his father Ahenesa demanded his due to him one [= on] his monthly sallery, and that the Company, Mr Wendover or any in the Company service should [n]ever be troubled in the least about his wife Boque.[17] To all this Ahenesas sonn Bobie tooke the fetish, and that hee would bring downe a trade, and wee to procure the same tooke the fetish that Ahenesas son or any hee sent to our fort should by us have and receive all civilllity whatsoever.

September the 3rd
Ahenesas sonn Bobie went away, with whome wee sent the aforesaid Black named Ba: Conto with our orders to give Ahenesa an account of our proceedings and what fetish his sonn Bobie hath taken in his behalfe, and that also wee desired ditto Ahenesa to confirm the same.

September the 9th
The aforesaid Ba: Conto returned from Ahenesa with 3 of his men whome sent us worde hee had not the least pretention either against Mr Wendover or any in this fort, and that hee approved of the fetish his sonn Bobie had taken in his behalfe and promised allwayes to confirm the same, and that hee had not nor never would have the least quarrell against the English here, and whatever stories wee heard from the Dutch, blacks or any other wee should not beleive them. Hee did assure us that if wee would procure him good bright musketts, powder and other goods, wee should not want either for slaves, or gold, but wee should have a constant trade. All these aforesaid is the certaine truth to us related in James fort att Accra the 9th September in Guiney 1681.

James Nightingale
George Phipps
William Pley

410. James Nightingale   James Fort, Accra, 10 Sept. 1681

I cannot but give your honour most humble and hearty thanks for all your kindness to mee. I desire your honour will be pleas'd to continue in the same practice, and on my side there shall be nothing wanting to answer your honours expectations, and shall at all times follow your commands. I send your honour a note which one Mr Beacon hath given Mr Frankland for 4 elephants teeth which ditto Frankland sent home upon his own account, also two kind letters your honour was pleas'd to write to him. I could heartyly wish, I had such a holesome advice given to mee, I

---

[17] But Ansa later revived his demand for compensation on this account (cf. no.440). Boque was held in pawn for the 100 muskets which Ansa had borrowed from the English in 1680 (cf. no.414, inclosure 3). She was eventually, in 1683, returned to Ansa (no.464).

doe assure your honour I should be glad to except itt, and at all times to follow the same. There comes likewise per this convert a coppie of an attestation of Docter Stone to the contrary of his former in the behalfe of Mr Francis Frankland to the contrary of mee,[18] as Docter Hulett was pleased to write Mr Frankland of, and also to inspect my actions, but the good God above has been pleased by his great mercy to lett the truth be known [as to] whoe are the persons that dealt with interlopers.

[inclosure]

Note

Mr Frankland and the Portuguese Governour Julian Campo de Barreto bought in company out of an interloper named the Blessing, Mr Edlin and Mr Harvey [commanding], about 200 iron barrs, whereof 60 found here since my last belonging to ditto Frankland. Besides I doe not reckon the muskets which ditto Frankland brought ashoare in Mr Wendovers time, and there is also reported that here is more goods at the Portuguese fort: to whome they belong I doe not know. I am very well satisfied that Mr Arthur Wendover bought some time agoe out of a Dutch ship some sayes, perpettuanoes, fine sletias and other goods, whereof at present is in the Portuguese forte 46 fine sletias, 5 sayes, and 7 perpetuanoes in the hands of Julian Campo de Baretto, which aforesaid goods your honour will be pleased to demand of Mr Wendover as belonging to Mr Frankland, and lett him give his note for the delivering of the same to ditto Julian Campo Barreto, that I may demand the same, alsoe give mee your order for whose account I shall dispose of them. Your honour will be pleased not to lett Mr Wendover know that I have any intelligence of what hee has done, for hee intends to keepe mee ignorant.

Captain Phypps will give your honour an account of all my actions and transactions, alsoe the proceedings here.

411. William Pley   James Fort, Accra, 28 Sept. 1681

According to that inviolable duty I am ever bound to beare you for your great and repeated favours to mee, I humbly presume to acquaint your worshipp with the transactions here, for the blacks, both Ahenesa's people and of the Dutch and Portuguese Towne and of other countries, came this morning in a kind of a mutinous manner, upon the reporte Bonete the black that came downe from Capo Corsoe gave them, that Mr Nightingale was to depart this place and Mr Hassell to come Chiefe. The Capisheers in generall declared upon their fetish that they would sooner die every man than admitt Mr Hassell to come on shoare, but would with their musketts with their whole force resist him to the utmost, and that if he did come on shoare, the fort should be forever in danger of treachery and never 1 oz[?] of trade should be admitted, for they all declared they loved Mr Nightingalle and

---

[18] Inclosed in no.401 above.

would venture their lives for him and bring him a good trade, but as for Mr Hassell they had not forgott their wives, children and friends that was carried away in his time, and that hee should never have one months peace here. I doe assure your worshipp from the bottom of my heart I doe not write this out of any feare from, or persuasions of Mr Nightingalle but purely out of duty and commands your worshipp hath been pleased to give mee to inform you of all transactions of moment, and leave itt to your worshipps pleasure, not doubting but you will please to confide in my fidellity both in this and my former letter (being not without sufficient witness in both), for I thank God I never did, and will imbrace the maxime that honesty is the best pollicy, and doubt not after your worshpp hath been pleased to putt mee right in the abuses put upon me per Mr Frankland as to the pottkeys etc. you shall find your favours not plact amiss, paying humble thanks I ought, for here I live here without expence in the least at the chiefs table, which most heartyly from the bottom of my soule thank your worshipp for, since I could not doe itt att Capo Corsoe. And I most earnestly (on that consideration) begg your worshipp to continue mee here, and if I in the least doe amiss either to the Royall Company or your worshipp I doe not desire the least favour as unworthy of soe much goodness.

I doe not put the Company to the charge of this canoe, for the Cabosheers send it with one of them in it to make a pallavre with your worshipp concerning the promises. I begg your worshipp not to take this amiss, being done out of pure duty (being their very words), and not for any other end. As soone as I receive any quarters sallary I will returne your worshipp the 17a I am indebted to the Steward. I begg pardone for my bad writting, the canoe being just goeing.

412. Ralph Hassell   James Fort, Accra, 7 Oct. 1681

These may serve your Honour for advise onely. I am I praise God in safety (though with difficulty) arrived here ashoare, for which I onely give God the glory, and humble thankes to your Honour. I write onely now per via advise that the people which your Honour did detayne yesterday arrived here with your Honours letter, which I thinke you did beyond expression most discreetly, and God alone be your adviser and councellour still to act good as you have in that onely thing to myselfe. The narrative shall be more ample for the future

[PS] Pray excuse brevity at present but after Captain Rickards departure shall inlarge. I have given Mr Nightingale a receipt for all things here that found. Idem ad eternum.[19]

---

[19] 'The same for eternity'.

413. William Pley   James Fort, Accra, 7 Oct. 1681

Mr Hassell arrived here the 5th instant, and had opposition by the Blacks at his landing, having small shott discharged at him, but is now safe on shoare. I am now sensible there was treachery used by those that ought to have done otherwise in that respect. Mr Wendover brought the sad news of my fathers death, who was my onely friend (my mother being dead before), and therefore I hope God, who is the father of the fatherless, will be pleased to heare my prayers soe farr as to recompence to you all your kindness to me in my sad condition, and I hope I shall never be unworthy of it.

I have been much aflicted with a relapse of my feavour since my last to your Worship but now I hope all is over.

[PS] By reason of my great sickness under which I lay and am yett troubled with, I had never the key of, nor did deliver any thing out of the warehouse, but James Mills in his time [did so?]. Mr Nightingale on a word or two would not signe it. Please to peruse the inclosed etc. Now all things are right and I have noates for all delivered and feare noe mistake etc.

[Inclosure]
I doe acknowledge William Pley by reason of his sickness, had nothing to doe in, nor did deliver any goods out of the Royall Company warehouse at Accra from the day of my landing there being the 18th of August 1681 till the time Mr Ralph Hassell had charge of the same, being the 5th day of October following.
Wittness my hand.
I doe acknowledge that Mr James Nightingale did confess that what is above written is true, but refused to signe it as he promised etc.

Ralph Hassell
Arthur Wendover

414. Ralph Hassell   [James Fort, Accra], 11 Oct. 1681

May it please your Honour that since the above have received the remaines of Captain Rickards cargoe and an account thereof have inclosed, with an account of all the goods in and about the forte, but cannot be certify'ed to whom they in part properly belong to, for noe one can give me a perfect accompt thereof. As for the things your Honour ordred in your orders that were at the Portugueese forte, [I] can learne nothing of neither will any one give me insight therein. I have likewise sent three receipts for 4 woemen slaves, which was all Captain Rickard would receive. I question not but Mr Nightingale will exclayme against mee, which I hope and humbley begg your favour to deale soe candidly by mee as to advise mee, and then shall give with Mr Pley a certayne relation of all occurrencys that hath hapned per Mr Wendover, who will follow to morrow night.

[Inclosure 1]

Accra October the 10th 1681

Received then on board the shipp Blessing, from Mr Ralph Hassell 4 Negroe woemen slaves, which are for accompt of the Royall Affrican Company of England

Samuell Rickard

[Inclosure 2]

Account of goods received from on board the Blessing, Captain Samuell Rickard Commander, for account of the Royall Affrican Company of England — vizt

216 musquetts matchlocks

100 narrow blew baftas

  20 sayes, some ratt eaten

  17 perpettuanes

  12 broad niccanees

  17 barrells powder

   8 narrow niccanees

   8 damaged Welch plaines

  10 pewter juggs

  20 tankards

   8 sletias, much soyld

  26 halfe firkins of tallow

  20 old sheets

1 box of beads, quantity contence 147 lb

The afore goods are received, wittness our hands this 11th October 1681

Ralph Hassell

William Pley

[Inclosure 3]

Inventory of goods in the Royall Affrican Companys warehouse of James Forte at Accra the 6th of October 1681 received from James Nightingale vizt

347½	iron barrs
24	sayes, and 12 fatham [= fathom]: 3 are quite ratten, and most worm eaten
16	perpettuanes
33	blew pottkeys
6½	paper brawles, all damaged
9	peeces tapseeles, whereof 7 are all broake and damaged
10	peeces niccanees, cutt and broake thee most part
24	blew baftas ⎫
29	ditto white ⎬ 53, some damaged
81	Guiney clouts, old
31	peeces of Welch plaines
100	peeces blew long cloathes
1	ditto white, rotten
6	old sheets

36	six pound pewter basson
4	halfe firkins of tallow
155	dozen old knives
366	musquetts
52	ditto damaged } 418
33	old carbynes
161	lead barrs
32¾	barrells powder
4	ditto, damaged } 36¾
34	brass kettles
4	chests corne
3	peeces course sletias
1	ditto in cartidges, quantity 25 dozen

Provitions received from Captain Bramfill

56	wormeaten stockfish
½	a small bagg of oatemeale
1	gallon vinegar
1½	ditto ranke oyle

Artillery

15	great gunns
2	pattareras[20] with broaken chambers
27	firelocks, 22 broake
1	halbert
5	powder hornes
60	great shott
	some small shott, part received from Captain Phipps
30	granado shells, small
1	St Georges flag
1	drum

Sundryes about the forte vizt

1	5 hand canoe
5½	cocarnutt trees
1	stacke wood
	some rope
4	iron crowes
3	pickaxes
2	sawes
1	axe

Companyes pawnes

Boquee, wife to Ahenesa, for	100 musquetts			
Agga for	0o	12a	0ta	
Aquerry for	1	08	0	} 3 canoemen
Asha for	0	7	6	

[20] A form of small gun (Spanish *pedreiro*).

1 sword for   1   0   0

Accompt of slaves belonging to the Company

3	Ardoe bumboyes[21]
3	women, their wives
23	women slaves
1	man
1	girle

Provitions

9	peeces of porke
8	hams ditto, dryed
½	hogshead pease
½	firkin of ranke butter
3	small potts palme oyle
1	barrell of flower

Old linning

4	old table cloathes
13	old napkines
2	pewter bassons
4	dishes
6	small porringers
10	plates
¼	chest of suger

Plate

1	punch bole
1	silver tankard
1	ditto porringer
3	spoones
1	forke
1	dram cup
	a small parcelle of earthenware
1	bed
1	Arda cloath
1	cott, lackerd
1	case, quantity 15 3 quart bottles
1	table
6	chaires
1	fowling peece

Cattle vizt

2	sheepe
3	lambs
2	boares

[21] See Glossary.

9	sowes
3	shoates
16	suckling piggs
2	goates
3	kidd

Wee whose names are under written doe acknowledge that all the foregoing and above written goods etc. are in James Fort Accra, wittness our hands this 6th day of October 1681

Ralph Hassell
William Pley

415. Ralph Hassell   James Fort, Accra, 18 Oct. 1681

These comes per Mr Wendover, who had come up sooner could hee have gott a canoe. These serve onely to advise your Honour of what wee want here and are in great want of, vizt a hogshead of tarres for the tanke and 1000 bricks to lay the bottom of ditto, 3 or 4 good locks, 1 good large lock for the warehouse dore, some large and short irons for slaves, for wee have none here, I bought 3 men and 3 women yesterday and am afraid of them running away for wont of irons to put them in; and if your Honour can spare some of your elme pipes for to repaire two flankers which are falling, with a mason to repaire them, also some good corne, for that we had per Captain Rickard being but 17 chests are all soe bad that the slaves will not eate it nor scarce the hoggs; also some brandy, for I found not a drop in the forte but a little I brought with me, which is allready expended. I thought good to advise your Honour that soe you might not blame me for not giving timely advise, but that crime shall not be laid to my charge, for per every oppertunity I will advise of affaires here.

416. William Pley   James Fort, Accra, 22 Oct. 1681

Your Worships kind letter I have received, for which I returne my most hearty thankes, it being a great cordiall in my trouble for my fathers death, and I shall ever pray for your life, health, and happiness since my well being here wholly depends on your generosity and goodness, which I hope I shall never misuse. As to Mr Hassells opposition [= opposition to Mr Hassell] at landing, when I writ your Worship, the palavor of the Cabbisheeers (which was the same day), God knowes I know nothing of any intrigue, but since tis too apparent twas contrived by James Mills, doubtless by the command of his then Master,[22] as the confession of some of the Blackes and other circumstances make apparent, but I hope all will prove

---

[22] i.e. James Nightingale.

insignificant and wee shall have a good trade (if I may measure the future by the present) to our masters profitt.

[PS] Desire your Worship not to declare (if possible) my words to Mr Nightingale for I am very loath in my condition to create myselfe the least enemy, though what I write is soe true that Mr Nightingale did protest he would not admitt Mr Hassell on shoare before he send his orders in a canoe, to what end I leave your Worship to judge.

417. Ralph Hassell   25 Oct. 1681

Since the above dated I received your honours of the 18th instant, and render your Honour the choycest of tenn thousand thankes for your cordiall expressions to me and I have donn what in me lyeth to render ample sattisfaction to your honours demands, and I will not add fuell to fire, for whome you guess is the whole agitator and whome your Honour has soe highly advanced, Mr Nightingale per name, did say to Mr Pley I should not come on shoar till I had sent him my orders, and upon that gave your honour for all your civilities many bitter curses, for what reason I know not. He would not give me any acccount of every particular mans concerns but said all are the Companyes, which Mr Wendover can give your Honour ample sattisfaction therein. I question not but he has been the hearauld of his owne actions and has sufficiently emblazoned his heroick deeds, thinking noe man able to agitate as he hath donn; but my halfe of this month will demonstrate I have past him, for I have nigh 12m of gold and 12 slaves, and what goods that are vendable for the purchasing more which I will here insert. As for the worthy gentleman Mr Mills, who did before my arrivall upon somewhat of a word given him per Mr Pley, waite for him on purpose to shoote him with 4 bulletts in his peece, and swore if he came downe would be his death.

What I have desired your Honour on the other side I humble begg you will send, for I cannot buy any more slaves till I have corne. I need not mencion what goods, but must submitt and say what you please to spare. I have not a good say nor perpettuanoe, nor sheet, sletia, brandy. Allejars are much in quest for slaves, soe is all goods. This is the needfull at present, with all the paper inke and wax I have [sic], soe hope a speedy supply. I humble begg your Honours favour with the continuance thereof, and I shall assuredly follow your commands in all things without the least breath.

418. Ralph Hassell   James Fort, Accra, 31 Oct. 1681

Yours of the 27th instant have before me, and in answer to your command of a former date have in every poynt hope rendred your Honour ample satisfaction, which I hope ere this has arrived you in salvo with Mr Wendover, who would have followed Mr Nightingale as I in my former advised but noe oppertunity proffered till that he imbraced per vio Anamaboe, and for want of a 2 hand canoe with 2 canoemen severall things may accidentally happen which requireth speedy advice, soe humbley begg that your Honour will agree for one and send downe at soe much per mensem as you thinke convenient, which will be cheaper then to send up a 5 hand canoe and thinke wee are beholden to them for the pay and laboure. The goods wee had that was good is most gone, soe humbley begg a speedy supply, vizt good sayes, and perpettuanoes, sheets, allejars, sletias, broad niccanees and tapseeles, and any goods, for slaves is to be had if I had these goods. As for necessaryes, corne is most wanting, 10 or 12 pipes of elmes if can be spared to build 3 flankers, which cannot be made use of for want of repaire, a 1000 of good well burnt bricks for to lay the bottom of the tank, with a hogshead of tarras and a bricklayer with a kill[23] of shells to make lime, for the tower is very leaky. If your Honour please to send these things, the charges elce will be little or nothing.

I have in this 25 dayes taken 12m 3o 8 odd mony, and bought 5 men and 6 woemen, and have turnd severall away for want of allejares and other goods above recited.

Immediatly on perusall of your Honours last I gott 2 fresh canoemen and sent them to Mr Shears, whose answere I have here inclosed.[24]

I hope will excuse me of neglect and cleare mee of what was not guilty.

[PS] Mr Pley presents his humble service to your Honour. Here is no brandy nor corne, this I humbley offer to your Honour in hopes of a speedy supply, with paper inke and wax.

419. William Pley James Fort, Accra, 12 Nov. 1681

Since my last to your Worship noe occurrances have happened here worth your perusall, as soon as any presents you shall not want the knowledge of them. My accompt of goods sold in the month of October and remaining the beginning of the next month is ready, most of which are damnified, and unfitt for sale, and wee waite your Worships pleasure as to a supply. I most humbley begg your Worship will please to give me some directions, as to the method of my particular accompt here, whether to send the delivery and remaines of the goods up, or whether my books (agreeing with Mr Hassells noates) will be sufficient for my discharge (if please God I live to see England) to the Royall Company, which obligacon (with those many past) will for ever give me sufficient cause to remaine your Worships most obliged and obedient servant.

---

[23] i.e. kiln.
[24] = no.518.

420.   Ralph Hassell   James Fort, Accra, 17 Nov. 1681

These at the request of the bearer I present your Honour with, having been severall times solicited thereto per severall of the blacks here. His request to your Honour is that you would please to see him in some manner righted, for Captain How an interloper hath paniard 3 Cabbisheers at Alampa,[25] one is his brother, who [i.e. How] is now gone to windward. I doubt it will much prejudice our trade at that place, for slaves are very plenty there, and this man hath brought some to me which I have bought, he is a considerable dealer and hath sold many slaves formerly to Captain Leo[?] Woodfine.[26] This he tells me is his only supplycation to your Honour. I am at a stand for want of good goods of all sorts, as advised in my two formers, one by Mr Wendover and the other per the canoe your Honour sent downe, of which I have not a word of the receipt thereof. Heer is slaves if I had goods as advised. Have nothing of news worth citeing.

421.   Ralph Hassell   James Fort, Accra, 27 Nov. 1681

Yours dated the 23rd instant received yesterday and then would have answered thereto, but could not procure a canoe and was loath to send the 5 hand canoe per reason of to great a charge, for I am loath to pay any more then what I am constrayned to doe. I perceive per your Honours letter that you are much incenced against me, per some buissey body who would be thought officious to gaine creditt for former errors hath been tampering with your Honour to doe me a prejudice per a damnable falce and erronius information. I here invoke God to wittness I did not buy anything of Captain How, but of Captain Rickard I bought a few small blankquitts, not considerable to the number you make mencon of, which I now protest in the presence of God I never made one ounce of, but have given them for dashes, and should I in the past abuse your Honours favour, which heither to hath been soe many towards me that I had need live an age to studdy gratitude, neither doe I know that they were ever accompted the Company's commodities, if I had I would not have medled with them, and should your Honour give creditt to all such stories that may be presented under the colour of fidelity to our Royall Masters interest your hands would have noe cessation from continuall perplexity. I doe now in the presence of the heavenly host and Jihovah protest that Ile not medle with or deale or none for me in my behalfe for one penny or any other summ with any interloper, and this I humbley offer to your Honours in hopes you will for the future have a more favourable construction of my intended cincerity, which are bona fide for my Royall masters interest, and in the end I hope it may be said of me fines coronat opus.[27]

---

[25] Cf. no.518.

[26] Sic: but other letters refer to the brothers John and Thomas Woodfine.

[27] 'The end crowns the work'.

422. Ralph Hassell   James Fort, Accra, 12 Dec. 1681

Yours of the 9th of November per Captain Giles Lawrance I have before mee ordering mee to afford my uttmost endeavour to purchase slaves, which I did but wanted goods to purchase them, alsoe to deliver him one moyetie of what I had of each sex, which I did divide in equall parts and cast lotts for him and Captain Woodfine, and haveing noe more then 6 men the halfe being 3, hee would not take any more then 3 woemen, for which I have taken four receipts and have herein inclosed three.

I have been long without a letter from your honour, which was the occasion of my silence. The 5 hand canoe with Captain Quow and Humphrey Davis arrived here on Satureday, bringing with them James Mills and Captain Lawrances boy, and within an houre after [I] sent your honours letter to Captain Lawrance to Mingo, who departed hence on Thursday last early in the morning, and yesterday his boate arrived and today have taken the aforementioned gentlemen and is gone downe. Captain Lawrance in a letter to mee, desires his service to be presented to your honour. This morning the Arda canoe arrived here and brings news of Thomas Gouldings death within 17 dayes after his arrivall, and alsoe Captain Rickards dispatch from thence, and that Captain Wyborne has settled a factory at Whiddah.[28]

I have here also inclosed sent Octobers and Novembers accounts to the 5th instant, whereby your honour will find due to my Royall masters 11m 3oz 9a 1ta and what slaves remaynes, onely what is aboard Captain Lawrance to be deducted and is not in those accounts because delivered the 8th instant. I humbly begg your honour to peruse what I formerly writt for both for necessaries and goods.

423. Ralph Hassell & William Pley   James Fort, Accra, 23 Jan. 1681/2

These are only and cheifly to supplycate you to give me a line of advice, for itt is long since have received one from you, which makes mee conjecture you are unmindfull of us here or at leastwise have us in great disrespect, for by Captain Woodfine had not a line directory for our proceedings, only an order to deliver him what slaves wee had ready and to take receipts for the same, which hee denied, only giveing one for 7 woemen and 6 men which I have here Inclosed sent your honour, takeing a coppy thereof under test for my security. Captain Woodfine stayed here not above 8 hours. Mr Wendover, his factor and mate came about an houre before the ship and carried the slaves in a 5 hand canoe. Mr Wendover informed mee hee had sworne against mee about a parcell of blanketts that came from on board Captain How, which hee said in the presence of the major part of the fort that you forced him to doe itt, else hee had not gon for Whiddah.[29] If your honour require

---

[28] Cf. no.479.

[29] Wendover had been appointed chief factor at Whydah (cf. no.484).

test of his word itt shall be at your service. I can produce evidence he never had come from England but for being sued to an outlawrie for perjury (my test is Mr Kirkam Junior in London), and I have in presence heard him objure both father and mother, and if such criminall oaths may be admitted I lay my hand on my mouth and with an humble silence submitt to your honours grave censure, and since per Captain Shears and Charles Towgood understand that your honours sent letters by him for mee which both Mr Pley and myselfe will aver I never received, although asked him for them, which how ill your honours may resent my silence, imputing it to neglect, I know not. I have inclosed sent an account of Decembers sales, which finding right please to noate in conformitie. I received from Captain Shears 20 sayes, and 20 red perpettunaoes, 66 chests corne, 1040 bricks. Musketts if your honours please to send that are good and bright, I can sell 500 in a month as I am promised, and all other goods will vend, powder excepted, for they have been glutted with that formerly. Ahenesa is now in battalia with his army marching towards the Achims.[30] If hee overcomes we may expect slaves, if [he is] over com a better trade for gold then hath been many years, and how to hope for success on either side is dubious, for if overcome these [Accra] people will never be in subjection as now they are, but will increase dayly more and more and old grudges will not be forgott. I requested your honour to send brandy, tarris, trees and other necessaries for rebuilding and finishing the tank, with wax, ink and paper, being now wholy destitute of either I must perforce hereafter continue silent unless supply'd. I humbly begg your honours favourable construction of all within mentioned, being nothing but verity, and with a full resolution to continue in my Royall Masters interest and advance itt as far as possible in mee lyes and with an unfeined resolution to serve your honour as your commands shall direct, being constant in my performances.

424.   Ralph Hassell   James Fort, 1 Feb. 1682

Your Worships letter of the 29th January I received, wherein as I find you are pleased soe far to creditt my former letter as to demand my atestation of Mr Wendovers words, soe I have here enclosed it with 4 wittnesses. And I assure your Worship I esteem it a very great favour that you were soe kind as to send a coppie of Mr Wendovers letter etc. and I hope my future actions will approve me what I profess as honesty and justice to the Royall Company.

Mr Shears delivered here 20 sayes and 20 red pepettuanoes, corne and bricks, for which Mr Shears hath creditt. The corne out of Captain Rickard amounted to noe more then I wrote your Worship. What slaves possible I can (now, or at Ahenesas returne) will purchase for my Royall Masters interest.

---

[30] Cf. no.425. Barbot also heard report of this campaign: 1992, ii, 604.

PS. All what things did appertaine to Mr Wendover which formerly have renderd an account are here, with increase of his cattle, and when you please to demand them shall be punctually according to command renderd to your Honour.

What musquetts wee have here are all out of order, elce could have vended them ere this time, hope a supply of 500 from your Honour, which vends now and nothing elce for slaves.

425. Ralph Hassell   James Fort, Accra, 23 Feb. 1681/2

Yours of the 11th instant per the Cabo Corso Briganteen, Mr Towgood Commander, have received, with 200 musquetts, 200 paper brawles, 40 sayes, 25 perpettuanoes, 100 herba longees, 50 Guinea stuffs and 30 blanketts, which I will use my utmost endeavor to dispose of for my Royall masters interest for slaves and gold, as your Honour directs.

Att present all manner of trade is soe dead that at all the forts here has not this two months taken 4 ounces. The reason is Ahenesa hath been out against the Arcanies and Akims, soe not any traders from any parts dare adventure to come downe, but this day news came that he had taken the Taffo country with some few slaves, the major part of the people fled for succour to the Akims.[31] This day 3 slaves was brought, 2 woemen and 1 man, but I bought them not by reason to great a price, which was 9 musquetts apeece, which in my apprehension is extravigant rates for my Masters proffitt. If Ahenesa is conquered this will certainly be a place of good and considerable trade, if not he will suffer noe Arcanie nor Akim to buy any thing here but what comes through his hands, which he makes double proffitt off, soe expect what the events will be and in the meane time hope for the best. [I] shall also follow your Honours order in demanding satisfaction of Ahenesa for the 100 musquetts.[32] Also inquired of the soulders here what man had the 50 musquetts, and the Gunner Thomas Barrett inform'd me it was Quobing, and that he delivered them himselfe, which shall likewise be demanded. I have paid him noe rent since I came nor has not been paid for severall months before except 1 benda per Mr Nightingale.

In your Honours you are pleased to charge me with extravigant expences at Christmas. It hath allwayes been acustomary to give more then what I charge in my account, and whosoever lived here will informe your Honour, and Mr Pley can verrifye the account in that respect and more then what I charge, soe begg your candor therein.

Your Honour writes and has likewise sent downe Humphrey Davis to be my assistant, but in what capacity I cannot imagine he is able to assist me as Mr Pley hath done, for I dare not trust him as a second to keep the key of the warehouse by

---

[31] i.e. Tafo, north-west of Akyem. The wording here implies that Tafo was allied with Akyem against Akwamu.

[32] Cf. no.407.

reason he had not given any security as Mr Pley hath, in whose fidelity and ability I could confid, and [he] always delivered every months account just to mee according to noeates given him, and your Honour does me a great diskindness in bereaveing me of his good company. I leave all the relation of affaires to his information. I have found all goods right that has bee under his management which has been all here, but this month I found a musquett under one of the Arda's bedds, and whipt him severely for it. He confest his crime and likewise charged a free black, Ashuma one of the black souldiers, to have been in confederacy with him in stealing 9 more, which he mistrusting run away the day before, but if I can catch him I will send him away on the Company account,[33] also 6 barrs of iron which is now wanting and 1 blew narrow baft which he threw over the wall when he went to turne them as they were drying, which wee here doe by reason of a damp warehouse every month. I have paid Mr Pley his sallery due, which was 2 months, vizt to the 1st of March. I humbley begg your Honour, if you please to grant it that I am per your Honour continued here, to send Mr Pley back againe as soone as possible, for Humphrey Davis is noe wayes capacitated to aid me, unless your Honour and worthy Gentlemen of Council please to order mee to deliver him the key of the warehouse and that I may be cleare from all things that shall bee wanting when you shall please to require an account of me. I dispatcht Captain Towgood in less then 24 houres and have supply'd all his wants for the furthering his voyage, as wood 2 5 hand canoe fulls, water and [sic =an] iron bound caske a tunn, and for himselfe dishes, basons, kettles, plates and spoones and all things towards housekeeping

Your Honours per Monsieur Barboate[34] I received but had not oppertunity to answer, and in obedience to your Commands I treated him with all the civillity I could, and [as] for the pacquett he gave me none, but he is gone windward in the sloope and suppose he may have sent what he promised as said he would. The French have great hopes to have bought the fort of the Portuguese but they obteyn'd not their desire.[35] I heare of noe place that they are minded to settle nearer then Alampo, which they tould me, that is Monsieur Penell and Monsieur Robellene, more ships were comeing and the new French Company did intend on there, which your Honour may hinder per presettlement and give somewhat of a dashey, elce afterwards wee must expect noe slaves thence. Mingo is the best place, for there is both gold, and the best in Guinea, and slaves, it is not above 2 leagues from Alampo, and if your Honour approves of the designe I will make inquiry therein, and imagine itt more feasable then Tanton Querry and of more considerable trade per 10 to 1, soe expect your resolve per next and leave it to Mr Shears and Charles Towgoods

[33] i.e. sell him to a slave ship.

[34] i.e. Jean Barbot.

[35] Barbot records visiting the Portuguese fort at Accra, but says nothing of any attempt to purchase it: 1992, ii, 434.

relation. I have inclosed my January account, in which you may perceive that there is small trade at present, and the reasons hereof I have before recited.

Charles Towgood tould me you desired a couple of good breading goates which I have of Mr Wendover's and are good, and now have sent your Honour and hope that they will answer what they have done here, for they were good here never bringing less then 3 and 4 apeice and now they are above halfe gone with young. Mr Pley had gone last night had not bad weather prevented him, soe hope your Honour will not chyde him in that point. I have not more at present to inlarge, having in all matters renderd your Honour a perticular account, but this only that when you are supplyed with sheets and sletias you will please to send some downe, being most inquired for here.

[PS] I have paid the 5 hand canoemen 3 dayes canky mony.

426. Ralph Hassell   Accra, 12 March 1681/2

These I humbly present to your Honour with all for covert of Charles Towgoods letters [sic],[36] the contents whereof I know not of what validity it may concerne my Royall masters interest. This is the first oppertunity I could imbrace by reason of a tempestuous sea which has broake all the canoes att Accra, not one either great or small has escap'd, the Companys 5 hand canoe in the night alsoe although haul'd above 6 foot above high water. This is a windward canoe that brought corne which I have seized on purpose to dispatch Charles letters, and hope your Honour will send her back with all expedition. I have also inclosed my February accounts, which indeed irketh mee to send per reason of soe inconsiderable incomes and soe great expences, which in noe way immaginable could be avoided, which if your honour pleases to cast your eye on will find nothing extravigantly charged, soe hope you'l not think mee culpable. Yett nevertheless though att present small trade is, I live in hopes better will come to make amends for the bad, soe that interlaceing the good with the bad it will in the end ballance expectations. I could have sold the musketts for gold but will not unless I have halfe gold, halfe slaves.

427. Ralph Hassell   Accra, 18 March 1681/2

Your Honours of the 13th and 15th instant is before mee. In the first your orders shall be punctually observed, and in the latter you please to express that the Companys stock is wasted per expences and that some other way must be found to increase a trade, alsoe why I made noe prevention to save the canoe, to all which I with humble submission desire to answer with your Honours permission. Imprimis, I am certaine that noe one here hath been more desireous to gaine your Honours

---

[36] Presumably = no.523 (transmitted from Alampo via Accra).

favour and my Royall masters good will per saveing of them money and not to be extravigant of others bulces which are soe far above mee which with a word may command all that I have from mee, and likewise I have never charg'd any thing extravigant in any of my accompts. Secondly, for a speedier way of finding an increase of trade, I have studied and ponderd on all immaginable meanes but nothing will be of a trade till the warrs are over, that the wayes may be free for up countrys to come downe, which I conjecture your Honour is sufficiently sencible thereof, which if you please to aske any black that can informe you of the same. Thirdly, for prevention of the canoes being broake, had I knowne that the flood would have come in the night I myselfe with all the helpe I could gett would have prevented itt, but this I humbly offer to your honour, shee was haul'd up as high as ever any canoe was yett att Accra, but soe high a flood I never yet knew. Your Honours to Charles Towgood inclosed Jamque[?] of the 13th date I sent immediatly away to him. These canoemen would not goe to Allampo, soe [I] was forced to take their canoe and hyre two others which I have paid, and suppose here is answer thereto inclosed, and by reason of your honours order to dispatch your last to him I have sent another canoe this morning to him.

428. Ralph Hassell   Accra, 25 March 1682

Your honours of the 21st instant have received (with one inclosed to Mr Charles Towgood) and marke well the contents and shall follow your honours directions therein. Have now likewise inclosed two of Mr Charles Towgoods.[37] Att present have nothing of news, only yesterday a few Anguinah men came downe and laid out above 10 ounces in sayes and brawles and Guynea stuffs. I alsoe sent a small dashey to the Queene of Anguinah per one Cabusheere of our towne, whoe has promised to bring trade. I desire your honour to send for some of the hogs that are here, for without a great deale of corne I cannot maintaine them, they increase soe fast. Yesterday 5 sows piged 30 and with what formerly that I have weaned and bred young and old there is upwards of three score besides 3 sows more to pigg, which stock if maintained would be a verry considerable income but with great charge here. I have destroyed none but have been verry carefull in preserving them.

429. Ralph Hassell   Accra, 3 Apr. 1682

Yours of the 28th and 29th last past I received, the first instant ordering mee to put what gold I had in cash of my Royall masters the Affrican Company of England on board Mr Towgood, which I have obeyed and likewise what good slaves shall be in the fort. The gold is the ballance of February's account, which if you will please to cast your eye on said account you'l find to be 12 marks, 4 ounces, 1 angle and 7

---

[37] = nos 525–6.

taccoes as per coppy of his receipt here inclosed, also 6 woemen slaves on board the Cape Coast Briganteen, Charles Towgood Commander. Mr Towgood hath had a brass kettle for the use of said briganteen. I pray your honour to send some more corne, for wee shall not have enough to last longer then this month. What slaves else remains are bad and have been severall times refused per the Companys ships, soe would not send any that are bad.

430. Ralph Hassell   Accra, 3 Apr. 1682

I have wrote your honour per Charles Towgood, Commander of the Cape Coast Briganteen, of this same date, wherein I gave your honour an account I had in persuance to your commands shipt on board the said briganteen 12 marks, 4 ounces, 1 angle and 7 taccoes of gold, with 6 good woemen slaves as per his receipt herein inclosed, which finding right please to noate in conformity, to which I humbley refer you. I humbly begg pardon for my brevity.

431. Ralph Hassell   James Fort, Accra, 22 May 1682

It is now full 2 months since I have had the happyness to receive a line from your honour, which indeed is the occasion of my silence. I am dubious all things with your honour hath not been according to your expectations, and the verity is yesterday the bad news of your honours sickness arrived per a Black that came from your parts, which informed mee per word of mouth that you had been soe for some time, which did not a little amaze mee and is the sole occasion of this and I humbly crave a word of advice of your health, for which I heartyly beg God of his infinitt mercy to restore you to your former health. This alsoe accompanys my last 2 months accounts, which should not have been soe long lacking had any oppertunity presented before this. Yesterday I bought 6 as good slaves as any I have seen in Guyney, vizt 4 men 2 woemen. Ahenesa hath taken Coma country,[38] and his partner Ancroffe hath routed all the people from Ningo to the River of Volta and all the Allampas are fled to a place about 4 leages leward of the River Volta to a place called Quitto,[39] att which place I beleeve there is good tradeing, and verry speedily the Allampas will returne againe. Had I a parcell of good sletias they would vend for 10a a peece and sheets for 24 per bendy. I have sold but 2 green perpettuanoes this month for 14a each, with some other small things, nothing but sletias and sheets are in request. Here is one Benjamin Houlding, a souldier that left 2 angles per month in England

[38] Cf. no.435 ('Commongs'); i.e. Kwaman, in the region of later Asante. Probably this campaign was a sequel to that against Tafo, in the same area (no.425).
[39] i.e. Keta. For the settlement of refugees from Le (Adangme) in the Anlo (Keta) region cf. Greene 1988. This evidence corrects the previous dating of Ansa Sasraku's campaign against Adangme to 1679, taken from an eighteenth-century source (as in Wilks 1959, 113–14). Cf. also nos 451–2, for a second Akwamu campaign against Adangme in 1683.

for three years, which time is expired and beggs your honour to consider him in the 2 angles per month, that hee may be paid here. I have formerly wrote for some brandy but have not as yett been supplyed, alsoe for some corne. I bought yesterday 6 chests for 2a per chest, or else I could not buy any slaves; it is very scarce here. I humbly begg your honour if the ship be arriv'd with timber you will please to spare some for this place, being in great want, will send the dementions per next after I heare of the arrivall.

432. Ralph Hassell   James Fort, Accra, 1 June 1682

Yours of the 17th last past yesterday arrived my hands, wherein you are pleased to tax mee with negligence in long silence, per which I perceive you had not received mine of the 21 past, in which I hope you'l be convinced that I was no wayes blameable. This I hope will arrive your honour in salvo per the hands of Mr Smith, whoe hath undergone lately a great deale of damage and hazard, but hope hee hath past the worst being now soe neare home. I know not what weather you have had att Capo Corsoe, for since my last wee have not had 24 hours of faire weather, which hath done us much damage, for almost all the out works is falen or ready to fall, which Mr Smith hath viewed and hope your honour if you have any spare timber to send some downe or order for the provideing, for wee are much necessitated here for timber and lime. This with Mr Smiths full relacons I hope of things in that respect will be sufficient. Mr Charles Towgoods vessell sprung a very great leake here, soe that I fear'd shee would founder, but I did my endeavour to prevent all damage and aided him with all assistance in sending 6 lusty men slaves to pump her, but now I hope shee will doe well, being gon downe to Tishen about 4 leages off[40] to borrow some helpe of the carpenter of another ship which is promised him. I tooke noe goods out of him as yett, haveing noe occasion att present for such goods as hee could spare.

433. Ralph Hassell   James Fort, Accra, 25 June 1682

These serves for covert to the two inclosed from Captain Starland and from Mr Towgood,[41] which last night late I received included in one from boath of them desireing mee to hasten them with all immaginable expedition, which I have done, not knowing the contents thereof but what Mr Towgood in his informed mee hee had sprung another dangerous new leake. Your honour in your last informed mee that Captain Shears would be ready to saile in 2 day's but as yett not arrived with any provisions towards erecting or supplying our buildings, which I have already begun and shall want good timber for all the 4 flankers, which 16 pieces 24 foot long will serve, if 23 foote some small baulks and boards with nailes, lyme to

[40] Teshi, east of Accra.
[41] = nos 512, 530.

plaister all the works; these provided the fort will be better and stronger then ever yett with a very small charge, for I have now 3 maisons att work and a carpenter which I borrow from the Dutchman.

I have now upwards of 50 slaves in the forte, which eats a chest of corne every day and I cannot gett any for money here. I have once sent my 7 hand canoe to Barracoe for corne and itt costs with charges 3a a chest, which formerly I bought for 2 here. This day I paid 2 paper bralls for 2 chests. And slaves comes in very plenty and I not haveing provisions to supply them, I must send my canoe to windward this night for more corne. They are somewhat deare in their slaves as yett, but the Portugueze nor Dutch buy's none soe I will lower them as much as possible I can. I give now not above 6 pezos 1 for men as your honour has rated goods, and question not but to have itt lower then 6 pezos for men and soe accordingly for woemen, but Ile not buy any but choyce slaves as hitherto have done. I have not now by mee 8 peeces of good sayes and all the green and blew perpettuanos are gone, and Guyney clouts, soe pray a supply of those goods and them that are good and all in cases or chests, for all the goods before the last parcell were without any, soe that here are very few good goods (though great quantity) but what are damag'd and of small validity. Itt is thought nay said that Ahenesa will speedily be att home with considerable quantities of slaves and gold which will be brought here, soe shall advise your honour as occasion serves. Mr Wendovers hoggs has come to great mortallity, for within this month of great raines there has dyed 15 breeding sowes, shoats, and 2 very large boars, besides piggs and most of the sowes with pigg, all well over night and dead in the morning. I wrote your honour for a butt of brandy but as yett Captain Shears is not come, which wee now much want. I have bought att great rates this 2 months out of the Dutchman and cannot be supplyed now; our people humbly beggs your honour to supply them these fogg times, for two are now sick. I had almost forgott to intreate your honour that above all things to send downe 10 paire of strong irons and 20 or 30 paire of short irons, for this day I have borrowed of the Dutchman, and some paper, for I teare my books for this, some iron wedges and a maule[42] to cleave rock's.

434. Ralph Hassell   James Fort, Accra, 5 Aug. 1682

Yours of the 2nd instant I have received, and your honour indeed may wonder att my silence, which indeed hath been occasioned by sickness and alsoe per a sting of scorpion on my right hand, which I could not till this day hold a penn in my hand, else had not been negligent in performing my duty. I have received from on board the Affrican Merchant, Captain Samuell Starland Commander, 25 perpettuanoes, 50 iron barrs and 50 Guiney stuffs,[43] and likewise have received from on board the

[42] maul, i.e. hammer.
[43] Cf. no.513, referring to the loading of wood, water and corn in the *African Merchant.*

Cape Coast Briganteen 25 perpettuanoes, 20 sayes and 48 tapsells,[44] and sayes will be wanting in a short time. I am extreamly troubled to informe your honour that on the 26th of July wee lost 13 men and 1 woeman which gott out of prison in the night, although a centry stood att the doore. They undermined the prison walls and gott out, which was the strongest place in all our forte. I shewed the place to Mr Starland and Mr Towgood whoe will render your Honour an account thereof. I have used my uttmost endeavour ever since and have sent to all parts and as yett cannot have any intelligence, which is a dayly and nightly perplexity to mee. I have gott up two flankers as high as the paveing and shall goe forwards with all vigour. Ahenesa will (as is reported) returne to Quomboe the next weeke and then may expect a supply of slaves. For upwards of 5 weeks here has been 3 or 4 interlopers which has given upwards of a bendy a head for slaves, soe that could not gett any. I have now putt on board 33 slaves [in] the Cape Coast Briganteen vizt 12 men, 20 woemen and 1 boy.[45] I have now sent May and Junes account, and tomorrow or next day another Capo Corsoe Canoe will goe hence and then shall send July's account, this being the last day. If wind and weather permitts the vessell will saile hence to Cape Corsoe. The irons, maule and wedges were lost, the canoe being kickadevood and staved, soe shall want those necessaries. This is all that offers att present, intending to write two dayes hence of all other things that shall in the interim present.

435.   Ralph Hassell   James Fort, Accra, 9 Aug. 1682

I wrote your honour of what you desired in yours of the 2nd instant, which beleeve may be with you ere this. Likewise of the loss of the slaves, which I have ever since endeavoured to regaine. I humbly begg your honour not to impute itt any wayes to my negligence, for I will in verryty certifie your honour that duely and truely a good watch both of whites and blacks is kept every night, and for the future if any slaves breaks through the prison I now have built I will be responsable for. Itt is 4 foot thick and 3 foot in foundation deepe. Captain Starland and Mr Towgood is now in the road windbound, they have in all about 100 slaves aboard both their vessells, and I supply their wants both with wood and water. If they stay here any time, I immagine Captain Shears may in a manner be up as soone as they with his loading of slaves per what I understand by a canoe last night from Allampo. Ahenesa will be att home this weeke with great quantity of slaves, and then shall render advice what progress hath made in his atcheivments. Hee hath conquered the Commongs, which was a verry greate people. When hee is att home and [I am] certaine thereof I will either send or goe my selfe if the people will admitt mee. I have here inclosed sent your honour my Jully's accounts as your honour demanded.

[44] Cf. no.531
[45] Cf. no.532.

436. Ralph Hassell   James Fort, Accra, 28 Aug. 1682

These are on purpose to acquaint your Honour that on Fryday last here came downe severall traders from Quomboe and laid out what mony's they had in say's, and have taken all that are good; and amongst the rest Ahenesahs cheife son with 30 or 40 men whoe were sent on purpose to carry mee up to Quamboe to treat with his father about the prizes of slaves and goods, there being verry greate quantity's of slaves there, soe I have sent up one of my boyes to enquire the verrity thereof. Hee likewise desired mee to write for sayes, sletias, course and fine, sheets and halfe barrels of powder, per reason whole barrels are too great a weight to carry soe far in the country, alsoe for currell if any att Cabo Corsoe. These are all that was desired, soe hope your honour will supply mee per Satureday next, att which time I expect the same persons againe, alsoe would desire your advice if convenient for my journey. I am willing to adventure for my masters interest any where, haveing been there formerly and had a kind reception. I have finished one flanker and another the beames are laid, and alsoe am now a breaking of stones to finish itt and soe goe on with what speede possible with the other works. Lyme is the only thing wanting and here is shells enough att the waterside about 5 leagues off to serve our turns if could but gett them here. Mr Shears hath severall times fetcht from thence, soe he knows the place verry well. Also [we need] a couple of good beams about 15 or 16 foot long for the tower, about 9 or 10 inches square. In my last I advised your honour that the wedges, maule and irons were lost, if slaves comes I shall want irons for have not above 10 paire that are good, soe a supply of all these are needfull. I shall from time to time render your honour advice as occasion shall proffer.

437. Ralph Hassell [to Agent-General & Council]   Accra, 2 Oct. 1682

Yours I have received saying [you are] admireing you heare not oftener from mee. Itt is now I must acknowledge a month since I wrote you last, which putting my Royall masters to 8a charge, and your honour formerly charg'd mee with extravagant chargeing in my accounts, for that reason I am as provident as I can, and would that I could in any manner save what expended that might be thought surplusage. In your honours last you ordered mee to send up my accounts with the ballance, I have made them up to the 5th instant, and what comes between this and then shall be transported to the next account. The ballance of the last account there is due 10oz 15a and odd tacco's, which I have not sent (for which begg your excuse) by reason that 12 day's hence is pay day and then must pay 11 oz and odd. If trade comes not I know not how men can live, for every thing of provisions is soe excessive deare that scarce a little corne but by the taccoe can be had heare. Most of all our people has been sick; Humphry Davis is now soe weake that I know not whether ever hee may recover. John Fishpoole died the 10th September, hee had of mee 8a before his death for pay, and itt wanted 5 dayes of a month. Hee left nothing but a few old cloaths which hee gave amongst the men to drink att his funerall, which was apprased at 8a.

[PS] I immagine Captain Nurse will saile hence for Cabo Corsoe in 2 or 3 dayes.

438.   Ralph Hassell [to Agent-General]   Accra, 2 Oct. 1682

Your particular letter per Captain Nurse I received and likewise your generall letter. In your letter your honour admires the hoggs, goates etc. were not sent up. I asked them to doe itt but they refused, haveing noe roome. Alsoe your honour is desireous to heare oftener from hence, which if you please to inspect in former letters you may see that your honour blames mee for too much charge in my accounts, and for that only reason I send noe oftener then you please to order mee, for 8a to carry a letter of noe consequence twice or thrice every month will amount to monys; therefore I humbly begg you not to censure mee negligent. I have now made up my accounts to the 5th instant and have inclosed sent them, per which your honour will see the scarcity of mony and slaves here, which is occasioned by shipps rideing here, for this month has layne one or two ships in sight and this day is a small ship come downe, which will make a bad trade for above this weeke longer here if hee stayes. Captain Nurse will have on board tomorrow if his sloope getts up (as she is in sight) the best part of 300 slaves, as I conjecture by their view. Hee purposes to stay about 2 dayes longer here.[46] I have not as yett put anything aboard him, only 2 men 2 woemen, till the day that hee sailes, which will be 2 dayes hence. Your honour with the Councill ordered mee to send likewise the ballance of my accounts per the canoemen, which if you please to view them you will find to be due 10oz 15a etc. to be due as the 5th instant and on the 14th will be pay day, att which time I must pay 11oz and odd, and if trading continues soe bad and should not have [money] to pay them the men might starve, for everything of provisions is extreame deare here, that itt is not hardly to be gott for mony, and through excessive heate can scarce gett water under 9 miles. Most nay all our men have been sick with one distemper or other. John Fishpoole, a souldier, died the 10th of September and Humphrey Davis is excessive ill, soe that now wee have here, now Christmas Cock works [sic], noe more than 2 that stands centinall of whitemen. This I thought good to informe your honour particularly of, as ikewise I have abreviated to your honour and Councill.

439.   Ralph Hassell   Accra, 16 Oct. 1682

Yours of the 12th instant per the hands of Mr William Masters I have received, and understand you are sorry I should have soe small a trade after soe great encour-

[46] Cf. no.628.

agement that I gave your Honour of a trade. In answer to which I humbly begg your favours to heare my reasons (which I doubt not but will in some measure render some small content to satisfaction). Imprimis, Ahenesa after his returne from conquest did desire mee to come up and agree for slaves, which I wrote your Honour and was denyed, and my not goeing there caused severall strangling[47] slaves to a quantity to Tishee, where many ships have gott many slaves and gives greate rates alsoe for gold. Here has not for above 3 months been less then 2 or 3 interlopers which have undersold the Company per much, which blacks will goe 2 or 3 leagues to save 6 tacco's. Alsoe Ahenesa is now in much feare of the Achims coming on him,[48] soe that within this weeke he hath given considerable quantity of gold and all his captivated slaves, soe these reasons pondered may with others for the future give you content. I have according to your commands received Mr Masters with as much allacrity as possible your orders could direct, and on sight did according to orders and have delivered him 7oz 9a 5ta in ballance to this day, which finding right please to note in conformity. I have through neglect (I must confess) omitted 28 halfe firkins of tallow ever since May account, not with any intent of fraud for they are all here and doe not vend. Mr Starland did receive of Humphrey Davis to pay your Honour 1o 11a 4ta, for which hee has had noe notice thereof. Hee is now indifferent well and presents his humble service to you. I purpose att the expiration of this month to send Mr Swindall the mony Samuell Stone owes him.

440. Ralph Hassell   Accra, 17 Nov. 1682

Since my last of the 16th October per Mr Masters have been silent, which was occasioned through [lack of] matter to correspond on, since which Ahenesa sent downe his son with upwards of 60 people desireing mee to come up to Quomboe to see a great quantity of slaves, sending one son as a pawne for my security, which though your Honour before denied yett thinking itt might prove for my Royall masters interest, I trespased on your Honours commands and went: where I had civill reception and am safe return'd, but old matters were there debated betwixt us, imprimis, why hee did not pay the debts due to the Royall Company contracted by Mr Wendover, to which hee made an answer Wendover owed him 25 bendy's for months custom of the forte, and that besides hee had layne with his wife, which he did expect [payment for?] according to the custome of the country. He demanded of mee custom ever since I was here, to which I responded I had not taken soe much money in my time, and itt was agreed hee should be paid on these conditions, that hee with his people should come downe and trade here att this fort only, and that hee should not hinder any other up country people from comeing downe. I tould him likewise that hee had been 10 months out of his country and that I had not seen

[47] sic: straggling?

[48] Presumably, in response to Ansa's campaign against Akyem earlier in the year (nos 423, 425).

any of his people, and what reason or with what face could hee demand a bendy a month thus. He answers hee was now return'd and would performe whatever hee had promised, provided hee might be supply'd att this fort with such goods as hee wanted, which I answered as far forth as Cape Coast could supply hee should not want if I saw he fail'd not of his word. Then wee proceeded to prizes of goods and slaves, hee demanded a bendy a head for a man and 6 pezos for a woemen. I tould him I would give itt him provided hee would allow mee my prizes for goods, vizt powder 7 pezos a barrell, 5 pezos for say's, 12a for perpettuano's, 3a for brawls, 3a carpetts, 9a fine sletias, 5a course ditto, and other goods to any amount per rates. If your honour thinks meet of this I begg a word of your advice and a supply of those goods I shall now write for per the verry first oppertunity. I have now in the fort 50 slaves and hope if you send a vessell downe with corne with expedition I shall gett more, I now desist for want of corne. I have sold this weeke to Allampo people 13 or 14 barrells of powder for slaves and itt is verry bad powder, or else might have raised itt to 7 pezos, soe begg a supply of good powder, full barrells and well hoopt. I have now sent up my October accompt the ballance whereof is 1m 7oz 3a, which finding all things right please to noate itt in conformity. The charges are much by reason of wood, trees and shells, for when a thing is once done well the proverb is tis twice done, and I would not have the same charge to be againe in my life time. I am now about the other halfe of the tower, being breaking stones etc. I humbly begg a supply of goods and necessary's undermentioned.

A box of white beads, some blew beads according to this patern and some biger, 80 tapsells, 40 good say's, 100 blanketts, 100 sletias fine and course, 20 or 30 barrells of powder full, dry and well hoopt in halves, quarters and wholes, 6 chests of sheets or more, some looking glases if any. All these Ahenesa will buy and desired to have them writt for. I humbly begg your Honour to spare if possible 2 hogsheads of tarris for the tank and halfe a sheet of lead for spouts.

441.   Ralph Hassell   James Fort, Accra, 16 Dec. 1682

Yours of the 22nd last past have now before mee, in which you verry much blame mee for my journey to Quomboe and say itt was not design'd for my masters interest. However itt be your good pleasure to conjecture soe, yett I know itt was [for my masters' interest], for two reasons I will demonstrate. First, as you are all men of reason what pleasure could you immagine I could take in soe unpleasant and tedious journey when itt hath been the death of one factor already, of which I had caution. Secondly, what delight could any man unless a prodigall receive in spending whatever hee had in the company of unknowne people, and such a one I am not, haveing not wherewithall to be lavish of, and likewise I went up to open the way that traiders might come to the forte and that none of his people should goe on board of ships to buy any goods nor any one for them, which I doe verry well know there doth, which in plaine is the ruine of all these forts. And as for prizes of slaves the agreement was on this condition, that your Honour would ratifie itt, and since your displeasure therein is knowne Ile not performe any contract and have bought noe slaves since. I did renew noe old thing about Mr Wendover and his wife, butt [it] being moved to mee thought good to informe you thereof, that I might have further inspection in that affaire. I have by Captain Churchey received his account [of?] debts on this day sennitt. On Monday last I sent a messenger to demand these debts and informe Ahenesah how ill hee hath served the Company in not rendering satisfaction all this time, but as yett I heare noe answer. My meaning by noateing my account in conformity is after examination thereof to make mee debtor to ballance thereof, and when you please to order itt and when your orders shall be obeyed. I find your displeasure greate likewise is extravagant expences. I know not of one angle but what was really expended and paid. I am heartyly sorry I cannot gett better traiding, which I have inform'd your honour above. In the margent you likewise order mee to send up Mr Wendovers goods att Accra. I know of none but houshold stuff, and 3 sowes, 12 piggs, for I never had any accompt from any that succeeded him, and if your Honour knowes what they are pray informe mee and send an oppertunity and they shall be sent up. I wrote your Honour per the last the great necesity wee stand herein for want of corne, yett have had noe supply. I can gett none here. Pray send for the slaves up or elce they will starve. I have here inclosed sent up Novembers accompt. I find errors in the goods sent per Captain Churchey, which please to rectifie. In the case no.447 is mentioned 30 blanketts, which all the men in fort can justifie there is but 25 and many rotton att the edges and much motheaten. Likewise in the case no.251 with chalke, for the black marke cannot be seen, is mentioned 20 good say's, in which case is not one good and I beleeve the case lay halfe up in buldge water or else under the fall of pump water. I open'd only the upper side and lett itt stand in the sun, both the wrapper and matt are rotton. In the chest of white beads no.167M I have not the contents, nor the prizes of looking glasses that I must sell for, I have ventered to sell 3 at 1a per piece. Likewise a barrell of tarras instead of a hogshead.

442. Ralph Hassell   James Fort, Accra, 26 Dec. 1682

Yours of the 19th instant have received and am much grieved, notwithstanding my sinceer (and not pretended) actions, should not prevaile to give you that content which I did hope might have reception. These accompanys Mr John Winder,[49] whoe hath been here 3 dayes ill of a feavour and was by mee desired to stay till hee had received a refreshment after a tedious voyage, and the rogues the canoemen would not be perswaded to stay for him, and other roguish actions which is to tedious to rehearse which [I] leave to his relation; and had they their desert (which I question

---

[49] Formerly RAC chief factor at Whydah, now on his way back to Cape Coast (cf. no.490).

not but your honours reason will retalliate) whipping is too good for them. Since the receipt of your honours I have examined the letters of the 22nd past, one which was the former mention'd but 25 blankquetts which arrived mee per the canoe on the 24th ditto, but the other per Captain Churchey arriveing mee the 9th instant of same date did mention 30, which I examined by, not noting the former, soe the mistake ly's in mee by not examining the orriginall, which fault pardon, although men ought to examine one with the other, which since I did and finding noe more to be placed to my debt I have torne the letter. I understand that Mr Towgood is now at Barracoe, whome I expect shortly downe and hope to ship what slaves I have on board him. I have not as yett any order for the delivery of them, hope may receive itt per him. This is what att present offers and for trade none presents in these parts to noe forts. I have bought but 1 man slave this month and gold soe inconsiderable I am afraid and ashamed to relate itt. The Dutch now proffers sayes according to their Generalls order 1oz and other goods farr below what wee can afford.

443.   Ralph Hassell   James Fort, Accra, 29 Dec. 1682

Yours of the 26th instant I received ordering mee to send up Mr Winder etc., which I had performed ere the arrivall of yours. Mr Towgood is now here, and shall according to order take out such goods as have occasion for.[50] Hope ere the arrivall of this you will meete with my former of the 26th instant per the party ordered to be sent up, I haveing given sufficient (and hope) orders to deliver him to Mr Thelwall att Annamaboe. Nothing of trade presents for want of sletias and sheets, which now is the only commodity here, and itt may be as great a drugg in 2 or 3 months hence as itt is now in request.

444.   Ralph Hassell   Accra, 31 Dec. 1682

Yours of the 26th instant ordering mee to secure Mr John Winder etc. have answered and hope is well with you. Likewise yours of the 16th ditto per Mr Towgood, of whome I have received 200 iron barrs and 2 chests of sheets for which have given him a receipt. Likewise have sent up by him the ballance of my Novembers accompt which is 3 marks, 4 angles and 4 tacco's, not knowing when I might meet with such an other oppertunity, and as soone as this month is expired my accompts shall not be wanting.

445.   Ralph Hassell   James Fort, Accra, 8 Jan. 1682/3

Yours of the 3rd instant have received late att night the 6th, in which you say you much admire why I should detayne the Royall Companys canoes, which indeed you may admire if itt were soe, for I did not desire one houre of their stay here more then till next morning till Mr Winders cloaths were washt and dryed, and that they

[50] Cf. no.550.

had letters for you I knew nothing thereof. As [for] the canoemen lett Docter Griffin aske the boatswain of the canoe if ever I opened my mouth about any letters or in the least way's offered them mony for the delivery thereof. I call God to wittness I never thought soe much, which I am per Mr Winder informed was said against mee, and that I put 2 of the canoemen in irons is as falce as the other; and to write the playne truth I putt 2 men in irons but they were not belonging to the canoes but passengers that were canoemen to William Parris, and 2 canoemen which belonged to one of the canoes stay'd behind, which went up with Mr Winder in the canoe and saved him 6 angles; and the other 2 were released the day after his departure and did offer to stay here and remaine with mee, but these 10 dayes [I] have not seen them. I wonder Mr Winder could not informe your honour thereof but because hee would have mee beare the blame in that, as hee doth the other in saying I gave him liberty to breake open your letters [which] is as erronious as any thing ever proceeded out of mans mouth: for how should I know that your honour would write mee, I have not the spirritt of devination and I think nay know my selfe not soe voyd of reason as to give that liberty to my father if hee were living, much less to any man thats a stranger to mee; and to salve himselfe thereof, in a letter of the 4th instant [Winder] desires mee not to denie itt, as itt stands to his future welfare or utter ruine, which letter I have taken a copie thereof and if you please shall be att your service, but the orriginall shall never be seen to prejudice mee in corresponding in soe basc actions. The sloope[51] hath been gon hence this 9 dayes and hope is with you ere this, and pray examine Mr Towgood about that affaire etc. The canoemen are in hast and will not stay, else should inlarge, which will per next which will be per via Annamaboe within this 2 or 3 dayes. I hope Mr Towgood hath delivered 3m 0o 4a 4ta ballance of Novembers account.

446. Ralph Hassell James Fort, Accra, 14 Jan. 1682/3

I wrote your Honour in my last that I would inlarge in my next, this being the sequall. Thought might have kist your hand ere this, but the canoe per via Annamaboe past unknowne to mee in the night. I suppose your honour hath heard how Captain Mingham and his Docter parted and the reasons therefore, hee haveing threatned the Captains death by poyson [he] was unwilling to carry him farther for feare his devilish threats might take place, and worke to strongly on such evill minded persons. Hee arrived here and not being well, stay'd 2 dayes and was blooded per Samuell Stone, and some of his men being sick aboard did desire the Captain that hee would speake to mee that Samuell Stone might goe with them in the ship. Hee made severall propositions to him before I knew itt, and [Stone] said if I would give my consent hee would goe, and being earnestly desired per Captain Mingham to lett him goe, I told him I durst not, unless your Honour would order

---

[51] i.e. the *Ann*, commanded by Charles Towgood.

mee. Hee offered mee and has given mee his obligation for 100£ sterling to indem-
nifie mee from the Company and your honour, and hope your honour will not think
itt ill done since hee is still in the Companys service and may be more beneficiall
in that imploy then here. I alsoe had one bendy to pay what he owed Captain Phipps
and myselfe etc. and one months pay that was due to him, and if that hee stayed
here on[e] hundred years in the capacity hee was in hee would never have paid what
he owed, although I gave him his dyett and cloathed him. I suppose your honour
has been informed per Mr Towgood how the slaves would have rose upon us, but
being prevented all is well. I have, humbley begging your pardon, put on board
Captain Branfill the 4 greatest rogues and 4 woemen, and have received in leiw
thereof 170 ounces of corrall, which hope will turne to better advance, for itt eats
noe corne, which now is deare. And the canoe which went up with Mr Winder
received verry much damage, soe that I could not mend her here, soe have sold her
to Captain Branfill for 8 sletias, which shall have creditt in this months account and
is more then her prime cost. I have hindred all canoes from tradeing with him in
this roade, soe that now hee is 3 leagues to leward at Tishee. The Dutchman here
paniard some goods that I had sold some Acquomboes, and I have donne the like
by him when I caught the goods hee sold, as hee did in my towne, soe pray informe
the Dutch Generall if hee gave him such orders, for I conjecture that hee doth itt
out of mallice that they bought them here, and Ile not be wanting to doe as he doth
after I heare your answer, neither will I release what I have till hee doth, because
hee made the first beginning. This I hope may find your honour with all Gentlemen
in prosperous health as itt now leaves mee. Here is now in this road and in this place
4 sayle of ships vizt Captain Branfill and 2 interlopers, whose names I know not
but one the blacks tells mee is one Salloway a Dutch interloper, and Thomas Travers
whoe arrived here yesterday. I have here inclosed sent my Decembers account,
which was forgott in my last, and humbly intreate your honour that Docter Askin
may be here in case of accidents, being now noe more then 6 whitemen.

447.   Ralph Hassell   James Fort, Accra, 7 Feb. 1682/3

Yours of the 20th past per Captain Cope have before mee, which gives mee to
understand your displeasure in detaining the Royall Companys canoes that came
from Arda neare 3 dayes, to which I object I detained them not one houre longer
then they had sufficiently refresht themselves, only desired them to stay, nay would
have had them but tarryed till next morning for Mr Winder, but my desire with them
was not prevailent enough, soe leave itt to your honours judgement. Likewise you
write you much admire parting with Samuell Stone one of the Companys servants
to Captain Mingham, to which humbly begging your pardon I reply itt was for these
reasons: first, haveing some of his sick people and himselfe not well did upon his
earnest entreaty grant him, which I doe immagine your honour would not have

denyed him had hee wrote your honour, which to further his voyage could not stay. Next, considering itt was to one of the Companys ships and was for the benefitt thereof, of the voyage, hee may as well be serviceable in that imploy as if here and if hee goes to England will be thought of not the worse by reason of serving in the ship for the Royall Companys benefitt. And as for the slaves which were delivered Captain Branfill (if you impute itt as a crime) itt being the first time, with humble submission beg your pardon and shall for the future be more cautious. I have according to order shipt on board the George and Betty, Captain Cope Commander, 27 slaves which hee himselfe accepted of vizt 10 men, 2 boyes and 15 woemen. What your honour desired about Mr Winders letter itt is enclosed,[52] and as to what goods hee landed here that arrived [in] my sight was some Arda cloaths and 3 remnants of silke of which I bought as much as would make a suite, his cloaths and such not worth your honours notice. I have enclosed likewise sent the 13a due to Captain Phipps's estate from Samuell Stone; alsoe my January's account.

[PS] Only sheets, iron barrs and tapsells are in request: this day have sold 24 tapsells. I am necessitated for a little inke.

448. Ralph Hassell James Fort, Accra, 20 Feb. 1682/3

Yours of the 15th instant I have received per the 5 hand canoe, with 3 whitemen, vizt Robert Crow, John Younger and George Browne. You seeme to be much concerned why wee have noe greater trade. I have given severall reasons in formers, as here being soe many forts soe neare that itt spoyles the trade, and that soe many interlopers comeing downe dayly to Tishee 3 leagues to leward, which causes soe great a resort of up country people to flock thither that in a manner all the forts are voyde of trade, for there they goe and noe one mollests them; but if here were good store of sletias and sheets they would vend suddainely. And as to what you write [that] you have not received above 12 or 13 marks in 16 months time, if you please to inspect a little farther you will find 16m 3o 15a 4ta paid, which indeed is a verry inconsiderable sume for the time, I wish cinceerly itt could have been 100 fold more, that then some creditt might redound to mee and not allways receive cheques and ill resentments. And as to what your honour blames mee in not sending Mr Windovers goods up I askt Mr Towgood to take them in, whoe told mee hee was soe full hee could not unless they were to put upon the spindle of his vaine. I have according to order sent up Christmass Cock, hope your honour will please to send him againe after the worke is finisht. The Portugueze are all goeing away and leave the fort to the Danes.[53] The Dutch Copeman here hath as I am inform'd wrote to

---

[52] Not preserved.

[53] The Danes reoccupied the fort on 26 Feb. 1683 (New Style: = 16 Feb. Old Style): cf. Nørregård 1966, 46. The wording here seems to contradict other accounts, which assert that the Portuguese had abandoned the fort earlier (29 Aug. 1682, according to Vogt 1979, 204), and that it was then occupied by the Akwamu, from whom the Danes subsequently recovered it.

the Generall to gett itt into their hands: itt stands the best for a leward trade, and if your honour thinks fitt intercept the Dutch. Thus much in breife.

449.　Ralph Hassell　　　　　　　　　James Fort, Accra, 8 March 1682/3

Yours of the 3rd instant per Mr Towgood is now before me. I likewise have received 6 cases of sletias course, 2 ditto fine, 10 barrells powder and 6 chests of sheets for the account of the Royall Affrican Company of England, which according to order shall endeavour to utmost of power to dispose of for gold. I have also sent up what goods are Mr Wendovers, only 5 old chaires and an old rotten table which I leave Mr Towgood to give his approbation of the vallue, also one forke that was stole within two dayes after my arrivall here. I have also sent the account enclosed of what is sent. I have now likewise sent 3m 4o 0a 8ta, which just makes up 20m. Had not the Dutch sent downe yesterday a vessell with the said goods that came from Capo Corso I might have sold all this month that came by the sloope. The sloope hath been here 2 dayes and upwards, but by reason of great raines, high seas and turnadoes could not adventure to unload any thing till weather presented, which was this morning. I shall send my February account per the canoe, which may arrive your Honour before this.

450.　Ralph Hassell　　　　　　　　　James Fort, Accra, 9 March 1682/3

Yours of the 3rd instant per the Ann Sloope have received, with 10 barrells powder, 6 cases of course sletias, 2 ditto of fine and 6 chests of sheets, of which I have sold 2 chests and want the prices of sletias. The powder will sell speedily for a benda per barrell. The Dutch accidentally next day received the same sort of goods, else should have sold most of the sheets ere this and sletias. All the mony I could make till the 7th instant, being 3m 4o 0a 8ta, I have per the sloope sent up as per Mr Towgoods receipt. This day arrived here two shipps, what they are I know not, which are traders and will imagine goe to Tishae. Nothing of moment presents but as any thing shall offer shall advise.

[Inclosure]
An account of Mr Wendovers goods sent per the Ann Sloop, Charles Towgood Comander vizt

1 silver punchbole with a cover	1 lackerd cott
1 silver tankard	1 feather bed
1 porrenger ditto	1 Arda old cloath
3 ditto spoons	1 case with bottles
1 dram cup ditto	1 fowling peice
4 pewter dishes	3 sowes
2 ditto basons	10 piggs
11 ditto plates	

As for the table and chaires they were not worth canoe hire aboard.

451. Ralph Hassell   James Fort, Accra, 14 March 1682/3

My last to you was of the 9th instant, in which was nothing of any concequence but what had wrote before per the Ann Sloope, Mr Charles Towgood Comander, hope ere this both are received, with the mony sent for my Royall Masters account and also the last months account. I had not wrote now soe suddenly but only for a supply of sheets, the former being all sold and am now importuned for more, if had 10 chests this day would have made good sayle, soe if your Honours will supply with what goods will vend, you need not question good sales and good mony. I have 4m now since the 7th instant for sheets and sletias and have refused good slaves for powder because of want of orders for buying slaves. I insert what is wanting underneath, which pray lett be sent and mony in a month shall not be wanting, as am promised. This morning came news from Allampa that Accruffee and Ahenesas people coming downe to Allampa, they [i.e. the Allampas] are againe fled over the river of Volta;[54] and 9 great canoes that came downe for cows and sheep are all return'd empty, only loaded with passengers,[55] soe that if you purpose to send there for slaves none at present are to be gott.

20 chests sheets att 7–8a
200 course sletias at 5a each
halfe barrells of powder, either empty or full, to fill what I have into, for they vend best

for the use of the fort
a barrell of mallageta
2 pickaxes and 2 shovells

452. Ralph Hassell   James Fort, Accra, 22 March 1682/3

Yours of the 19th currant per Mr Towgood in the Ann Sloope have received, with 8 chests of sheets, 8 chests of sletias and 12 halfe barrells of powder, all in good condition, only tooke a little wett per great seas coming on shoare, all which according to order shall dispose of to my Royall Masters best advantage. I have likewise followed your orders in sending up what gold I have and have not left one ounce in the fort, the sum now sent is just 5 marks, which finding wright please to advise per next the receipt thereof. Your Honours mention nothing in yours about the receipt of Mr Wendovers things sent per your orders in the sloope. The very next day after the departure of the sloope, being the 9th instant, Ahenesa went to

[54] Cf. no.431.
[55] Cows, sheep and other animals were imported into Accra from Allada to the east, evidently by canoe (cf. Tilleman 1994, 30, 38), so that the disturbances in Adangme interrupted the supply.

fight to Allampa, elce should have made a large sum. Just as his fetish tells him he must goe, noe one knew the day before thereof, soe uncertaine he is in all his actions of warr that noe councill is to determine the success apparent either maligne or otherwise, but only the dictates of a few braines.

[PS] Here is 2 brass pattareras with 2 chambers [with] the mettle soe bad [we] cannot use them; also 1 gun about 500 lb which wants a vent, soe beg an exchange or elce order to send them up.

Pray furnish me with a little inke, 2 shovells, 2 pickaxes, 300 barrs iron.

453.   Ralph Hassell   James Fort, Accra, 5 May 1683

Yours of the 3rd instant is now before mee, to which shall according to commands answer. Oppertunity before could not find place to answer to your Honours per the letter per Woolliford, likewise per Captain Lowe, occasioned thus, vizt on the 7th past haveing occasion to goe into the warehouse in the morning to deliver some goods sold, tooke the key out of my breeches pockett and staid there but a verry small time. When I went above I found my scretore open, and mistrusting I was wrong'd (or my masters leastwise) and upon search found what I would not, for weighing the Companys money I found wanting upwards of a marke, and upon examination understood itt was a free boy that lived with mee. I went and demanded him of his freinds and they denyed him, on which loath to be wrong'd I caus'd all the guns that could beare on the towne to be shotted and fired, which were accordingly performed; and about 3 or 4 hundred appear'd against our fort with small armes and fired. I made as good work as could and did maintaine a fight for 3 dayes, but the rogues all shelter'd themselves in the Dutch fort att last, and when they saw that I would have my money againe they called a pallavora and sent the money, but what I now insist on is for the payment of my powder and shott, which still they denie, yett am freinds and have a good correspondency with them, soe if your honour thinks convenient to desist of my demands I humbly crave a word. And I think there is Accra's enough in Cape Coast to satisfie 2 barrells powder and shott,[56] which will be better then meddle with them here, for reasons your honour knowes, vizt spoyle of trade etc. These are the cheife and only reasons has hinder'd and prevented mee from wrighting, and [also] their hindering the Companys pawnes from comeing to mee when sent for, which if your honour please to weigh in the ballance of your reason will find itt not to be suffered where a fort is. The Dutch Copeman writt his brother about my fireing in his towne, suppose your Honour has advice thereof but wee are much together; I have now his carpenter and cooper both

---

[56] i.e. they could be 'panyarred', or seized against payment.

att worke and hee hath two of the Companys Black maisons for him. I perceive per your honours that itt is your honours pleasure I should buy slaves att the rates of goods 3 lb prime cost,[57] soe desire an invoyce for direction for such goods as have here as per account, that I may know the better to govern my selfe thereby, for goods in England rizes and falls. I have here likewise sent the key of the warehouse and desire itt may be mended, a peece is broken almost off. I have alsoe sent up the last months account and this months, ending this day, per which your honour will find due to the Royall Affrican Company 8m 1o 2a 1ta, which if your honour had ordered itt up per any one that could give a receipt for't should have delivered itt. The Dutch have little or noe goods here. Your honour is pleased to say you will supply mee with what goods I want, which is only sheets and good sayes. I have sayes as per account 42, but 20 I wrote were received per Churchey in the case which are all much damnified, and have not 10 good ones in the Castle. The Dutch has sold sayes as long as had any goods att an ounce, and I never abated of 18a according to your orders for what were good and will not abate but rather rise. Redd perpettuanoes ly's by and spoyles, soe per permission begg what may sell for and other damag'd goods, which doe my endeavour. I purpose to make a generall sale of damag'd goods and cleare the warehouse when the up country people comes downe, that they may give notice thereof, but the waters are soe high and cannot pass as yett. It was in Mr Amy's time[58] accustomary once every yeare that soe what were a little damaged might not be quite spoyle'd and lost, and I beleeve here is sayes now that was in his time to my knowledge 4 yeares. Your honour may perceive per my March accompts how sheets sold, and if had twice as many more they had all been sold att same rates; I suppose there is a good quantity att Cabo Corsoe. I want carriages for most of the guns in the fort, if any spare ones pray lett mee not want. Likewise powder in halfe barrells; plank[s], if any some deales, for spouts to convey water into the tank; 6" [and] 8" nailes 12 per hooks and hinges for doores. The raines are verry much with us, haveing not had this 10 dayes one faire day. This I humbly begg may find a favourable reception, being the verryty of my silence and truth of all the Royall Companys concerns, and as quick expediated answer as your Honour could desire, which per the carrecter you may perceive.

454. Ralph Hassell   Accra, 14 May 1683

Yours of the 12th instant I received last night, and had then made answer thereto, but the weather proving bad and the canoemen weary deferr'd itt till this morning.

---

[57] 'Prime cost' was the value of goods in England, as opposed to their 'trade' value on the African coast. £3 prime cost per slave remained the standard RAC calculation later in the 1680s (cf. Davies 1957, 236–7). This presumably represented a shift in accounting conventions, slave prices being earlier calculated in terms of gold.

[58] From the context, presumably a former chief factor at Accra.

I am sorry to heare that Captain Lumly come to that bad fate,[59] but understand per the Serjant of Axim which they brought downe to Tishae that they gave him his ship etc. againe and [he] related all accidents that happened from Axim to this place, which is too tedious to relate and indeed doe not remember all, being spoken in Dutch. Yesterday morning one of them [i.e. the pirates] with Captain Thompsons ship past by in the offing, and the Brandenburger,[60] and about 11 a clock stood into the shoare and came to an anchor at Tishee, and about 3 a clock the 3 hand canoe past by here, and question not but arriv'd a day before the ships att Arda and hope Captain Lowe will be well provided for them ere they come.[61] Captain Summervill as per said Serjants report inform'd them that Captain Lowe had above 300 marks of gold of the Companys aboard, which made one to hast soe suddainely away, the other is now att Laggue. When the sloope shall arrive will observe all your honours orders in order to her protection and alsoe to the Royall Companys concerns ashoare, and desire noe better sport then to see them land 100 men, for I with the Dutch have given small matter to oblige the blacks and alsoe have promised powder and armes if occasion should bee, which doe not feare in the least. They take noe goods nor slaves from any but gold and plate etc. I have been this 3 dayes much troubled with the bloody flux, which has not yett left mee and weakens mee much.

455. Ralph Hassell   James Fort, Accra, 22 May 1683

Yours of the 11th instant per Mr Towgood I have before mee, in which you admire I could not secure money from my boyes. Your Honour may be assured I keepe itt not soe slightly as may be by you conjectur'd, but as itt was the Companys money I ought to endeavour the regaining thereof. I have not hindered noe trade thereby, for the Accraa's have noe money to trade withall; and as I wrought all differances are att an end and itt is better to make rogues to comply with foule meanes then by flattery, for being once brought under subjection a yoake seemes not weighty etc. I have according to order sent up the ballance of my last Months accompt being 8m 1o 2a 1ta per the Ann Sloope, Mr Charles Towgood Commander, and made as quick dispatch for him as possible could. Had your honour wrote for ballance of accompts to this day your honour should have had 3m more which have by mee; and question not but should within this 3 dayes had money enough to pay the people on next Fryday, for sheets are only now good, and sayes I question not but will vend att the rate your honour setts, 1oz. One chest of sayes I begg your Honour to enquire of Mr Towgood, which I opened and hee saw was not good, which I am apt to creditt were sayes has long layde by, and were damaged and much discoloured. Have not

---

[59] He had been attacked by pirates (cf. no.556).

[60] Presumably one of the ships in Groeben's squadron, which went on from the Gold Coast to purchase slaves at Allada: Jones 1985, no.3 (Instructions to Mattheus de Voss, 17 May 1682); cf. also Groeben 1985, 54.

[61] But it did not, and he was not (cf. no.637).

as yett opened any more. Slaves are verry scarce and cannot procure any att rates proposed, unless had powder to advance other goods. I could have sold severall barrells this month at 2oz per barrell, but will not disfurnish the fort. [We need] a bale of green perpettuanoes, 300 good iron barrs, and shott from 2 lb to 6 lb, for have but verry few left. Nay in verrity shall have noe occasion for any unless have not timber or new carriages, for to my knowledge never this 4 years was any to supply this place and can scarce play a gun on what wee have. This I wright if any occasion should happen, but as long as under your honours command here none shall ere possess but the Royall Company. I have given an accompt to Boby, Ahenesahs sonn, that on the last of this month all goods both little and much damag'd should be sold, and hee promised to bring downe severall men that are considerable traiders with him and give notice thereof to the adjacent country's. I desire your honour that all the articles that were made by your honour (for good disapline and government of men att Cabo Corso vizt for goeing into towne without my knowledge, whoreing and keeping wenches in the fort, swearing etc.) may be sent mee sign'd by your Worship and Councill, which Ile see performe'd. I have received all things exprest in your honours that were aboard the Ann Sloope. I am much in want for some padlocks; I have sent both the lock and key of the ware-house, the brazeing the key was too weake which would not turne the spring etc. The fiscal of the Mina is here att Accra and the Copeman and hee hath sent both to mee and Charles Towgood to accompany them this afternoone, which purpose to doe.

456. Ralph Hassell   James Fort, Accra, 12 June 1683

Yours per Captain Lumley of the 11th past and 24th per the ketch, Mr John Groome Commander, I have received. I would have followed your honours order in the delivery of the slaves to Captain Lumley, but hee would allow mee but 4 course sletias a piece, one with another, att which rates cannot procure more, neither doe I know when shall att the rates proposed. The raines have been soe greate in the country that noe people can come downe, only yesterday some people came which layde out about 5 bendy's in sheets and one barrell of powder. The last weeke Atta Barba came from Anguina, but I had sent twice before for him to come downe and open the way for a trade from thence, for many up country people come there, as the Akims, Taquoa [var. Toquoa][62] and other nations, soe hee sayes after your Honour pleases to considder itt and send for him hee will waite on you att Cabo Corsoe to discourse farther about other affaires, soe per returne of this canoe I expect to heare what your honours good pleasure is. I wrote your honour in my last per Mr Towgood for iron barrs and green perpettuanoes but as yett have had noe

---

[62] Not identified, but cf. 'Tocqua' in a map of 1746, shown inland of Kabestera and Angona (Kea 1982, 29–30).

answer, which begg a supply for I have none of those that are good. I have alsoe enclosed my May's accompt which is less then what I expected, which was occasioned per raines above recited. I am straitened for corne, not haveing above 6 chests in the fort, and here is none to be had for money att any rates; soe begg a supply within this weeke, elce must send what slaves I have to Cabo Corsoe in the 5 hand canoe for they will be starv'd elce. Captain Groome is now at Tishee, and I admire hee hath not sent a canoe to informe your honour what trade, for I told him I would deferr wrighting till hee sent. George Browne saith that hee left but 4£ per anno to his wife in England, but they that cast his sallary up makes itt to be 4£ 12s 7½d, soe that itt will att 13 months per anno amount to 7a 8ta per month but it is sett downe noe more then 7a 6ta per month.

457. Ralph Hassell   3 July 1683

Yours of the 23rd past per Mr Towgood and of the 28th ditto per John Lord in the canoe is now in view and according to your orders have donn what you required and commanded, and with all doe as much wonder as you admire why noe more money is remitted, which I with submission reply if trade presents not, I am noe quiner [= coiner?] of gold (which expression pray pardon). In mee lyes noe fault for itt would certainely redound much more to my creditt and advantage that more money presented, and will per Mr Towgood remitt 12m of gold which I have now by mee, and would per the bearer if you had in the least commanded I would have obeyed. Have now under command of the Royall Companys fort the sloope,[63] and Mr Towgood waites only your orders for proceeding, not that I detaine him but desire that all things may be don for the best, and desire your Honour soe to censure. Shall per Mr Towgood more largely answer, this only begg 30 or 40 chests of sheetes as soone as possible, for they are much enquired after and have none left and itt will be a meanes to put other goods off. Have nothing elce to add only to request suddain newes of the pyrates arrivall, that soe I may give advice to Mr Groome and Mr Harper, whoe hath wrote me to send them word.

458. Ralph Hassell   James Fort, Accra, 9 July 1683

Yours of the 7th instant received yesterday, and immediatly gave the canoemen cankey money and dispatcht them to Mr Groome.[64] In answer to your honours of the 23rd June, I wonder what should be the reason why my waights doe not hould out with those att Cabo Corsoe, being the Companys weights given to master of a ship, or elce certainely greate waight is made att Cabo Corsoe, for I made good weight here. Yett nevertheless I have sent up the money wanting, which is 9a 5ta. Alsoe now per Mr Towgood my Junes accompt with the ballance thereof being 12m

[63] To protect it against the threat from pirates: cf. no.558.
[64] Cf. no.561–2.

1o 5a 2ta. Alsoe you seeme to admire why I take noe more money, considering the quantity of goods I have, which I must acknowledge I never knew this place better furnished for upwards of 4 yeares then now itt is, but if traders are not suffered to come downe, whoe are hindered per Ahenesah, elce Arcany's and Ackims would bring twice as much trade here as att Cabo Corsoe, and all what ever hee buy's hee makes them pay treble the prime cost here. I have likewise shipt what slaves Captain Charles [Towgood] would chuse, which is 4 men, 8 woemen and 1 girle,[65] and also two carriages for guns, one is for a saker the other a minion. And as for my complayning of goods being damnified, please to send any of your Councell to inspect them whoe may be competent judges and sett rates on them, Ile be responsable for what hee or they shall vallue them att provided they sell for as much. Your honours orders I have sett up att the gate and am seveere in seeing them prosecuted according to order, and not one free woeman I suffer to lye in the fort, which seemes tedious to those soe habbituated and make them raile against mee, speaking hardly about itt, which I question not but your Honour has heard thereof or will suddainely, yett nevertheless Ile performe your commands. Have received every thing per the sloope as your honour advised. As for the nero and strafino corall I expect within this day or two a marke for the moiety, which will answer what I expected, which will doe more then purchase 4 slaves. Atta Barba is now with mee and has brought 5 bendy's for sheets, and had I 50 chests I would sell them in a months time and other goods with them. Hee purposes to Cabo Corsoe next weeke; this night he goes to Barracoe. Have dispatcht the sloope with wood water and corne sufficient for the slaves, and alsoe spar'd 1 iron bound teirce and 1 barrell which I expediated as soone as received your command.

459. Robert Young   Accra Fort, 11 July 1683

This serves only to acquaint you that on Tuseday night my selfe with Mr Nightingale and the soulders landed here and delivered Mr Hassell your order for the delivery of the fort, which hee noe sooner read but hee immediatly caused the souldiers to be drawne up and delivered mee the key of the fort, and as soone as I had possession I read my owne orders before all of them in armes and commanded them that they were in my orders, to dismiss their armes and immediatly to gett their things ready and repaire on board the sloope; but a great sea riseing and night comeing on I sent them away before itt was darke. And likewise this day two men which I understand had turned the master of the small Barbadian interloper, his mate and carpenter out of the ship in this roade, the master comeing on shoare made his complaint to Mr Hassell, whoe with a greate canoe went on board with him and went in. Mr Hassell haveing given his canoemen a signe, they seized them and threw them overboard. The master haveing gott possession of his ship againe is

[65] Cf. no.559.

weighed and gon off the coast. Wee shall make an end of inventorying the Companys goods today and shall if weather permitt send Mr Hassell away in the sloope to morrow night. Here arrived in the roade an English canoe from Ardra but can not say any thing of the newes because shee was afraid of the sea which went on shoare, but there is noe whitemen come with them. Wee have sent up to give Ahenesa ackey and to acquaint him of our arrivall here. Our trade att present is not verry good for gold but indifferant for slaves. The fort is almost as bad as the Danes hill,[66] one flanker is fallen in, but the best is, the tank houlds water verry well and wee should not be behoulden to none but that wee want good spouts, and if your Worship thinks fitt to send a few deales downe, Ile doe my endeavour to gett them made by the first carpenter that comes downe. Here is some lyme Mr Hassell left to repaire the fort, which shall begin to doe as soone as hee is gon. Here is abundance of goods, but most of them damnified but what Charles [Towgood] brought downe this last time.

460.   Robert Young & James Nightingale   James Fort, Accra, 12 July 1683

This accompany's Mr Hassell whoe imbarques along with Mr Towgood,[67] and according to your Worship and Councills orders have sealed his chest and scretore up and have delivered them to Charles to take care of the seale of them. I was forct to seale them with Mr Hassells seale, because mine with Mr Nightingall's was on board Mr Sheares, but I shall send itt up enclosed in a letter by Captain Quow. I with Mr Nightingale have given him a receipt for all the goods and what wee found in the Castle. I hope wee shall have itt in a little better case then itt is at present.

[PS] I have received of Mr Hassell 3 marks, 2 ounces and 1 taccoe of gold for the ballance of his account and have taken Charles Towgoods receipt for the same.

461.   James Nightingale [to Agent-General]   James Fort, Accra, 13 July 1683

I render your honour humble thanks for your kindess I have received, but especially for your fatherly advice, and pray doe not doubt but that in all things I shall be verry obedient to your honours commands and will with the assistance of Mr Robert Young my Cheife doe my utmost to promote my masters interest. I have heard the Dutch Copemen say just after Mr Hassells departure that Mr Hassell had advice of our comeing 3 day's before our arrivall here. Your honours will heare all the actions and transactions against Mr Hassell of the people which are sent up, I doe assure your honour the one will betray the other. In the interim I refer the rest to our generall letter.

[66] i.e. the Danish fort at Accra.
[67] Cf. no.559.

462. Robert Young & James Nightingale [to Agent-General & Council]

James Fort, Accra, 13 July 1683

This accompany's Captain Quow and Tom Amamaboe, and have sent enclosed the inventory of the remaaines of the Company's concerns in this place, and likewise Mr Hassells accompt which [we] brought from Cabo Corsoe with us, and since his departure in one of the roomes we have found a chest where was 30 peeces of Cape Verd cloaths belonging to Mr Hassell, the Serjant and some others, which they bought of an interloper, but most damag'd, and likewise in overhauling the warehouse wee found 31 brass kettles which had formerly been in his account but not in this that we had with us, and have sent likewise a paper enclosed of what George Browne sayes against Mr Hassell, and as soone as hee is any thing well shall send him up per first oppertunity. Wee need not write any thing of the damaged goods for your Worship will see that per the invoyce. As concerning the trade wee can say nothing to att present, haveing not heard from Ahenesah but expect them dayley. Wee desire your Worship to send downe per first conveyance some iron, blew pautka's and sheets which the natives now enquire after, and by that time hope shall have some money to send up. All things seeme to stand verry well between the natives and us, they being verry well satisfied att Mr Hassells departure and our comeing. Questioning not but through our endeavours to bring a good trade againe.

463. Robert Young [to Agent-General]   James Fort, Accra, 13 July 1683

I thought fitt to acquaint you how our guns are here, one has a drill broke in itts vent and one a hole in itt's side and another that is soe thinn that noe body durst fire itt, and the two pateraro's are the same mettall as the gun which broke on the tower, nor is here one inch of match nor one good truck[68] to any of the carriages, nor one bed nor coyne,[69] all being soe rotton that wee are almost afraid to fire them for feare that they should fall to peeces, therefore if your Worship thinks fitt to send downe the two gunns that came out of Mr Groomes ship they will be halfe the defence of the fort, with some match, 2 linstalks,[70] 2 shovells, 2 trowells and one pickax, and shall send these mentioned up per first conveyance.

464. Robert Young   James Fort, Accra, 22 July 1683

Your Worship and Councills letter dated the 20th July I have received, and this serves to acquaint you that according to your order I have sent up per this canoe Thomas Barrott and George Browne. Mr Hassells boy Toby is in the sloope with the two pawnes your Worship writes of, I doe not know (but here is but three) but

---

[68] i.e. wheel.

[69] quoin, i.e. wedge.

[70] linstocks, i.e. staffs to hold matches.

Mr Hassell and this Thomas Barrott sent one to windward to purchase a 2 hand canoe but hee is not return'd as yett, soe shall send these two in a small canoe with a letter to your Worship, as judgeing itt to be the best, for should I goe to take them here they would give notice to the other which may be one, but as soone as hee comes downe shall secure him till further order, and according to your orders shall send tomorrow morning Boquee up to Ahenesa with a man along with her, and to acquaint him that itt is your possitive order shee be releast.[71] As concerning the trade itt is but little att present and the goods which att present vend most is as formerly wrote, as iron, sheets, powder, and some enquire after blew pautka's. Wee have taken upwards of 2 marks, but paying the people here, that is in pay, hath diminished a little. Here is noe trade come from Quomboe as yett, his sonn and the man which alway's was our messenger is up in the country, but when itt doth come itt is all att once. Wee have purchased 7 slaves and could have had more, but wee stand for one man and one woeman, men slaves being verry scarce here. Here lyeth Agent Pearson and Captain Parris. Mr John Groome hath filled some water here and hath taken in some wood and doth intend for Cabo Corso, his goods being much damag'd, but hath 30 odd verry good slaves in and some gold. I have put on board him 3 old gunns and 2 patteraro's for to be delivered ashoare att Cabo Corsoe, they being not fitt for any service, and according to your order I shall sett the people to repaire this fort and will be as spareing in the charges as possible and will not lett the Companys slaves build the Dutch fort, and lett ours fall. Your Worship would doe us a kindness if you can spare 3 or 400 hundred of bricks, 2 shovells, 2 trowells, 1 pickax, with 2 small gunns with things appertaining, and 6 of the Companys musketts new and well fixed, for here is not one muskett fitt to use but a man snaps almost a hundred times before itt will fire. Not else att present to inlarge but wishing for a good trade, which shall not want for my endeavouring for to gett itt.

465. Robert Young   James Fort, Accra, 2 Aug. 1683

Your Worship and Councills letter dated of the 26th July I have received, and according to your orders I have proceeded in the seizing of what I mett with in this fort or the towne, which is as followeth, one old man of Mr Hassells which hee kept for a sentinall, one woeman of Thomas Barrotts and one small boy, and likewise his wench being his slave, and have enquired of the natives of the Dutch Towne and can learne noe more but that they have one slave of his, a man and one woeman pawn'd to him for an ounce, which slave hee hath already delivered mee and hath promised the ounce for the woeman. A Monday here arrived from Ahenesah his two sonns with some Arcany Cabasheers and they tell mee that their father Ahene-sah saith that if I have good goods I shall not want for a trade both for money and

---

[71] Boque was Ahenesa's wife, held in pawn for 100 muskets supplied on credit: cf. nos 409, 414 (inclosure 3).

slaves, and I acquainted them that I had your Worship and Councills promise for what goods I wanted and have made them wellcome. They enquired for sheets but wee haveing none, they have bought some sayes, some powder and some musketts. Not elce at present to enlarge, haveing not as yett a trade to my mind but itt doth not want for my endeavours, Captain Pearson lying in sight and the other interloper and gives a bendy for woemen and a bendy 4 angles for a man in goods or gold.

466. Robert Young   James Fort, Accra, 8 Aug. 1683

Your Worships and Councills letter dated the 3rd of August came safe to my hands, wherein I understand that the sloope is not gott as yett noe higher then Amersa, and that by her shall receive the goods I formerly wrote for. Wee doe take some money although the Dutch hath been supplyed with sheets, iron barrs, sayes etc. 3 dayes agoe by their sloope, and shall use my utmost endeavour to purchase as many good slaves as possible, and as cheape as I can. One ship lying in sight and giveing those rates, wee buy none, but Ahenesah hath promised mee to gett some slaves, against the sloope comes. I would desire your Worship to send downe one chest of good bright musketts, for they would sell here, these being old and have been a long time here. The Dutch sells their musketts and sheets for slaves and disposes of them [i.e. slaves] againe to the interlopers, which hope for the future may be but few. I would desire your Worship not to forgett to send downe the trowells and other materialls.

Slaves bought: 2 men, 6 woemen and 1 boy.

467. Robert Young   Accra, 24 Aug. 1683

Your Worships and Councills letter dated the 22nd August come safe to my hand, and am glad the sloope is arriv'd soe that wee may be supplyed with goods and materialls which wee have wanted ever since my arrivall. As to slaves wee have purchased 4 men, 6 woemen and 1 boy, and might purchased more but that had not goods suiteable, which the Dutch furnish themselves with all nations and especially of late both English and Dutch, their boates comeing and landing their goods on shoare. And according to your order have sent Mr Nightingale up per the 5 hand canoe and Mr Harper along with him, they being as yett here, and am heartyly sorry for the death of Mr Stapleton whoe was a good servant to the Company, and as acquainted you formerly have lost one here by an unhappy shott, but they are all fledd and gon, but hope with the assistance of Bobee to gett one if not two of them. And have likewise sent per Mr Nightingale my July account with the ballance being, 1 mark, 6 ounces, 14 angles and 7 tacco's. Not elce att present to inlarge but desireing to dispatch the sloope with goods.

468. Robert Young   [Accra], 2 Sept. 1683

Your Worships and Councills letter dated the 27th August by the sloope I have received, with the receipt for the ballance of my July account and likewise 10 chests sheets, 2 cases of sayes, 1 chest of musketts, 5 barrells gunpowder, 200 iron barrs, and 4 yards of green cloath for Ahenesah; alsoe 300 bricks, 3 shovells, 1 pickax, 3 trowells, 2 small gunns, with a spung, 30 minion shott, 20 faulkon ditto, 10 deale boards, 2 scaynes of match, 2 linstalks, 2 old carriages, 12 granado's, and 6 old musketts that will not fire, as your Worship may see per the returne of them, for there is abundance such here already, but the musketts I desired in my letter to be sent downe, were 6 new musketts well fixt.

[PS] The sloope staying a day longer then expected by reason of the sea, soe have sent my August account with thee ballance per James Bayly.

469. Robert Young   Accra, 13 Sept. 1683

Your Worships and Councills letter dated the 29th August by Captain Doegood I have received, with 2 cases of sayes, 200 iron barrs, 5 chests of sheets, 30 pieces allejars; and your Worships and Councills order of the 2nd September to deliver one man and one woeman slaves, but hee [= Doegood] did protest here that itt was your Worships promise to him, if that Captain Bell did not take any off, then hee was to have 4 (Captain Bell did not come neare this place but went directly downe in the offing as far as wee could see him), and have the Company[s] creditt for the goods in leiu of them; and a letter by Mr Harper of the 3rd instant whoe you order to live here as my seacond and shall pay his sallary as itt is mentioned; and likewise a letter of 4th instant being an order to purchase as many slaves as possible and to ship what slaves is here on board Captain Draper for Cabo Corsoe (and have sent Mr Sheares and Mr Groomes letter down to them). Captain Draper wanted powder to purchase some slaves att Barracoe and upon his receipt have spared him 3 barrells of the damnified powder, takeing his receipt for the same. Here is att present verry little trade. Agamaco is gon up to Ahenesah but is not as yett returned. The bricklayer is not come downe, which wee much want.

470. Robert Young   Accra, 23 Sept. 1683

Your Worship and Councills letter dated the 14th September by the 2 hand canoe with an express came safe to my hands, and have ever since my arrivall here given an account to your Worship and Councill how things have stood here by all canoes that were bound up, and since my last to your Worship have put on board Captain Draper, 4 men, 10 woemen and 2 boyes,[72] and if I might have disposed of powder

[72] Cf. no.573.

should have purchased some more, and for other goods wee have quantity's by us, but as for the Guyney stuffs that your Worship mentions in your letter there hath been none disposed of or enquired after since my arrivall, and shall use my endeavour to keepe the prizes of goods up as much as possible. I sent up my August account per James Bayley, which since per your letter I understand is delivered but have as yett noe receipt for the ballance and doe wonder the money should not hould out weight, itt being 3 angles over when weighed itt here, as James Bayley see when I delivered itt to him, and itt agreeing with these weights in the former; and since your letter dated the 18th September, where I find to be on board the sloope 15 barrells gunpowder and 4 chests musketts, but the musquetts for the forts use are not come which are mentioned in the letter and [I] sent the former that hee brought per the returne of him, and shall use our endeavour to dispose of the powder and musketts which are now come downe (but there is 22 that their stocks are broake) for slaves but as yett have purchased noe more then 1 man and 1 woeman. The people that were seized are all on board Captain Draper, but only [= except] Mr Hassells whoe is one of our centinalls and cannot with conveniency part with him, but if your Worship orders him up shall per the first oppertunity that presents send him; and for the goods which your Worship was pleased to mention in your letter, here at present noe trade soe cannot answer in that respects, but if any be enquired after shall write to your Worship of itt. I have sent Agamaco to Ahenesah to know why the trade to the waterside is stoped but is not as yett return'd. I can not dispose of Daniell Roe's things here, they being intermixt with the things of Thomas Barrotts, soe have put them on board the sloope alltogether and have dispatch her away. Captain Thomas Draper hath been gon from hence this 8 day's.

471. Robert Young   Accra, 29 Sept. 1683

Your Worships and Councills letter dated the 26th September by Thomas Plumer in the 9 hand canoe came safe to my hands, with 10 barrells gunpowder, 5 chests containing 3025 sheets and 1 case containing 25 greene perpetuano's on the Companys account. I beleeve wee might dispose of some broad tapsells but for fine sletias there hath been none enquired after. Course sletias your Worship may send some downe per first oppertunity with some Guyney stuffs. Your Worship and Councill hath lowered the goods to undersell the Dutch, which wee shall follow and shall use my endeavours to assist the vessells as much as possible. I sent Mr Shears's letter to him att sea, whoe departed from hence the 17th att night,[73] and likewise Mr Groomes to leward.[74] I find that Captain Draper had noe occasion for the powder your Worship was pleased to mention by itt's arrivall. The trade here is

---

[73] sic: presumably miscopied for '15th' (as implied in no.470 above); Draper was at Beraku by 16 September (no.573).
[74] Groome was at Alampo (cf. no.569).

by Ahenesah stop'd by reason of the Dutch, and they did not take soe much this month as paid their souldiers. Aggamaco is come from Ahenesah and itt's their danceing time, but hee saith the Dutch are the occasion of soe little trade and hath not don well by them which makes his people not to come downe to the waterside, and shall use our endeavours to dispose of the damag'd goods. I shall according to your order put on board Mr Groome what slaves I have when hee comes up, which att present is but 2 men and 2 woemen and att present can verry ill spare them, being just now a rebuilding the flanker which is fallen downe.

472.   Robert Young   Accra, 9 Oct. 1683

Your Worships and Councills letter of the 4th currant came safe to my hands, and doe use my uttmost endeavour to dispose of the Companys goods as fast as possible, which if itt continues as this month begins, wee shall have an indifferant good trade, although the Dutch hath since our last supply of goods made a pallavora with his Cabasheers to the intent that they might hinder our trade, and hath gave out that whoever hee be that comes trade with us or is the occasion of the up country peoples comeing here hele fire their hourses and turne them out of the towne, which keeps the blacks much from their usuall tradeing with us, and hath promised to protect them against Ahenesah and to take them in his fort if occasion serves; and shall according to your order put what slaves I have in the fort on board Mr Groome, which att present is but 2 men and 6 woemen. I sent a 2 hand canoe up with Mr Groomes letter[75] the 1st instant but is not as yett return'd, nor heare noe tideings of her, which makes mee doubt that shee is not arrived.

473.   Robert Young   James Fort, Accra, 22 Oct. 1683

This accompany's James Bayley in the ketch,[76] by whome I have sent my September accompt with the ballance and what slaves I had by mee, being 2 men, 8 woemen and 1 boye, and have spared him 12 chests corne for his voyage up, with some wood and some water.

474.   Robert Young   James Fort, Accra, 23 Oct. 1683

Your Worships and Councills letter dated the 18th instant by James Bayly came safe to my hands. This morning the ketch weighed from hence and hath taken in 12 chests of corne, some wood and water, and have likewise put on board her what slaves I had by mee in the fort, and likewise my September accompt with the ballance, and shall use my endeavour that the Dutch may as little undermine us here

---

[75] = no.569.

[76] i.e. the *Adventure*, commanded by John Groome

as possible, though they give all the encouragement immaginable to doe it. I shall want per the next some sheets; our powder and musketts doe not att present goe off by reason of the Dutch whoe undersells us, and an interloper lying in the roade, just goeing off, sells powder for almost prime cost, and his musketts at 18 per bendy. Mr Groome is come ashoare with Docter Meade, haveing noe conveniency to doe any thing for him there, and questions not but in grace of God that hee may doe well though att present is very weake.

475. Robert Young   James Fort, Accra, 1 Nov. 1683

Your Worships and Councills letter dated the 25th October by Captain Browse came safe to my hands, with 10 chests sheets containing 650 on the Companys accompt. This accompanys a 2 hand canoe and to acquaint you of the death of Mr Groome whoe departed this life the 29th October about 7 a clock in the evening, and have sent his booke of accounts that every thing might be made even betwixt the Company and him, and what is due to him did desire mee to receive for his wife and children, and what debt hee owes for mee to satisfie them. I have likewise sent an inventory of what things hee hath here and desire your Worship will send an inventory what hee hath on board the ketch.

VIII

OFFRA AND WHYDAH

The section of the West African coast east of the River Volta was probably already becoming known to Europeans by the 1680s as the 'Slave Coast'.[1] The RAC correspondence, however, does not employ this terminology, calling it rather the 'Coast of Arda', after Allada ('Arda'), the principal African state in the region. The RAC had re-established a factory at Offra ('Ophra') in Allada in 1674,[2] and this still existed at the beginning of 1681. In May 1681, an attempt was made to establish a second factory in the neighbouring kingdom of Whydah ('Whiddaw', 'Guydah' etc.), to the west; but this proved abortive, the RAC factor left there, John Thorne, being recalled to take over the factory at Offra in August of the same year. At the beginning of 1682, the RAC again sent people to occupy Whydah, but the chief factor designated for Whydah, John Winder, initially took up residence at Offra, and moved to Whydah only in July 1682. At the time of the latest correspondence preserved, in June 1683, both the Whydah and Offra factories were maintained, although the possibility of withdrawing the latter was under discussion. It was, however, evidently abandoned soon after. The trade at Offra and Whydah was solely for slaves; gold was available only as a re-export, being brought by some European traders from the Gold Coast to be exchanged locally for slaves.[3]

The correspondence from the Offra and Whydah factories is not preserved as completely as that from the establishments on the Gold Coast. In part, this reflects their greater distance from Cape Coast Castle, and the lesser frequency of communication with the latter. Ships which had once left the Gold Coast to the eastward did not normally pass back up along the coast. Offra and Whydah depended for their communication with the Gold Coast mainly on African canoes and canoemen, which were regularly brought from the Gold Coast by European ships for use further east and returned home when their employment was completed;[4] alterna-

[1] The earliest use of the term 'Slave Coast' so far traced is in a work published in 1697 (Tilleman 1994, 32, 34). Barbot in the 1680s, however, already used a similar term, 'Captive Coast [Cativos Kust]' (1992, i, 231).

[2] Law 1991a, 126.

[3] For discussion of this trade, including references to it in these documents, see Law 1990b, 105–6.

[4] Other Gold Coast canoes traded to the Slave Coast independently: see further Law 1989.

tively, letters were carried by ships departing from the coast to the island of São Tomé, where they were evidently passed on to local shipping for transmission to the Gold Coast. In addition (and partly in consequence of this pattern of shipping and communication), it seems that the Slave Coast factories for most purposes reported directly to the RAC in England, rather than through Cape Coast Castle.[5] The correspondence from Whydah reproduced here, indeed, includes some letters sent to the Company in London, which were copied for information to Cape Coast.

In addition to the RAC's factory in Offra, the Dutch West India Company also maintained a factory there, which is mentioned in several of these letters. When the RAC began to consider a factory in Whydah in 1681, it was noted that there were already a French and a Portuguese factory there (no.479). The French factory here had been established in 1671.[6] The Portuguese factory may have been established in 1680;[7] it was evidently ephemeral, however, since in November 1682 it was reported to be empty, there being no Portuguese in Whydah.[8] At Whydah, as reported in this correspondence (no.479), the RAC had been preceded by a rival English factory, established by the interloper Petley Wyburne in November 1681.[9] Three of the letters preserved in this correspondence were from Wyburne, rather than the Company's own factors. The RAC evidently demanded that Wyburne should withdraw, but Wyburne himself refused to leave (nos 491, 495), and the RAC's own factor claimed to be powerless to remove him (no.490). He was still there, trading in competition with the RAC, at the end of 1683.[10]

The RAC correspondence for 1681–3 is less illuminating about the indigenous politics which formed the background to (and, in some measure, a determinant of) the patterns of European activity on the Slave Coast. Other evidence shows that, when the Company began trading at Whydah in 1681, the Governor of Offra had initially forbidden the carriage of slaves there;[11] but by the time of the first letter in the series reproduced here, in May 1681, 'free trade' between the two places had been re-established (no.476). Subsequently, in December 1681, there is reference

---

[5] Cf. Davies 1957, 250.

[6] Barbot 1992, ii, 635–6.

[7] Verger 1968, 159–60 (n.20), citing a nineteenth-century source. Verger himself is sceptical about this report; but it is supported by the contemporary evidence of the English correspondence.

[8] Celestin de Bruxelles, Whydah, 2 Nov. 1682, in 'Documenta' 1915, 358. It is noteworthy that Barbot, who visited Whydah in April 1682, makes no reference to a Portuguese factory there, though this may reflect the fact (which is clear from Celestin's account) that the latter was situated in the capital inland, rather than at the coast where the French factory was.

[9] The English factory at Whydah noted by Barbot in April 1682 (1992, ii, 635) was presumably Wyburne's rather than that of the RAC, which (despite earlier attempts) was not effectively established until later in the year.

[10] Wyburne was eventually forcibly removed from Whydah, in early 1686: PRO, T70/12, Edwyn Steede & Stephen Gascoyne, Barbados, 27 April 1686; T70/11, Henry Nurse et al., Cape Coast Castle, 19 March 1686).

[11] Law 1990a, no.7 (William Cross, Offra, 13 June 1681).

to a war 'among the Blacks', which evidently involved a threat of attack on Offra, since the English factory there had to purchase gunpowder for its own defence, and to a subsequent meeting of repesentatives of the kings of Allada and Whydah to make peace with Offra (no.480, with inclosure 1); but the context and significance of these events is not explained. Other evidence shows that the rivalry between Offra and Whydah for control of the European trade was complicated by tensions between Allada and Offra, with Whydah recurrently supporting the latter in rebellion against the former,[12] so that the threat to Offra in 1681 may well have come from Allada rather than from Whydah. In the following year Allada was reportedly urging the RAC to establish a new factory, at Apa to the east, on the grounds that the route to Whydah was unsafe, traders running the risk of being 'panjard [kidnapped] and robed' on their way there, very probably (though this is not stated) by the people of Offra (no.484). This implies both that Allada was then sending its trade to Whydah rather than Offra, and that its policy was to establish access to the coast independently of Offra, rather than to favour the latter.[13]

476.   John Thorne   Agriffie in Whidaw, 24 May 1681

Att our arrivall at Whidaw Captain Lowe came to an anchor, and by his and Mr Gouldings[14] order I was sent on shoare to learne how affaires stood here and att Ophra and att which place was most probability of his quick dispatch, and next day returned on board againe with answer from the King that if Captain Lowe would come on shoare himselfe hee would contract with him for his whole complement of slaves,[15] whereupon he and Mr Goulding went on shoare and the King likeing his cargoe promised him his slaves in 26 dayes, which might have been accomplished had there not come two interlopers, a Portuguese and a French ship into the roade. Captain Lowe haveing gott goods on shoare, Mr Goulding bought slaves at Sabba [var. Saba] the Kings house, and I was ordered at Agriffie the lower towne,[16] where when wee had purchased his whole complement of slaves hee would have had the remaines off againe, but finding it something difficult, and Captain Lowes ship springeing a great leake, twas thought most convenient to leave the goods on shoare and mee with them then to delay time for the aforesaid reasons.[17] I have built

---

[12] Cf. Law 1991a, 238–45. These tensions ended in the destruction of Offra, in 1692.
[13] Cf. the situation in 1671, as described by Barbot 1992, ii, 636.
[14] Thomas Goulding had been sent to take over as chief factor at the RAC's factory at Offra, but (as noted later in this letter; cf. also no.477) died shortly after his arrival there.
[15] If this means that the king himself was to supply all the slaves, this was not the usual practice. Barbot says merely that 'the king ordinarily does more trade than any of his subjects' (1992, ii, 637). On this issue, see further Law 1977.
[16] i.e. Savi, the royal capital, and Glehue, the coastal town where the European trade was centred.
[17] Cf. no.592.

noe house yett but if your worship think itt convenient to settle here I desire you to send mee orders for itt, and another man which is a good accountant, which I judge may be very beneficial for the Royall Companys interest, this place being not above 4 or 5 hours journey from Ophra and the charges being the same at both places.[18] Besides the King [of Whidaw] and Phidolgo[19] [of Ophra] are great friends againe and are desireous of a free traid againe.[20] I have only the 3 hand canoe left and the great canoe went downe to Ophra and was staved in goeing ashoare with the goods, the weather being very bad and Captain Lowe unwilling to stay by reason of the leake, and I understand there is never a canoe att Ophra and desire you will be pleased to send one by the next ship.[21] As for the canoemen, I have not paid them their halfe pay,[22] because they would not goe downe to Ophra with the canoe and neglected their busieness here for the 3 last dayes. I have been downe at Ophra and find the factory was all burnt downe but is almost finished againe and a very secure trunck built and things very well settled. I find Mr Cross to be a very civill gentleman and none that is as well deserving as capable of the place. I was ordered to be accountable to Mr Goulding att Ophra, but hee being dead and Mr Cross succeeding[23] have brought them to him [i.e. Cross], whoe hath sent them up with his owne.

477. William Cross   Ophra in Arda, 18 Aug. 1681

I humbley presume to give your worship the trouble of these few lines to certifie you of my departure with Captain Branfill, and how hee made a shift to pick up his slaves in about 20 days with those goods and some money [which] hee brought;[24] but tis very inconvenient for a ship to come here without booges, and if you send none by the next ship, you must hardly expect any slaves; but if you purchase any [booges] att the Mina Castle (where I heare there is plenty) you may be sure of slaves in a very short time, and if you send but halfe the cargoe of the next ship in booges,[25] any other goods you have will goe off except iron barres. I am sorry I am to send you the unhappy news of Mr Gouldings death, whoe died on the 5th of May

---

[18] Contrast Barbot, ii, 658, who reported that charges were much higher at Offra than at Whydah; also no.493, which says that costs of porterage from the beach to the Company's factory were lower at Offra.
[19] See Glossary.
[20] When Low went to trade at Whydah, the Fidalgo of Offra had initially closed the paths there, but subsequently relented and allowed slaves to be supplied to Low at Whydah: cf. Law 1990a, no.7 (William Cross, Offra, 13 June 1681).
[21] A canoe was supplied to the Allada factory from Anomabu in May 1682, presumably in response to this request: cf. no.274.
[22] Canoemen hired from the Gold Coast for service on the Slave Coast were paid half their wages in gold on recruitment, and half in goods at the end of their employment: cf. Phillips 1732, 229.
[23] Cross had in fact been chief factor at Offra prior to Goulding's arrival, and resumed the post on the latter's death.
[24] Cf. no.596.
[25] This recommendation is repeated in no.494; cf. also Law 1990a, no.3 (William Cross, Offra, 13 June 1681); Barbot 1992, ii, 657.

last, hee lay sick but 4 dayes, all which time I had the Dutch docter with him, who att first comeing told mee he was a dead man, after hee understood what hee had taken, which was too large a potion of some physick hee brought downe here with him, being enough for neare three times takeing, as the docter told mee, and being not sick before found nothing to worke upon but an empty stomack, yett held him vomitting for two dayes or more and the rest of the time lay speechless and in 4 dayes died about 3 in the afternoone. Captain Lowe tooke in his slaves at Whidda, where hee left Mr Thorne and Robert Chapman with the remaines, but upon Mr Gouldings death and my goeing home hee [= Thorne] is come downe to Ophra to take possession here, who is a man that is very capable and deserving of the place and one that knows the custome of the country, which is not presently found out by a newcomer, and if your worship please to send downe another man to him that is an accountant, I doe not question but hee shall manage the Company's affaires here better then anyone you can propose to send downe. Captain Low had promised the King of Whiddah to settle a factory there, for which reason would not lett bring away what goods were on shoare after hee had bought his slaves, but was forced to leave Mr Thorne with them, an account of which you will find in his letter, and likewise an account of which goods hee put on shoare herein inclosed. Since I am goeing home, I think tis most convenient for mee to carry my accounts home to the Company, and not trouble you with them. I dispatched Captain Bowler from hence with 87 slaves[26] according to your worships order in Mr Gouldings letter, and the directions Mr Nightingale gave, which has took up almost all the booges Captain Lowe put on shoare, soe that I shall leave Mr Thorne very bare, if you doe not send him some recrute very speedily. Wee had noe goods before but iron barrs, for on the 12th of March last happened a great fire which burnt down almost all the whole towne together with our factory, but I have neare built itt againe and built a very secure warehouse, which I have covered with iron barrs to secure the goods from a second fire, if it should chance to happen. All our goods in a manner were burnt except iron barrs, of which you will find an account by Mr Thorns receipt of the remayns here. I have Mr Gouldings papers and a bill of ladeing for 529 slaves[27] which I have put up to carry home to the Company, but cannot find among them all the account of the particulars of canoe hyre you paid, 4 ounces odd angles, which I have sought after very carefully, finding you writt so earnestly for itt. The great canoe was staved upon the breakers in comeing ashoare, and wee had a 7 hand canoe here before, which broak loose from Captain Lowes sterne in a tournadoe, soe that att present wee have none but the 3 hand canoe to helpe our selves, and I have bin beholden to the Dutch for Captain Bowler and Captain Bramfill both, for the use of their canoes, whoe had 3 very good ones, but I have broke two by the

[26] Cf. Law 1990a, no.7 (William Cross, Offra, 13 June 1681), which incorrectly gives the number of slaves shipped aboard Bowler as 187.

[27] i.e. those taken by Captain Lowe (cf. no.592).

badness of the weather. You may be pleased to send Mr Thorne a good canoe or two with some paddles, here are 13 canoemen already which are pawnes to the Company, soe that then hee shall have occasion for noe more, but if you send any send noe more free men for they proved themselves rogues to Captain Lowe.

PS. Your worship may be pleased to understand that when you send any ships for this place to consigne them to the factor, for if you raise the price of goods (as I have lately seen) the Blacks will never lower them againe.

[Inclosure]
Ophra in Arda, 18 Aug. 1681
Received by mee John Thorne of Mr William Cross for account of the Royall African Company of England these goods following vizt.: 2 men and 2 woemen slaves, 961 pounds of booges, 12 old musketts, 1 kittle, 32 lead barrs, 2752 whole barrs of iron and 65 pieces ditto which doe contain 30 whole barrs which are for sale, with 380 that covers the trunck for the security of the goods from fire, which are in all 3090 iron barrs, I say received by mee the day and year above mentioned.

John Thorne

In the presence of us   Andrew Bramfill
                        Andrew Crosbie

478. John Thorne   Ophra in Arda, 19 Aug. 1681

I hearing of Captain Parris quick dispatch last voyage att Whida, encouraged Captain Lowe to take in his slaves there, but after hee had gott his slaves, haveing promised the King to settle a factory there, hee [= the King] would not lett the goods which were on shoare be brought off, whereupon Captain Lowe and Mr Goulding ordered mee and Robert Chapman to stay with them there, an account of which you will find herein inclosed. It being put to Mr Croses choise to goe home or stay, hee sent for mee downe to Ophra to take possession of the Companys concerns, which libberty I could hardly obtaine because of Captain Low's promise to the King, but was forced to come away without my things, neither can I gett the other man away, but think it convenient (with your worshipps order) to keepe both places, for I find them very civill and obledgeing there, and a place as plenty of slaves as this, and are within foure hours journey one of the other, and by keeping both places will be a furtherance of the dispatch of all ships you shall send downe; by which if you send booges a good quantity, with allmost any other goods you have you cannot want slaves, for they are very plenty. I humbly begg of your worshipp to send downe a man or two, and one in the roome of James Boyde, for hee has been very falce to Mr Cross, and promised the Blacks 12 slaves in goods, if they would send him [= Cross] away, and make the other cheife, so that hee might have the command of the factory, to imbazle thee Company's goods as he pleased, but some of the Blacks haveing a kindness for Mr Cross came and told him of itt, whereby itt was prevented, this is the greatest occasion of his [= Cross's] goeing home now as hee himselfe has told mee, and as far as I understand this rogue has the same designe upon mee, for I have heard some inclining of itt, and am sencible by the very same craft this factory has often been ruinated, and the Company not only lost their goods, but a great many honest men their lives, therefore I hope you will be pleased to take itt into consideration. Wee have great occasion for a canoe or two, and some paddles, the great canoe was staved upon the breakers, and a 7 hand canoe which was here was broken adrift in a turnadoe, soe that at present wee have great want of canoes, and you had as good send noe ships as noe canoes, for without them nothing can be done. Pray send some booges by the next shipping, and they will put off any goods you shall send downe besides, without them you must expect little to be done, for tis all one their money here, as silver and gold is wth us.

[PS] Mr Goulding died on the 5th of May last and Mynher Lunk the Dutch Copeman[28] about a month after.

[Inclosure]
Agriffie in Whidda 20 April 1681
Warehouse is debtor to severall goods in the possession of mee John Thorne for account of the Royall Affrican Company of England,
vizt.

	Value of goods in slaves
344 small brass panns att 40 pound per slave	08½
006 course sletias att 4 per slave	1½
002 longcloaths att 1 per slave	2
008 broken bunches of beads vallued att	00½
101 iron barrs att 12 per slave	08½
490 mannilloes att 220 per slave	02½
003 pintadoes with 50 odd manilloes	01
013 musketts vallued att	02
631 pounds of booges att 78 lb per slave	08
082 kettles great and small vallued att	08
001 piece of red cloath received from Mr Cross vallued	02
078 pounds of booges received from ditto	01
	45½

	No.of slaves
Per contra is creditor, Whidda 1681	
By 2 kettles and 2 musketts sent Mr Cross att Ophra	01
By 2 course sletias paid for the use of the trunck	00½

[28] Lonq, chief factor of the Dutch factory at Offra.

By 2 slaves in brass pans paid Captain Blanko[29] for 2 slaves shipt

    on board Captain Low   02

By goods paid for 22 slaves sent to Mr Cross att Ophra and shipt

    on board Captain Bowler, July the 7th   22

By goods paid the canoemen for worke done on board Captain Lowe

    to the vallue of   08½

By 48 gallons of brandy for the use of the factory for 4 months

    att 12 gallons per slave   04

By 312 pounds booges for my owne diett att 78 lb per slave for 4 months   04

By 78 lbs booges for Robert Chapman his diett for 4 months

    att ¼ of a slave per month   01

By 20 lbs booges for Andrew Crosbies diett for a month   00¼

By 2 slaves bought, remaining for the use of the factory   02

By 22 lbs of booges for slaves victualls and cloaths   00¼

By hammacks and dasheys to the King and other great men in red cloath

    and booges   03

Balance at Ophra in Arda, August 20 1681   48½

By ballance of the gaine said account the Royall Affrican Company is debter to mee 3
slaves   errors excepted, per mee John Thorne

August 14th and 17th. The 2 slaves bought for the use of the factory died of the small pox.

479. John Thorne   Ophra in Arda, 4 Dec. 1681

Heareing of Captain Parris quick dispatch last voyage att Whidda, I encouraged Captain Low to take in his slaves there, and comeing to anchor in the road I was sent on shoare by Captain Lowe and Mr Gouldings order to know how things past as well att Ophra as Whida and in which place I might best and soonest purchase his slaves, and the next day returning on board againe with answer from the King that if Captain Lowe will come himselfe on shoare hee would agree with him for his whole complement of slaves, whereupon Captain Lowe and Mr Goulding went on shoare and the King likeing his cargoe promised him his slaves in 26 dayes, which might have been accomplished had there not come two interlopers into the road, a French man and a Portuguese. Captain Lowe haveing gott goods ashoare Mr Goulding bought slaves att the Kings house att Sabba [var. Saba] and I was ordered at Agriffie the lower towne, but after hee had gott all his slaves, and haveing before promised the King to settle a factory there, hee [= the King] would not lett the goods which were on shoare be carried off, whereupon Captain Lowe and Mr Goulding ordered mee and Robert Chapman to stay with them there, an account of them you will find enclosed herein. Therefore if your worship be pleased to settle

[29] i.e. Portuguese *branco*, 'white': this translates Yevogan, 'Chief of White Men', a title used in both Allada and Whydah for the official who dealt with European traders: cf. Law 1991a, 206–7.

a factory lett mee have your order for itt, that I may make provision for the reception of any ships you shall be pleased to send. I have little to say in the praise of the place, only itt is something more healthfull then Ophra and is a place of free trade for all ships that comes. There is two factory's already, a French and a Portuguese, and interlopers dayley frequent the place. I have done my best to prevent them, to the hazard of my life by one Captain Beacon, who sett a pistole to my breast but I prevented his designe, for the Blacks will have noe striveing one with another but will have all ships trade that comes.[30] Therefore if your worshipp please to continue this place at Whidda itt will require two whitemen, for I have but two with mee, for itt being put to Mr Crosses choyse to goe home or stay he sent for mee to Ophra to take possession of the Companys concerns, the which libberty I could hardly obtaine because of Captain Low's promise to the King, but was forced to come away without anything for my necessaries, neither can I as yet gett the other white man away, though I have made tryall to the loss of all that I brought out of England with mee. If both places be kept itt will be a meanes to dispatch ships the sooner, for there is butt 4 or 5 hours journey betwixt them and you cannot miss of slaves att either place if you send any quantity of booges, and they will be a meanes to put off almost any other sort of goods except iron barrs. A note of what goods is vendible you will find inclosed herein. Wee have great occasion for a canoe or two and some padles. The great canoe was stav'd upon the breakers and the 7 hand canoe broke away from the sterne of Captain Low's ship in a turnadoe, soe that wee have great need of canoes and you had as good send noe ships as noe canoes. For canoemen I have 13 here, and if you send downe any more pray lett them be pawnes, for those which came with Captain Low proved rogues. For the last 3 dayes when there was most occasion for them, could not gett them to carry off the slaves, to Captain Lowes great damage, but was forced to hyre others, for which offence I hope your Worship will be pleased to take itt into consideration. Captain Lowe departed from Whidda the 20th Aprill last with his complement of slaves and sent Mr Goulding on shoare att Ophra, and what goods came on shoare there Mr Cross I hope certifies you in his letters, and likewise of Mr Gouldings death, hee being spectator, and therefore needless to insert itt here, and of his charges in rebuilding some small part of the factory, and what hee hath left mee to build, which will cost 26 slaves to compleat itt, and I have not wherewithall to pay for itt, but the Blacks are soe civill to stay till the next ship comes. Captain Parris lately arriv'd at Whidda, where in a short time gott his complement of slaves and departed the 20th of this instant, leaveing Mr Wyborne to settle a factory, and the said Mr Wyborne is now building a large house for the reception of interlopers. Captain Rickard departed hence the 12th November haveing gott his complement of slaves in 20 dayes for

[30] This policy was formalized in 1703, when the king of Whydah required the local representatives of the various European nations trading at Whydah to sign a formal treaty guaranteeing the neutrality of the Whydah road, even in times of war in Europe: Law 1991a, 152; cf. also Barbot 1992, ii, 645.

money and what goods hee brought with him, for I had not any goods to supply him with all but iron barrs, and they will not off here upon any account.[31] Pray be pleased to send downe money to pay the souldiers their wages, for here is two which are 12 months behind and the other 6 months and myselfe likewise, for I want cloaths and other necessaries. The Phidalgoe would desire your Worship to send him a dram cup.

[Inclosure]
An acccount of what goods are fitt to purchase slaves att Ophra in Arda:
Booges, all sorts of brass bassons great and small, and sattin, all sorts of flowered and stripd silks, red cuttanees, ginghams, chercolees, sallampores, all sorts of linnen, longcloth, Holland, muslins, white baftes, pintados, chints, linnen printed, beads of all sorts, chiefly yallow, lamon and greene, rangoes, cases of spiritts, brandy, musketts 200, powder 20 barrells, lead barrs 400, what linnen you send lett it all be white.   John Thorne.

480.   John Thorne   Ophra in Arda, 18 Dec. 1681

This comes with the accounts of Ophra and to certifie you how things are with us att Arda, haveing no knowledge of men [sic — omission?] a canoe goeing from Widdaw, by reason of the canoemen which went in her were those which came downe with Captain Lowe and they haveing soe plaid the rogue with him I durst not send any letters by them if I had known of her goeing, for fear of their miscariage. These accounts att Ophra may seeme something strange to your worship, if you had butt seen what condition I found the factory in and what bad customes factors had brought up here since I went home, not knowing how to deale with the Blacks, for they are a very encroching people to men that are strangers to their customes, and I have been forced to be att an extraordinary charge in reducing them to their former customes againe and I hope to continue itt whilst I have the power in my hands, but if your worship send another above mee I doe not know how hee will deale with them, for the Blacks will not lett any instructions to be given to a new Cheife but will make him condition with them before hee shall have any considerable discourse with the old Cheife about their customes, but I hope the next account will be more easier to the Company then this, for the charge hath been ogmented in regard of an unhappy war which broke forth among the Blacks and I was forced to give 2 slaves for one barrell of powder for to secure the Companys concerns.[32] If Mr Wyborne please, who is the bearer of this letter and accounts, hee can give you certifection att large.[33] The same thing is by masters of ships as by a

[31]Cf. no.599.
[32]Cf. the enclosed accounts, under date 4 Dec. 1682.
[33]Cf. no.481, which explains that Wyborne did not in the event deliver the letter, but sent it by Yankey, an African employee of the RAC.

new factor, for when they have the cargoe in their owne disposeing the Blacks will have things att their own rate, knowing that they know nothing of the customes of the country.

I would desire your worship to send booges downe by the first oppertunity for I have none for my present use but am forct to borrow of the blacks, and they will not lend above 50 lbs of booges for a slave and att the arrivall of a ship will have 78 lbs for them, for I have not any goods that I can put off for booges but to great loss. James Boyde humbly requests of your worshipp to send him your discharge for hee is willing to goe home, his time being expired. If you please to send him his discharge pray send two honest men downe which can wright, for John Waterhouse is dead and shall have but two left which is not enough for this.

PS. Here is a great man who desires your worship to send him a drum and hee will send you a slave for itt.

[Inclosure 1]
Ophra in Arda, August 1681
Warehouse debtor to severall goods of the Royall Affrican Company's of England in the hands of mee John Thorne

			Value in slaves
18th	To 961 pound of booges att 78 lbs per slave	. .	012
	To 4 slaves for the use of the factory	. .	004
	To 12 old musketts vallued att halfe a slave	. .	000½
	To 32 lead barrs att 16 per slave	. .	002
	To 3090 iron barrs att 12 per slave	. .	257½
20th	left in my hand by Captain Branfill		
	To 116 nicanees halfe of them damnified, they that were damnified were vallued att 9 per slave and the other were att 6 per slave	. .	015
	To 96 red comiters vallued att 10 per slave	. .	009^{6}/10
September the 12			
	left in my hand by Captain Rickard		
	To 9 iron barrs		000¾
	To one halfe piece damnified scarlett vallued att one slave and a halfe		001½
	To 3 damnified allejars vallued att halfe a slave		000½
The sum in slaves is			304½

Per contra creditor
August 1681

26th	By 100 lbs booges paid for Captain Branfills charges of carrying of goods from the waterside to the factory	001¼
	By 4 slaves for 4 months dyatt for myselfe	004
	By 3 slaves for 4 months dyatt for 3 white men	003
	By 1 slave and a quarter paid to the watchmen and to the slaves in the house for dyatt	001¼

30th	By 1 slave in booges given to great mens servants	001
	By halfe a slave in booges paid for a man that was	
	panyard carrying a letter for mee to Whidda	000½
September		
6th	By 3 slaves in booges towards building the factory	003
18th	By 3 slaves for getting me some part of my things from	
	Whidda, the rest being lost	003
	By 7 slaves in iron stole away when the factory was downe	007
November		
12th	By 1 slave paid to a Docter for looking after sick men	001
14th	By 1 slave in iron to buy oyle for the use of the house	001
15th	By 1 slave in committers given to the great men of the towne	
	when I tooke the Companys concerns into my hand	001
December		
4th	By 1 slave bought for the use of the factory	001
	By 1 barrell of powder bought for the use of the house,	
	cost 2 slaves in niccanees	002
9th	By 24 niccanees sold for 48 gallons of brandy for the use	
	of the factory for 4 months	004
12th	By 2 slaves in musketts bought for the use of the house	002
	By halfe a slave in committers given to the King of Arda	
	and to the King of Whidda when their people mett to make	
	peace with the Phidolgoe [i.e. of Offra]	000½
	036½	

By ballance of the gainsaid account remains in my hands, errors
excepted   267½

John Thorne.

[Inclosure 2]
An account goods left in my hands by Captain Bramfill:
112 narrow niccanees, 12 ditto damnified, 96 red comitters[34]

The goods which Captain Rickard left in my hands:
halfe a peace of damnified scarlett, 9 iron barrs, 3 damnified allejars, 1 broken 7
hand canoe

John Thorne

Ophra in Arda 18 Aug. 1681
Received of Mr Cross for account of the Royall African Company these goods vizt.:
4 slaves, 961 lbs booges, 12 old musketts, 32 lead barrs, 3090 iron barrs.

Testes   John Thorne
Andrew Bramfill

[34] Cf. no.596.

481.　Petly Wyborne　　　　　　　　Judeah alias Whidda, 8 Jan. 1681/2

The bearer Yanky hath been here some time to come up to the Gold Coast with mee, but I not being ready and here being a blacks canoe comeing up Mr Thorne sent to mee to send Yankey, which I now doe with your letters by her. Some small time since I have been att Ophra, where I saw the Companys factory and a considerable parcell of iron in itt but very little other goods. Slaves are to be had here if they that wants brings goods fitt for the place, as booges, brass, linnen, pintadoes, beads, etc. If itt lieth in my power to serve the Company or yourselfe, there is nothing wants but your commands or oppertunity, and assure you I will faithfully.

482.　John Thorne　　　　　　　　Ophra in Arda, 23 March 1681/2

I received your letter per Mr Arthur Wendover, which orders my departure off the coast for England.[35] I would most willingly have compplied therewith could those persons you have sent down discharged the debts I have bin forc't to contract with the blacks, for want of booges or other goods to maintaine the factory, but till that is complied with they will not lett me goe. I have obeyed your orders in delivering an account to Mr John Winder of all the Royall Company concerns that have been in my charge, copies whereof I have sent to Capo Corsoe, and have always endeavoured to give advice of affaires here as well to the Agent and Councill as to my masters in England. I am sure I have been at great charge and have lost considerably since I came downe last, by sollicitous dilligence in the Royall Company service, however I see my honest endeavors have been ill represented or not well accepted. When I was ordered from Whidah to Ophrah by Mr Cross I lost the greatest part of my things to the vallue of 14 slaves, they being seized on by the King of Whidah, for noe other reason then my leaving his country, for the service of the Royall Company. I hope some consideration may be allowed for it, otherwise people will have little encouragement to serve the Company. I likewise paid 2 slaves for a flag and staff, which never was put in my account. I am heartily sorry I am turned out of my imployment without any reason given. I will obey your order as soone as possible I can, which cannot be until the ballance of my account is sent downe which I owe to the Blacks of this towne, having borrowed it out of necessity. I much admire I could receive noe answer of my letters and accounts which I understand were received at Capo Corso. It would have been a great satisfaction if I could receive your approvall of my accounts, or otherwise what you could object against them. Here is likewise 21 slaves due for building the house which must be paid before I can goe off, having engaged to the blacks before they would undertake to

---

[35]Wendover had been sent to supersede Thorne as chief factor, but was himself shortly afterwards superseded by John Winder, mentioned below (cf. no.484).

build. Mr Smith has been here and have seen the conveniency of it and is able to give his oppinion of it.

483.   John Winder   Ophra in Arda, 23 March 1681/2

This accompanies Mr John Smith,[36] who will give you an account of all transactions since our departure from Capo Corsoe Castle, and in what condition the Royall Company affaires are at present upon this coast, which for want of goods is soe bad, that I know not how to maintaine myselfe and the rest of the Royall Company servants, finding noe goods in the possession of Mr Wendover (though falsely inform'd he had brought a supply from Capo Corsoe). By the approvall of Mr Smith I came to Ophra, to take account of what goods was in this factory, where I found none but iron and a small parcell of lead, which is soe great a drug that I cannot buy provisions with it but at great loss. Mr Thorne upon my comeing shewed me his accounts to the 18th of December last, copies whereof he advised me were sent to Capo Corsoe. I punctually discharged your commands in acquainting him with your orders for his departure off the coast, he express'd much willingness to be discharged and told me he would goe off in Captain Thomas Woodfine, as required, provided I could pay those Blacks the booges he had been forct to borrow of them for maintenance of the factory, and himselfe his sallery, otherwise he could not gett away, the blacks being resolved to be satisfied before his departure, which having noe effects to doe, must be forc't to continue till the Agent and Councills further order. Mr Thorne hath made up his accounts to the 18th instant, when he delivered the keys of the trunk into my possession, I being detained here by the Phidalgoe, who is very sorry that the Royall Company should have any thoughts of settling at another place, this having been the residence for their people this many years, soe will not lett me leave it, but hopes the Royall Company will alter their resolution and continue their trade with him.[37] My humble advice is that goods may be speedily sent down, with a factor to remaine as second to me, and that both this place and Guidah be continued, the one under the other. By examination I find that Mr Thomas Goulding died about the begining of May last. Mr Thorne being then at Guidah, he declares he knows nothing of his concernes, Mr Cross having taken Mr Gouldings estate into his hands, which was left him as I understand by his last will. Captain John Woodfine is ready to saile, of whome I have demanded bills of loading for his slaves, but he possitively denies to give any, having bought his Negroes himselfe. Captain Thomas Woodfine continues still at Guidah, in great distress for want of goods to purchase his complement of slaves. He hath severall times sent his boat to this place to offer gold for Negroes, the Dutchman have sent him some

---

[36] Smith had been sent from Cape Coast to install Winder as chief factor at Whydah: cf. nos 484, 492–3.
[37] Cf. no.492 (with response by Winder, no.493) for the allegation that Winder colluded with the Fidalgo in remaining at Offra.

and promises more, but at a very extravagant rate. I received your letter of the 24th February last per Captain Daniell Gates, who arrived at Guidah the 20th instant, I shall comply with your orders in demanding bills of loading for his slaves, when he hath his complement, and proceed further as your letter directs. If he comes hither I shall doe my utmost endeavour for his dispatch, otherwise I shall be incapable of doeing him any service. Mr Smith has taken charge of the hogshead brandy sent from Capo Corsoe with me, which he will give an account of at his returne. I shall att all times endeavour to promote the interest of my masters, and doe hope that you will think fitt to send downe supplies, that I may have encouragement in their service.

[Inclosure 1]
Goods proper and vendible at Arda
booges
long cloathes
broad baftas and narrow white halfe baftas
pautkeys
sletias fine and course and muslin diaper
bag Holland
sletia Holland, fustian and tufted Holland
allejars
pintadoes all sorts
chinches [= chintzes] all sorts
ginghams
chercolees all sorts
brass panns
beads
rangoes
manilloes bright, 2 or 3 casque
powder, 10 barrells
musquetts
cases of spiritts
brandy, a good commodity to sell
printed callicoes
all sorts of silkes and sattins
a good 9 hand canoe with paddles

[Inclosure 2]
Goods in the Royall Company factory at Ophra
2796 barrs of iron
32 barrs of lead
23 musquetts
½ a barrell of powder

1 brass kettle
1 iron pott
3 slaves for the use of the house
1 paire of stilliards
John Winder

[Inclosure 3]
Ophra, January 18 1681
Warehouse debter to sundry goods of the Royall Affrican Company of England in the custody of me   John Thorne

	To 244 slaves & ½ of iron	244½
	To 32 lead barrs vallued at 16 per slave	2
24th	1 man slave died that belongs to the factory	
	246½	

Royall African Company of England debter to 13 slaves worth of booges to me, which I borrowed to maintain the factory, whereof 1 slave of them was expended in November and 3¼ in December   13

Per contra creditor

Jan. 18	By 1 slave & ¼ of iron sold for the monthly expence	
1681/2	of the factory in brandy	1¼
	By ballance remaines	245¼
	By 1 slave in booges for my own diett for a month	1
	By ¾ of a slave for three whitemens diett for a month	
	vizt. Robert Chapman, James Boyde, Andrew Crosby	¾
	By ¼ of a slave in booges paid to watchmen per month	¼
	By ¼ of a slave in booges for they in the house for	
	victualls and cloathes	¼
	By ballance remaines in booges, 6½ slaves	2¼
Feb. 18	By 1 slave in booges for my own diett for a month	1
1681/2	By ¼ of a slave in booges for Robert Chapmans diett	
	for 1 month	00¼
	By ¼ of a slave in booges for the watchmen per 1 month	00¼
	By ¼ of a slave in booges for they in the house per month	
	for victualls and cloathes	00¼
	By ¼ of a slave in booges for Mr Winders diett per week	00¼
	By ballance remaines 4½ slaves in booges	02
	By 1 slave and ¼ in iron barrs for the monthly expence	
	of the factory in brandy	01¼
	By ballance remaines 244¼ [sic] of a slave in iron	

Ophra   Warehouse debtor to severall goods of the Royall Company of
March 18 England in the custody of me, John Thorne
1681/2   By 244¼ slaves in iron   244¼
              The remaines of the booges that were borrowed   4½

                                    Per contra creditor

              By 6 slaves in iron paid towards building the factory   06
              By 1¼ slave in iron sold for brandy for the monthly expence
              of the factory   01¼
              By ¼ of a slave in iron given to the canoemen that day
              the Phidalgoe made his custome   00¼
                                                                                           7½

              By ballance remaines 236½ slaves

              By 1 slave of booges paid for[?] the Phidalgoes yearly custome   001
              By 1 slave in booges given the same day to the Phidalgoes people   001
              By ½ of a slave in booges in extrordinary expences when
              Mr Smith came here   00½
              By 1 slave in booges for my own diett per month   001
              By 1 slave in booges for Mr Winders diett   001
              By ¼ of a slave for Robert Chapmans diett   00¼
              By $^{1}/_{10}$ of a slave of booges for the slaves of the house $00^{1}/_{10}$

                                                                                           $4^{4}/_{5}$

By ballance of the againe said accompt remaines in the factory 236½[sic?] slaves in iron

Witness my hand   John Thorne

484.   Arthur Wendover   Appa,[38] 17 July 1682

You may justly blame me and wonder at my bouldness for goeing to Appa in a
canoe that belongs to Captain Wyborne, and also conclued twas on his account and
in his service. But I shall endeavour to make you sincible of the contrary, and give
you an account of a more honourable a designe than you may or are aware of, and
I doubt not may if not neglected prove very advantagious to my masters the Royall
Company in whose service I am, and should be heartily glad and as willing as
anyone to venture for their advantage my person, as far as my life and health will
permitt me, under God etc.
     In January last past it was your pleasure to send me Cheife to Guidah on the
coast of Arda, and did also deliver me a letter for Mr Ralph Hassell Cheife of Accra,
which it seemes was not delivered,[39] upon which neglect your Worship thought fitt
to withdraw me, and to that intent did send Mr John Smith, to place Mr John Winder

---

[38] Near Badagry (in modern Nigeria), east of Offra.
[39] Cf. no.423.

in my stead, and me returne with Mr John Smith to Cape Coast per first oppertunity of the canoe, and also did order me to deliver whatt concernes I had of the Royall Company: which was soone done, for haveing nothing I could deliver nothing, but only 8 damaged barrells of powder which Captain Lawrance left, because Captain Wyborne would not buy them, those they had according to your Honours commands. This hard dealing is enough to breake the hearts of any one, and hath been almost the breaking of mine in this case, and doubt not but your thoughts are as mine, for a burnt child dreads the fire. I humbly beg your pardons, Gentlemen. The letter you are all very sincible that twas particularly about my own business, twas to order Mr Ralph Hassell to take the produce of what goods I had to dispose of there, for account of the Company, and although I did not deliver the letter, neither did I on the other hand take the least thing to the vallue of one cracra, but left all as they were. There is neither Mr Hassell nor Mr Pley, nor any one can say I did, soe that hope this may in part give your Worship some satisfaction. I should not have doubted nor have had any feare in mee but would have gladly delivered the letter, but having a knave to deale with all and the blanketts sticking in Mr Hassells throat,[40] that I could scarce gett a word from him nor a good looke, nor victualls nor drinke, that I did expect no other, butt all the ill usualls imaginable as could be owne to a man, which was the reale cause and is the truth and nothing but the truth (as God shall helpe me). Now being put out of all imployments, and having nothing to doe but walking from place to place and spending my time in idleness, which life was a burthen to me, and being often at Cricry [var. Guidah],[41] for generally there was the most company, always one Commander or another begging of Captain Wyborne his assistance to furnish them with slaves, for goods and gold, whoe always was ready to imbrace their desires with his promises in great measure, and indeed to speake the truth was commonly as good as his word, being there I made a very neare inquiry into all matters; and understanding that there was a place to leward called Appa from whence he gott a great many slaves, some coming by land others by sea, made me admire that men should see their own goods goeing to this place and bring slaves for the produce, when they might as well themselves send their boats and purchase them themselves, for I believe if a canoe may goe a boat may doe the same (I am sure their ships will not faile them), but they doe soe deale on this place Guidah and Ophra that they thinke slaves are not to be hand past [var. below] these places. Then there is another dependence, Captain Wyborne being there they cannot faile, whoe getting their goods into his hands makes his owne advantage, a benda a head the least price for all sorts, men, women, boys and girles. That men of reason and of understanding should see themselves soe bubled,[42] I am

---

[40] As made explicit later in this letter, Wendover had accused Hassell of purchasing blankets from an interloper.

[41] 'Cricry' (i.e. Glehue) is probably the correct reading, one copyist having presumably failed to recognise the name, and substituted the more familiar 'Guidah [Whydah]'.

[42] bubbled, i.e. cheated.

sure tis much to the disadvantage of the Royall Company and owners, I shall
instance in several particulars by and by.

Seeing how causes went and nothing to do, I desired the favour of Captain
Wyborne that I might goe to Appa per the next canoe, which he readily granted
mee, telling me the canoe would returne in 10 days, which time I thought would
not be long, and knowing that Mr Smith would not goe this month, I did adventure
at which place I am now, of which I shall give you the following account and the
great advantage that may be made on all accounts whatsoever. Appa is about 30 or
40 leagues at the most from Guidah and is very remarkable for ships to find, there
being a single cocarnutt tree standing in the middle of a small bay, and a flag staff
by that one [= on] which they hang up an old clout, itt makes off to sea very woody
for it is a woody place, but I shall advise the Phidalgoe to make a new St Georges
flagg. The Phidalgoes towne is about 3 miles from the sea, which is incompassed
round with water and small riverlett issuing from the great river, and is mightily
full of ba[m]boo trees which afford wine much like unto palme wyne, of which
baboos they build all their houses. There is also a very famous river that goes to
Boneen,[43] from whence comes all sorts of cloathes and are sold cheap for any sorts
of goods. Boneen is 2 dayes journey from this place per land, all goods that comes
to this place are conveyed to the Phidalgoes towne by water, they having canoes of
40, 50 and 60 foot in length. There is noe need of anyones taking care of goods
when ashoare as to watch them, for the people are so just that they may be trusted
with unsold gold, their honesty is to admiration, and the Phidalgoe takes all the care
upon himselfe. Here is good conveniency of wooding and watering just by the
seaside. These people never goe to sea in their canoes, for the river being soe large
and affording very much fish as mullitts and there is one sort of fish that is large as
a good handsome hoge, eats much like our sturgeon and is as good in my judgement, for that if any vessell intends for this place they must be provided with a
canoe and men, which said canoe may returne fraighted with Boneen cloathes (and
other sorts as the place can afford, which may be much to the advantage of the
Royall Company my masters. It is also the chiefest markett for slaves (or the fairo
as the blacks call it),[44] from whence the people of Guidah and Ophra are furnisht.
Assinah voulgarly called Ardau Grandy[45] and other ajacent places from whence
comes most slaves are ajacent to this place, soe that slaves cannot be wanting and
are not, and to be bought for a more reasonable rate then either at Guidah or Ophra;
of rates shall give you an account how I have seen them bought. The Phidalgoe is

---

[43] i.e. Benin, the 'river' being the coastal lagoon. For the importance of canoe-born communication
along the lagoons between Whydah/Offra and Benin, including further reference to the role of Apa, cf.
Law 1983.

[44] Portuguese *feira*, 'market'.

[45] 'Ardau Grandy' (i.e. Great Allada) was the royal capital inland; 'Assinah' (more correctly, as later in
this letter, 'Assimah') was an alternative name for this town, which occurs in other sources in other
variants (e.g. 'Assem', in Delbée 1671, 417).

very desirous of a trade and also the people. Once in 15 or 20 days you shall see the river full of canoes and like unto the River of Thames, some with slaves others with clouts, others with sheap, goats, henns, others with corne etc.

The Phidalgoe is a very good man, and lives in great splendour and much honoured by all his people — your trade is wholly with him and noe man elce, he takeing charge of all, soe the trouble is but small.

The Cappusheers are a very good honest people, very laborious alwayes, and for the Phidalgoe or else themselves, their business is cheifely in building, which they doe very famously and very large houses, and as for the common people they seldome or never trouble you, for they come not within the Kings Court, but they are generally honest, which thing is a rarity amongst them: tis not soe at Guidah, them knaves are always stealing and bringing troublesome palavoras to their King, which is not here. Goods bringing from the Appraye[46] very reasonably with abundance of care, and delivered safe into your house. As for the base exacting of custome as the King of Guidah doth demand, I doe not as yett understand that they desire any, and I shall not make enquiry for feare of putting them in mind of such an evill habuit, but I doe believe the Phidalgoe doth expect something, and also the Cabbisheers, which will not be much. I can assure your Worship this that slaves are not wanting at this place, and could the Phidalgoe have any encouragement and his people they would make it their business to turne the trade. Also the people of Assimah or Uper Arda and severall neighbouring Phidalgoes have been with me, and beg heartily that ships may come, for it is soe far for them to go to Guidah, and likewise they run the hazard of being panjard and robed of their goods and slaves (which are all very good reasons in my opinion). And as for the injuries done to the Royall Company, I shall instance in these particulars; Captain Thomas Woodfine, Commander of the Sarah Bonadventure, sold the 3 peices of scarlett cloath to Captain Wyborne for 9 slaves, and also 3 pieces perpettuanoes and 1 piece of say for one, which 3 pieces of scarlett cloath I saw sold for 22 by one Cocarham, a person that belongs to Captain Wyborne, and his [= is] brother to Hansco, a very honest fellow, and very willingly would be imployed in the Companys serice; and also Captain John [Woodfine] of the John Bonadventure and Daniell Gates, Commander of the Allapeen, sold sundry pieces of silks to Captain Wyborne, they being somewhat damaged, which the other person sold as followeth, 1 piece of yellow sarcinett slite and damaged containing 48 yards ¾ for 5 slaves, one piece of green very slite containing 37 yards ½ for 4, one piece of pinke colour and 1 piece cherry containing 37 yards for 5, one piece of skie sarcinett slite but a pleasant colour and good containing 39 yards ¾ for 5, 1 piece of flowered colour and good containing 13[½] yards[47] for 2 slaves — which goods at Guidah where blowne upon and slited as if they had cost nothing, nay upon the scarlett cloath the King spit upon it, for

---

[46] Portuguese, *a praia*, 'the beach'.

[47] Emendation required, from comparison with the postscript to this letter.

noe booges noe slaves, without you will pay the twice the worth of them in other goods. Tis otherwise here, for anything goes off, booges not coveted, but good rich silkes, and all sorts of linnins, noe one sort excepted as I know of unless it be iron barrs, and they shall not stick ahand, neither any other thing rather then not trade, the people are soe willing.

And having now made you sincible of my goeing to Appa and upon what account, which was noe other then to see what manner of place it was and what sort of people, also if that the place were a place for trade or not, which were my cheiefe intentions, and noe other ends in the least but to make the strictest enquiry as possibly I could, that I might be capable of giveing account of a place that may soe much to the advantage of the Royall Company, which is the truth (as God will help me), having given this account I shall leave it to your wise and prudent considerations and shall remaine here untill your further answer and make what inspection possible I can into the trade; and accordingly shall act and doe as you advice.

[PS] I must acquaint your worship that I have had two tedious fitts of sickness since I have been here, which have much weakened me, but I thank God am very well recovered, and in a good way to gaine my strength againe. The Phidalgoe was my docter, for every day he makes me one thing or another to take, but what it was I can never tell, also water to gargal in my mouth, and would alwayes see me take them before he would goe. In perusall of yours by Mr John Smith I understand that Mr Ralph Hassell should say that the oath which I did take upon the account of the blanketts that I was forced to doe the same, but I must be so bold with him as to tell him that he is a base knave and a most horrible notorious lyer, for all the time that I was at Accra last I scarce changed one word with him, for he would not speake to me. And likewise Mr Pley doth confirme the same, he knowes to the contrary, but I pitty him, he dirst doe noe other wayes. For Mr Hassells part tis like him, tis the real effects of his heart and minds, also his maxims of advice to all to deny itt and confirme it with oaths, but I would have Mr Hassell to know that I understand my selfe better then to be made a knight of the past, or to be forced to sweare upon any account whatsoever. He may sweare by the eternall God if that he pleaseth, he never bought any blanketts from Captain John How, and Mr Pley may also sweare he never had them in possession. According to the the oath that I did take, which I did voluntarily, I say that Ralph Hassell Chiefe of Accra did buy from Captain John How 102 blanketts att 3a per blankett, whoe lay at anchor off Lague, this was the 2nd day of October ([16]81), and brought them ashoare and put them into the warehouse in Accra fort;[48] which is truth as God shall help and the whole truth etc. Being at anchor at Wyamba Captain John How came aboard Captain Thomas Woodfine[49] and saluted me per the salutation of informer, for Mr Hassell had

---

[48] Cf. nos 421, 423, for Hassell's rebuttal of this charge.
[49] Wendover travelled to Whydah on Woodfine's ship (cf. no.602).

acquainted him how squares had gone; and I suppose delivered the blanketts back againe, for he told me that he was fully satisfied.

Accounts of the rates I have seen paid for slaves at this place Appa
Silks, 1 piece yellow, damaged, containing 48 yards ¾ for 5 slaves; 1 piece greene containing 37¼ yards[50] for 4 slaves; 1 piece of pink and 1 piece cherry, damaged, containing 37 yards for 4 slaves; 1 piece of good slite skye containing 39 yards ¾ for 5 slaves; one piece flowred ditto, good, containing 13 yards ½ for 2 slaves.

All sorts of silks sell well here, especially those that are very rich and gaudy. Sundry other sorts of goods vizt a piece of fine scarlett cloth, 7 slaves; 12 iron barrs, 1 ditto; 3 cases of spiritts, 1 ditto; 2 red perpettuanos 1 ditto; 3 fine India carpetts, ditto; 6 narrow pintadoes, ditto; 4 silke allejars ditto; 12 small baftas, ditto; 4 chints, ditto. These goods I have seen bartered for slaves per Cockro and for the rates above mentioned, butt for the rates of others I cannot tell as yett, but doe presume to be all one, nay and rather cheaper, for good goods they covett much, gaudy and rich, although anything is vendible here, rather than want a trade the people are so desireous. I doe believe that Welch plaines would sell well here, by reason they make all their rich cloathes of them,[51] soe that care must be had to the severall sorts of colours, red, green, yellow, blew, purple and orange, and the Phidalgoe gave me a cloath made of Welch plaine which is very handsome.

[PPS] I had neither inke nor paper but only this one sheet per chance, and am forced to write with gunpowder steeped in water, soe desire to be excused for this foule page[?].

At the request of the Phidalgoe he desires me to write for the severall particulars as followeth — fine linnins of all sorts, as fine sletias, fine muslings, also beads of all sorts, small and great. I saw sold an head of beads of an gold color, transparent, large the size of a white pea, this bought 1 slave. With beads, the small ones, they adorn their cloaths and make capps in the shape of a sugar loaf and adorne them as thicke as possibly they can in sundry pretty formes, which show very glorious. Your atlas silke are desired, also booges, which doe encourage much.

485. Andrew Crosbie [to Royal African Company in England]

Guydah, 1 [sic] Sept. 1682[52]

Whereas Mr John Winder, your honours cheife factor for this coast, was upon the 15th of this instant September panyard by the Blacks in order to his being sent home

---

[50] sic: but 37½ yards earlier in the same letter.

[51] The use by local weavers of thread unravelled from imported woollen cloth was also noted at Whydah by Phillips 1732, 227.

[52] This date is clearly wrong, since the letter itself refers to events on 'the 15th of this instant'. Note also that no.486, bearing the same date, is said to be transmitted by Captain North, and a later letter (no.487) refers to a letter sent by North dated 26 September.

in the ship Thomas and William, the reasons whereof shall in short give your honours and thereby endeavour to cleare myself of those aspertions hee already has or may further cast upon mee.

Firstly: Att his first comeing here from Ophra to this place, not well considering the interest of your Honours in studying and consulting the humours and dispositions of these people, whoe will neither be slighted by a high and lofty carridge or abused by bad language, in both of which gave too much liberty to his selfe, by which hee hath for ever lost the love and good will of these people, although the breach for the present be seemingly made up, there being not one upon the place from the King to the poorest can afford or give him a good word.

2ndly: By his becomeing debtor to one Captaine Bebe[53] for 15 slaves which was a long time before paid and then not to his [= Bebe's] satisfaction, I doe presume might be a great part (and by the disgust the blacks had before taken against him) of his being panyard, and for whatt hee may possibly say of my selfe being concerned therein, itt was soe farr from mee that when heard itt [I] did endeavour and partly effected the composeing of the business, and now must give your Honours an accompt of his suspistious asperscons cast upon mee. For some time past your honours factory here lead voy'd, in which time did give the utmost of my assistance to all masters of ships in your Honours service, by which meanes was gratified by one and the other to the vallue of 7 or 8 bendy's, possibly more, 7 whereof lent to Mr Winder, for which received his noate to be paid mee againe, but some time after when hee had my money in possession told mee hee had seazed itt for your Honours account, which seemed more then unkind, of which doe leave your honours judge. Seeing hee was like to leave the place [I] did tell him if might have my monyes [I] would trye and endeavour to compose his business, which did endeavour and partly by my meanes itt was effected, and to what other callamnys hee may loade mee with, as seeing interlopers and the like, I doe here declare the contrary, but can bring with good proofe the same thing upon himselfe, which hereunder in short shall give your Honours an account of in three articles.

1st. Upon the 14th day of August past, here being in port an interloper called [blank], one Fullwood Commander, whoe wanting some assistance, Captain Wyborne not being here, Mr Winder did him what kindness lay in his power, by first of all in paying his customes to the King, which was paid out of your Honours warehouse in 9 lb of boogees and 9 yards of silke, which contracted the familliarity betwixt them (things not here going to his satisfaction), that hee agreed to put 40 slaves on board of him and soe leave your honours factory here, 8 of which was put on board, in which time Captain North came in hither with some goods for your honours account [and] the business was made up and declined.

2ndly. Captain Shepheard here leaveing some few remaines of booges, the said

---

[53] Also mentioned in Winder's accounts (no.487, inclosure 2). Barbot also refers to 'Captain [or Prince] Bibe': 1992, ii, 635, 642.

Mr Winder caused them to be carryed to Captain Wyborns to serve and for the use of interlopers.

3rdly. Upon the 17th instant I doe know and can attest hee served and supplyed a Portugueze vessell with 6 slaves, notwithstanding your honours ship in port, which is all att present I shall trouble your honours with, notwithstanding could attest and averr severall things more.

486. Andrew Crosbie [to Agent & Council at Cape Coast Castle]

Guydah, 1 [sic] Sept. 1682[54]

I humbly presume to offer to your serious view and judgements the foregoing copie sent to the Company by Captain North, as well for my owne justification as for endeavouring the prevention of the ruine of the interest of their honours here in this place by Mr Winder, whoe never from the first day hee came hither tooke the right way or course to preserve itt, by his alwayes quarrelling and not agreeing with the natives here, since which hee hath acted many more ill things to the prejudice of the Company, as Mr Armitage if hee please can testify of, as enticeing away Captain Norths man,[55] not to serve the Companys interest but his owne, for that Mr Winder tould me that expected a New England man here and did designe to put on board some slaves of her and send him along with them. And then his carrying out the Companys goods in the night to Captain Wybornes house, trucking of them away for gold and cloaths to the ruine and prejudice of the trade here by selling att and under rate, only for to gett gold to have carryed him off, with many more ill things of the like nature, and for whatsoever hee may impeach mee of I durst refer myselfe to your Worship or any person here that is concern'd in the Companys service. The grounds of his disgust and hatred your Worship may perceive by mine to the Company. Not else, but as have soe shall still faithfully endeavour the full discharging of my duty, and the obeying in all things Mr Armitages commands.

487. Timothy Armitage [to Royal African Company in England]

Guydah, 24 Oct. 1682

In my last bearing date the 26th past per Captain North gave your Honours an account of the then present needfull, and did hope by this conveyance might have given your Honours a satisfactory account of the well settlement of this your factory, which doe now find will never be effected as long as Mr Winder tarry's upon this place, his humour not suiting with the nature and disposition of the blacks here, whoe has noe love or kindness in the least for him. They have since my last to your Honours endeavoured a second time sending him off, by pigniaring of him

---

[54] Cf. n.52 above.

[55] Cf. no.490 (naming this man as Daniel Roe).

with a possitive resolution that hee shall not remaine upon this place. The reasons of their disgust against him I have endeavoured as nigh as possible to gather from them, which goes here inclosed, the most part of which I must assert the verrity thereof, as can likewise Captain Ambrose and Mr Thomson,[56] both whome as well as myselfe have endeavoured to secure your honours interest by counselling of him upon a consultation together held the 21st instant to cause those goods that were carried down to Captain Wybornes in the night time out of your honours warehouse to be brought up againe, and to apply himselfe to the Agent and Councill at Cabo Corsoe, by takeing the oppertunity of a canoe now going thither, to both which he would not agree nor assent, but has and does endeavour to convert the said goods into gold to your honours prejudice, pretending your honours are more indebted to him, as your honours may perceive by the inclosed account, which hee gave mee to send home to your honours when [he] thought to have gott his passage upon one of these two ships now in port, vizt the Goulden Fortune and the George.[57] I have as bounden drawne up some objections against his said account, which together goes here inclosed for your Honours better government. I am sorry should have soe just occasion and soe bad a subject to enlarge upon, and soe soone contradict my last, but shall as soone as may be dispatch away the canoe to the Agent and Councill, whose further orders shall here attend; and shall per Captain Ware give your honours a more full account.

[Inclosure 1]
Hereunder follow the reasons of the disgust the Blacks has taken against Mr Winder, vizt.
1st. When he first came to settle amongst them his bad language and carriage suited not their humours, which occasioned a small breach.
2ndly. Upon which he left their towne and the Companys factory and tooke up his aboade for some time att Captain Wybornes house, whome they knew was not concern'd in the Companys business, which created in them a great dislike to him, they being naturally covetous of trade.
3rdly. His endeavouring to gett into their debts, and actually running into one Captain Bibbees debts, when afterward they understood hee did it with a designe to goe off with one Fullwood, an interloper then in port, to which end hee had actually put aboard 8, and laid under an obligation to make itt up 40 slaves.
4thly. His cutting of sletias and lessening the bunches of beads, which they looke

---

[56] Thomson was factor on the ship commanded by Robert Ware (cf. no.489).
[57] The *Golden Fortune* was commanded by Lott Ambrose, mentioned earlier in this letter; the *George* may have been Robert Ware's ship.

upon as an absolute cheate to their country.

5thly. His carrying of goods out of the factory in the night time to the Lower Towne and to Captain Wyborne's house,[58] which soe far as I can perceive have been the cause that have soe much insenced them against him.

In Guydah the 19th October 1682   Timothy Armitage

[Inclosure 2]

1682	Royall Affrican Company debtors	lbs	Slaves
July	To account of booges paid for 16 gallons brandy	90	
	To paid the cost of 6 hamacks	100	
	To paid account of sending to Ophra upon severall pallavoras	125	
	To petty charges for this month	75	
August	To paid for entertaining Captain Attwell etc. people	90	
	To my owne diett for the months of July and August	225	
	To petty charges for this month	115	
September	To expended on account of Captain Norths people	90	
	To paid for iron worke for the factory	200	
	To mine and Mr Armitages diett this month	180	
	To petty charges for this month	205	
October	To mine and Mr Armitages dyett this month	180	
	To petty charges for the same month	031	
		lbs 1706	18.86lb
July 9	To given the King upon account of building the factory, in silke		2:-
September 16	To more paid the King and Cabasheers when was pigniard, in silke		2:-
	To brandy 77 gallons expended in the months of July, August September		4: 13gal
	To more paid the King and Cabbasheers when was pigniard, in beads		2:-
October 24	To 10 white long cloths paid for 450 lb booges for the use of the factory		$6^2/3$
	To paid the King and Cabasheers in part for building the house		5:-
	To more paid on account of the same		4:-
	To paid severall carpenters on account of worke done		

---

[58] This implies that, whereas Wyburne's factory was in 'the lower towne' (i.e. the coastal village of Glehue), the RAC factory was elsewhere. This is corroborated by Celestin de Bruxelles, 2 Nov. 1682 (in 'Documenta' 1915, 358), who implies that the English factory (together with the Portuguese) was at the royal capital Savi. Later in the 1680s, however, the RAC factory itself was located at Glehue. The transfer may have occurred in 1684, when the RAC chief factor at Whydah reported that he was 'busied about building an house': Law 1990a, no.18 (John Carter, Whydah, 11 Dec. 1684).

in the factory   2:-
To 5 white long cloths paid Andrew Crosbie his wages for
6 months to the 8th instant   3^1/$_3$
To paid Francis Caple his wages for the same   3^1/$_3$
To delivered Captain Ambrose 10 blew long cloths and
8 fine sletias   9^1/$_3$
To paid Captain Bibbee for his assistance in the Royall
Companys service   1:-
To my owne sallary from the 29th January to the 29th instant,
which is 9 months att 3 slaves per month   27:-
To my dyett for 5 months at Ophra and expence of brandy   10:-
To expence of brandy for this month   1:-
                                                      slaves   100^2/$_3$

1682	Per contra is creditor		
July 9	By booges received from Captain Shepheard	1100 lbs	
September 24	By ditto exchanged for 19 white long cloaths	450	
27	By ditto received from Captain North	156	
		1706	Slaves
			18.86lb

July 9	By silke received from Captain Shepheard, 62 yards ⎫	
Sept 27	By ditto received from Captain North, 203 yards ⎭	13¼
July 9	By 21 pintado's, all broken, received from	
	Captain Shepheard	2:-
September 24	By 25 ditto narrow received from Cabo Corsoe	3^1/$_8$
July 9	By 7 sletias, damnified, from Captain Shepheard	1:-
Aug 27	By 60 peeces ditto received from Cabo Corsoe	20:-
July 11	By 16 gallons brandy as per contra	1:-
Aug 27	By more 61 gallons received from Cabo Corsoe	3:13gal
	By 559 pounds of beads received from Cabo Corsoe	14:-
Sept 24	By 25 peeces of white long cloaths⎫	16^2/$_3$
	By 50 peeces herba longees ⎪ Received from	7^1/$_7$
	By 25 silke ditto ⎬ Capo Corsoe	3^4/$_7$
	By 25 chercolees att 5 per slave ⎪ by ship George	5:-
	By 25 strip'd silkes ⎪	5:-
	By 25 ginghams ⎭	6¼
September 27	By 31 blew long cloths from Captain North	10^1/$_3$
	By 31 iron barrs from ditto	2:-
	By 980 rangoes, white small and broken, from ditto	2:-
	Slaves	133^2/$_7$

In Guydah 19th October 1682

[Inclosure 3]
Objections to Mr Winder's account under date of 19th October sent home to the
Royall Affrican Company

his charge to the Company   lbs
July   6 hammacks charg'd att

			Objections	lbs
	booges	100		
	sending to Ophra etc.,		3 hammacks costing booges	21
	booges	125		
	petty charges for this month	75	not expended more then	10
	entertaining Captain Attwells		I can say little to	
	people	90		
Aug.	petty charges this month	115	I can say little to	
	entertaining Captain Norths		I can say little to	
	people			
	iron worke for the factory	200	I can say little to	
Sept.	petty charges for this month	115	not expended more then	6
Oct.	more for this month	31	I can say little to	
	Booges lbs	1036	can say little to	

Slaves
att 90 lbs booges per slave is 11½

Slaves

	To the King upon account of		
	the house, in silke	2	nothing paid upon said account
	to the King and Cabasheers		
	when was pigniard, in beads	2	nothing paid upon said account
	to given the King when was		
	pigniard, in silke	2	nothing paid upon said account only 12 yards of silke given the King for a datig [= dashey]
	To 9 slaves paid acount of the		
	house	9	of which only 7 slaves is paid
	To Andrews and Franks		
	wages for 6 months	7	not yett paid
	to my dyett etc. att Ophra for		not paid as hee having left your honours in
	5 months	10	debt att Ophra
	To carpenters worke in the		
	factory	10	not paid more then 1 ounce of gold
	To his sallary, 3 slaves per		
	month to be paid here	27	I can say little to
	Slaves	73½	

In Guydah the 22d October 1682
Timothy Armitage

488. Timothy Armitage [to Royal African Company in England]

Guydah, 28 Oct. 1682

The foregoing is coppy of my last per Captain Ambrose, which doe confirme and should herein have sent your honours copie of the within mentioned, but that was hindred by Captain Wares sudden departure, occasioned by the non setlement of your honours affaires here, which now doe hope in some short time may be put into some better posture, Mr Winder haveing delivered to mee what remaines of goods in your honours warehouse, which is verry inconsiderable, as your honours will perceive by the inclosed account taken, the which have passed to your honours creditt, as shall likewise doe all the goods consign'd or left here. Mr Winder design'd to have come home in Captain Ware, now upon departure, but that hee absolutely refus'd to take him in, the reasons whereof he will give your honours. I doe hope may perswade Mr Winder to goe for Cabo Corsoe, in which shall use the utmost of my endeavour, and as oppertunity presents keepe your honours advised. Since mine per Captain North, which gave your honours an account of what goods most in demand, here is noe alteration. And as for a further account how things has been here manag'd, doe referr your honours to Captain Ware, Captain Ambrose and Mr Thomson. I hope in 2 or 3 day's to send away the canoe to Cabo Corsoe to the Agent and Councill, to whome shall give the needfull, assureing your honours that as far as in mee ly's nothing shall be wanting for the promoteing of your honours interest.

[Inclosure]
In Guydah the 24th October 1682
Received from Mr John Winder upon account of the Royall Affrican Company of England vizt
12 narrow pintado's
2 white long cloaths
11 halfe pieces blew ditto
13 herba longees, damnified by the worms
18 yards of flowred silke
23 three yards plaine ditto
2 chests beads containing 345 pounds
rangoes, white and small, 1260
rangoes more 900, broken, white and small

per Timothy Armitage

Slaves standing out, which were acknowledged before the King and assured to be paid att the arrivall of the next Companys ship, 15

489.   Timothy Armitage [to Agent and Council, Cape Coast Castle]
Guydah, 28 Oct. 1682

My last was under date of the 27th past,[59] copie whereof must here omitt in regard of the shortness of time that at present offers, occasioned by a great differance

[59] Not preserved.

betwixt Mr Winder and the Blacks here, as your Worship may perceive by the above copie and inclosed sent home to the Company by Captain Ambrose, there being no reconciling of itt; since which hee has delivered what goods remaining in the warehouse (although very inconsiderable) into my custody, which shall be disposed of to the most advantage of the Royall Company, an account whereof goes here inclosed. Hee would willingly have gon off in Captain Ambrose or Captain Ware, but neither of them would receive him, itt being our generall advice that hee should apply himself to your Worship and Councill, causing the goods hee carried out of the factory in the night time to be brought in againe, which hee will not be perswaded to, but supose hee will take the next oppertunity to goe off. Shall endeavour as much as in mee ly's to maintaine the Companys honour and interest, although hee has left mee very little to doe it with, as your Worship will perceive, and in goods that will not readily vend. This comes via St Thoma per Captain Ware, whoe has this day gott his complement of Negroes aboard if not more, haveing left behinde him only 21 iron barrs in the factory. I have obeyed your Worships order in requiring bills of loading from them, but itt is refus'd by all. To prevent the Companys goods from being made use of I doe humbly offer my opinion that your Worship send down copie of their invoyces of what goods aboard of them for the purchaseing their complement of Negro's, by which shall be able to make some computation; for that if they have any remains they will rather sell them for gold then leave them in the factory for the Companys use, as Mr Bathurst in Captain North did, whoe sold upwards of 500weight of booges, cutt the Companys sletias, sold severall remnants amounting to 11 peeces to Mr Winder, whoe will not denie itt, by which the trade is almost ruin'd. In 2 or 3 days hope shall dispatch the canoe, by which shall give your Worship a more large account how things goe here. In the meanetime humbly crave further orders for the settleing of this place, which in time may prove a place of as great consequence as any place upon the coast of Guyney. Doe likewise crave positive orders for the putting of any slaves aboard any ship or ships, and the quantity.

490. Timothy Armitage   Guydah, 5 Dec. 1682

Inclosed goes copie of my last via St Thoma per Captain Ware, who departed this place thee 3rd instant, although had all his Negro's aboard the 28th past and upon thee same day took his leave of this our towne, although tarryed below att Captain Wybornes severall day's, which with his leaving behind but 21 iron barrs in the factory creates the suspition in mee of his haveing many more slaves aboard then his complement, for that Mr Thomson whoe acted and did all the business in the buying the slaves, upon the 28th instant told mee that then they had their full complement, when that I was assured hee had not disposed of in silke more then 2 slaves, and what became of the rest I leave your Worship to judge, as likewise a parcell of corrall and some muzlins which were not here disposed of. As not seeing their invoyces could not make any computation, but tooke notice of what goods they had, an account whereof goes here inclosed, with their prize how disposed of, by which your Worship may see whether they have done the Company right or not. I doe not remember that did see any other sorts of goods but what is here specified. The wrong Mr Bathurst did the Company in selling their booges for gold, cutting their sletias, have in mine of the 28th October past given your Worship an account of, copie whereof goes here inclosed, as likewise copie of last to England with Mr Winders account etc., whoe (although much against his will, haveing endeavoured his passage upon all ships that has bin her, as well interlopers as Companys ships) comes in the canoe, whome I safely wish with your Worship. What goods he tooke out of the factory in the night time hee has disposed them the major part for gold, and the rest for cloaths, with an intention to have seen England before Cabo Corsoe, although now prevented. I must needs acquaint your Worship that many day's before I arrived here in Captain North that hee had contracted with one Fullwood, an interloper, to have put aboard 40 slaves, and to have went with them himselfe to Barbado's, whereof I am sencible that 8 of them was actually put aboard. Together with Mr Winder comes one Daniell Roe whoe left and ran away from Captain North, whome Mr Winder has entertained ever since; his designe in itt (I am inform'd, if things here went according to his expectation) was in some short time to have sent him away with slaves for New England in a New England man hee expected downe here, of which as bounden thought myselfe obliged to give your Worship an account, leaving the sequell of all things to your Worships prudence. I have likewise sent you up in the canoe one Patrick Welch, whome I understand ran away from the Castle to the prejudice of the Companys interest, hee was brought hither by one Wood, an interloper, and putt aboard of one Wilcocks now in port, whoe turned him here ashoare upon some differance happening. I did hope, as your Worship may perceive by the inclosed copies, might have sent you up the canoe before this, but that the canoemen did evade itt by the non properness of the season of the yeare,[60] with the like excuses, and have been forced to furnishe them in order to their dispatches as att bottom, of which your Worship may please to take noate. I now question not in the least, but that the Companys affaires here will be in a mighty good posture and condition, and hope towards the maintaining of which your Worship will consider a fresh supply, Mr Winder haveing left nothing behind him that will att present purchase victualls, allthough have and shall ever endeavour the maintaining the Companys, their rights, honour and privilidge here, and the true discharging of those bonds and obligations under which I lay, which hope time may veryfie. As to the removing Captain Wyborne in complyance to your order, I see

---

[60] Navigation by canoe along the coast was feasible only in the dry seasons, as during the rains the passage of the entrance to the River Volta was dangerous (cf. Bosman 1705, 328); it was now around the end of the lesser (September/November) rainy season.

not how myselfe or any other in the Companys service can effect it, soe long as the Companys ships doe maintaine and uphold him and supply him with guns, all sorts of ammunition, with other materialls, as Captain Ware has latly don. I have wrote to Mr Thorne severall times but as yett can gett noe account from him of what number of barrs remaine in the factory, although hee writes mee word is willing to goe off and shall, if can gett leave of the King, send Andrew Crosbie thither to take an account and endeavour their disposall for the Companys use. What goods most in demand your Worship will find att foot hereof, for which goods slaves can never be wanting, although there should come downe never soe many ships, and question not but in a verry short time this place may prove of verry great importance to the Company. And if they should altogether quitt Ophra, this place is sufficient for to slave all their ships, for that they doe and must send their slaves from Ophra hither, and that if your Worship and Councill thought itt convenient and approved thereof here might be alway's in bank 100 slaves to supply upon any occasion any of the Companys ships according to your order and directions, which presume your Worship will find itt in time much to the Companys interest.

[PS] May itt please your Worship, there is great occasion of brandy here in the factory.

[Inclosure 1]
Captain Norths canoe is debtor
To oyle   ¼ of a slave
To booges for sayles   10 lb
To canky mony and wood   10 lb booges
To a rope for a grapline
Captain Wares canoe is debtor
To oyle   ¼ of a slave
To canky mony and wood   10 lb booges

[Goods vendible]
booges
sletias
white long cloths
white and green beads
allejars
pintado's, white ground
rangoes, large and red
red corrall, long beads
silke longees
callico's, with all sorts of white ordinary lining

[Inclosure 2]

Accompt of the prizes of goods for which Captain Ware disposed his cargoe as followeth vizt

chinseys, 4 peeces per slave
fine muzlines, 2 peeces per slave
allejars, 4 peeces per slave
pintado's broad, 5 peeces per slave
fine sletias, 3 peeces per slave
course ditto, 2 peeces per ditto[61]
herba longees, 8 per slave
silke ditto, 7 per slave
iron barrs, No. 16 per slave
beads, 40 lb per slave
rangos, 200 per slave
white and blew long cloaths, 1½ per slave
silke, price uncertaine, from 15 to 20 yards per slave
In Guydah the 5th December 1682

491.   Petly Wyborne   Guydah, 8 Dec. 1682

I received a letter from your Honour and Councill dated the 12th of September. As for Captain Parris leaveing me heare,[62] itt was because I would not goe further with him. For the Royall Companys service, I respect itt as I ought to doe. I have had a letter by Captain Price from my brother Wyborne,[63] in which I understand the Company hath spoke to him to write to mee to serve them and that hee is intreating them about my former losses, of which I expect to heare farther by the first and then shall be able to give you a better satisfaction. However my concerns are too greate here to leave this place untill I goe off the coast. If your honour and Councill think mee fitt to serve the Company here or att Ophra and allow mee assistance, I will endeavour to sett theire affairs in a right posture and render a just accompt, or if you doe not think fitt to intrust mee if you are pleased to send an honest ingenious man that will heare my advice, I will be as faithfull to him as I would be to my brother, and be as just to the Companys interest as if I received their pay. I beseech you be pleased to beleeve me, as I am upon my owne account here soe I doe all that I can for the good of trade, and if I doe well for my selfe I must doe well for the Company. For your being my enemies itt would trouble mee verry much if I deserved itt, but if itt be as I am to the Companys interest I shall be thankfull to you, for I am sure I have done them more true service then hath been don to them since

---

[61] sic: but this can hardly be right. In 1681 coarse sletias sold at 4 per slave: cf. no.478, inclosure.
[62] Cf. no.480.
[63] Petley Wyburne's brother was Sir John Wyburne, a prominent captain in the English navy (and friend of Samuel Pepys).

I came here by all their servants besides. It would not become mee to wright the least ill of any of the Companys servants, but to see their trade and our country's creditt, that mought be soe great here, abused by horne mad,[64] brandy mad, boy mad, treacherous and foole mad men, hath made mee ashamed and troubled sometimes — treacherous by bribing the blacks to quarrell with their fellow servants and turne them out to gett themselves into their places, by insnareing one another into ill actions and then wrighting against them, by informing the blacks of the vallue of goods against their masters and all other peoples interest that trades. Here is one Crosbie, whoe the people would have sent away from this country severall times before Mr Winder came downe, but I would not suffer them, and since by his informing the blacks of what your factors or masters of ships doe or say, and alsoe informing in trade, that hee is in such favour that Mr Winder told mee that he would verry willingly have him up to Capo Corsoe with him, but hee beleeved the people would not let him goe. Mr Armitage pretends that hee desires verry much that hee could send him, but when I had spoke to the Blacks and they had consented if Mr Armitage and Mr Winder would desire itt, Mr Armitage then told Mr Winder that hee could not send him yett, but hee would in a short time. I doe verryly beleeve Mr Armitage had rather Mr Winder had run off from the coast then to Cabo Corsoe, this fellow was verry helpfull in getting Mr Winder out of his place. Pray beleeve I had rather see the Companys interest goe forward then any other nation.

492. John Thorne Ophra in Arda, 28 Jan. 1682/3[65]

February the 12th 1681/2 Mr John Winder in the night came to Ophra and the next morning showed me your Worships order, the which I most willingly complyed with, and he forthwith desired that the Phidalgoe might have notice of it, that your Worship and Gentlemen of the Councill had thought fitt to make him Chiefe factor on the Coast of Arda, and [he] desir'd he might have his residence here at Ophra and to be secured, otherwise Mr John Smith would have him to Guidah, he [= Smith] being the only man he was to suspect, as haveing notice of it before from Mr Spurvay. A letter of the 14th came to Mr John Winder from the said Mr John Smith to desire Mr Winder to looke after the debts which is owing to the Royall Company, unto whome I gave a particular account of all. The 22nd came another letter from Mr John Smith to Mr Winder intemating that Captain Thomas Woodfine had altered his mind and was resolved to take in his complement of slaves at Guidah, and wished Mr Winder to neglect noe time but come away as soon as possible might be. Mr Winder having received this letter makes all the meanes that might be to the Phidalgoe, telling him that Mr Smith had sent for him to Guidah with an intent to withdraw this factory, and therefore desired he might be protected

[64] Normally used of one made mad by cuckoldry; but here perhaps more generally, 'sex mad'.

[65] This and the following letter refer retrospectively to events during the first half of 1682.

by him, which being granted by the Phidalgoe Mr Winder then writes to Mr Smith that he was retain'd by the Phidalgoe and could not possibly come to Guidah. Mr Smith sent severall letters to him to come to Guidah and at last came himself, but was forced to goe back without him. I asked the reason of his being soe unwilling to goe with Mr Smith, he told me Mr Smith had a mind to keepe him at Guidah and come to settle here himselfe, and that he had received severall abuses by whitemen att Guidah and held it not a place fitt for a factory, in regard they had soe raised the prices of slaves to 25 per cent dearer then they are at Ophra.[66] Mr Smith not satisffied with Mr Winders staying at Ophra, thinking the Phidalgoe had kept him by force contrary to his owne will, was resolved to fetch him away in the night, the which resolution he put into practice and came to Ophra in the night with a spare hammack and men arm'd, and being without sent Francis Capell to the factory to acquaint Mr Winder with his designe, and desired Mr Winder to come to him with all speed. Mr Winder haveing received this message went along with Francis Capell to Mr Smith, and as he went acquainted some of the Phidalgoes people which lay at the gate (as they doe every night) that Mr Smith was come to fetch him to Guidah. This notice being given the towne was soone up in arms, which Mr Smith found to his cost, and seeing he could not gett Mr Winder away return'd to Guidah againe and began to make preparation to goe to Cape Coast, which after some time proceeded on his voyage. He being gone Captain Shepheard arrived about the 20th of June in Guidah Road, and goeing on shoare there was forc't to send for his goods, for the Blacks would not suffer him to goe on board againe before he had began to trade with them. Captain Shepheard then sent Mr Winder your Worships letters, which haveing received [Winder] sent Robert Chapman in a canoe on board to desire Captain Shepheard to bring his ship into Ophra road, where he would be ready to doe him all the service he could as per order from your Worship, but where he was he could not assist him in any thing, besides if he could come might do the Royall Company great service in it, for here was 30 slaves owing to the Company which would be shipt on board him, or if his goods should fall short might be made good by iron barrs, which with his other goods would be put off and not otherwise, but Captain Shepheard being on shoare before Mr Winders letters came could not comply with his desires, but writt him a letter and sent it by Robert Chapman who was then on board that in regard he could not comply with what Mr Winder had write him of, nevertheless he would send him his remaines to Ophra if he would send the said Robert Chapman for them, and withall order him to give a receipt for what he received, and it would be as well as if he had did it himselfe. Mr Winder haveing received Captain Shepheards letter was willing to goe on board of him, and

---

[66] Cf. the statement of Captain Lowe, in the following year, that prices were 20% higher at Whydah (no.627). A significant increase in prices is confirmed by comparison of the slave prices assumed in John Thorne's accounts both at Whydah in 1681 (no. 480, inclosure 1) and at Offra earlier in 1682 (no.483, inclosure 3) with Winder's accounts for Whydah in the second half of the year (no.487, inclosure 2): e.g. from 78 to 90 lbs of cowries per slave.

desired me to speake to the Phidalgoe for him, but when the Phidalgoe heard he would goe on board a ship in Guidah road began to be doubtfull of his returne and refer'd his answer till another time, but Mr Winder being urgent with the Phidalgoe made him the more distrustfull of his comeing againe, which I told Mr Winder of but he told me that if I could gett leave of the Phidalgoe for him, he would become bound to me in a 200 pound bond,[67] and likewise would give the Phidalgoe 60 slaves, that is the 30 that he owes the Royall Company and 30 more in iron, if he returned not againe but went on shoare at Guidah. On these considerations the Phidalgoe granted leave with my engagement together. He went on board and haveing been on board 2 dayes but the King of Guidah heard of it, and told Captain Shepheard if he would bring him on shoare he would give him a slave for his paines, the which Captain Shepheard soone put into practice and gott him on shoare, to the great loss of the Royall Company, for as soone as this Phidalgoe heard of it he sent for his 30 slaves in iron, which I kept him from for severall months and told him did believe Mr Winder would come againe, and had kept them yet in the factory had not Mr Armitage sold 500 bars to the French Merchant[68] and he comeing to demand them the Phidalgoe said he would be paid first the 30 slaves due to him which Mr Winder contracted, and soe forc't me to pay the 30 slaves in iron. He being paid I refused to give the French Merchant the barrs Mr Armitage had sold him till further order from your Worship. I often desired Mr Winder to take some care for my departure from this place but he put me of from time to time, and told me would waite your Worships further order, he not finding me guilty of any thing of what was laid to my charge. The letter that came to your Worship in Andrew Crosbies name is false, he denyes it and saith he never writ any. Mr Smith and Mr Winder both questioned him about it and had his answer. When Mr Winder was gott to Guidah I often moved my willingness to be discharged and to goe home according to your Worships order. I also desired him to take some care to send booges downe to maintaine the factory, [he] have[ing] then soe many in his hands, and not let the Companys barrs be sold at soe pitifull a price as 3 lbs of booges per barr,[69] but neither Mr Winder nor Mr Armitage would give me any answeare to what I writt, though severall desired, and might have had my passage in a Dutch ship if it had not been both theire neglects. I have been ever willing your Worships orders should be obeyed in things soe far as ever I was capable, for I hold it as great a crime to disobey lawfull authority as to take part in any unlawfull authority. My humble request to take some consideration of this place, either by sending some releife or by other meanes to withdraw it. If it be your Worships pleasure to with-

---

[67] sic: but £100 in no.493 below.

[68] i.e. the chief of the French factory at Whydah.

[69] For some discussion of the exchange rate between iron bars and cowries at this time, cf. Law 1991b, 249–50.

draw it, send but some goods that is vendible here to put of this iron and you may have the slaves sent to Guidah or elsewhere.

I have sent your Worship the coppy of Mr Winders contracts made to the Phidalgoe and my selfe.

[Inclosure]
A copy of the contract Mr John Winder made the Phidalgoe of Ophra:
On consideration that the Phidalgoe hath promised me to goe on board Captain Richard Sheppards ship the St George, I doe promise not to goe on shoare at Guidah, but after some small stay on board the ship to return againe to Ophra; and if I shall act any thing contrary to my promise, doe hereby oblige myselfe to the said Phidalgoe in the debt of 30 slaves, and doe give him free liberty to take the same in iron if I shall faile to returne, in witness whereof have hereunto sett my hand dated this 27th day of June (1682).

The copy of Mr John Winders condition made to me [John Thorne]
The condition of this obligation is such that whereas the above said John Thorne shall upon the special request and intreaty of the above bounden John Winder use all his endeavour to prevaile with the Phidalgoe of Ophra to permitt the said John Winder to goe aboard the St George in the road of Guidah upon the said Coast of Arda, whereof is Commander under God Richard Shepheard, and hath engaged his estate to the said Phidalgoe that the said John Winder shall returne to Ophra and not goe on shoare at Guidah aforesaid, that then this present obligation to be void and of noe effect, or else to stand and be in full force and vertue.

493.   John Winder[70]   Guydah, 15 March 1682/3

Whereas John Thorne in his letter of the 28th January last accuseth me of the following misdemeanours:
1stly. That upon my arrivall at Ophra the 12th day of Febuary 1681/2 I desired the Phidalgoe that I might reside in his country and that he would protect me from Mr Smith, whome I pretended was my enemy and would have me to Guidah; of which (he saith) I had advice before from Mr Spurvay.
2ndly. That I received a letter from Mr John Smith the 22nd following wherein I was desired by him, to make all possible hast to Guidah, did acquaint the Phidalgoe that Mr Smith had sent for me with an intent to withdraw the factory from Ophra, and that I againe desir'd his protection, which being granted, he saith I wrote to Mr Smith that I was detained by the Phidalgoe and could not possibly come to Guidah.
3rdly. Being demanded by the said John Thorne, why I was so unwilling to goe

---

[70] Following his deportation from Whydah in December 1682 (no.490), Winder had been reappointed chief factor there early in 1683: cf. Law 1990a, no.8 (Henry Greenhill et al., Cape Coast Castle, 19 April 1683).

with Mr Smith when return'd to Guidah from Ophra, I answered Mr Smith had a mind to keepe me at Guidah, and come to settle at Ophra himselfe, that I had received severall abuses from whitemen at Guidah and that I thought it not a place fitt for a factory, in regard the prices of slaves was exhaurted to 25 per cent more then at Ophra.

4thly. That Mr Smith came to Ophra in the night with a spare hammack, and being without sent Francis Capell to the factory, acquainting me with his designe and desireing me to come to him, which (he saith) I did, and as I went acquainted some of the Phidalgoes people therewith, whereupon the towne was up in arms and Mr Smith forct to goe without me.

5thly. That Captain Richard Shepheard being arrived at Guidah I desired John Thorne to speake to the Phidalgoe to lett me goe on board him, but he being doubtfull of my returne was unwilling to lett me goe, upon which he saith I proffered him a bond of 100£,[71] and another to the Phidalgoe of 60 slaves to be forfeited if I did not returne, upon which consideration leave was granted to me.

6thly. That the said John Thorne did often solicite me to take care for his departure from Ophra and that I would send him booges to maintaine the factory, and not lett the Companys barrs be sold at soe pittifull a price as 3 pound of booges, to which (he saith) I never returned him an answer.

To which particulars I returne these answers:

To the 1st. I acknowledge I arrived at Ophra around the time John Thorne mentions, but that I had any intention to reside there I utterly deny; neither did I ever request the Phidalgoe to protect me from Mr Smith, having no other intention but to returne to Guidah as soone as I had completed my business, and acquainted the Phidalgoe with the Agent Generalls and Councills instructions; and as to what he saith that I had notice from Mr Spurvay of Mr Smiths ill intentions towards me, I call God to wittness I never received any letter from him in my life; neither doe I remember I ever soe much as mentioned his name to John Thorne.

To the 2nd. I acknowledge that I wrote to Mr Smith in answer to his of 22nd February that the Phidalgoe did detaine me, and that I had soe great a watch over me that I could not possibly make my escape, but that it was my owne contrivance, I againe call God to wittness, tis a most notorious lye, and I hope not to be credited; since Thorne doth attest in the 5th article, that I went on shoare at Guidah, and forfeited bonds I had given for my returne.

To the 3rd. I acknowledge I did often say that I thought Ophra more convenient for the Companys factory then Guidah, by reason of the cheapness of carrying goods to the factory from the waterside was not soe great, and that slaves were to be had there at a far lower rate. As to what he saith that I told him of Mr Smiths designe to keep me at Guidah and settle himself at Ophra, I doe attest that the said John Thorne did endeavour to perswade me Mr Smith had such a designe, which I never

---

[71] Cf. n.67 above.

credited, knowing he did it on purpose, to alienate my affections from the said Mr Smith.

To the 4th. I can safely take my corporall oath,[72] that when I went out of the factory to Mr Smith, I did it with as real a designe to make my escape with him to Guidah as ever I did any thing in my life, and might have gon away had not Thorne sent the Blacks to panyare us.

To the 5th. I acknowledge it true, and that I did give a bond of 100£ to John Thorne and of 30 Slaves to the Phidalgoe for my returne to Ophra, without which I could not possibly escape, and here I desire John Thornes roguery may be taken notice of, for if he had noe designe to prevent my goeing away, why did he make me give him a bond to assure him of my returne.

To the 6th. I confess I never sent John Thorne any booges, it being contrary to my orders to send any goods or any person there till he was gon off.

494.   John Winder   Guydah, 24 June 1683

Your severall letters of the 17th and 19th of Aprill, with those of the 10th and 12th of May, lyes now before mee, haveing in pursuance to your orders therein specified, don my utmost endeavour for the dispatch of the Royall Companys ships that are lately gon from hence, and should have ere now dispatcht the canoe with advice had the weather been a little more favourable, but the canoemen have been forct to stay some time to repaire the canoe, much damag'd by her often oversetting in these boysterous seas. I am most heartily sorry I am forct to give you account of the unhappy misfortune befallen the Royall Company by Captain Lowe and Woolli-fords ships being taken, as also per the loss of the Blessing. I shall forbeare to trouble you with every particular circumstance hereof, because itt is largely ex-press'd in the inclosed from Captain Lowe to the Agent,[73] and only acquaint you in the generall that the 16th ultimo in the evening the two pyrates mentioned in your letter of the 12th ditto came downe to this roade, and tooke Captain Lowe, whoe made some small resistance. Captain Rickards people cutt their cable and went out of the roade, but before the ship came ashoare tooke the gold out and left her, which [ship] is lost, and not anything saved out of her. The mens intent was to run away with the gold, in order whereunto they gott aboard the Dutchmen in Ophra roade, but by the endeavour of Captain Rickard and myselfe and some small matter given the Phidalgoe for his assistance (whoe I must needs say was verry helpfull to us) part of itt is recovered, and one bulse containing 28 marks, 3 ounces and 7 angles sent the Royall Company by Captain Woolliford. The rest Captain Rickards has carried with him in the Merchants Bonadventure, whoe departed this roade 5 dayes since. Captain Woollifords men left the ship, which the pyrates tooke the next

[72] i.e. oath by the corporal, the linen cloth used in the mass.
[73] = no.637.

morning with all the gold in her, they pretended they would have fought but that 12 of their guns were in the hould, which was the occasion of their flight.[74] Perhaps itt may be immagined that itt was my fault hee was not gon off with his complement before, but I call God to wittness I did my utmost endeavour, as Captain Lowe and Rickard will justifie to the Royall Company, and doe affirme that would hee have been ruled by mee hee might have been dispatcht. Att my arrivall with him, I found the trade much altered in my absence, the people craveing to have the measure for booges altered, and the price of slaves in many goods to be advanc'd, which I refused to doe, itt being your express order to depress the price, and not to advance itt,[75] by which meanes I bought but 50 slaves in 3 weekes, but when I had brought the people to their former customes and they were content to sell their slaves att the old rate, Captain Woolliford came ashoare, and in a great passion tooke the business out of my hands[76] and immediatly chang'd the measure and brought up a custome of shakeing itt, whereby itt is become neare 90 pounds, and farther gave 3 fine sletias and halfe, which was never before more then 3, the like in allejars halfe a peece more then usuall,[77] whereupon I demanded the cargoe ashoare which you were pleased to consigne mee per bill of loading, but in the presence of Captain Lowe and Captain Rickard, hee absolutely refused to deliver itt to mee, saying that haveing possession hee had 11 points of the law, and that hee would make use of that part of itt which was most ready to buy Negroes, the rest hee would deliver mee when hee had his complement, since which the pyrates came downe, by whome he says he was plundered and the goods lost, though I can prove that part of the cargoe consign'd to mee was sent to windward in his boate without my approvall, which was sunk per the pyrates, and for anything I know, might be a greate occasion the ships were taken, for the people in the boate inform'd the pyrates in what posture the ships lay, with their yards and topmasts downe, and many of their men on shoare. I have acquainted the Royall Company att large herewith[78] and have given them coppie of his bill of loading for the goods, with bills of loading for the slaves hee said he had aboard, and those aboard Captain Lowe, the same you will receive enclosed, and have likewise sent others to the Royall Companys factors in the West Indias according to your order. I found Mr Armitage ready and willing to comply with your order in all things, and doubt not would have been verry helpefull to mee had hee lived, hee departed this life the 15th ultimo, haveing laine sick above 10 days, and by mee and others often advised to settle his estate, and make up his accounts with the Company, which hee neglected to doe,

---

[74] Cf., in addition to Captain Lowe's account (no.637), accounts by the other two captains involved, William Woolliford (no.632) and Captain Rickard (Law 1990a, no.10).

[75] Cf. Law 1990a, no.8 (Henry Greenhill et al., Cape Coast Castle, 19 April 1683).

[76] Cf. Woolliford's counter-claim, that Winder had refused to assist him in obtaining slaves (no.632).

[77] Cf. Law 1990a, no.11 (John Winder, Whydah, 15 July 1683).

[78] = Law 1990a, no.9 (John Winder, Whydah, 4 June 1683).

however after his decease in the presence of severall English men, I inventory'd what concerns of his was in the factory, and have taken itt into my possession, of which the Royall Company and his freinds in England shall have a just accompt. I have now no person with mee whom I dare trust (except William Belwood), haveing sent Mr Still to Ophra, and the rest that came downe with mee I find to be such sottish fellowes, that I dare not be out of the factory an houre unless I leave Belwood att home, for which reason I most humbley intreate your favourable construction for my non complyance with your order in sending him up, for I can at present as well spare my right hand as him. Captain Quow hath been att Ophra, being ordered by mee to proceed according to your instruction, hee will give you an account of the Phidalgo's answer to his pallavora. I likewise desired Captain Rickard to acquaint him with every circumstance of your order, and hee tells me that the Phidalgoe replyed that the first ship of the Companys that goes thither shall have Thorne aboard, provided they will carry him to England and not to Cabo Corsoe, and that hee will comply with all your demands whensoever the Company begins to continue their trade with him. If I might advise, I think itt would not bee amiss to order one ship thither for tryall, and accordingly the Royall Company may proceed with these people. Mr Windover continues still at Appa about 15 leagues to leward of this place.[79] I have informed Captain Wyborne according to your order, that hee [= Wendover] is considerably in the Companys debt and that if he detaines him itt will be att his own perrill, to which hee returned that hee was not anywise imployed by him, and promised mee to use his endeavour to gett him heither, when he doth I shall comply with your order in sending him to Cabo Corsoe. The present you were pleased to send the King of Guydah was thankfully received per him, with many promises of continuing a faire correspondence with the Royall Company, but if masters of ships have liberty to give what they please for their slaves and spoyle trade att their pleasure, the endeavours of the factors they have will be frustrate, and this place in short time of noe advantage to them. Andrew Crosbie went off in Captain Churchey, and Robert Chapman is dead. Captain Wyburne is lately returned from a place called Abree, about 16 leagues to windward of Guydah, where hee hath been about 6 weekes buying slaves for Captain Booth, an interloper.[80] I understand itt is a good place for slaves, and doe know that Wyburne intends to settle a Whiteman there, but had I your order I would prevent him, or att leastwise

[79] Cf. no.484.

[80] Cf. no.627 (giving the name of this place as 'Abrew'), which states that Booth's ship also was taken by the pirates. A source of 1690 mentions 'Aboré' as 'a village of Great Popo' (Debien & Houdaille 1964, 168). Another account of the taking of Booth's ship places the incident at Little Popo, west of Great Popo: PRO, CO1/13, 'Narrative of Thomas Phipps concerning pyracies committed by the pyrate Hamlyn upon the Coast of Africa', 24 Oct. 1683.

share the trade of that place by hoysting a flagg there for the Royall Company.[81] The cheife goods they covett are booges, tapsells, allejars and pintado's. I have enclosed return'd your letter to Captain Waugh, who was gon off the coast before the pyrates came downe. I heare he gott his slaves att Quitto, a place about 5 leagues to leward of the River of Vallta.[82] Hee came not downe to Guydah, but I am credibly inform'd hee sent mee a letter which Captain Woolliford intercepted and never came to my hands, soe can give you noe further account of him. Captain Lumley arrived here two dayes since, whoe I doubt not may have his complement in 10 dayes, he giveing the same rates that others have don before him, without which nothing is to be don, unless these people see that wee can send our ships to Ophra. Had I a good supply of booges, I might probablely, when ships are absent, bring them to the old rate, and I am sure, could in 10 dayes time, noe ships being here, purchase a good parcell of slaves for the next ship that came. The goods most in request att present are booges, corrall, white baftas, broad pintado's, white ground, allejars, sletias, white pautkaes, and brass panns. If your Worship would be pleased to entrust me with a small parcell of each, itt shall be my greate care to imploy them to the utmost advantage of the Royall Company, and desire that I may have a proportionable part in booges, for without halfe in halfe noe slaves are to be had, and I doe hereby reiterate the promise I made to you att Cabo Corsoe of being faithfull to my masters and not to convert their stock to the use of interlopers.

495.   Petly Wyborne   Guydah, 26 June 1683

Your letters of the 30th December and 23d March I have received, which binds me soe much to serve you that I shall never be able to performe my duty, but will to my power. I have never refused the Companys service nor I never will, but truely without a verry great loss I cannot leave this place in a little time, not soe soon as to have oppertunity to waite upon you att Cabo Corsoe before you goe, if you goe when your first three yeares is out. In what I can be serviceable to the Company here, I will and doe itt faithfully, The Dutch are setleing a factory att Popoe, which they have had formerly, itt is 8 leagues from this place.[83] I have an acquaintance about 8 leagues to windward of itt.[84] The cheife people have obliged themselves to mee, I know itt is a place that in a short time would be verry convenient for the

---

[81] But later in 1683 Winder reported that he could not settle 'Abron [= Abren]', because of lack of goods and 'a fitt man' for the job: Law 1990a, no.12 (John Winder, Whydah, 14 Oct. 1683).

[82] i.e. Keta. Cf. also John Waugh's own account (no.636).

[83] i.e. Great Popo. The Dutch factory here had been destroyed in a local war in 1680 (Law 1991a, 143). The WIC had instructed its factor at Offra to investigate the possibility of re-establishing the Popo lodge in 1682 (Van Dantzig 1978, no.14: Instruction for Martin Witte, 3 July 1682); but this was not in fact done until 1688 (cf. Law 1991a, 143). Barbot's reference to a Dutch factory at Popo (1992, ii, 621) is evidently copied from earlier sources, rather than reflecting the situation when he was there in 1682.

[84] i.e. at 'Abren' (Little Popo), as reported in no.494.

Company, being well managed, there is noe gold but there is aggree[85] and slaves, corne always is plenty; I have some trade with them, I send from Guydah to this place by river.[86] If I can serve the Company in settleing a factory for them and you are pleased to send a quallified man or two for that purpose, I will not question the doeing of itt. I question not but I could send you a letter to Accra within land. Mr Winder shall want nothing I can serve him in. I trouble you not with account of pyrates because he tells me hee doth.

[85] Akori ('aggrey', 'cori' etc.) were beads originating from the Slave Coast, which Europeans had earlier purchased in large numbers from Benin and Allada, for re-sale on the Gold Coast. This, however, is the only allusion to them in the 1681–3 correspondence, so that it is clear they were no longer an important item of trade for Europeans. By the late seventeenth century, the trade in akori was probably mainly in African hands: cf. Law 1991a, 149, 192–4.

[86] i.e. by the coastal lagoon.

IX

SHIPS

As was noted in the Introduction, a large number of the letters in the Rawlinson collection (145 of 640 in 1681–3) were received not from the RAC's factories in West Africa, but from ships operating along the coast (or, sometimes, from factors accompanying such ships, who were temporarily onshore). These included both locally based vessels — characteristically, smaller craft such as 'brigantines', 'sloops' and 'ketches' — which undertook coasting voyages from Cape Coast Castle, to both east and west, and ships involved in trans-Atlantic voyages.

COASTING VOYAGES

The *African Merchant*, Commander Samuel Starland

496. Samuell Starland   From aboard the Affrican Merchant, 3 Aug. 1681

Yesterday I received yours from Commenda by the hand of Captain Bracons[1] couzen, and according to your orders I shall doe the utmost of my endeavour. When he brought the letter hee told mee that Captain Bracon would have mee send 100 of niccanees ashoare, but hee sent noe money soe I sent him none. And this morning hee came a board with money for 100 and would have had 50 more without, and said that Bracon was very angry, for it was your order that hee should have what hee sent for, but I have sent him none as yet nor shall not without your order. Wee are now about a league to windward of the Mine and in hopes within a day or two to fetch Commenda, which has seemed to mee a very long passage. As for the prizes of good[s] I can give you little account at present, onely this, wee have had severall canoes aboard, I could have sold halfe the powder at 5 pease 2 angles per barrell for noe more, and severall of the blew baftes the broad at 5a and the narrow att 2½a, and most of the best knives at 1a per dozen, but what the prizes will be att Commenda I know not as yet.

[1] The principal merchant trading with the English at Komenda (cf. section II).

497.   Samuel Starland
                From aboard the Affrican Merchant, Comenda Road, 6 Aug. 1681

I received yours dated the 3rd of this instant, and that night I gott into Commenda road. I have disposed since of all the niccanees I had and 4 barrels powder, 1 say, 1 gingham, 1 piece of baft broad. This day Captain Bracon came aboard, whome I treated according to your worshipps command as well as the shipp could afford, him and all the rest of his friends. If you think fitt to send mee any more niccanees, which I find here the onely commodity att present, be pleased to let mee have them soe soone as your worshipp can, I beleeve I may dispose of as many more as I had and according to the raites I gave you an account of before, I find the same proffers here by most that come aboard. I onely gave you an account in my last of what I had found betwene the place I then rid att att [sic: and?] Cape Corsoe, not that I intended to trust any goods ashoare or sell any under the rates I had your order for.

498.   Samuell Starland
                From aboard the Affrican Merchant, Commenda Road, 28 Aug. 1681

These are to give you notice that I sent the canoe a Satureday up to Captain Woodfine to give him an account that you would not have him dispose of any of his goods till advice from your worshipp, and the last night about 8 a clock she came aboard againe, otherwise I had sent her downe before now. A Sunday Captain Brakon was aboard of him. I desired to know the reason wee had noe trade here, hee told mee because our goods was att too deare a rate. I desired him for to tell mee the prizes that they would give for such goods as I have a board, which according to his price I have here sent your worshipp an account, per 1 say 1o 2a, 12 musketts per bendy, per one barrell powder 1o 4a, per 1 gingham 5a, per 1 broad baft 5a, per 1 ditto narrow 3a, 1 pewter jugg 4a, per 1 dozen knives of the best sort 1a, for the other 6ta, per 1 lead barr 1a, which hee saith hee can buy soe out of the Company ships and out of interlopers a great deale cheaper. He saith if wee can sell them soe, that they will come here before any other shipps. I have now on board 15m 4o 7a of gold and one man slave.

499.   Samuell Starland
                From aboard the Affrican Merchant, riding off Cormanteen, 28 Aug. 1681

These are to satisfie you that wee have possession of the small shipp with little damage, onely the master of her wounded in the hand, but on our side noe hurt at all.[2] There is all their men come in the canoe, onely two which is left aboard. According to your order I have sent the key of the masters chest to your worshipp,

---

[2] Not explained; possibly an interloper arrested by Starland.

hee desireing that hee might bring itt up with him, and I have also the supracargoes chest a board of mee. I cannot give your worshipp any further account as to what she has aboard as yett. I begg your worshpps order in what I shall doe.

500. Samuell Starland   From aboard the Affrican Merchant, 29 Aug. 1681

Yours of the 28 instant I received, and according to your order I shall use the utmost of my endeavour that nothing be imbarked by any of our people. I have ordred the boatswaine to suffer nothing to goe out of her, and likewise I told their owne two men which is aboard her to see that nothing be disposed of. I have taken all the slaves I found aboard her aboard mee, there being 8, 1 man 4 women 3 boys, and the next morning I understood by them there was 10 aboard, the other two being carried aboard Captain Rickard that night she was taken by his canoemen. Yesterday I was aboard him to see if they were there, and hee told mee that they came contrary to his order or knowledge. The rogery I find was in the canoemen, itt being in the night they thought not I beleeve to be discovered. Captain Rickard told mee I might have them or leave them aboard, hee beleeveing that your worshipp would order him the rest, if not he would give a receipt for them, they being 1 woeoman 1 boy, soe I left them aboard. I hope to be up in 2 or 3 dayes if anything of a land breeze presents.

501. Samuel Starland   Anishan, 27 Sept. 1681

I went this morning ashoare to Annamaboe and shewed Mr Thelwall your worships order which you gave me, and he ordered mee to goe to Anishan to Mr Richards there to heare what he and the Curranteere has done about the shells,[3] which accordingly I went and spoake to them, and the Curranteere saith that to morrow he will come aboard mee and goe downe in the shipp and send his people away by land.

502. Samuell Starland   Affrican Merchant, Amersa, 30 Sept. 1681

These are to give you an account that this morning the canoe came on board without any shells and understand by them that the Cabisheer will not lett any come off under the raite hee had before soe desire to knoe what I shall doe as soon as you please.

[Starland was still at Amisa collecting shells on 11 Oct. 1681, but hoped to complete the work within a week (no.241). In November, he called at Komenda and delivered goods there (nos 37, 39.)]

[3] i.e. oyster shells, burned to make lime for building work; cf. no.238.

503.   Samuell Starland

Aboard the Affrican Merchant, Anamaboe, 2 Jan 1681/2

This afternoon I received your commands, and if that I had had anything that had been worth troubleing your worship with I should have sent you word. As for the interlopers threatning to lay mee aboard, hee was att the same time more afraid of being laid a board himselfe, for hee presently waid and stood off to sea and I after him for the space of two hours, and then I stood in againe and about an houre afterwards he tackt and stood in againe and came to an anchor, and the next morning I waid and came to anchor alongst his side, and yesterday about 3 a clock hee waid and this morning wee see him att anchor a great deale to leward off of Amersa. Mr Shears was this morning aboard and told mee the blacks were very unkind to him att Annamaboe, but hee went this morning ashoare to Agga.

504.   Samuell Starland

Aboard the Affrican Merchant, Annamaboe, 5 Jan. [1681/2]

These are to give your worship an account that the interloper is now att anchor as far to leward as wee can well see him, and another ship that came to an anchor by him yesterday in the afternoone but what hee is I doe not know. I sent your worship an account before by the same canoe that brought the letters which was writt by Charles [Towgood], and I have lain here ever since in expectation of your worships further order. In my last I forgott to give you an account that Captain Woodfine would desire your worship to tell his brother not to goe ashoare to Annamaboe upon any account whatsoever, for hee said that the Blacks would certainly murder him. I have sent per the canoe the boatswaine to bring downe the boate if your worship pleases, for if wee should breake a cable wee should want her very much. Mr Richards this morning sent aboard two men in irons desireing mee to keepe them aboard, they being two of the blacks which endeavoured to panyar him.[4] Haveing not elce to give your worship an account of, but wishing you your health which I understand by Charles you want at present, which I hope will not be long.

505.   Samuell Starland   Aboard the Affrican Merchant , 11 Jan.1681/2

This morning I received your worships orders for to goe to Amersa[5] and shall make the best of my way thither. I have sent the 2 hand canoe up, and desire your worship would bee pleas'd to order us some shovells, for wee have not one aboard. I sent this morning aboard of Captain Gates to borrow some of him but hee has none aboard, and without them I know not what to doe.

---

[4] Arthur Richards, RAC factor at Anashan; but the correspondence preserved from Anashan (cf, section III) does not allude to this incident.

[5] The oyster-fishing centre: hence Starland's need for shovels.

[In early March 1682, Starland was at Anashan, where he took in corn (no.178.)]

506. Samuell Starland   Wyamba Road, 27 March 1682

These are to give your Worship an account that I have no more then 5 slaves as yett, 4 woemen and 1 man. I lay 2 dayes off Tantonquerry but noe canoes came off, soe I went downe to Lague and lay 5 days there and bought but 2 slaves, soe I came downe to Wyamba, where I have now layn 10 dayes and bought but 3 slaves, but I had a verry faire prospect of purchaseing 30 or 40 if that the Ancrongs had not come soe soone uppon them,[6] for the night before there was two of the Queens[7] men came downe and 12 (whereof one lost his head the next morning) slaves that would have been there the next morning, but the Ancrongs came upon them an hour or two before sun riseing. I was then in the towne, for I lay that night ashoare. The people of Wyamba being surprised ran away soe fast as they could, without any resistance at all. They have killed a great many of them and carried a great many away. I have lost one of my canoemen, whether hee bee killed or carryed away I cannot heare, but they have cutt off Mattees head, his body lies in the bushes. Myselfe with the other canoeman lay in the bushes about 6 or 7 hours and then wee gott out and went for Barracoe some 5 leagues to leward of Wyamba. I lost all my cloaths only [= except] shirt and drawers with 4 ounces of the Companys that I had received ashoare, which if I live to see your worship I shall give you a farther account. I designe tomorrow morning to weigh and turne up as far as Momford to see if I can buy any of those slaves they have taken.

[PS] It was Fryday last.

507. Samuell Starland   Momford Road, 3 Apr. 1682

Your Worships of the 29th of March I received, and according to your order in takeing care of not being supprised I shall take all the care I can. The 28th of March I waied from Wyamba and the 31st ditto I came to an anchor a little to the westward of Momford, where I sent my canoe ashoare with Parrett in her to see if they had any slaves, and when hee came aboard hee told mee that hee see the canoeman ashoare which I lost att Wyamba, but they would not lett him come off except I would pay for him as much as another slave. I have not concerned myselfe in itt, I desire that your Worship would be pleased to order mee what I shall doe in it.[8] The last night about 7 of the clock three of our gudgings broake away from our sterne

---

[6] Akron, west of Angona. Cf. the earlier Akron attack on Winneba, in 1681 (no. 385).

[7] i.e. the Queen of Angona, to which Winneba belonged (cf. section VI).

[8] This canoeman was subsequently ransomed by Richard Thelwall, chief factor at Anomabu (nos 279–80).

post, and one we had lost before, we haveing only the upper one left, and wee were forst to gett our ruther in upon deck and have noe way to hang him againe. Your Worship was pleas'd to order mee to Accra, but if I should goe downe now I should be in a bad condition for to gett up to Capo Corsoe againe. I doe not question but to hang him againe upon 3 gudgings more besides that as is left, if I can gett up to take all our things out and bring her by the head. I have noe more slaves aboard then what I gave your Worship an account of in my last. I shall lie still here till I have your Worships order what I shall doe.

508.   Samuell Starland & Arthur Richards[9]   Anishan Road, 4 May 1682

These are to give your Worship an account that this morning the Curranteer and Cabisheers of Anishan held their pallavora with severall of the Arcanies, and when satisfaction was demanded for their tradeing with interlopers their answer was that the loss of their goods they thought was enough, and as for any other satisfaction they would not give any thing. They have nothing to say to Mr Richards, only that hee had made them pay for that hee had given them before, and for the townes people they say that they had noe hand in the matter, soe this is all the satisfaction that I heare is like to be given by either of them. Mr Richards this afternoon sent off 13 iron barrs and towards night came off himselfe, hee told mee without any hinderance att all, and tomorrow morning I intends to goe ashoare againe and if hee finds not other satisfaction intends for to send off all the goods if not prevented. The demand made by him was that those two Anishan people that was the first actors should be turned out of the towne, and that the second of the Arcanies and the two that were taken with the goods should be sent up to your Worship, and 40 marke of gold should be paid besides. I have the Curranteer's sonn board still and the Braffo's sonn, soe expecting your Worships further order, haveing not elce to give your Worship an account but leaving the rest to Hansico.[10]

509.   Samuell Starland   Anishan Road, 12 May 1682

I hope this will find your Worship in better health then I heard by Captain Sheppard hee left your Worship in. I am sorry I should give your Worship the trouble of this but necessity forces mee to doe itt. The 5th of this instant att night wee sprang a great leake, and have been ever since endeavouring to find itt but cannot. Wee make between 4 or 500 stroaks a glass and have done ever since itt first began, soe if your Worship pleases to order mee up to have the advice of a carpenter and for to take

[9] Richards was in charge of the RAC factory at Anashan, but had come on board the *African Merchant*, as explained in this letter, intending to abandon the factory if a dispute with the local people was not resolved: cf. also no.182.
[10] Cf. no.183.

out our caske, that wee may have roome to trench our ballis [= ballast?] fore and aft, I doe not question but wee may find itt.

510. Samuell Starland

Aboard the Affrican Merchant, Barracoe Road, 30 May 1682

These are to give your Worship an account that the Wyamba people have all left that place and are gon to Barracoe. I came to an anchor in the roade the 24th instant and sent my canoe ashoare. They met with two men just att the landing which gave them that account, soe next morning I waid and ran downe to Barracoe, where severall of the Wyamba people came off, and some of them which were taken by the Accrongs[11] that had redeem'd themselves, they give mee an account that the Lague and Momford people doe threaten very much what they will doe to the first Whiteman they can take, or if your Worship should send downe any great canoe to leward that they will use the utmost force to take her, and sweare they will cutt of the heads of any Cape Coast people they can light of. The Wyamba people sayes that here is some of them ly's lurking to and again about about the towne. I had a letter writt 3 day's agoe to have given your Worship an account of this, because I heard Mr Towgood saying hee intended to water at Wyamba, but [through] the badness of the weather I could not send the canoe. The last night came to an anchor here Mr Towgood, and this morning sailes. If any of the ships come downe itt will not be safe for them to send their boats for water at Wyamba. Since I came to an anchor here I have bought 6 men slaves and taken about 5 marke of gold. If your Worship pleases for to give me a line or two in order what I shall doe after delivered the remaines of the goods to Mr Hassell,[12] whether I shall lye there till further orders or make the best of my way for Cabo Corsoe, for I have nothing mentioned in my orders.

511. Samuell Starland   Aboard the Affrican Merchant, off Accra, 11 June 1682

These are to give your Worship an account that yesterday waighing of our anchor wee broke our cable, the currant runing soe strong to the eastward and the wind att S.West wee could not fetch our buoy, soe wee bore away for Accra and fired severall gunns for to gett a canoe off to see if there were any anchors to be gott there, for wee have never a one now and but two thirds of a cable, but wee could not gett any canoe off that night, soe wee stood off to sea all night and in the morning wee stood in and fetcht a little to windward of Accra, and in the afternoone wee had a 2 hand canoe came off to us. I sent to Mr Hassell to see if hee had any or could gett one, soe if this comes to your Worships hand you may know wee have not gott any. Wee

---

[11] In the attack reported in no.506.
[12] Ralph Hassell, chief factor at James Fort, Accra.

must be forc'd to goe to Allampo to Mr Towgood to gett one of him if hee has not lost one. If your Worship can gett one from any of the ships to send itt downe, and a cable with itt. If wee should gett one from Mr Towgood hee will have but one left, which if either of us should have the misfortune to break a cable I know not what wee should doe for one. I have now on board 9 marke of gold and 13 slaves. A Tuseday last came aboard Mr Smith from Arda,[13] very ill, and is here now. Wee have had very bad weather here. Hee presents his service to your Worship and hopes to bee with you very shortly, hee has had a very hazardis and tegious passage, being absent from Whydah since the 18th past. I sent my 2 hand canoe up to your Worship 11 dayes agoe but have not heard of them yett.

512.   Samuell Starland   Aboard the Affrican Merchant, Allampo, 23 June 1682

These are to give your Worship an account that the 12th instant I came to Allampo, where I found the Cape Coast Briganteen and gott an anchor out of her, but being very much wind and a great sea I was forc'd to buy an anchor out of a Dutchman that lay here, by reason the anchor that I had from the Briganteen would not ride the ship.[14] The 18th came to anchor here the Arcanie Merchant, and hee tooke up my anchor which I left att Barracoe, which I have now on board. I would have turn'd up to Accra before now but the currant has run very strong to leward ever since I have been here, but the first oppertunity I shall make the best of my way up thither. I gave your Worship an account by a letter I sent ashoare to Mr Hassell that night I came off of Accra, desireing him to send itt up by a canoe. I have not seen my canoe nor canoemen never since that I sent them from Barracoe.[15] I should have given your Worship an account before now if that I had had a canoe; if shee be att Capo Corsoe if you please to send her downe for I have a great miss of her. If you please if any oppertunity presents for to send mee downe a cable, for the anchor I bought is upwards of 500 weight and I feare if I should come to an anchor in stiff grounds my cable will hardly weigh him.

513.   Samuell Starland   Aboard the Affrican Mechant, Accra Road, 6 Aug. 1682

Yours of the 2nd instant I received. I should have given your Worship an account of my proceeding severall times before this if that I had a canoe or Mr Towgood [had one], but I could not gett any between Allampo and Accra. I have been from thence [= Allampo] ever since the 26th of June and have made the best of my endeavour to gett up according to your worships former order. The 2nd of this instant I came to an anchor in the roade of Accra to gett a little wood and water and

---

[13] John Smith had been at Whydah, trying to establish an RAC factory there (cf. nos 492–3).
[14] Cf. no.530.
[15] For the reason, cf. no.620.

some corne, which I am now supplyed with from Mr Hassell, and tomorrow if wind and weather permitt I shall make the best of my way for Cabo Corsoe. I have now on board 50 slaves, some that I tooke out of Mr Shears in his goeing downe and what I have bought my selfe, and 12 marke in gold.[16]

514. Samuell Starland   Morea Road, 23 Aug. 1682

These are to give your Worship an account that wee find the currant runs verry strong to leward which forceth us to ride here, wee haveing noe more then 2 day's corne aboard for the Negro's and Mr Towgood about the same quantity, Mr Shears haveing had none this 3 dayes but what wee have spared him between us. I have now aboard 50 slaves, 21 that I had out of Mr Shears[17] and 29 of my own.

[Starland proceeded to Anomabu, where he landed goods for the factory, but died there on 22 September 1682 (nos 293, 297–8).]

Unidentified vessel[18]

515. George Phipps   Annamaboe, 17 Aug. 1681

I mett Mr Nightingale off the Morea and delivered your orders to him and accordingly wee proceeded on our voyage, onely stay here to take in fresh canoemen for the 7 hand canoe, be assured your orders shall be justly observed by [myself].

516. James Nightingale   Annamaboe, 17 Aug. 1681

According to your honours orders have settled Mr Shears att Wyamba, but not with litle trouble, I was forced to goe 15 miles by land and back againe. Your honour will find by Mr Shears letter that I have made agreement with the Anguinnas, Laguers, Accrongs and Wyamba people and made them take their fittish to be true and trusty to the Royall Affrican Company of England and all their concerns.[19] I mett with Captain Phipps about Morea and very sorry to heare the ill management of Accra fort. Notwithstanding I am tyred of my travell will and shall obey your honours order to the utmost of my power. I intend to goe ashoare att Wyamba and

[16] Cf. no.434, referring to the landing of goods by Starland..

[17] Cf. no.522.

[18] This voyage may have been made in the canoe referred to in no.515, rather than in a European ship. Phipps and Nightingale were sent to reorganize the RAC factory at Accra, where they arrived on 18 Aug. 1681: cf. no.406.

[19] Cf. no.385.

see how things goe there. If I see Mr Shears will goe hee may, if not convenient may stay, notwithstanding if any thing should happen I will order him to come att Accra.

[In fact, Phipps and Nightingale did not go on shore at Winneba, though they spoke to Shears there (no.386); they arrived at Accra on 18 Aug. 1681 (no.406).]

The *John*, Commander Hugh Shears

[Shears had been at Winneba in August 1681, though whether he was then commanding the *John* is not certain (nos 385–8). He arrived at Anashan in the *John* in late September 1681 (nos 237–8.]

517. Hugh Shears   Anamaboe Road, 9 Oct. 1681

As for your letter and order I have received with men and goods, and as for two of our men I have sent your worship in this boate, and as for having care of the vessell I shall doe my best, as for my advise to Captain Lawrance and Captain Woodfines mates shall not be wanten, and at all oppertunities I shall give your Worship an account of our proceedings, and as buying what I can for your Worship I shall doe my best

[PS] Now just departing for Amersa.

518. Hugh Shears   Alampo, 30 Oct. 1681

This is to give your Worship an account that this morning I have received your order dated the 27th of this instant, the which in the morning wee shall begen to make our best way for Cabo Corso. As for slaves wee have gott but 34 men, 12 woemen, the cause of nott gotten of slaves is that there lyes a Portugeze and he gives for a man slave 1 bendy and for a good women 7 peze, and likewise Captain How an interloper hath panyard or kept on board 3 Cabbisheers,[20] the caws [= because] of it wee dare not venter on shoare. Likewise at Mingo lyes another Portugeze and a Frenchman distance from Alampo about 4 leagues.

[PS] As for getten of slaves as wee turne up wee shall doe our best.

[20] Cf. no.420.

519. Hugh Shears   Aboard the ship John at Annamaboe, 2 Jan. 1681/2

This is to give your worship an account that the corne is on board, which is about 80 chests, soe haveing nothing elce to doe I waite your worship and Councills order. One man is sick, the which I have sent to Capo Corsoe, the which I would have your worship send another man in his roome or order to take out of Mr Starland, and one man more if you please to send would not be amiss, and order the gunner to send mee 6 granadoes more and 6 pound of brimstone if you please, for I have heard that an interloper will be on board of us, likewise if your worship can send mee one small grapnell. The anchor that was mended at Capo Corsoe the first time wee putt him on ground is broke as itt was before, the which I have put on shoare at Annamaboe but there are not coales to mend it.

[According to Starland's report (no.503), Shears went aboard Starland's vessel at Anomabu, and landed at Egya on this same day, 2 Jan. 1682.]

520. Hugh Shears   Aboard the John, Alampo Road, 30 Jan. 1681/2

This is to give your Worship and Councill an account that all the goods are disposed off, all to 1 barrell of powder and 13 musquetts. Wee have on board 26 men slaves, 23 woemen and 1 girle. Soe this night if God willing wee shall beginn to make our best way for Capo Corso. Mr Towgood carryes the account with him.

[In February 1682, Shears was at Accra, where he delivered goods for the factory, and from where he was expected to return to Cape Coast (nos 423–5); on 30 March he was at Anomabu, where he also delivered goods ashore (no.266).]

521. Hugh Shears   Commenda Road, 4 Apr. 1682

This is to give your Worship an account that wee came into this road Monday last about 4 of the clock in the afternoone. As for Mr Nightigall hee has done what hee can to gett corne but cannot gett it at that rate that your Worship has ordered but they will not sell under 2 angles per chest, and that on shoare for they will not pay canoe hyre, soe haveing nothing else to trouble your Worship withall but waite your Worships further orders.[21]

[On 15 April 1682, Shears was at Komenda, and sent to Cape Coast to ask whether he should proceed west along the coast (no.528). On 3 June he was back at Anomabu, where he delivered a letter from Cape Coast (no.275; cf. no.619); he left Anomabu back to Cape Coast on 24 June (no.278).]

---

[21] Cf. no.65.

522. Hugh Shears   Morea Road, 23 Aug. 1682

This is to give an account of our proceedings the which I have sent inclosed, and
our bad success in our slaves. Of 24 that was put aboard Mr Starland there are 3
dead, 2 men and 1 boy,[22] and of 55 that I bought after there are 2 men dead, not for
want of that wee had [sic]. If your Worship please send us some corne for wee have
none. If your Worship think convenient to send for the slaves, for I beleeve the
currant will run for some time, which if itt does with these winds itt is but in vaine
to way, and likewise wee have no wood nor canoe to send for what wee want. If
your Worship hath any canoe to spare if you please lett us have her, I have not stopt
att any place that I could gett one. July the 25th the carpenter run away on board of
one Allin, the which by noe means could gett him againe, the cause he saith is that
your Worship fired att him and that hee was taken by the Kings ship by the Companys meanes.

[PS] Departed Allampo July the 27th.

[By September 1682, Shears had transferred to command of the *Cape Coast*
(no.304). The *John* may have been decommisioned, since a sail from it was
later in use on the *Cape Coast* (no.535).]

The *Cape Coast*, Commander Charles Towgood, then Hugh Shears

[In February 1682 Towgood was at Accra, where he delivered goods
(no.425).]

523. Charles Towgood
                    Aboard the Cape Coast Briganteen, Allampo Road, 5 March 1681/2

I thought itt convenient to give your worship an account of my proceeding in this
place. I have been here this 10 dayes and att my first arrivall found a French man
here with 4 othere ships about 4 leagues to windward of mee. The French man had
nothing but bouges, which the natives wanted at that time to buy corne, soe that as
long as hee lay here I could not gett a slave;[23] and the day before hee went away
which was Fryday Captain Gates came to anchor here,[24] and hee gives such rates
that I am like to lye here a considerable time, besides his pintados are broad and
mine are all narrow and hee gives as many of his for a slave as I can of mine, soe

---

[22] Cf. no.514.
[23] This ship was one of Jean Barbot's squadron, though Barbot himself did not arrive at Adangme until
later (1992, ii, 440).
[24] Cf. no.613.

that I cannot expect to sell any of mine till his bee all gon and then hope they will goe off. I have made shift since hee has been here to gett 8 good men, 6 woemen and 2 boyes with 2 girles, 18 in all which are all verry goode slaves; but I have been forc'd to give 1 angle upon a head for a man more then what your worship has allowed or elce they would have gon aboard Captain Gates. I intend the first oppertunity of a wind to turne up to Ningo, a place 4 leagues to windward of this place, where I understand there are a few slaves, for I cannot expect to gett many slaves here as long as hee lies here without I could give as great rates as hee, which is a bendy a head. I wish I had a few green and blew perpettuanos more, for those that I had of that sort which were 8 are all gone and they aske for them now extreamly. Just now my canoe came from the shoare, but the sea runs so high that they are not able neither will they venture to bring off a slave. They have promised to bring mee about 10 or 12 as soon as they can gett off.

[PS] This goes by my canoe as far as Accra and then to goe up with the first conveniency. Robert Crow lies very ill of a voiolent feavour.

524. Charles Towgood   Allampo Road, 17 March 1681/2

Last night about 8 of the clock I received your Worshipp and Councills orders, which I will follow the first oppertunity that presents.[25] I wish itt had come 2 or 3 dayes sooner, for there was a 2 hand canoe on board mee that belong'd to Morea which I could have detain'd with ease. About 10 dayes since I sent your Worship a letter, itt bare date the 5th instant, itt went in my canoe as far as Accra, and then to be sent up with first convenciency; wherein I acquainted your Worship of the great prices Captain Gates gave and of his pintados being broad and mine narrow, which hindred the sale of mine, but hope I shall put all off when hee is gon, which will bee tonight. I have on board att present 40 good slaves, most of them men and boyes, but as I acquainted your Worship in my last I have been feigne to give 1 angle upon a head for a man more then what your worshipp allowed mee, and glad I could gett them soe too, hee giveing a bendy a head in all goods. I hope to have the rest of my slaves in a small time if the bad weather does not hinder the bringing them off.

[PS] I wish I had a few more irons for I beleeve I shall have occasion for them, haveing but 25 pairs aboard and some of them the rust has eaten quite out, for when I goe to make use of them they breake in the eye of the shakle.

525. Charles Towgood   Allampo Road, 19 March 1681/2

This morning I received a letter from your worship and Councill with an inclosed

---

[25] i.e. to panyar canoes belonging to the Dutch: cf. no.264.

for Captain Gates, who sailed from hence a Fryday haveing 156 slaves, hee putting on board mee his remains with a letter for your Worship, which I send here inclosed with the letter that came from you to him. His remaines was only 16 Guyney stuffs for which I gave him a receipt.[26] I have on board att present 45 good slaves, most men, and hope to have as many more by that time your worship has ordered mee to depart from hence. A Fryday morning dyed a woeman which I bought but 2 dayes before, shee was as likely a slave as any I have on board, alsoe very sullen and would not eate, for the Docter opening of her found her verry sound but starv'd for want of eating. This morning I sent one whiteman ashoare to stay till I sailed, for they sent off word they would not bring off a slave before I sent one, for feare of being panyard.

526. Charles Towgood   Allampo Road, 24 March 1681/2

I intended to have followed your Worships order which bare date the 15th instant tomorrow morning if I had not received your orders to the contrary about 4 hours since (which bare date the 21st instant), with 10 pairs of irons, but nevertheless seeing noe likelyhood of getting slaves here, there being noe slaves in the towne and 2 English interlopers lying here and the French sloope, and my water spending and noe likelyhood of getting more here, I intend to depart the first oppertunity of a breeze with what I have (which is 50 good slaves) and make the best of my way for Capo Corsoe. I shall likewise take what care I can to secure the Companys vessell and concerns against all Dutch sloopes and canoes that shall oppose mee, to the best of my power. Since my last which bare date the 19th instant there died one of the best men that I had on board of a voiolent feavour, his tongue being scorched in his mouth, the reason I know not, only beleeve twas through the Negroes beating of him when hee was panyard.

[At the beginning of April 1682, Towgood was at Accra, where he embarked gold and slaves (nos 429–30).]

527. Charles Towgood   Commenda Road, 13 Apr. 1682

This serves to acquaint your Worship that last night about 7 a clock I came to an anchor in this roade, and this morning early I went ashoare to acquaint the traiders of my comeing and told them what goods I had and the prizes, but their answer to mee was that they did admire that your Worship did send noe more goods to the factory ashoare, for then they would give those prizes, but to come aboard they would not to buy goods att those rates, when they could buy them cheaper else-

---

[26] Cf. no.614.

where, soe that I wish your Worship would order mee up higher, where I beleeve I should make a quicker dispatch then to stay here. There has not a canoe been aboard to day, for here lyes 2 interlopers, one is Aushhead of Redriff, the other is a Burmudian. This goes by my canoe, which I have lent to Mr Shears because shee is not able to carry mee anywhere, shee being all to peeces; soe I shall borrow his canoe if I have any occasion, and I would pray your Worship that if you have anyother that you can spare that you would be pleased to send itt by the canoemen, I not knowing what to doe without one, and that your Worship will be pleas'd when you order Mr Shears downe, to order him to lett mee have one of his slaves hee haveing 3, I haveing great occasion, makeing 500 stroaks a glass.

[PS] If your Worship please to order mee that if any corne presents In the time of my stay that I may buy itt, I will.

528.   Charles Towgood   Commenda Road, 15 Apr. 1682

This morning I received your Worships and Councills letter dated the 14th instant, upon which I went ashoare to acquaint the people of itt, but they told mee they would buy all the goods, says, perpetuanoes and blanketts excepted; but I find in your Worships letter that only sayes and perpetuanos were excepted, and likewise that if they did not comply with that, that then I should ply up to windward with Mr Shears, which I am ready to doe, but only thought itt convenient to give your Worship advice and waite for your answer and that if your Worship order mee to deliver these goods ashoare, whether I shall goe up to windward with the remaines or what I shall doe, I only attending your Worships further orders.

[PS] Mr Shears presents his service to your Worship and desires to know whether hee shall goe to windward without mee if that you order mee otherwise. I would desire your Worship that if you can spare another canoe that you would be pleased to send itt in the roome of this that comes downe, shee not being able to swim above water.

There is more in this pallavora then I can immagine about these goods.

[PPS] Since the wrighting of this letter the blacks sent word that they would not take the great basons. And just now arrived here the Arcanie Marchant, Captain Attwell,[27] soe I sent the canoe on board him to know if hee had any commands for Capo Corsoe, upon which hee sent mee a pacquett which I have forwarded to your Worship.[28]

---

[27] Cf. no.615.
[28] For Towgood's activities at Komenda around this time, cf. also no.67.

529.   Charles Towgood   Charles Fort, [Annamaboe], 27 May 1682

Haveing an oppertunity by a canoe that came from Cabo Corsoe this day, thought itt convenient to give your Worship advice of my proceeding here. I am just now goeing aboard intending to saile, haveing gott my wood and corne, but faine to give great rates for itt, there lying 3 ships here; I should have had itt before now but that the bad weather that has been here for 4 or 5 days hindred them from bringing itt; which bad weather I am afraid will be a great hinderance to mee att Allampo.

> [Towgood proceeded to Beraku, where he arrived on 29 May, and left there on 30 May 1682 (no.510). Around the beginning of June 1682, he was at Accra, from where he called at Teshi (no.429).]

530.   Charles Towgood
                        Aboard the Cape Coast Briganteen, Allampo Road, 23 June 1682

I had given your Worship an account of my proceeding before now but that bad weather hindered it. I haveing been here this 3 weeks and have gott noe slaves by reason of 2 Dutch ships that has been here that had great store of cowries, and likwise 2 English interlopers, but nevertheless I had gott slaves if the Dutch Companys ships had not given the Negroes greate dasheys that they should not come aboard of mee; which I should not have knowne but that the Negro's themselves told mee that the Chiefe Cabusheers of the towne would prendee them a cow if any came aboard of mee with slaves. Since which time one of the Dutch ships is gone and the other has but few good goods that is fitt for this place, soe that I should have had slaves but that Captain Attwell came downe just as I had made the pallavora (which was a Sunday last) and gives such greate rates that I cannot expect to gett any, soe that I intend to turne up to windward with first oppertunity about 6 leages to windward of this place, where there is both gold and slaves, hopeing to dispose of most of my goods. Mr Starland about 12 day's since came to this place without an anchor, soe I lent him one of mine to ride by for the present, haveing but one left myselfe, since which time hee procured one out of one of the Dutch ships but gave a very great rate, which hee could not helpe because my anchor would not ride him, hee driveing athwart the Dutchmans harse; soe hee intends likewise to turne up to Accra with the first conveniency.[29] I beleeve Mr Smith inform'd your Worship of the great leake I sprung att Accra, since which I have sprung another, they are both in the worst places of the vessell to be come att, one of them being in the very scagg [sic: = ?] of the sterne post, the other in the stem or rather between that and a false stem, which cannot be come att without cutting some timbers, which will endanger the vessell. The force of itt wee have stop't by stuffing in a great quantity of tallow and coales beate together, nothing else being to be done. Captain Attwell told mee

[29] Cf. no.511.

that your Worship ordered him to putt his remaines aboard of mee when he had done here, because your Worship cares not how little goods goe to Arda,[30] soe that I intend if your Worship doe not order mee to the contrary to come downe when he is ready to goe and take them in.

531. Charles Towgood
Aboard the Cape Coast Briganteen, Accra Road, 6 Aug. 1682

I received a letter from your Worship and Councill directed to Mr Starland and mee dated the 2nd currant, wherein your Worship admires att my soe long silence, which should have been but that (wee have been turning up ever since wee received your last letter, hopeing to have gott to Accra before this time) my canoe being bad and Mr Starland haveing none, durst not lett her be absent from the ship for feare of anything that might happen in her absence. Since I have been here I have gott wood and water from the forte, which I wanted extreamly, and taken all the slaves that Mr Hassell had in the forte that was any thing likely, that is 12 men, 20 woemen and 1 boy, in all 33, and have on board att present 28 good slaves, soe that I hope with what slaves I shall gett in turning up and what Mr Starland and what Mr Shears will gett will make a good quantity. Mr Shears haveing purchased about 20 odd slaves comeing downe, which hee putt aboard of Mr Starland, desired a few goods of mee to make up a full complement att Allampo, which I spared him, that is 20 sayes and 20 perpettuanoes,[31] and likewise lett Mr Hassell have 1 case of sayes, a bale of perpetuano's and 48 tapsells, which I tooke their receipts for.[32] I intend God willing in company of Mr Starland, wind and weather permitting, to depart this place tomorrow morning.

532. Charles Towgood
Aboard the Cape Coast Briganteen, Morea Road, 23 Aug. 1682

I seeing noe likelyhood of getting into Cape Corsoe roade, by reason of the strong leward currant and small land breeze, I thought itt convenient to know your Worships pleasure, whether you will have the slaves to Capo Corsoe or whether I may carry them downe to Captain Nurse att Anamaboe, for I have but one day's corne aboard and Mr Shears has butt a meale, and that I spared him this morning. I have on board 31 slaves of mine and 32 of Mr Hassells, I had 33 of his but one man died yesterday morning.[33]

---

[30] To which Attwell was bound.
[31] Cf. no.513, though the number of perpetuanoes is given there as 25.
[32] Cf. no.434.
[33] Cf. no.434.

[PS] This comes by the Docter, whoe did desire to be the bearer for he has a request to your Worship.

[On 8 September 1682, Towgood was expected at Komenda, to embark the RAC factory there (no.83). At some point, he presumably returned to Cape Coast, and command of the *Cape Coast* was assumed by Hugh Shears. Towgood himself commanded the sloop *Ann* from December 1682 onwards (nos 549–59) On 15 September 1682 Shears was in command of the *Cape Coast* at Anomabu, where he took in corn (no.304).]

533. Hugh Shears   Allampa, 30 Sept. 1682

I have received yours dated the 27th of this instant, wherein your Worship commands mee to make the best of my way which I can unto Cabo Corsoe, which by the grace of God I shall accordingly performe, for praise be to God I have att this present 65 verry good slaves, and 3 slaves more I was forc'd to pay upon Captain Wares account, for the Negro's kept Captain Nurs's man and mine which wee gave for pawnes, and would not permitt them to come aboard, for Captain Ware did panyar 3 freemen and slaves, and wee had much adoe to gett them to trade with us. I cannot sell one of the musketts, they are soe verry bad, and I have sold verry few of the perpettuano's red, by reason that they have warrs in the place where they vend them. I have been verry lame in my right hand, which hath been a greate hinderance of trade and forceth mee to make use of the Docter in writting unto your Worship, but praise be to God itt is upon the mending hand.

534. Hugh Shears   Annamaboe Road, 29 Oct. 1682

Haveing received your Worships order to deliver what slaves the sloope could take in, which Mr Carter told mee 60, which I deliver, 25 men, 30 women, and 5 boyes, Fryday last att night, soe haveing nothing else to trouble your Worship withall att present, hopeing for your good health hopeing tomorrow or Tuseday at farthest to waite on your Worship.

535. Hugh Shears   Mine River, 28 Nov. 1682

This is to give your Worship an account [that] as soon as I received your Worships order I sent the canoe on board of Captain Branfill with your letter, and last night hee sent his boate and his 2 carpenters and 1 barrell of pitch and 1 barrell of tarr, and likewise according to your Worships order have sent Joseph Ferera and Bostian, and if your Worship have ocam [= oakum] send itt in this canoe, for wee want and shall want itt dayly and I desire your Worship lett us not want itt, and if your Worship have any wait nailes and small spikes wee shall want them for the bottom of the vessell.

[In January 1683, Shears was reported to be sailing west along the coast, and to have reached Cape Three Points (no.86).]

536. Hugh Shears
From aboard the Cape Coast Briganteen In Succondee Roade, 24 Feb. 1682/3

This is to give your Worship an account that last night wee came into this road, and here wee found Captain John How and Mr John Groome, but as for Mr Groomes ship is in peeces or in bulge[34] ashoare, and the wind proved easterly, I thought itt good to save what things wee could of that remaines. There are some of the men would willingly serve your Worship if you be please to entertaine them,[35] if not that they may come and stay att Cabo Corsoe till they can gett a passage to goe home or elcewhere. Wee lay att Cape Appalonia[36] 10 dayes, and in that time the 8th vessell, and wee sold only 25 barrells powder and some sheets and 10 three pound basons, the powder att 1o 12a 0ta a barrell, and could gett noe more because the other ships sold at 1o 8a -ta. And as for treating with the natives, wee did what wee could, but they will not lett any man to settle on shoare because the country people are their masters[37] and then they shall gett nothing to live on, and they say they must looke to themselves and doe not want ships to goe on board of. Mr Sanders is dead, hee dyed the last Sunday. Since I have sold 40 odd perpetuano's, as for sayes they proffer noe more then 14 angles a piece. Iron and tallow they doe not take. For today, sold one barrell of powder att 1 ounce 10a, and since wee came from Dickiscove sold the remainder of the sheets, soe wee have tooke noe more then 14 marks and odd ounces att present.

[PS] Captain Quow presents his service to your Worship.

537. Hugh Shears   Off of Annamaboe, 27 Feb. 1682/3

This is to give your Worship an account of what befell us since our departure from Cape Corsoe, for haveing noe land breezes but the wind att S.S.W. [var. W.S.W.] and S.W., could make no orphing [= offing] without a greate loss, and the currant runs to the eastward verry strong, and the more wee towed thinking to gett to windward, the more wee goe to leward, soe now wee lye to an anchor here off shoare about 3 legues, expecting the currant to about or a turnadoe. I ashure your Worship wee have used the best of our endeavours to gett to windward but cannot att present. Our mainsaile is too little and foresaile verry bad, and if not for the name

---

[34] Presumably bilge, meaning that it was holed in the bilge.

[35] The commander of the ship, John Groome, seems to have been among those who did so, commanding the locally based vessel the *Adventure* from June 1683 (cf. nos 560–9).

[36] Cape Apollonia, between Axim and Assinie.

[37] Referring to the recent conquest of this area by Adom (cf. section I).

of a mizon [= mizzen] wee were as good have none, being a small saile and old that belonged to the John.

[On 23/25 April 1683, Shears was at Sekondi, where he assisted in an abortive attempt to establish a factory (no.1).]

538.   Hugh Shears
From aboard the Cape Coast Briganteen off of Dickiscove, 15 May 1683

Yours I have received, and as for the ships your Worship wrights of, wee did not see nor heare of them before this present that your Worship gave us notice of itt, and as for what care possible for the preserving the Royall Companys goods, I shall use my best endeavour and if not possible, they shall have little benefitt by us. I have heard by the blacks of a ship cast away to windward, which I suppose these rogues have taken and sunk, for they took severall goods on the shoare and Sunday last wee tooke up a muskett chest empty. Sorry I am for what hath befell Captain Lumley and the rest.[38] As for Succondee people they would have us stay till the people come out of the country that they have sent up, I would have the Cabosheers come on board but they would not, but sent the Teetee, but hee spake as before mentioned. Tomorrow God willing Captain Quow and Captain Coffee shall take their journey into the country, for God willing wee shall gett in with the sea breeze today. As for tradeing is but bad, for wee have taken noe more as 4 marks.

539.   Hugh Shears
From aboard the Cape Coast Briganteen, Succondee, 21 May 1683

As for sending into the country by the way of Dickiscove I did what I could, and likewise Captain Quow and Captain Coffee, but they would not, the cause that the waterside people threatened them and told them that if wee sent that the Addoomes would come downe and destroy Succondee and afterwards destroy Dickiscove, but they told mee they would venture them, soe I would leave a Whiteman and only goods to maintaine him, and your Worships people should goe where they pleas'd and they would send guides with them, the which I told them I had not order for itt. Fryday last came the Braffoe of Succondee and the Tetee came up to Dickiscove to us, and would not goe on shoare before wee went downe to Succondee and then not without the flagg, because the Addoomes had threatned them, soe yesterday they sett up our flagg, and afterwards came a Cabosheer that was sent from the Addoomes to see the flagg sett up,[39] [he] came on board with the Captain of the souldiers and their wives and attendants, because they say they were never on board

---
[38] They had been attacked by pirates (cf. no.556).
[39] The Sekondi people had earlier pulled down the English flag (no.1).

of a ship before, but I rather beleeve they came to see what would be given them, the which I could not doe otherwise but to give them a dashey on your Worships behalfe, soe this morning the abovementioned Cabosheers hath taken Captain Quow and Captain Coffee up in the country with them and they say they will be here a Thursday next. If you please to send mee an order, for in my last your Worship doth not mention James Parris what shall be don with him, nor what goods shall be left to maintaine him on shoare, but if your Worship thought fitt to send a man att once and goods, itt will be less charges to him and to avoyde further trouble and expence for the future. This afternoon is come a great boate and a great canoe from the Mina to take their goods away, which now they brought some to the waterside. Pray dispatch the canoe. As for the 2 ships wee know not what they were, but [they] have taken the Serjant of Axim with them and taken Agent Pearsons small vessell and fought a Dane that they have robbed likewise, but the men is gott on shoare as the blacks saith.

540. Hugh Shears
From aboard the Cape Coast Briganteen, Succondee, 26 May 1683

Yours I have received dated the 24th of this instant. As for what the Dutch doth intend to doe I know not att present, but they have carryed away their goods but the whitemen stay here still. As soone as Captain Quow and Captain Coffee comes I shall talke with the Cabbasheers about what must be given them only, and as for dashy's given when the Factor comes I shall doe my best to helpe him, and as for the Cabasheers that tooke the fetish for the Dutch I cannot as yett resolve you, but they make a show all in generall to be verry glad for the English settleing here. As for disposeing of goods I must not expect to dispose of noe more whilst I lye here, for Captain Clarke arriv'd here on Thursday last, whose factor goes in this canoe. I have disposed about 7 marks in goods. I have sent your Worship a tortell. This instant came Captain Quow and Captain Coffee out of the country and hath some of the Addoomes with them, and they will prendee the Cabasheers 4 cowes and 1 bendy of gold for pulling downe our flagg staff, and as for what elce att present I cannot satisfie you because the people are weary, but tomorrow wee shall be better satisfied and then I shall send a canoe. This canoe I would detaine till tomorrow, but Captain Clarke would needs send your Worship your letters.

541. Hugh Shears
From aboard the Cape Coast Briganteen, in Succondee Roade, 29 May 1683

Yours this morning I have received, and as for your better satisfaction I have sent your Worship Captain Coffee. As for Captain Quow I keepe him here till I heare farther from your Worship or a factor comes. As for Tickadoe[40] hee sayes the

---

[40] Ruler of Adom, at this time in control of Sekondi (cf. section I).

Cabosheers are his slaves and they have taken his tongue out of his mouth, meaning they have pulled downe our flagstaff, for this time they shall pay for itt, but hereafter for the least offence, hee will send for them in the country, more he sayes as soone as your Worship begins to build hee will send downe one of his sons to live with the factor. Captain Clarke saith hee will assist the factor in any thing on shoare and put any goods that is consign'd to the Castle with his boate on land if you please. I can doe nore more good here at present, for goods I sell none, but I spend on shoare which I am not willing, but cannot helpe itt for if I goe not on shoare they will come aboard, and they waite by the waterside for the factor to come.

542.   Hugh Shears
From aboard the Cape Coast Briganteen, in Succondee Roade, 8 June 1683

Willingly would I heare a word or two from you as concerning this place, that I may satisfie this man that is sent out of the country, for here hee stayes with att least 50 men to waite on him, for to settle the factor that your Worship intends to send to this place and to order the townes people what hee thinks good in his behalfe.[41] What your Worship pleaseth that I shall that I shall doe as concerning this man, whether hee shall goe in the country to his master or stay here any longer, for I beleeve he begins to be weary of staying here soe long. As for the Dutch the remainder of their goods and slaves went away yesterday, one Whiteman still remaining. The sooner your Worship sends, the less charges itt will be, for I assure your Worship I have been att charges this 3 weeks wee have been here since wee came from Dickiscove, and as wee lay there passed by land a Dutchman from Occada,[42] and as I was told hee said to the Blacks of that place that the Generall of Cabo Corsoe gave them only a flagg but would not settle the place this 2 or 3 yeares, and lett them not have the occasion to say the same by this place, for they take all occasion to doe what ill they can.

543.   Hugh Sheares
From aboard the Cape Coast Briganteen, in Longo [sic: = Ningo] Road,
29 July 1683

This is to give your Worship an account that Satureday last was sennitt wee came to Allampo and abode 4 day's before wee could buy one slave, though there were slaves on shoare and severall brought on board and carryed away againe, because they would have 7 peaze for a man and 6 for a woeman, for they say the interloper gives a bendy for a man and 7 peaze for a woeman, besides dasheys that they give, and have carried severall slaves by land to Accra to the ships that be there, soe if

---

[41] Cf. no.2.
[42] Akwida.

your Worship and Councill please to consider on itt, lett me heare as soone as possible, for if I could give the above mentioned prizes I might have 50 or 60 slaves on board and most men. Soe on Thursday last came from Allampo to this place, but all one, soe wee have bought noe more then 14 slaves which are 10 men, 4 woemen for these goods as follows: 11 sayes, 1½ barrell of powder, 3 allejars, 13 musketts, 36 sheets, 1 Guyney stuff, 3 paper brawles, 9 iron barrs.

544. Hugh Sheares
   From aboard the Cape Coast Briganteen, in Allampo Roade, 6 Aug. 1683

Yours I have received dated the 3rd of this instant, and shall doe my best to purchase slaves and as cheape as I can, but as yett I have noe more then 26 slaves on board, the reason one Mr Parris that came from the Barbado's lies at Tisha and gives 9 peaze a head for slaves, but I heare that most of his gold and goods are gonn. Agent Pearson came into this roade yesterday but will not stay as I heare. I doubt not but to purchase a considerable parcell of slaves in short time, for I expect the people out of the country every day and severall slaves on shoare, but because that Agent Pearson is here they aske greate rates for them, expecting hee will give as Mr Parris did.

545. Hugh Sheares
   From on board the Cape Coast Briganteen, in Allampo Roade, 25 Aug. 1683

Yours I have received dated the 22nd of this instant, and have according to your order sent my brother in this canoe. As for slaves I have purchased noe more then 62, that is 27 men, 20 womene, 5 boyes, for these people doe not understand to trade, for they are new come out of the country to live here, and two or three that speakes Portugueze cheate the boores of a third or a quarter part of their goods they sell the slaves for. The other people that lived here before is fled to leward of the River Volta att a place called Cetta,[43] and the trade that was here before is now there. Att first when wee came here they were most men slaves, but now hard to be gott. As for slaves I shall doe my best to gett as many as I can, but I am forct to come to windward to gett water, now under saile to goe as far as Tisha.

  [On 13 Sept. 1683, Shears was off Accra (no.572).]

546. Hugh Sheares
   From aboard the Cape Coast Briganteen, Tisha roade, 22 Sept. 1683

Yours I have received dated the 4th and 14th of this instant. As for giveing your

---

[43] i.e. Keta: cf. nos 431, 451.

Worship an accompt, I should willingly doe, but itt cannot be without charges, of my proceedings. I have purchased noe more att present then 87 slaves, whereof was of men 38 and woemen 44 and boyes 5, and of the men 2 are dead; in gold, 6 marks, 5 ounces, and 12 angles, that is all; and expedition I shall make all what is possible and purchase slaves I can in our way to Cabo Corsoe.

[PS] The canoe came but this morning because itt blew hard and greate currant.

Remains	36 men
	44 woemen
	5 boyes
Gold	6m 5o 12a -ta

547.   Hugh Sheares
                From aboard the Cape Coast Briganteen, off of Accra, 28 Sept. 1683

Yours I have received dated the 26th of this instant, and shall doe my best for to gett what slaves I can. Slaves are verry scarce here, for I have bought but one woeman since I gave your Worship the last accompt and about 10 ounces of gold. Now wee are under saile bound up to Barracoe to see what wee can doe there as for purchaseing slaves, and likewise to water and wood, for water to leward is deare and not good, and to lye here att Accra I see itt is but in vaine for I see noe slaves on shoare.

548.   Hugh Sheares
                From aboard the Cape Coast Briganteen, Barracoe Road, 10 Oct. 1683

Yours I have received dated the 4th of this instant, and shall doe my best to make what hast possible up to Cabo Corsoe, but since I received your order I have had noe oppertunity, but only yesterday but blowing weather and leward currant. I have laine 9 dayes att Barracoe and have not bought one slave of them, soe I have noe more then 90 slaves and 9 marks, 3 ounces, 15 angles of gold, soe hopeing to see your Worship in good health with the rest of the good men in a short time.

The *Ann*, Commander Charles Towgood

549.   Charles Towgood
                Aboard the Ann Sloope now under saile off Shumah, 5 Dec. 1682

About 2 hours since I received your Worships letter by Captain Coffee, wherein you admire of my not adviseing your Worship how tradeing goes to windward; which should not have omitted but that I sent word on Thursday last by Docter Griffin how that I had sold 22 perpetuano's att 10 angles and that Captain Brackon had promised mee to come off againe on Fryday to buy some say's, but hee was not as good as his word for hee came not till Satureday, and then hee would have had more perpetuano's and narrow niccanees if I would sell them att 3 angles, which is as Captain Bramfill sells, but for say's hee told mee the traiders was not come out of the country nor would not be there till Monday, soe I would lett him have neither perpetuano's nor niccanees unless hee would take say's, for there is noe feare but that the perpetuano's will goe off, being all the goods they aske for unless it be sheets, and the price for the one is 10 angles and the other 32 for a bendy, Captain Branfill selling att the same rate and, which is worse, on Sunday morning the Negro's came aboard and inform'd mee that both the interloper and Branfill had lowered their say's to 14 angles, which I would not beleeve till I went aboard of Branfill and see itt don before my face, soe that seeing little hopes for mee to sell any there unless could sell as cheape as hee I weighed the next morning, being Monday. I went to windward and that night gott to Shumah, where Captain Coffee found mee at 4 a clock this morning, haveing been under saile an houre before, and your Worship ordering mee to send word immediatly I have therefore sent my canoe downe to Commenda (with this letter) to desire Captain Brackon to forward itt by land by one of his boy's, and I would desire your Worship that you would be pleased to send two or three words to Commenda to meet mee there when I come downe, that I may know what I may doe, for if once the say's were gon, which hope I shall put off to windward, I doe not question the sale of the rest. Here inclosed is an account of the prices of goods sold by Captain Branfill. Not else at present to informe your Worship of, only that there is 3 ships upon the coast besides Branfill, all interlopers, 2 of which are att Commenda the other at Dickiscove, one Thornton master, besides two Brandenburgs which went from Commenda to windward last weeke.[44]

sayes att 14 angles each.
perpettuanoes att 10a, blew and green.
sheets, a chest for 4a, that is 32 a bendy and one over.
iron barrs, 24 for a bendy
niccanees narrow 3a, or 10 per bendy

550. Charles Towgood
From aboard the Ann Sloope rideing at Dickiscove, 7 Dec. 1682

Your worship and Councills letter of the 6th instant came safe to my hands by a canoe from Commenda, and shall take all care immaginable for the sale of the goods to the best advantage. Yesterday in the morning I came to this place, and

[44] This was Groeben's expedition, which was at Komenda around this time, prior to going westwards to establish the fort at Gross Friedrichsburg: cf. Groeben 1985, 42–3.

presently after the Cheife of the towne came off and told mee that hee would send up into the country and in 2 or 3 day's the traiders will be downe and buy goods, that is perpetuano's, niccanees, sheets and barrs, but for sayes they did not aske after nor have not don between Cape Corsoe and this place, nor as I understand as far windward as Ashinee but there they goe off att an ounce, and for perpetuano's they say they will give but 10 angles for blew and green, but red they will not take, yett I doe not question to putt all the perpetuano's off with the rest of the goods; and I hope when the traiders come downe to put off some say's too. I doe not heare of any more ships upon the coast then what I inform'd your Worship in my last, which I hope will make the goods off the faster. Thornton the interloper ly's here getting of corne and the Brandenburgs lies about 2 leagues to leward.[45]

[PS] I paid the canoe, the men telling mee twas ordered by your Worship to Brackon [that] I should doe it.

551.   Charles Towgood
                    From aboard the Ann Sloope in Barracoe road, 26 Dec. 1682

Haveing the oppertunity by Mr John Winder, whoe came from Accra to this place this morning,[46] I thought itt convenient to informe your Worship of my proceeding, which has been verry bad as yett, for I have not taken one angle since my departure from Capo Corsoe, there being noe money all the way downe, I stoping at all places but noe canoes from any place till I came here, which was about 4 dayes since, and upon my comeing they told mee they had sent up to Anguina to informe the Queen of my being here and that in 3 or 4 dayes the traiders would be downe, but I see noe likelyhood yett, soe intend to stay to see what this morning will produce and then downe for Accra. Slaves they have some but most for powder, which they want extreamely. I would faine put off the sayes if I could before I came up but I am affraid I shall not, this place failing of money, which was never known before. There came in company with Mr Winder Patrick Welch and hee [= Winder] fearing hee would make his escape from him desired mee to take him aboard[47] and [I did] the sooner because Andrew Johnson lyes verry sick, whoe I am afraid must leave ashoare att Accra for his recovery.

[PS] Just att the closeing up of my letter came off a canoe from shoare to tell mee that the reason that the bores was not come downe was because they were fighting with the Mumford people and would be downe tomorrow.

---

[45] Probably at Butri: cf. Groeben 1985, 43.

[46] Winder was on his way back to Cape Coast from Whydah, where he had been removed as chief factor (cf. no.490).

[47] Welch was being returned to Cape Coast as a deserter (cf. no.490).

552. Charles Towgood
From aboard the Ann Sloope riding in Accra Roade, 29 Dec. 1682

I received your Worships letter of the 26th currant for the secureing the persons that Mr Hassell should send aboard att Barracoe, but the night before they parted from mee, only [= except] Patrick Welch, which I shall take care to secure as I inform'd your Worship by a letter sent by Mr Winder, as likewise a full account of my proceedings, which beleeve your Worship have received ere this time, tradeing being verry dead everywhere. The reason of my long stay att Barracoe was because after I had been there 3 or 4 day's and had noe trade, the Queen sent downe her man to excuse itt and withall to tell mee that I should have money the next day, but twas noe such thing for I did not receive one angle, soe I came for this place and gave Mr Hassell your Worships letter, but hee tells mee hee will take none of the goods, only sheets and iron barrs.[48] I shall make all the hast up that possible I can as soone as hee hath taken the goods out, without your Worships orders to the contrary. The letter I received last, as also that of Mr Hassells, was broke open, and asking the canoemen how twas they told mee that Mr Winder mett them and oppened the letters.

553. Charles Towgood
From aboard the Ann Sloope in Commenda Road, 9 Feb. 1682/3

Although I have informed your Worship of my proceeding by Mr Shears, yet thought itt convenient to give your Worship an account of itt myselfe in wrighting, for since my departure from Cabo Corsoe I have taken about 12 ounces of gold, most of which has been for sheets, of which I have only 40 remaining, haveing sold only 7 perpettuanoes and ½ a barrell of powder, although I lay 2 dayes between Shuma and Commenda, and one day att Shumah, the rest of the time I have layne here. Here lyes att present att this place 2 interlopers, the one Captain How and the other Captain Price in Finchams Catt, the latter of which came yesterday, but I beleeve neither of them has taken any money since they came here, for I have not seen one canoe goe aboard of them. Yesterday by a canoe that came from windward I was inform'd that there was a Companys ship att Dickiscove that would be downe about 4 or 5 dayes but the Commanders name I cannot informe my selfe of. The same canoe told mee that Ashenee was all destroyed by the up country people about 10 or 12 dayes since.[49]

---

[48] Cf. no.443.

[49] In late 1682 Groeben heard that Assinie was at war with Albani ('Abeni') to the east (1985, 39); but Albani was on the coast rather than 'up country', so may not have been responsible for the attack recorded here. Cf. also Barbot 1992, ii, 337, who refers to the destruction of Assinie in 1681 — perhaps an earlier episode in the same war.

554.   Charles Towgood
                    From aboard the Ann Sloope in Commenda Roade, 11 Feb. 1682/3

Your Worhips of the 10th currant came safe to my hands, and soone after came into this road. The ship that had given himselfe out to be a Royall Companys ship but proved to be an interloper, one Booth Commander, having for his mate Singleton that was formerly in the Royall Companys service. As for goods I heare not of any thats more vendible then those I have on board but am not like to sell any, for as the Negro's tells mee Captain Price sells for 13 angles a say and 8 per perpetuanoe. As to narrow niccanees I have not been asked for one since I came here.

555.   Charles Towgood
                    From aboard the Ann Sloope in Commenda roade, 24 Feb. 1682/3

According to your Worships desire of the 10th instant, thought fitt to acquaint you that narrow niccanees and narrow tapsells are in great demand, for now the Arcanies are come downe, but I cannot expect to sell any of those goods I have on board by reason the two ships that are here sell cheaper then I can, vizt sayes att 12 and 13 angles and perpetuano's att 8 and 9, but I beleeve they have almost don for they sold greate quantity's yesterday of both sorts, besides other goods; soe that after they are gon I may be in hopes of selling my goods if nothing comes downe in the interim, for I heare there are two at Dickiscove. I have not sold any thing since my last to your Worship, onely one halfe barrell of powder and the remainder of the sheets, for there has been noe trade to speak of since before yesterday. Just att my closeing up of the letter I received one from your Worship and Councill wherein I was ordered to procure one barrell of pitch and one ditto of tarr, which I have don out of one of the ships that is here, but would not pay for itt before acquainted your Worship with the price vizt one barrell of pitch, 1 ounce and one ditto of tarr halfe an ounce, soe shall only stay for your Worships further orders. I would have sent this by the same bearer that brought yours, but hee was gon before I received mine, for I did not receive itt before 10 a clock this morning.

[Towgood was at Accra, where he embarked John Winder's effects, on 9 March 1683 (no.450); at Anomabu, where he took in corn, on 11 April (no.346); and at Komenda, where he delivered goods and took in gold, on 21 April (no.109). He re-entered Komenda Road on 8 May, perhaps to evacuate the RAC's factory there (no.112). By 11 May he was at Anomabu, where he delivered a letter (no.341).]

556.   Charles Towgood
                    From aboard the Ann Sloope under Annamaboe fort, 12 May 1683

I would have writt to you this morning by Mr Thelwalls boy but that hee was gon before I came ashoare; however I am verry sorry that I have displeas'd your Worship with my stay att this place, which I could not helpe for twas 8 a clock before I came to an anchor here, I being becalmed which forct mee to itt, a little before which time 2 French men came to anchor off of Anishan, as likewise Captain Lumley. I kept a light for him till 11 a clock to come into the roade this morning (for twas calme all night). I see the two ships aweigh as likewise Captain Lumley, one of the two ships standing to windward and the other to leward, but presently the ship that stood up tackt and stood downe againe and Captain Lumley being taken astayes, was forc't to stand up, att which time the Frenchman was almost aboard him with a red ensigne but our King's jack (with which hee tooke all the ships), and presently fired a valley of small shott and three great guns with shott, att which time Captain Lumley answered him in the like with two pateraro's and some small armes and then the Frenchman fired about 8 or 10 guns shott and all as likewise about some 3 or 4 valley's more of small shott, which carried away Captain Lumley's foot of his maine sayle out of the bolt rope and as I beleeve kill'd Captain Lumley, for I presently see the ensigne struck halfe mast downe and the ship yeilded to the Frenchmans boate which presently went aboard of her, and soone after Thomas Amamaboe came from him to mee and told mee to goe under the forte, which [I] was ready to doe before but could not for had noe wind, but I sent ashoare a note by him to Mr Thelwall to send mee off some great and small canoes, which hee did, which towed us in under the forte, where wee now lye, and presently I see the Frenchman take the two interlopers without fireing a gun, the one being Captain Summervill the Scotch man, the other Captain Lowes brother Thompson. I likewise understand by the Blacks that they tooke a Dutchman up to windward and left the men ashoare at Succondee. I suppose the biggest of the two ships might have about 28 or 30 gunns, being well mann'd to sight. I only stay here for your Worships further orders, for itt will be in vaine to goe before the Frenchman be passed by Accra, which I beleeve will be in a day or two. Not elce att present to informe your worship of (though I wish I had not this).

557. Charles Towgood
From aboard the Ann Sloope under Annamaboe forte, 15 May 1683

These few lines serves to acquaint your Worship that yesterday, there comeing a ship into Anishan roade from leward, I thought itt convenient to send a canoe off to her to know what shee was, fearing itt was one of the ships the French had tooke, which att the returne of the canoe I found to be soe, but not in the custody of Frenchmen but return'd againe to the right Commander, Captain Summervill, of whome I received a noate sign'd by himselfe and Captain Thompson. which note was as followeth. After my sad usage, with the loss of all my provisions, sayes, goods &ca, I am arrived with my men severly punished att this place, acquainting you that Captain Lumley ly's at Daggue desperately wounded himselfe, his ship disabled for want of sayles, all his provisions, water &ca taken out, Captain Thompsons ship taken and carryed cleare away, himselfe and most of his men on board mee. Soe hopeing that there was a canoe dispatcht away that day (that I was taken) downe for Guydah to advise Captain Low and the rest of them of these pyrates, that they be provided to receive him, for hee threatens to surprize them and hath taken Agent Pearsons tender and doth force the master to tell him every ships force, and alsoe doth say that Captain Lowe hath a gold chest aboard for the Company which they are resolved to have.[50] These are the verry words I received from Captain Summervill in his note, which thought convenient to informe your Worship of. Not elce but stay for your Worships orders what to doe.

[Towgood was at Accra, delivering goods, on 22 May 1683 (no.455); but then returned to Anomabu on 29 May, leaving there on 30 May, after taking on more firewood (nos 346, 510).]

558. Charles Towgood
From aboard the Ann Sloope in Accra Roade, 3 July 1683

Your Worship and Councills letter of the 28th past I received by the bearer hereof; and as to secureing the Royall Companys sloope, I shall take all the care immaginable by runing in as neare the shoare as possible, upon first sight of the pyrates; for I doe not intend to move from hence till I am certified they are passed by, or till I have further order from your Worship. However if I had a designe to weigh, to doe any good upon itt I could not, the currant runing soe strong to leward and the weather calme. The night after I parted from Cabo Corsoe, I was taken with a voiolent ague and feavour which continued with mee every day till Sunday last, since which time I have not had any thing of itt, and hope I shall have noe more, although I am verry weake and cannot gett anything in this place to helpe mee, the Docter haveing nothing to give mee. Mr Hassell informes mee that your Worship has ordered mee to take in his slaves, which I designe to doe, but if I have a long passage up, as I am afraid I shall (because of the calmes), I shall want water, haveing but 4 hogsheads aboard. Not elce to informe your Worship of, but hope the news that Mr Groome writes to your Worship is not true,[51] for I cannot heare any thing of itt here by the Dutchman nor of the canoe that brought itt.

559. Charles Towgood
From on board the Ann Sloope in Accra Roade, 11 July 1683

Your Worships and Councills letters of the 7th and 9th instant I received, the one

[50] As indeed, they did (cf. no.637).
[51] Cf. no.562.

by the 2 hand canoe the other by Captain Robert Young, and did my endeavour to follow the orders of both, for I had both the gold and slaves aboard and was gott out of Accra roade when received that by Captain Young, and according to orders I weighed and went into the roade againe, where I now lye to attend him, but expect to sayle to morrow night, Mr Hassell embarqueing with mee (whoe complyed with his orders in all things),[52] att which time I hope I shall have a windward currant, which oppertunity I shall not lett slip. I have on board 12 marks, 1 ounce, 5 angles, and 2 tacco's of gold from Mr Hassell, and 4 men, 8 woemen, and a girle slaves.[53]

[This last letter implies that Towgood intended to sail from Accra back to Cape Coast Castle (where Hassell was to be delivered); but by 8 Aug. 1683 he had reached no further west than Amisa (no.466). Later in the year, he went east to Whydah, where he took in slaves, and from which he departed back for Cape Coast in October 1683.[54]]

The *Merchant's Adventure*, Commander John Groome

[Groome had presumably arrived on a different ship, which reached Sekondi in February 1683, but was reportedly 'in peeces', and was presumably abandoned (no.534). He was then given command of the ketch, the *Adventure* (or *Merchant's Adventure*), for a voyage to the east: on 29 May he took in corn at Anomabu (no.346), and on 12 June he was at Teshi (no.456). David Harper, who had served in the RAC factory at Komenda in 1682–3, evidently accompanied Groome in the capacity of factor.]

560. David Harper
From aboard the Merchants Adventure Ketch att Allampo, 30 June 1683

Your honours of the 28th ditto I have received, and am sorry to hearc of the pyrates returne upon the coast, but hope God will preserve us out of their unmercifull hands. As to an account of our proceedings here, be pleased to know that wee had noe trade to windward of Accra, and what wee had since was most at Tishue.[55] All the goods sold for gold are 15 pieces sayes, 3 perpetuanoes and 8 Guyney stuffs, amounting to Mk2 1o 8a 8ta, the which money Mr Groome hath sent up per bearer. There are 18 slaves aboard, which were puchast one with another for 5 pieces sayes,

---

[52] Cf. no.460.
[53] Cf. no.458.
[54] Law 1990a, no.12 (John Winder, Whydah, 14 Oct. 1683).
[55] Teshi.

5 barrells powder, 105 sheets 7 pieces Guyney stuffs, 17 pieces course sletias, 12 iron barrs. Wee arrived att Allampo 2 dayes agoe (expecting better trade then to Windward), where there are slaves to be purchased but they rate them att 7 and 6 pease per head, men and woemen, vallueing our goods noe higher then att Cabo Corsoe, soe that there is little hopes of doeing any good except the prizes be advanced. Alsoe the Portugueze is here, whoe buyes all up att the Blacks rates with the best of goods. The goods most desired here for slaves are powder, musketts, good sayes, tapsells, allejars, sheets and sletias.

561.   John Groome
            From aboard the Marchants Adventure Ketch att Allampo, 30 June 1683

Your honours of the 28th of this instant I received and by the whiteman in the 3 hand canoe, which am heartyly glad to heare all is well at Capo Corsoe but am verry sorry to heare that the pyrate is to windward againe, but being forewarned by your Honours letter doe fully resolve to burne or put ashoare before I will be taken by him. According to your honours order I have sent by the whiteman in the 3 hand canoe what gold I have taken, which is but little itt being 2m 1o 8a 8ta. The whiteman seeing itt weighted and sealed itt, being upon the Royall Companys account, and as for the trade wee have had, has been verry small, till wee were past Accra, for wee had not tooke one ounce of gold till wee came to Tisall [sic], where wee found but small trade for gold and slaves, for they houlding them att such deare rates that my purchase of slaves is but small, there being but 18 in number. The goods that purchast them are 5 sayes, 5 barrells of powder, 17 course sletias, 105 sheets, 12 iron barrs and 7 Guyney stuffs. I being in hopes of haveing a better trade att Allampo then I found to windward, I made the best of my way downe, where I did arrive 2 dayes agoe, where I find that there is slaves but they houlding them up att such deare rates that wee cannot purchase any but for powder, for they vallue our goods att noe dearer rates then they are att Cabo Corsoe and att them rates they hold their slaves att 7 peazes and 6. I am certainely inform'd by the Blacks that this last night there was a Dutch canoe passed by from Ardra, whoe gives account of 2 English ships being taken,[56] but the Dutch escaped. I find but little encouragement of staying here, therefore doe God willing intend by the first oppertunity up to Accra, where I doe hope I shall have further order from your honour to advance upon the price or to come up to Cabo Corsoe. The goods that are good here and the usuall commodity's as good sayes, powder, tapsells, allejars, good musketts, fine sletias.

---

[56] Cf. nos 494, 637.

562.   John Groome   Allampo, 9 July 1683

Your Honours of the 7th of this instant I received, which I am heartyly glad to heare
that the news of Ardra is not true,[57] and likewise I shall use my great care and
dilligence in preventing all pyrates surprisalls. I have used my best endeavour to
gett up to Accra ever since the 1st of this instant, but by reason of a streame setting
strong to leward and noe land breeze have been rather a looser than a gainer,
although itt was this day I being under sayle standing into the shoare when the
canoe came aboard, I being some 4 miles to windward of Allampo. And while I was
standing in, the Portuguze waighed and made the best of his way for Ardra, hee
purchaseing some 70 or 80 slaves att this Allampo, but the rates hee gave was verry
greate, hee giveing for a woeman slave 7 peazes, which was little under 2 sayes,
and 2 sayes for a man, likewise advanceing upon all other goods. I shall give your
honour account att my returne; I made itt my business to know the reason wherefore
hee did soe much advance upon slaves above the Companys price, his answer was
hee gave not above 7 peazes 2a for a man and 6 [peaze] 1 angles for a woeman,
considering he bought the sayes to windward for 14a and other goods verry cheape.
I finding the currant to continue to leward and the Portuguze being gon, Mr Harper
and I did consult what to doe, and did think itt the best way for the Companys
interest for him to goe ashoare and see wheither they would lett us have slaves att
your honours rates or noe, if not to take my first oppertunity to gett up to Cabo
Corsoe according to order.

563.   David Harper   From aboard the Adventure Ketch at Allampo, 9 July 1683

Your honours of the 7th instant I have this day received, in answer whereof please
to know that since my last to your honour wee have endeavoured our uttmost if
possible to have purchased some slaves for the Royall Company att this place, but
itt proved in vaine by reason of the Portugueze paying such unreasonable rates, for
his lowest prizes were 2 sayes, 4 tapsells or 3 perpetuano's per head, whereupon
Mr Groome hath don his utmost to gett againe to windward, but the leward currant
being strong and land breezes but small, have gott not above one league to windward of Allampo. While wee were this morning under sayle the Portugueze tooke
his departure to Ardra, haveing carryed some 70 or 80 slaves from this place. Upon
receipt of your honours have resolved with Mr Groome to stay here some dayes
longer. In the interim I designe ashoare tomorrow to see if possible I can purchase
some slaves att your honours rates after the Portuguze is gon, and if I can doe noe
good Mr Groome will according to order take the first oppertunity of a windward
currant to gett up, without which the ketch is like to gett but little ground.

---

[57] But it was (cf. no.637).

Att my comeing ashoare shall learne what goods are most in request here and advise your honour accordingly att my returne.

[On 22 July 1683 Groome was at Accra, taking in wood and water, and intended from there back to Cape Coast (no.464).]

564.   David Harper
From aboard the Adventure Ketch in the roade of the Oystershell Bank,[58]
5 Aug. 1683

Your Honours of the 3d Instant I have received, but am sorry wee did not know your honours orders that wee were further to leward. The goods most in request to leward of Accra and att Allampo for slaves are powder, sayes, tapsells, sheets and some allejars and this I am verry certaine of, haveing been 3 day's ashoare att Allampo, but could not buy one slave, the reason was that our powder was gon before and the say's soe verry much damnified that they did not goe off there, and for the tapsells they would not take less then 4 peeces for 1 slave. There is now 32 slaves aboard, but the currant goeing strong to leward and all the provisions for the slaves expended, Mr Groome thought fitt to come up him selfe that hee might know your honours further orders, haveing with him the money in cash and an account of the goods that are disposed of, and if itt should please your Honour to order the slaves ashoare, sending downe a cargoe of sayes, powder, sheets, and allejars I doubt not but wee shall purchase a cargoe of slaves that will answer your honours expectation.

565.   John Groome   Annamaboe, 8 Aug. 1683

This last night haveing received a receipt from the Bumboy of 32 slaves, I doe find that 4 are mentioned as old, wherefore I confess that one is worse then I expected, and as for the men [blank] is verry young. Therefore humbley begg your honour will consider the low rates I was constinted to, and if any of the slaves doe not answer expectation your honour will pass itt by, and for the future shall take greate care to buy none but what I shall be well satisfied will answer your honours expectations. I doe understand that my mate is to be cleared to come to Cabo Corsoe, therefore I desire that your honour will assist mee with one hand more in his roome, for I doe intend this night or tomorrow morning to sayle. I desire that you will please to send mee downe brandy for the voyage, on account of the Royall Company, or an order whether I shall charge as much as I was allowed last voyage.

---

[58] i.e. off Amisa.

566.   John Groome   Accra, 24 Aug. 1683

Yours dated the 22nd of this instant I received, and according to order I have
dispatcht up Mr Harper by the first oppertunity. And as for the slaves I have on
board is 4 woemen, 1 man, besides 1 marke, 4 ounces of gold; for att my arrivall
att Barracoe, the sea being soe greate I could not make noe greater dispatch in my
watering and wooding then I did, but did use my best endeavours to bring downe
the Anguina's: which day they came downe Captain Draper came to an anchor in
the roade,[59] which was a greate hinderance to mee, for had not hee came downe,
my purchase of slaves had been a grete deale more then they are, and when I came
downe to Accra I was encouraged by the Cabasheers of the Dutch Towne to have
both slaves and gold, which fell out to the contrary, for the same day the traders
came downe, old Cabasheer Will[s] sonns fell foule of one of the Whitemen, which
Captain Young endeavouring to bring the man in, that first gave the abuse, had one
man kill'd, and since noe canoe will come aboard of mee, and Captain Young does
require mee to continue till hee receives a letter from your honour.

567.   John Groome   From ashoare att Allampo, 15 Sept. 1683

Your honours of the 4th of this instant I received this day, being ashoare att Allampo, useing all the endeavour that possible lyes in mee for the purchase of slaves
according to your honours command, but Allampo is nott the place that itt has been
in other times, for if a man can have 3 or 4 slaves one day hee must waite 4 or 5
more before hee has one. I have now on board 25 slaves, there being 11 men, 11
women, 2 boyes, 1 girle, and doe hope by the next windward currant to be comeing
up for Cabo Corsoe with 50 or 60 slaves in. Not elce to acquaint your Worship but
that slaves are att very high rates if good.

568.   John Groome   Allampo, 18 Sept. 1683

Since my last letter from Accra I have had noe oppertunity of sending to you, but
the 14th of this instant, being ashoare att Allampo received yours dated the 4th of
this instant, the man comeing by land with itt, and by the same bearer I sent your
honour a letter, giveing you account of my proceeding in trade and what slaves I
have purchased in men, woemen, boyes and girles. And att present am ashoare
useing my best endeavoure for to answer your honours commands. I have aboard
28 slaves, there being 12 men, 13 woemen, 2 boyes and 1 girle, and may purchase
more woemen but I doe forebeare because I would have them bring one man with
one woeman. I am in greate hopes by the full of the moone or the next windward
currant to be comeing up for Cabo Corsoe with 50 or 60 slaves in or more. As for

[59] Cf. no.570.

my proceeding downe to Allampo contrary to your command, was upon the account of purchaseing of slaves, for there is none to be had att Ningo but what comes
from thence, and I did not purchase a slave ashoare. And Allampo is [not] the place
that itt has been in other times; for the slaves I first purchased, the man that sould
them sent his men with the goods up in the country for the purchaseing of more
slaves, and are not come downe as yett, but I am in hopes that this weeke may
proove better then the rest of the time has. Not else to acquaint your honour with
but that slaves are att verry high rates and specially them that are good.

569.   John Groome
                From aboard the Adventure Ketch, Allampo Roade, 29 Sept. 1683

Yours of the 26th of this instant I received, which accordingly to your Honours
commands shall use my best endeavour to the purchaseing what slaves I can in my
comeing up. I have now aboard 45 slaves but not according to your honours desire,
for men are verry scarce and especially those that are good. I was in hopes for to
have had an oppertunity for my getting up this full moone, but the currant has noe
wayes abated and as for land breezes I have had none, whatever there is to windward, I beleeve the wind has tooke a lese to blow att S.West and constantly a verry
hard gale soe that I have broake my cable noe less then 4 times: not elce to acquaint
your honour with but will take all oppertunity's in getting up.

[Groome evidently set out back for Cape Coast, but got only as far as Accra,
where he died on 29 Oct. 1683 (nos 474–5).]

The *Unity*, Commander Thomas Draper

[Draper arrived at Sekondi, apparently from the west, so perhaps from England, on 8 July 1683 (no.8). On 11 August he was at Anomabu, where he
landed goods (no.361).]

570.   Thomas Draper   Unity, Barracoe, 25 Aug. 1683

Yours came to my hand the 25th of this instant, and am verry sorry to heare of the
sudden alteration, not forgetting to returne your Worship thanks in minding of mee.
As to affaires here, Atta staide here till the 24th and then tooke his journey for the
country and carryed Captain Quow with him, promiseing to be downe againe a
Monday next. Hee hath ordered that the boores shall not trade with mee, till hee
comes out of the country. Itt lookes as if here will be but small encouragement as
to Negro's, hee importuning mee to sell my staple commodytys for gold, which I

have denyed him. They stand for 7 peaze for a woemen. Powder I doe want. I have purchased but one slave as yett and are most woemen here alsoe. Captain Groome gott 5 here.[60] Atta sayes you promised to trade halfe money, halfe slaves. Pray per next [tell me] where [= whether] I shall trade for money or noe.

[PS] Atta is angry hee forgott.

571. Thomas Draper   Unity, Barracoe, 29 Aug. 1683

This is to acquaint your Worship of my bad success here, and how I am deluded along by Atta from day to day and noe hopes of any slaves. Here is but 2 att this time that I have seen here, and one they will not sell without powder and the other hee stands for 1 say, 3 brawles and 2 barrs of iron, but Atta has spoyled mee in telling the people how goods goes there att the Castle, beateing downe mine and endeavouring to raise the price of slaves. I doe think to be at Mumford, before the returne of the canoe, but I would willingly have your Worships orders what to doe, for here is noe abideing for slaves. Here is now Atta and Captain Quow have been up with the Queene and shee hath sent downe to cleare the place att Wyamba.[61] I may take a little money if I would sell goods for itt. I begg your Worships leave to goe to some other place or to come up, for which I shall waite your leisure. These people waite the coming of interlopers; that's the cheife of their discourse.

572. Thomas Draper   Accra, 13 Sept. 1683

Yours of the 2nd instant I received, and according to your Worships order I am now att Accra and find that slaves are verry hard to be gott, likewise by reason of the late desturbance,[62] that I gott but 8 as yett and to goe any lower [along the coast] I doe not intend, for Captain Sheares lyes in sight and writes word hee has gott but one slave since hee came there. That the next morning I intend to waigh and spend one weekes time more att Barracoe and then to returne to your Worship, without further orders comes to the contrary.

[Draper left Accra road for Beraku around 15 Sept. 1683 (nos 470–1).]

573. Thomas Draper   Unity, Barracoe, 16 Sept. 1683

Yours received dated the 14th instant, and I have not slipt any opertunity when I had itt, to acquaint your Worship how affaires stood with mee, and if I had, itt had

---

[60] Cf. no.566.

[61] Presumably in preparation for an attempt to resettle the factory there. The 'Queen' referred to was the ruler of Angona, to which Winneba belonged (cf. section VI).

[62] Presumably that in May 1683, recorded in no.453.

been a greate negligent in mee for soe doeing. I am now come to Barracoe and they doe promise to helpe mee with 8 or 10 slaves, how true itt is cannot tell but will stay one weeke to see the event of itt, and then make the best of my way to your Worship. Itt cannot be expected that where the factory's are and soe many ships comes, to gleane much after them. The slaves I have received on board from Captain Young att Accra the 24th [sic: = 14th?]. This morning I am makeing the best of may way to your Worship. I have purchased but 12 slaves. The canoe could not stay, forct to send this letter.

[Draper reached Anomabu, presumably on his way back to Cape Coast, on 1 October 1683, and took in corn there (no.371).]

TRANSATLANTIC VOYAGES

The *Edgar*, Commander Charles Bowler

[Bowler was at Anomabu, where he picked up oyster shells, presumably for use in Cape Coast, on 11 February 1683 (no.210). Having presumably called at Cape Coast in the interim, he was back at Anomabu on 25 February, as reported below, to embark James Nightingale (earlier RAC chief factor at Komenda and Accra), who served as factor for his voyage until May. Robert Hollings, who had served with Nightingale in the RAC factory at Accra in 1681 (no.396), was probably also a locally–based RAC employee serving temporarily on Bowler's ship.]

574. James Nightingale   Annamaboe, 25 Feb. 1680/1

I have according your Honours and Counsells order delivered your letters to Mr Thelwall and Mr Hassell. Mr Thelwall will deliver mee the sheetes ordered both from Annamaboe and Agga. Captain Bowler came into this road about 2 a clock. The Captain wants bagges for his corne.[63]

[Around the beginning of March 1681 Bowler supplied goods to the RAC factory at Anashan (nos 120–1), and was subsequently off Egya, which he left on 3 March (no.382.]

575. James Nightingale   Wyamba, 9 March 1680/1

Accordinge your Honours order [I] delivered the 5 hand canoe in all hast to Mr

[63] Cf. no.214.

Franckland att 8 a clock at night, but he did not depart the shipp tell morning. Have sent per ditto canoe for the 200 pieces brawlls and 20 pieces long cloths your honour ordered me to receave from Mr Windover, butt yett noe more from ditto Windover than 120 pieces brawlls whereof above 40 pieces damnified, and allso 20 pieces long cloth all damnifyed.[64]

Wee have alsoe a great quantity of damnifyed tapseels good for nothing at all, eatten up by the worme, they came 5 or 6 years agoe per Captain Powlegrines [var. Polgreen].

As to our proseeding I hope will goe on well, butt at our comeing in this roade we found 2 English interloopers which gott all the slaves that was at the water side, but I comeing ashoar hinderd their design, alsoe spoke to the natives to cut away their boats, but they [= the interlopers] came to understand the same [and] went away from thence to windwards.

The Queen of Anguina will be downe with me next Fryday and then I hope will bring downe some slaves, but they are very deare. The interloopers have given 2 ounces of gold for a slave.

Heare came by yesterday a canoe from Alampo, the canoe men reportes that att ditto place is 6 sayles of shipes, 2 Duch 2 English interloopers and 2 Portugees. The slaves there are dire [= dear?] and full of the small pox, the onely commodity there is coures [= cowries] and long cloths, the which we have not aboard. Notwithstanding I doe assure your Honour and Counsell that I will doe my utmost indeavour for the creditt and proffit of my masters the Royall Affrican Company according to mean capassety.

Wee want here iron barrs and would have sent for the same to your Honour and Counsell, but Mr Franckland beeing one board of our shipp tould Captain Bowler and his mate it was but a folly to send to your Honour and Counsell for any more goods, you had entrusted with me so much goods already, and that I was a pittiful rasskall, and when I came to Accra [he] would kick me downe stayres, and that if had but spooke to your Honour you would putt him in my place, and severall other words not fitt to be write. I doe assure your Honnour that itt troubles me much to see a man affront his fellow companyon undeserved, I desier God to doe by him as he would be done by. Soe having noe more att present onely hope God Almighty will bless your honour and Counsell in all health and prosperity, and assure yourselfe and Counsell that there shall be nothing wanting to dispach Captain Bowler what lieth in my capascity.

[PS] Mr Bicknall will give your Honour a furder account. Pray excuse me this, being ritten on my hast.

Mr Bicknall has delivered Mr John Hilliard abourd the shipp Edgar, [he] came last night here.

---

[64] Cf. no.393.

Captain Bowler desiers your Honour and Counsell to give him a receipt for his slaves, corne [and] mallegettee which he bought out of his windward cargo.

576.   James Nightingale & Robert Hollings   Alampo, 25 March 1681

This brings an account of our proceedings since wee left Caboe Corsoe. To mention the number of Negroe slaves wee received from Annamaboe may be unnecessary, wee proceed to relate what Negroe slaves wee purchased at Wyamba and soe leeward to this place. Our purchase at Wyamba was in all 13 Negroe slaves. Some time wee spent there, for that the natives promised a great trade for slaves, if wee would stay, which when wee found frustrate, wee sail'd downe to Accra. Here indeed wee had the choyce of 19 Negroe slaves, out of which wee could hardly find 7 fitt to be putt aboard shipp. Wee fear some may be conceald, for what reason know not, the fault is not ours. From Accra wee received 120 pieces brawles, and those much damaged; wee likewise received 20 pieces of long cloth, in which but 4 pieces vendible. This is not the way to dispatch the shipp, her demorage[65] approaching, and the charge great, besides our cargoe on board is not vendible, the one halfe. By invoyce inclosed is mentoned what goods wee want, without which wee cann proceed noe farther, and it may be supposed the Royall Company will enquire the occasion of payment of freight more then by bill of lading shall be made manifest. This is what we ought to acquaint your Worshipp with, to avoid prolexity is our care. Wee are now promised a quantity of slaves if goods to purchase them. Wee wait your Worshipps answer.

[Inclosure]
An account of what goods wee want for dispatch of the shipp Edger, Captain Charles Bowler Commander

In primis   tapseeles broad
                nicconees ditto
                sheets
                long clothes white
                cowries
                allajares
                sletias fine
                musqueets bright
                boysadoes
These are the severall sorts of goods inquired affter here.

---

[65] i.e. payments made in compensation for delay beyond the contracted time of dispatch.

577. Robert Hollings   Alampo, 25 March 1681

Per this conveyance your Worshipp will receive the needfull menconed as to the ships dispatch. I have farther thought it requisite to acquint your Worshipp of our way in negotiacon, vizt Mr James Nightingale continued ashore at the severall places of trading, for which there is an absolute necessity, per reason wee meete interlopers, Portugues and Dutch ships, where wee come. I send him what goods he writes for, and soe far as I can yett perceive hee does use the utmost of his endeavour for the Royall Company intrest. I goe some times on shore to inspect his actions, and shall continue in the same while wee are upon the coast, and at the shipp[s] dispatch shall carefully render your Worshipp a faithfull accompt of all transactions etc.

578. Charles Bowler   On board the Edgar, Alampo, 25 March 1681

My occasion of my writing unto you at present is that my time groweth very short according to charter partye, which is not above 7 dayes longer affter the deate hereof, and therefore I desire your Worship and Councills letter for my security for the 20 dayes of demorage by order in Charter partye by the Royall Affrican Company of England there, which I think my selfe not secured without your Worshipp and Councills order, for at this time wee have on board of our ship but 101 Negroe slaves on board, which is not one third part of our complement, but wee are promised the rest in 4 weekes time after the date hereof. If itt be nott, it will be for want of good goods, and if it should please your Worship and Councill I was informed at Accra that Mr Thelwall had purchased about 20 slaves, which would doe me a great kindness now in our destress, and one thing I would desire your Worship if you please to send me a receipt for the 22 slaves that I bought to windward, malligeeta and corne, which you [have] the account of it with you.

579. James Nightingale   Alampa, 6 April 1681

My last to your honour was the 24th March, wherein I desired of your honour more recrutt of goods by reason sayes, perpettuanes, Ginny stuffs, Welch plaines, knives doe not goe of for slaves, and the Dutch shipp lying heare with good cowries, long cloth, fine sletias, bright musquetts, also gives a great rate for slaves, putts me to a stand, also is heare 2 English interlopers which gives 2 ounces of gold for a slave. Therefore pray consider in what a condition wee are in. I doe ashure yor honour I doe my best indeavour.

The Negroes promises faire, but currant goods purchases slaves, which are broad tapseeles, long clothes white, sheets, brawles, fine sletias, broad nicanneese, allejares, read ground pintadoes, bright musquetts, but especally cowries. Wee have not above 135 Negroes aboard, but the people of the countrey which are gone for slaves are not come downe. Wee expect them dayly with a good quantity, and then will doe my indeavour.

Your honour is not unsensable how far wee have gott in the 20 dayes of demorage after the 64 according to charter party, therefore pray lett me have your Honours and Councills order if you thinke it convenient for Captain Bowler to stay longer upon the coast then the 20 dayes. It would be a great shame, also noe little charges to our masters that the first ship by your Honours dispatched from Guiny should goe without her complement of slaves or there about.

My small oppinion is this, that if your honour keepe the shipp longer then the 20 dayes, and send some of the goods afore mentioned, especially broad tapseeles and some other of those which are in the Castle, I doe beleeve by degreese and good industry wee may gitt the ships complement of slaves or there about, in 6 weekes time.

In my last I forgott to mention of 5 pieces of sayes and 24 blew potkeys I sent to James Mills and Galansa at Wyamba in the 2 hand canoe,[66] with an order to dispose of them for slaves against the canoe comes backe, and if I find good trade would send the 5 hand canoe with more goods, by reason sayes doe not goe of here, I ordered him likewise if could git noe slaves for the goods, to dispose of them for gold, and send it per the 2 hand canoe, for gold will purchase slaves heare. I doe ashure your honour and Councill that I study every way to gitt slaves for the ship.

I have been like to dye, and had a fitt for 24 houres [so] that I was forsed to be tyed hand and feeit, but praised be God I am very well recovered. I could right your honour a great deale, but will leave it tell I see your honour in parson.

580.   James Nightingale & Robert Hollings   Alampa, 11 April 1681

Our last unto your honour was dated the 25th of March and the other the 4th instant, wherein wee gave your honour a full account of our proceedings, also what sorts of goods wee wanted for the purchaseing of slaves, but as yett not received any answer. Wee have aboard 140 slaves, and doe what wee can to procure more, with those goods which are vendable. Captain Bowler intends to saile this day sennet for Acra, and there to land the remains, and there to depart the coast without your Worshipp and Councell order him to the contrary of staying. In the meane time wee will doe what wee can for the ships dispatch. Soe having noe more to inlarge onely refer our meane capassity to your honours further order, which shall be punctually obeyed.

---

[66] Cf. no.394.

581. Charles Bowler to James Nightingale [on shore at Alampo]

On board the Edgar, 20 April 1681

These few lynes are to certifie you that I am resolved to saile to morrow night for Accra, and therefore I desire you to dispatch your buisness to morrow, and come off, for I see noe hopes of the 15 hand canoe comeing downe.

582. James Nightingale & Robert Hollings

Edgar, between Accra & Wyamba ½ way at 10 a clocke at night, 25 April 1681

Last Saterday wee sailed from Alampa and came the last night about 2 a clock in the morning off Accra. Wee sent presently our canoe a shoare to see what orders where there, wee received your Honour and Councells letter dated the 21st instant wherein wee heard the loss of the 15 hand canoe, goods, white men, and slaves, wherefore wee are hartyly sorrey. Per inclosed comes the coppy of Captain Bowlers note, allsoe [that] of Mr Wendover,[67] the aforesaid Bowler saying that he wanted water to supply his complement of slaves and that would stay noe longer then the 20 dayes according to charter party without he had your Honours and Councells order thereunto, with a proviseall that the Royall Company should pay him.

Wee being at Alampa did our best to gitt what slaves wee could, but wanting a supply of goods was a great hinderance to us, but seeing your Honour and Councill did your indeavour gives us some hopes. The inhabitance at ditto place seeing wee had noe goods vendable beguane to play the rogue with Nightingale a shoare, but with much trouble gott all safe off. He himselfe both goeing ashore and coming aboard was most drounded.

Wee have aboard in all about 200 slaves, and wee will doe what wee can to procure more at Wyamba while ditto Bowler gitts his water, and I will give him noe dispatch till furthur orderd of your honour and Councell. If wee must procure slaves at Wyamba, wee will want broad tapseeles, bright musquetts, brawles and sheets. If your honour and Councell order us to sell those goods for gold which wee cannot for slaves, will follow order, perhaps wee may gitt slaves for gold. At Accra are 4 English interlopers and 2 Dutch ditto. Per the next shall give your Honour and Councell a further account, in the meane time wee will doe what wee can, but if the ship stayes wee will want those goods afore mentioned ...

583. Charles Bowler

On board the Edgar between Accra and Wyamba, 25 April 1681

These few lynes are to certifie you that I sett sail from Alampa a Saterday last, being the 23rd instant, I waiting some sartin [= certain] dayes expecting the 15 hand canoe

---

[67] = no.395.

with a supply of goods which I did understand by your Worshipps letter, but seeing noe hopes of her coming I thought it convenient to make the best of my way for Wyamba to fill our water againe, but by the way of Accra. I doe understand of your great lost of the 15 hand canoe, the which I am hartiely sorry for it, and I understand by your last that Mr Wendover wrotte you concerning Mr Kyte that I would not take him in,[68] which is abominable lye, I onely denying his great cheste which would take up more rume than a tun would containe, which Mr Nightingale and Mr Hollings was at present and ditto Nightingale did order Mr Wendover not to lett him imbarke upon noe interloper what soe ever. Concerning your last letter the 21st instant to Mr Nightingale, I understand you have given order not to dispatch me untill I have my complement of 320 slaves, whereof I have not above two thirds of them yett and my time by charter party hath been out this 6 dayes and my provissions groweth short, and I cannot continue myself upon the coast not above 18 or 20 daies longer at furthest without a supplye of provissions, and further I desire your Worship and Councells order for the time that I shall lye upon the coast in purchaseing of slaves above charter party mentioning. I shall make all the dispatch I can in filling of my water and I desire your Worships answer of this in tyme of watering.

584. James Nightingale & Robert Hollings   Wyamba, 7 May 1681

This conveyance brings the several coppyes of what wee wrotte you upon the receipt of yours mentioning the unfortunate loss of the 15 hand canoe etc. Per ours to your honour at that time you will find how affaires where with us at that time. According to the dates of them wee have expected some answer, for the want of which Captain Bowler is very impatient, not knowing what it may meane, and likewise his provissions growing very short he is compelled to depart the coast. Wee have desired of ditto Bowler this morning how long he intends to stay for answer from your Honour, he replyed that in his letter bearing date the 25th ultimo he hath signified his mind, the limitt of which time he is resolved not to exceed now, fearing that his with our letters of the same date may not come to hand. Wee have this possitive answer from him, that within 5 dayes from this date he intends for Accra and there to land the remaines, soe go off the coast with those Negroes that are on board, Mr Nightingale having refused to take the goods ashore at this place, it beeing as he sayes besides his orders to doe it. Wee have been heere this last time about 11 or 12 dayes. Indeed our trade gives but little incoura[ge]ment, wee having purchased few slaves. The Queen of Anguinna came to this towne on Thursday last, has promised the payment of some part of her debt to the Royall Affrican Company of England, and as the Negroes say is ready with her pawnes for the settlement of a factory here. She likewise promises the best of her indeavour for procuring slaves.

[68] Cf. no.394.

She hath allready done this for us (there being an English interloper who came down here the 4th insten, one Richard Lumley Commander) to put one of the natives in irons at the factory, for sending a slave aboard of him, and has commanded that he be put one board of us. Wee have had an ill accident befalling us aboard, which is the loss of a hogshead of our Negroe brandy, and likewise a great part of our Negroe bread has been throwne over board since wee came here, it being old bread when bought in England as may be beleeved, and not fitt for use. There is absolute necessity for a recruite of brandy for the Negroes, without which if wee depart the coast it may be the loss of many of our Negroes in the voyage. This being the needfull wee humble desire your Honour may be pleased to send us a speedy answer.

585. James Nightingale   [Wyamba] 7 [May 1681]

At my coming downe here found a shoare a person by name Nicholas Bartrell, whome came from Accra under protection of our flagg desiring your honour be pleased to entertain him in servis of the Company or else to give him his discharge, as he sayes Mr Wendover denied him the same, hee being lodged at a blackes house. I desire your Honours order what to doe in itt.

586. James Nightingale   Wyamba, 11 May 1681

Your Honours and Councells much esteemed dated the 6th and 11 of Aprill, allso the 3rd and 7 instant received: wherein I understand your Honours great care and indulgency in ordering me to dispatch Captain Bowler with his complement of slaves. This is to answer that I have done my utmost indeavour and will continue in the same practise. As to our progress at this place, wee have had noe more than 3 slaves, interlopers lyeing here to windward and leward hinders us much.

The Queene being heare as I wrote your honour before hath promised to us some part of her debts, allso pawns for the factory, and to procure slaves, the two first I am certaine but the last I question much to procure as many slaves as wee want. She promise faire but they are blackes, I give them but little beleeve. I doe ashure your honour I will doe my uttmost indeavour. Your honour has been pleased to mention that there was suficient suply of goods sent before, you will find that I will give your honour and Councell a good and just account of what received, sould and remaines when I come to Cape Corsoe.

I shall according to your honours order dispose of noe more goods for gold then will procure slaves. Your honour has been pleased to mention of our progress at Alampa, itt being small incouragement for our Company, and that in all that time I gott but 140 slaves. [I] answer pray consider what ships has been there and the rates they have given, you will finde I have done my indeavour. I am of the same opinion that interlopers will be prevented to come to Guiny by their own imployers when the day of account comes. Your honour has been pleased to mention of the 7 instant that you dayly expected what success wee had at Wyamba. I have given your honour a full account the same day per our 2 hand canoe, also that Captain Bowler will stay noe longer then 5 dayes after the same date. I have showne your honour and Councells order to Captain Bowler that he should not goe of the coast, with[out?] his slaves or thereabouts, if did it was upon his own account. I doe beleeve ditto Bowler rights to your honour himselfe. He has the 2 letters, one to the Company, the other to Mr Steed and Mr Gascoyne. Being sworne one of your honours Councell to be true to our masters the Company, am bound to follow the same. Your honour will finde per attestation my meaning. I take God Allmighty to wittness I would doe noe man any rong, but instead, would take his place. I give your honour and Councell humble and harty thankes that you have been pleased to lay your commands upon me; there shall be nothing wanting what my meane capassity can procure. If wee stay heere shall want musquetts, but especially tapseeles, and as for giving your honour and Councell a certain account of what slaves to procure in such a time or such a time [I] can not doe itt, when I was heare last with the Portugueese [I?] gott 58 slaves in one months time. Pray lett the rest of the out factorys send what slaves they have.

The sea running here mighty high, the 2 hand canoe could not goe before, nor can I gitt well aboard. In the meane time I doe what I can, gott this day 2 girl slaves, part of the Queens debt.

587. Charles Bowler On board the Edgar, Wyamba Road, 11 May 1681

The ocasion of my writing unto you is that I understand by Mr Nightingales letter from your Worship that you doe intend to detain me heare at Wyamba untill I have my full complement of slaves, which I doe want at present about one 120, for I have a areyfd [sic: = arrived?] at this place 15 dayes and wee have goten but 3 slaves in all this time and therefore I thinke it impossible for to gett [them] here if wee laye here this 3 months longer, for the Queene and the Atta is come downe from Anguina to this place, and I doe not heare of any slaves that they brought with them, and if you will force me to stay for my full complement you must to gett them your selfe or at the other factoryes, for here they are not to be gotten, and I must needs tell you I have not above 4 months provissions left in my ship and therefore I cannot stay much longer nor will not, weather you give me my dispatches or not, for I have fulfilled my demorage dayes in charter party and 20 dayes more besides and our Negroes corne spends apace to. Wee have had a great mischance aboard concerning a hogshead of Negro brandy which is leaked out and wee shall want it very much for them, and farther I doe acquint your Worshipp that some of our Negroes hath goten the small pox and the longer wee stay I feare will be worse.

588. Charles Bowler Wyamba, 15 May 1681

Yours I have received dated the 9th instant, and as for going to Accra I was intended for heare. We have been at Wyamba 19 dayes and purchased noe more then 6 slaves and wee have had 7 dead aboard, and therefore I think it will be little proffitte either for Company or owners of our lying heare, having noe assistant from your honour or from any othere factoryes, and as to my provissions I brought anough with me if you had complyed with charter party. As you say I complaine of a months time of demorage, but the Company will find 45 dayes from this deat; and as for my going to Arda I am very free to [do so] with a provisor I might have my complement of slaves, but how they will be gotten without goods I know not, and for me to goe from place to place to be lead by the nose as I have been allready, I am quite aweary of it. If your honour had send goods for Arda there might be some hopes of purchasing of them, for Captain Bell lay a considerable time for want of goods to buy his slaves, and I dont understand how wee shall gett them without goods to. I am willing to goe downe to Arda for the rest of our slaves, for they are not to be had heare at Wyamba, but I desire your honours order for what quantity of time I shall stay at Arda if slaves to be had, if not to depart the coast.

[PS] I hope your honour will not be unmindful of a hogsheads of brandy for our Negroes, for there is a great necessity for itt.

589. James Nightingale   Wyamba, 15 May 1681

Your honours and Councells dated the 9th, 10 and 12 instant came safe to hand, allsoe a chest of musquetts, 25 tapseeles, 5 men and 9 women slaves, all aboard Captain Bowler. In answer to your honours of the 9 instant is this, Captain Bowler is very free to goe to Arda, as he sayes, but wants goods for ditto place as per his letter. My humble desire is that you would be pleased send your positive order what I shall doe with the remaines of the Companys merchandies, eather to put them ashore heare or att Accra. Alsoe if Captain Bowler goes to Arda if I should consigne ditto Bowler to Edwin Steed and Stephen Gascoyne Esquires, the Companyes factors at Barbadoss, with those slaves he has on board or not, I being very dubeous in this case because your honour has ordered me before not to dispatch him before he had 300 slaves or there about or else your positive order.

I have given Captain Bowler your Honours 3 letters, and sent yesterday the 2 before. As to your Honours of the 10 instant I shall do my endeavour for Captain Bramfill after Captain Bowler is gone from me according to order. In answer of your Honours of the 12 instant shall acte for my masters good as much as possible can. In the 9 hand canoe will send Nicholas Bartrell, which departs tonight. If your honour please to have 7, 9 or 11 hand canoes pray give me order to buy any of them and what I shall give for them. In the meantime desire your possitive order, which shall be all wayes obeyed.

[PS] The 14 slaves above are 1 man, 6 woemen from Mr Thelwall,[69] and 4 men, 3 woemen from Agent Generall and Councell.

590. James Nightingale   Wimba, 20 May 1681

Your Honours and Councels of the 18th instant I have received, also 14 men and 11 women slaves, but send [back] per bearer 2 men delivered in the 9 hand canoe, by reason indeed they are not good, also Captain Bowler saies hee cannot take them aboard, for hee will not give a receipt for them.

Captain Bouler intends to sayle for Accra this night, there to land the remains and soe to sayle for Arda. I have given him the letter to Mr Goulding.

I shall according order accompany him to Accra there to take a receipt of the Companys remains.

After getting what slaves at Accra shall within 3 days after arrived there consigne what slaves are abord to Edwin Steed and Stephen Gascoyne Esquires, the Compaany factors in Barbadoes.

As to Mr Wendover delivering slaves abord of interloopers, denieing to me them for the Compaany use, I doe believe your Honour had an accompt before now, and as for the future to come shall hinder as much as possible I can.

Shall also deliver the letters to them directed.

As touching the canoes:
11 hand canoe ....   Mk -...7...11
7 hand ditto, 3 pieces sayes, or   4....2
(The 9 hand canoe is not yett come)
If your Honour likes them at the above rates pray send your order and men to fetch them away. The owner of thee 11 hand canoe will give the other sayes.

[Inclosed]
James Nightingale to Mr Bucknell   [Undated]
I send per bearer 2 men slaves, the receipt for the men is in the Agents letter. Pray bring those 2 slaves to Caboe Corse again [in] the 9 hand canoe. You will likewise receive 6 pieces of irons.

    [Bowler proceeded back to Accra, where Nightingale left the ship in order to
    take temporary charge of James Fort (no.396).]

591. Robert Hollings   Ship Edgar, Accra, 23 May 1681

I need not mencon any thing more relateing to our proceedings since we left Cape Cors Castell, wee having from time to time advized your Honours of the severall

[69] Cf. no.225.

occurrences in the voyage to this place, where tis ordered that wee shall have our dispatches and then to sayle to Arda to compleat our number of 320 Negroe slaves, of which wee now want 87. Per the bills of ladeing and the account, your Honour will perceive how many received on bord at all places, out of which are deceased in all 19, vizt 8 males and 11 females, of which number 6 were received from Cape Coast Castle, and 1 from Accra. In the account your Honour will find to be short in the tapseels 11 pieces, I doe sweare I saw noe more, not 1 piece than specified in the account, and beleive that they came not on bord. I wish Mr Bridge had taken receipt (as the usuall manner is) for the goods so put on board, then the error would have been manifested with ease, of the sort of goods many came loose on bord, all the other answering the invoice, except the afore menconed tapseels. Your Honour etc. may perceive by the severall letters sent you that slaves were not easily pur-chased where we have been, and truly I am glad we have so many on bord, which had not been purchased had not Mr Nightingale been acquainted with the coast and likewise industrious in this affair.

[Bowler then proceeded to Offra, where he collected a further 87 slaves, and from where he departed in June 1681 (no.477).]

The *Merchant Bonadventure*, Commander John Lowe

[Lowe was at Accra, where he delivered letters and took in cowries, in Feb-ruary 1681 (no.391).]

592.   John Lowe & Thomas Goulding[70]

On board the Marchant Bonadventure, 18 Apr. 1681

This day wee parted with Whidaw with 529 slaves on board, but the ship hath sprung a very great leake, as much as two pumps can keepe her free. Now wee intended for Ophra to put the remaines on shoare. Wee have left Mr Thorne and Robert Chapman with the remaines of the goods wee had ashoare att that place [= Whidaw], the King haveing such a desire to have a factory settled there, and finding itt something dubious to gett the goods off without some time, the ship being leakey, we told the King [we] would referr the further settleing of itt till further order.

Our oppinion in itt is that itt will very much advance the Companys interest, by the great quantity of slaves that is to be had from that place, and the great awe to Ophra, who att present slites our English factory and nation and dus not allow halfe the libberty to us as to the Dutch, provided that that factory be accountable to

---

[70] Goulding travelled with Lowe to take charge of the RAC factory at Offra.

Ophra (and dependant upon that), besides the better convenience for getting of water for shipping and not above 6 leagues from Ophra.

Now if this concor with your prudience itt will be convenient that you send downe another man to Mr Thorne whoe is an accountant.[71]

The *Alexander*, Commander Andrew Branfill

[Branfill delivered goods to Anashan on 10 May 1681 (no.129) and Anomabu on 12 May (no.225).]

593. Andrew Branfill   [Place unknown], 23 May 1681

I thought convenient to give you a line concerning my slave cargoe, weather it be thought by you and Councell most for our Companyes interest to carry the remaines home or to put them ashoar if any remaines be.

[Concerning] the 45 sletias, I signed for fine sletias but find 15 corse and the other 30 to be a kind of dowlas and not fine sletias, I question weather they will answer expectation. I understand Captain Bowler is going off the coast, I hope you will be pleased now to lett me see some of your assistance concerning getting my slaves. I am now going to Tantumquerey. After I have had a vew of the place and find how the people are afected Ile give you my judgment according to your desire.

594. William Todd   Alexander, [Tantonquerry], 2 June 1681

The Captain according to your worships request came to anchor before Tanton-query, where one of the chiefe men came a board to give the Captain an invitation ashoare and told us of much slaves they could procure in a little time for us. The Captain prest him to send the slaves aboard, but nothing would satisfy them, with-out the Captain or myselfe goeing ashoare first, soe I went ashoare and severall of the cabasheirs came to give me their hands, and was verry kind to mee the time I was ashoare. Wee have laid in the road 10 dayes and has got no more but 9 slaves of them. The King is up in the country and sent one of his men downe to tell the Captain he would come downe shortly with slaves, but there being very little money wee thought not worth the while of staying any longer, yet I doe beleeve that if a factory were setled here there might be good store of slaves procured, and in time might be a place of good trade.

I greatly feare that wee shall be put to a nonplus in procuring of our slaves, for nothing goes off wth us, but sayes, perpetuanoes, sheets and some tapsells. Paut-

---

[71] Cf. Thorne's account, in nos 476, 477, 479.

keys, fine clouts and committers wee have not sold one since wee left Cape Corso roade.

[PS] The Captain gives his humble service to your worshipp and hopes you will not forgett in assisting him with some Negroes.

595.   William Todd   Allampo, 13 July 1681

Haveing the oppertunity by a Dutch man to convey this to Accra I thought good to give your worship an account of our proceedings. The Captain is now very ill and in a feavour. Wee have now about 200 slaves but abundance of them woemen, our goods not being very proper to purchase them with. As for the long blew cloths, pautkeys, pewter, none of them is vendible here. Niccanees narrow sometimes wee get two or three off, as likewise the pintadoes. If you would doe us the favour as to lett us have 100 pieces of your fine sletias and 150 of your broad niccanees by the first itt would doe us a great kindness, either of the Companys account or elce the Captain will exchange pautkeys, fine clouts, committers belonging to the windward trade at prime cost with your worship for them, and likewise let the canoe that comes with those things may take up the remaynes with the helpe of our long boate to Accra, for the ship cannot turne itt up haveing no land breezes.

[PS] If your worship please to send these things by a 5 hand canoe to let the canoe attend of us 10 dayes will doe us a great kindness.

596.   Andrew Branfill   Ophra in Arda, 18 Aug. 1681

[I] thought fitt to give you a line to satisfie you of my proceedings. I am now in good health, praised be God for itt, and have all my slaves on board and have put my remaines on shoare, which is 125 peeces narrow niccanees and 96 comitters, here at Arda, and Mr Thorne hath signed the wrightings you sent to goe home with mee.[72] I have nothing of news to wright.

PS. 12 of the narrow niccanees above specified which is out of the Castle are stained or damnified.

The *Unblessed Blessing*, Commander Samuel Rickard

[Rickard took in corn from Anashan in June 1681 (nos 135–6, 228).]

597.   Samuell Rickard   From aboard the Unblessed Blessing, 13 Aug.1681

These give you an account that Mr James Nightingale hath been on board us in his

[72] Cf. no.477; also 480, inclosure 2.

passage to Wyamba, that our boate hath been that way 15 or 16 dayes, [it?] hath sent me up 4 men 4 woemen Negroes. Find slaves hard to come by both at Annamaboe and all other places. Have now on board 153 Negroes, 100 of them woemen kind. Have disposed of almost all our goods except powder, gunns and iron, and baftas. Sletias and sayes being the principle goods where the shipp lies. If you please to help mee with more sletias and sayes, allejars or such goods as you have it may be I may purchase more slaves at Annamaboe.

I heare of a case of sletias at Annamaboe, which if you please to order mee ly convenient to receive I sell them for 8 angles, in account you can gett noe more for them ashoare. I have indeavoured to gett what slaves I can for money, knowing that I have not goods to procure above halfe my number, and have laid out 8 marke. Find I cannot procure Negroes without goods and know not where to goe or how to come by my number, being well inform'd that both French and Dutch, as far as Arda, doth blow upon gold without goods, there haveing been soe many att the say [= essay?] before mee. I find I cannot sell gunns, powder or iron, which goe a great way in the vallue of my less than 600£ cargoe. I am in great straite, not knowing what to doe. My provisions goes short for white men, haveing laien 90 odd dayes since I came to Capo Corsoe, and on my voyage to this time, 9 months. I intend to come to Capo Corsoe about Monday or Tuesday next.

[PS] My yaule went yesterday to our long boate. At her returne I intend for Capo Corsoe.

598. Samuell Rickard   20 Aug. 1681

Our number of Negroes are not much increased. Since I came to Capo Corsoe I have received from Mr Richards[73] 10 sletias, being I think all that is unsold. Pray please to lett my mate receive the 20 peeces of sayes, some allejars and what Negroes you have for us, all which will be to the furtherance of [myself].

[Rickard was off Kormantin on 29 August 1681 (no.500); in September he received one slave supplied from the factory at Anashan (no.149, 154); and in early October was at Accra (no.414).]

599. Abraham Wise   [Ophra in Arda], 14 Nov. 1681

My humble service to you to informe you of our affairs here in Ophra in Arda, is that Captain Rickard hath gott his slaves through some trouble, his goods being short in answer to the quantity of Negroes, but good fortune attending mett with slaves for money. The King of Arda hath received goods for 5 slaves but since cannot heare from him, soe that wee are forct to leave them, and one with the

---

[73] RAC chief factor at Anashan (cf. section III).

Phidolgoe that hee had sworne us out of, not knowing how to helpe ourselves, soe that wee have all our slaves except those 6. The factory is very badly furnished, having nothing but a few niccanees and some commetters and iron, which is noe commodity att all.[74] They ashoare in the factory is well and hath been very kind to us. Our Captain hath been very sick but att present indifferent.

The *Vine*, Commander Abraham Cooke

600. Abraham Cooke   [No place], 19 Aug. 1681

These are for to acquaint you that I have been out of England ever since the 18th May and I was the last ship that came away. I thought Captain Finey and Captain Lawrence had been here, for I have seen noe ships since I came out sea [until?] the last night that I see your pink and 2 interlopers that are now in the ofing for your ship fired then out of the place whence they lay att Commenda. I am bound for Old Callibarr[75] for the Company, the ships name is the Vine, the ship that Captain Bramfill commanded last. If you please to have mee come ashoare I will if you send a canoe off to mee, and I shall stay till I have your answer.

The *Lion*, Commander Giles Lawrence

601. Giles Lawrence   The Ship Lyon, Dicky's Cove, 26 Aug. 1681

In conformity to the Royall Companys orders I send this express with the letters received from them for you; and allthough an entire sale be not as yett procured to the cargoe committed by them to my disposall, I despaire not but in a few dayes there will, and then to be capacitated with the oppertunity of kissing your hands att Capo Corsoe. Intrim corne being here att one angle and halfe per chest, please to favour mee with the price, and plenty itt may being with you, for my governance.

[PS] What endeavour I have used itt hath not been possible for mee to purchase more than 5 negroe persons.

[Lawrence was off Anomabu, where he delivered gunpowder to the RAC factory, in Oct. 1681 (no.246); and later at Accra, whence he departed for Ningo on 12 December 1681 (no.422).]

[74] Cf. no.479.
[75] For English trade at Old Calabar (for slaves) at this time, cf. Barbot 1992, ii, 672; Latham 1973, 17–18.

The *Sarah Bonadventure*, Commander Thomas Woodfine

[Woodfine was at Anomabu by 10 December (no.251), and left there around
the beginning of January 1682 (no.254). Arthur Wendover embarked at Accra, to go to Whydah, where was to take over as RAC chief factor (no.423).]

602. Arthur Wendover   Wyamba Road, 5 Jan. 1681/2

This day att 11 of the clock, I came safe on board the Sarrah Bonadventure, and to
Captain Thomas Woodfine Commander did deliver to himselfe the 2 boxes (the
Royall Companys pacquett) and alsoe your worships particular letters. For the
aforegoeing particulars made mention of, here is the receipt inclosed for them
according to your worships orders

[Inclosure]
According to your desire I have sent up the Quarrenteers man, and had you commanded a greater matter itt should have been obeyed   Thomas Woodfine

[In March 1682 Thomas Woodfine was reported still at Whydah, trying to
complete his complement of slaves (no.483).]

The *Charles*, Commander Edward Hill

603. Edward Hill   Annamaboe, 25 Jan. 1681/2

These may acquaint you that I have this day begun to take in my corne and doubt
not but to have itt all in this weeke. And for slaves some few to be purchased, if had
goods which they demand or give the price in gold as other ships give, which is 7
pease 2 angles for a man and 6 pease and 2 angles for a woeman. I have little
remaines on board which these people requier. I humbley desire you will please to
supply with the goods following, perpettuanoess green and blew, tapsells, sletias
of either sort, allejars, Guyny stuffs, powder and sayes. Whatt I have remaining on
board is iron, sheets, pintadoes, red perpettuanoes, and some few sayes. I intend
my long boate up to morrow for water. If your honour thinks convenient for to send
mee these goods aforementioned she shall leave the water caske, and come up for
them the next day. Captain Woodfine hath all his corne in, but when hee intends to
sayle I know not.

604. Edward Hill   Annamaboe, 26 Jan. 1681/2

Yesterday I wrote to your Honour at large as to the price of slaves. I assure you
theres nothing wanting on my part, without tools I cannot worke. Captain Woodfine
gives the prices I advised yesterday in gold, and hath sletias and allejars, which are

the goods every one demands. When he goes hence I know not. These come by my longboat, who will receive what goods your honour will please to order me; and for the prices of slaves in gold please to give me your order, which shall be duely observed. What slaves are here to be had the interloper at Amersa and Captain Woodfine sweeps them all away.

605. Edward Hill   On board the ship Charles, Anamaboe Road, 31 Jan. 1681/2

Yours of the 26th instant I received, with the goods therein mentioned, and shall duely observe your orders for the disposall of them. As for the sletias they are all gone, soe desire I may have a supply of both sorts, having sent my boat up to receive what you please to order me. I want now 120 chests corne to compleat my complement, which is ready.[76]

606. Edward Hill   Anamaboe, 10 Feb. 1681/2

Yours by my long boat I received, and according to your desire I have put Nevin on board Captain Gates.[77] This comes by my mate, and desire may have 20 peeces blew and green perpettuanes; as for redds, they will not goe here.

607. Edward Hill   Anamaboe, 3 March 1681/2

The red perpettuanos and fine sletias [I] had from you two dayes since, I have disposed of all to 6 peeces of both sorts, and desire may have a supply of 30 peeces of each more, with 10 blew and green perpettuanos. I had sent my boate this morning but the sea breeze blowing all night, was doubtfull of her getting up in time.

[Hill was reported to have left Anomabu for Cape Coast Castle on 11 March 1682 (no.264); but he was back at Anomabu, taking in slaves, on 13 April (no.269).]

608. Edward Hill   25 Apr. 1682

Haveing received 44 chests of corne and 16 slaves from Mr Richard Thelwall I have accordingly signed bills of loading for what slaves on board vizt 147 men, 160 woemen, 21 boyes and 16 girls, in all 344.

[PS] The slaves from Anamaboe were 8 men, 8 woemen.

---

[76] Cf. no.259.
[77] Cf. no.612.

The *John Bonadventure*, Commander John Woodfine

[Woodfine was at Komenda, landing goods for the factory, on 2 Dec. 1681, intending to go from there west to Takoradi (no.46). At some point he took in wood from Anashan (no.171), and on 2 Jan. 1682, he was reported to be at Winneba (no.167). John Smith and John Winder embarked with him to go to Whydah, where Winder was designated to take over as RAC chief factor (cf. nos 484, 492–3).]

609.   John Smith & John Winder
                    On Board the John Bonadventure, Wyamba Road, 30 Jan. 1681/2

This may serve to acquaint you that wee safely arrived on board Captain Woodfines ship this noon, who designes to saile tomorrow morning for Accra, where he will stay some houres, and soe proceed on his voyage for Arda. Wee heartily wish your Worship and all the rest of the gentlemen health and happiness, and hope to discharge our business to your satisfaction, at least shall endeavor soe to doe.

PS. Mr Smith desires you will let Mr Young know that Mr Page sayes he left the scales and weights belonging to him, in his chamber.

Captain Woodfine presents his humble service to your Worship, to whome I have delivered your letter for Mr Steed and likewise your noat concerning Mr Page, which he shewed to him, and Mr Page promised to write your Worship.   JW

610.   John Smith & John Winder
                    On board the John Bonadventure, Accra Road, 1 Feb. 1681/2

Yesterday about 4 in the afternoon wee came to anchor in this roade, and did feare wee should not have an oppertunity to send a letter ashoare, which might advise you of all transactions here, but Mr Pley and Mr Towgood comeing aboard, did resolve to give you an account of the incouragement Captain Woodfine gives us in our business, who (by his words) wee very much feare hath some underhand dealing with Petly Wybourne and Mr Wendover,[78] and are confident he will doe us no good, and (it may be) all the hurt he can. If wee had goods in our hands whereby wee might have made interest with the Blacks, it would have been much better, for we have little or noe hopes of getting any thing out of Mr Wendovers hands, and unless your Worship doe speedily send downe one of the vessells with supply the Company concernes at Arda may wholy be ruined, Mr Wendover being informed of our comeing by a canoe that went from aboard Captain John Woodfine some houres before our arrivall. Wee most earnestly desire your Worship to be speedy in

---

[78] Wendover was chief factor at Whydah, due to be superseded by Winder. The allegation of collusion with Wyburne, the interloper established at Whydah, is supported by his subsequent actions (cf. no.484).

sending, for Captain Woodfine swears Mr Smith shall not have the canoe, unless he paies him 11 ounces of gold, having paid the money himselfe for the Company use. Wee shall upon all occasions doe the best we can, and send advice by all oppertunities.

[John Woodfine proceeded to Offra, where he was reported to be 'ready to sail' in March 1682 (no.483).]

The *Allapeen*, Commander Daniel Gates

[Gates was at Anomabu on 11 Jan. 1682 (no.505).]

611. Daniell Gates   Aboard the Allapeen, Anishan Road. 1 Feb. 1681/2

I have gott aboard from Anishan 135 chests corne and there is about 15 chests more ashoare which I intend to fetch of tomorrow morning in my skif, and that is all I am like to gett here.[79] I intend to fall down to Anamaboe tomorrow in the afternoon. I would desire you would be pleased to send me downe what course sletias, clouts and brawles you can spare me, for I have bought but 2 slaves since I came, and I want those things to put of those goods that I have aboard, or elce I am likely to lye here a great while for a few slaves. I hope you will consider of it.

[By 12 Feb. 1682, Gates had taken in 215 chests of corn from Anashan (no.175).]

612. Daniell Gates   Aboard the Allapeen, Anamaboe Road, 18 Feb. 1681/2

I have received yours by Captain Hills boat, and John Nevin in irons, and according to your order I have sent up your irons in Captain Hills boat, and have put on him a paire of our owne, and doe desire to know how long I must keep him in irons.[80] I have gott but 23 chests of corne from Anamaboe as yett and slaves are very scarce.

[Gates now went west to Komenda, where he took in corn on 20 Feb. 1682 (no.60), before proceceding east to Adangme.]

613. Daniell Gates   Allampo, 6 March 1681/2

Haveing this oppertunity I make bold to trouble you with two or three lines to

[79] Cf. no.171.
[80] Cf. no.606.

acquaint you I am now riding at Allampo. Here is 2 Portugueze more and 2 interlopers. The Frenchmen went from hence on Satureday last. Negroes are very hard
to be gott and att very great rates, for the Frenchmen has cleared the towne of slaves,
they haveing a great many booges.[81] Here is nothing goes off att present but
musketts, and I could wish all my pintados was in musketts, for I cannot sell one
nor doe know what to do with them. I have bought but 8 Negroes since I came here,
for they doe aske after the rate of a bendy and better a head for a man slave. I would
desire you if you have any oppertunity to send mee some musketts in the roome of
my pintados, for there is nothing but musketts and booges goe off here.

614. Daniell Gates   Aboard the Allepeen, 17 March 1681/2

These are to acquaint you that I am now under saile, I haveing purchased as many
slaves here as with those I had before makes the number of 156 Negroes, and I have
left my remaines with Mr Charles Towgood, the Master of your briganteen,[82] and
have taken his receipt, the remaines being 16 Guynea clouts.

[Gates proceeded to Whydah, where he arrived on 20 March 1682 (no.483).]

The *Arcanie Merchant*, Commander Thomas Attwell

615. Thomas Attwell   From aboard the Arcanie Merchant, 15 Apr. 1682

These are to lett your honour understand that wee fell in with Cape Mount[83] the 8th
of March and that now praised be God wee are safe arrived off Commenda, with
great part of our cargoe, finding tradeing to be very dull to windward, hopeing that
I may find amendment for itt here. As for Negroes and corne none to be gott att any
rates, haveing in all my time of trade purchased but one Negroe, hopeing that you
[sic: = they?] may be plenty below for interlopers are soe thick that there is noe
getting any thing there without a man gives twice the vallue.

616. Thomas Attwell   Anamaboe Road, 25 Apr. 1682

These are to informe you that I have had corne profered mee, but their price is soe
high that I am afraid to deale without your honours advice. They doe aske mee 3
angles per chest but I beleeve I may beat them downe to 2½, which is the interlopers
price and they are corned in a short time, soe it is my opinion that if your honour
hath thoughts of corning mee with olde corne I beleeve you must give the interlop-

[81] Cf. no.523.
[82] Cf. no.525.
[83] In Sierra Leone.

ers price, if not more. However I desire that you would be pleased to give mee your order, which I shall observe.

617.   Thomas Attwell   Anamaboe Road, 28 May 1682

These are to lett your Worship understand that here is very little corne offers as yett, and the rates that your Worship and Councill hath sett on the goods that I have to purchase corne and slaves the Negroes will not meddle with them nor sell slaves att the rates as your Worship hath limitted, and for corne they doe desire gold as well as goods. Therefore I doe desire of your Worship and Councill how to act, for I have been a considerable time on the account of getting corne and slaves already, which your Worship is very sencible of, and I am afraid that I must be forc't to buy my corne with gold and put the most part of my goods ashoare.

[Attwell proceeded to Adangme, where he arrived on 18 June 1682 (no.512, 528), and was at Whydah in August (no.487, inclosure 2). His safe arrival in Barbados was reported back to West Africa in the following year (no.6).]

The *St George*, Commander Richard Shepherd

[The *St George* was rumoured to be west of Komenda in February 1682 (no.58). Shepherd took in corn at Anomabu on 28–29 May (no.274). He presumably went from there to Cape Coast (cf. no.272); but he was back at Anomabu by 3 June, when he delivered a letter there (no.275).]

618.   Richard Shepheard   Aboard the St George, Annamaboe Road, 4 June 1682

Yours I have received of this same date by my chirurgeon, wherein you doe desire my company up to Capo Corsoe Castle. I would willingly have waited on your Worship but I have been very ill ever since I came last downe with a strong feavour, but I hope the voiolence of itt is over, for itt begins to breake out in my lips. As for my dispatches I desire your Worship would be pleas'd to send them downe by the bearers[?]. As for the child Letitia Croxton, if you please to send her alsoe downe with her effects by my boate with one of your owne people with her I will here signe to your obligation, provided itt oblidges mee to keepe her no longer then till shee be of age to provide for herselfe if itt run to the age of twenty, provided she doe not contract marriage before that time. I have received noe woeman slave upon her account as yett. I hope your Worship will be pleased to send the 2 slaves downe in my boate, soe craving your Worships pardon I cannot waite upon you.

619.   Richard Shepheard   Aboard the St George, 6 June 1682

This inclosed is one I writt you of the 4th instant att receipt of yours by my Docter and I expected to have sent my boate up that night, but you are very sencible that wee have noe oppertunity of good weather and itt is very uncertaine when wee shall have any faire weather, and for my comeing I dare not venture, as not being well. Soe if your Worship pleases to send my dispatches and what else you please by Captain Shears, for I understand he is a comeing downe, and if your Worship sends any body downe with the child I will endeavour to send them up againe in my boate.

[Shepherd proceeded to Whydah, where he arrived on 20 June 1682 (no.492).][84]

620.   Richard Shepheard   [Guydah], 5 July 1682

These bearers is Captain Starlands canoemen, whoe were not able to gett aboard their ship, their canoe being broake, and I passing Allampo in the night could not put them aboard, whoe was constrain'd to take their passage with mee to Guydah, where I have purchased all my slaves in 14 day's and now am ready to saile. I have left the remaines with Mr John Winder,[85] and reffering you to his letters I take leave.

Unidentified ship, Commander Richard North

[North was at Anomabu, where he delivered goods, on 6 July 1682 (no.282).]

621.   George Bathurst   Annamaboe, 16 July 1682

Captain North being very weake, hee desired mee to acquaint your Worship that hee hath received from Mr Richard Thelwall what corne hee hath, which is but 76 chests,[86] whereas your Worship promised him his whole complement of 500 chests att his first arrivall here, which I suppose might have been procured had not your Worship stinted Mr Thelwall to buy att a lower rate then other men have. And now the interlopers have bought up almost all, soe that there is noe probabillity of getting soe much old corne here as will serve for the voyage. Therefore his desire is that your Worship will supply him some other way with old corne, or else send an order that hee may have 50 chests more added to what you have already ordered, by reason of his long stay here, to have the new corne well cured, and likewise below to procure the rest of his slaves will with what hee hath already be the

---

[84] The report of the *St George* being in sight of Komenda on 24 June 1682 (no.70) must be an error.
[85] Cf. no.480, inclosure 3.
[86] Cf. no.284.

occasion of expending much corne upon the coast, which hee leaves to your Worships consideration.

622. Richard North   Annamaboe, 5 Aug. 1682

God be praised I am in pretty good health and faire way of recovery. I give you many thanks for my beere. I have now on board 300 chests of corne, and fetch itt as fast as they on shore drie itt. I have consulted all the ways I can immagine and cannot find the cargoe I have for Arda sufficient for the purchaseing of my complement of 450 slaves. May itt please your honour to order some ogmentation to my cargoe, for if any thing remaines itt shall be certainly left in the hands of them you have ordered itt to. The reason of my being soe urgent upon you is because I would not goe off the coast dead fraigted.

623. Timothy Armitage   Anamaboe, 5 Aug. 1682

Yours of the 31st past have received, and shall as oppertunity presents keepe you advised as well from Arda as from hence, [87] God sending us safe thither, being very sollicious (which shall be attended with the best of my care and dilligence) for the interest of the Royall Affrican Company there, whome I shall likewise hold advised from time to time as occasion serves, for the promotion of whose interest, humbly begg your Worship would please to take into consideration for a supply of some booges (as may be thought meet) to goe along with mee, for that Captain North tells mee shall fall short of goods whereby to purchase his slaves. And moreover if your Worship would please to consider the bad or ill circumstances I may there be under for want of them, as comeing a stranger into the place. And itt may probably soe happen that what already consign'd Mr Winder or myselfe may goe towards the compleating of Captain Norths complement of slaves, when shall be incappacitated to doe the Company that service which otherwise I might doe. And itt is likewise feared that neither the sletias nor the beads will goe off alone. I humbly desire the perticulars of their cost for my better government in their disposall, because doe understand that the sletias are high prized goods and of severall rates. Captain North may in 5 or 6 day's be dispatcht from hence, haveing in about 300 chests of corne aboard.

624. Richard North   Annamaboe, 9 Aug. 1682

After a months tarry tomorrow God willing shall have all my corne in, and this weeke doe intend to saile. I make bold to trouble you, if have any service to

---

[87] Armitage was travelling on North's ship to Offra in Allada, where he was to serve in the RAC's factory.

command pray advise. The time I have waited for corne as you are sencible has been a great detriment to mee and rest of my owners. As for what I writt to you in my last, but not answered, to desire your Worship to grant mee some ogmentation to my cargoe, which if you please to consider will be noe disadvantage to the Royall Company nor you.

[North proceeded to Whydah, which he left on 26 September 1682 (no.487). He was reported to have arrived safe in Barbados, and thence to Jamaica, around January 1683 (no.6); but was subsequently reported taken by pirates in the West Indies (no.633).]

Unidentified ship,[88] Commander Robert Ware

625. Robert Ware   Anamaboe, 21 Aug. 1682

These are to lett you understand that this morning early I began to take a part of my corne aboard and hope may gett off 200 chests this day, and if the weather continue in 3 dayes or 4 att most to have all on board. I am afraid that the quanitity of corne your Worship hath ordered Mr Thelwall to deliver mee will fall short of my expectation, and therefore desire your Worships speedy order for 50 more.[89] I am much afraid that Mr Richards will faile of his promise as to a canoe; for I understand that his people went to fetch her out of the woods but on Thursday last, but how long shee may be getting downe to the waterside is not yett knowne.[90] Hee informs[?] his people shee will be up in 3 dayes but itt is doubted by most people here. If hee come not according to his promise wee shall endeavour to purchase one here, which if procured will come att noe less price then a pound of gold, but she is a large canoe, therefore I earnestly begg your Worships advice by the first. The 3 vessells which were to leward are now in sight and suppose may gett into the road to day. I hope to see your Worship about Fryday next God permitting.

[Ware had completed his corning at Anomabu by 23 August 1683, and was due to sail from there, to Cape Coast, on 30 August (nos 290, 292). He subsequently proceeded to Whydah, where was reportedly 'upon departure' by 28 October 1682 (no.488), but did not actually leave until 3 December (no.490).]

---

[88] Possibly the *George*: cf. no.487.
[89] Cf. nos 289–90.
[90] Cf. no.190.

The *Golden Fortune*, Commander Lott Ambrose

626. Lott Ambrose [Annamaboe], 13 Sept. 1682

Yours received by the bearer this day att noone with 9 letters more inclosed, which shall take care to deliver according to instructions. I have not as yett gott above two thirds of my corne aboard, because Mr Thelwall could not assist mee before todaye with his canoe.[91] I hope I may be ready to saile on Fryday next. I have spoken to Mr Thelwall about my canoe but find noe probabillity to be furnished with staying 8 or 10 day's and if soe can be upon noe certainety. Therefore desire your honour to send your orders downe to Mr Thelwall to furnish mee with his canoe; and if not furnished here with a canoe may be a great means towards the ruining of my voyage. I am confident if have any long stay upon the coast, as in all probabillity I shall, I must want corne if your honour orders noe more, and if soe when come to the Islands must putt the Company to a greate deale of charge to be furnished there. This thought good to informe your honour, desireing answer by him that accompany's the bearer.

[PS] I desire your honour to send a receipt for the chest of wine and caske of mum, includeing the cheese and firkin of butter.

627. Lott Ambrose [Annamaboe], 15 Sept. 1682

Yours came into my hands last night, and as to the canoe that Mr Thelwall hath which your honour thinks will be to bigg, as I beleive few goeth with lesser. Itt would have been far from my thoughts to write to your Honour concerning Mr Thelwalls canoe if a lesser could have been any wayes produced. I have made all the inquiry I can here, and from Lague have notice there is noe less then a 11 hand canoe to bee had there, and to goe downe without one will be verry uncertaine of being furnished there, for every man will serve himselfe first in such cases, and besides because of the abundance of shipping that I suppose to lye there now, I shall not make too much hast downe to the factory if can find any prospect without any long stay on this side of itt to be furnished. As to my corne, of the complement that that you ordered Mr Thelwall to deliver mee there is about 6 chests lost, the canoe sinking goeing off. I desire that you would be pleased to order that to be made good.

[PS] Pray be pleas'd to send a receipt for the cheste of wine and caske of mum, because certainly the Company will question the delivery of itt, although you doe acquaint them in your letters. Be pleas'd to send speedy answer because I intent to saile tonight.

---

[91] Cf. no.293.

[Ambrose had completed his corning at Anomabu by 16 Sept. and left there on 18 (nos 295–6). He proceeded to Whydah, which he left in October 1682 no.488).]

The *Mary*, Commander Henry Nurse

[Nurse arrived at Sekondi on 5 July 1682 (no.73). He was later at Anomabu, from where he sailed on 29 August (no.292).]

628.   Henry Nurse   From aboard the Mary, Accra Road, 1 Oct. 1682

Yours I received bearing date the 29th September, and glad to heare of your honours health. I have aboard about 210 slaves. I have been to leward of Accra some 4 leagues but now rideing att Accra, and as soone as my sloope comes up from Allampo I shall make all the hast I can up to Cabo Corsoe, for my time growes short as to charter party, but I may stay longer if I think fitt for the Companys advantage, which will be chargeable to the owners if I should stay longer. I hope to make up 300 Negro's before I goe off the coast.[92] As for your hoggs and goates I will bring up what Mr Hassell will put on board mee.

[Nurse was back at Anomabu, taking in corn, on 19 October 1682 (no.304). His safe arrival in Barbados was reported in the following year (no.6).]

Unidentified ship, Commander Andrew Branfill (second voyage)

[Branfill was at Mina on 28 November 1682 (no.533); off Shama on 5 December (no.547). He subsequently took in corn, as reported in this letter, probably at Anomabu.]

629.   Andrew Branfill   No date [Dec. 1682]

Yours of the 16th instant I received, and as to the corne when you see my charter party you will be better satisfied. I hope by the latter part of this week I shall be ready to draw an exact account of my remaines, which I suppose will be sayes, perpetuano's, iron, Guyney stuffs, broad allejars, tallow, lead, musketts, Welch plains, manillo's, and paper bralls, which if you please to take and give mee 25 per cent advance they will be yours, if not I must dispose of them as well as I can.

---

[92] Cf. no.438.

[Branfill was reported to be on the point of departure from Anomabu on 2 January 1683 (no.314); and was at Accra later in the same month (no.446).]

Unidentified ship, Commander William Maple

630.   William Maple   Cabo Corsoe Castle, 15 Jan. 1682/3

I doe acknowledge to have received from the Agent Generall and Councill one man slave (in leiw of a man slave that ran away from on board my ship) with this condition, that if the said slave be not retaken I doe hereby oblige myselfe to make satisfaction to the Royall Affrican Company for the slave received by mee from the Castle, as wittness by hand

William Maple Junior
Wittness William Pley

[Maple left Anomabu on 16 January 1683, bound for Angola (no.317).]

The *Lisbon Merchant*, Commander William Woolliford

[Woolliford was at Anomabu, 20–23 March 1683, landing goods and taking in corn (nos 326, 327, 329.329).]

631.   William Williford   [Guydah], 9 May 1683

This is to acquaint you that the canoemen have been att Mr Winders[93] command ever since I have been here and not att mine. When I had any occasion for them to carry my slaves off I was faine to come capp in hand to them with a greate many faire words, and their crye was they should displease Mr Winder, and now they are with you requite them as you think fitt. Mr Winder is now out of your reach and hee will doe what he lists.

632.   William Williford   [Guydah], 9 June 1683

This is to acquaint you of my condition and of Mr Winders kindness to mee, whoe made mee lye 5 weeks without any slaves and hath strived to sett the King and all the Cabasheers against mee what he could, and hath endeavoured to ruin and destroy mee and my ship ever since I have been here; and when Captain Lowe and Captain Rickard came downe hee bid mee shift for my selfe and gett slaves where I could, for I should have noe trade here if itt lay in his power to prevent mee,

---

[93] John Winder, RAC chief factor at Whydah.

Captain Lowe and Captain Rickard bringing gold downe with them if in case their cargo's should not hould out, and they were men for him, but I haveing none was forct to shift for my selfe.[94] May the 16th the pyrates came downe and tooke our ships about 5 a clock in the afternoone, I being ashoare getting what slaves I could and 2 of my boates man'd and gon to windward seeing to purchase what slaves they could, but the pyrates interrupted them of their designe for they tooke them and sunk the boates and all the goods. The same day the ships were taken 12 hours after I received a letter per a canoe but then itt was too late, but if I had received itt 12 houres before I had saved all the gold which is now lost. The next day I went aboard of the pyrate and with much adoe I gott my ship, but their intents were to burne them all. They tooke away one ankor and cable from mee, and all my bread and most of my beefe, and destroy'd most of my water caske and every thing that I had aboard.[95] I have now 306 slaves aboard and doe intend to sayle a Saturday if wind and currant present. Mr Winder owes mee 18 ounces of gold and I cannot gett one cracra of itt.

[Woolliford departed Whydah early in June 1683.[96] He was at Principe by 22 June (no.639).]

The *Hopewell*, Commander Richard Lumley

[Lumley arrived at Cape Coast Castle on 1 May 1683 (no.334), and was intended to go on to Anomabu for corn (no.337). But on 11 May his ship was attacked and plundered by pirates off Anashan (no.556). David Harper was a local employee of the RAC (chief factor at Komenda earlier in 1683) who (as explained in no.633) went on board Lumley's ship after this incident.]

633.   David Harper   From aboard the Hopewell, 15 May 1683

I came this evening aboard of Captain Lumley, whoe I found under saile off Amersa and is now up with Anishan, and I hope tomorrow shall be in Cabo Corsoe Roade. The Captain is wounded in the right shoulder but there is good hopes of his recovery. The Royall Companys concerns are nothing embazeled, only the sayes and sheets hee had from Cabo Corsoe are taken away. They conjecture the pyrate is [blank], for they came from the West Indias and carry's a ship of 30 gunns and 150 men of all nations. They tooke Captain Norths ship before they came from the Indias, and have taken severall of good vallue since they came upon the coast. His seacond was a Dutch interloper of 24 gunns they tooke to windward, and they had

---

[94] But cf. Winder's account, no.494.
[95] Cf. the accounts by Winder and Lowe, nos 494, 637.
[96] Law 1990a, no.9 (John Winder, Whydah, 4 June 1683).

of him 70 Mk in gold, and have given him Captain Thompsons ship with both interlopers cargo's for a recompense, for the pyrates covett only gold and sayes, they will have the Companys gold they understand is att Arda if itt costs their lives. Captain Lumley presents his humble service to your honour and the rest of the Councill, desireing your honour will please to send off Docter Meade to search his wound, which his owne Docter cannot well doe, being hurt in the thumb. They have robbed Captain Lumley and all his folks of all their owne concerns and the ships furniture and provisions, soe that hee is in a verry low condition. Hee desires Docter Meade may be off with speede and bring off with him a case of lancetts and a douzen of fowles.

634. David Harper   From aboard the Hopewell, 16 May 1683

Captain Lumley heartily thanks your honour for your care in sending of Docter Meade, whoe hath searched his wound and will give your honour an account of his personall estate. The Captain saies they have left him one sett of sailes att the yards which are verry old, haveing been two voyages upon the coast before and are now soe much damnified with shott that they will not carry him off the coast, wherefore hee earnestly desires your honour would lett him know by the first what you please to command him, the Royall Company's cargoe for slaves being nothing embazled. Your honours commands are humbley desired.

[Lumley took in corn at Anomabu on 29 May 1683 (no.346). He proceeded to Whydah, where he arrived on 22 June 1683 (no.494), and from which he departed with his complement of 260 slaves in July.[97] Lumley himself died en route to Cape Lopes, which his ship reached in August (no.639).]

The *Seven Oaks*, Commander Thomas Pearson

[Pearson was reported west of Komenda on 12 April 1683 (no.107), and was a victim of the attack by pirates, who captured his attendant boat, off Anashan on 11 May (no.343). He was subsequently at Accra, 22 July (no.464), and arrived at Alampo on 5 August 1683 (no.544).

As is explained in this letter, Pearson had been Agent-General at Cape Coast in the 1660s (for the Company of Royal Adventurers Trading into Africa, the precedessor of the RAC), and had presumably been requested to give his evidence regarding rival Dutch and English claims to certain places on the coast.]

[97] Law 1990a, no.11 (John Winder, Whydah, 15 July 1683).

635.   Thomas Pearson   From aboard the Seven Oakes, 22 May 1683

Yours of the 7th currant came safe to my hand by Mr Shears. I am verry glad to heare of your health, which God continue and send you safe to England where, since it cannot conveniently be here, I hope I may have the Honour of your company. In the interim soe neare as I can remember concerning Agga Annamaboe etc. are as followeth. In June 1667 I arrived att Cabo Corsoe Castle, att which time wee had warr with the Dutch, then finding Agga demolisht and in said warr Annamaboe deserted,[98] and being courted by the natives of both places to settle, finding them to be much for the Companys interest did send whitemen and house slaves to both places. Some time after I had severall threatnings from the Dutch that if I did not deliver the possession of the said places, they would gaine them by force of armes. That not takeing effect in greate grandure they protested; that was answered; still they protested, in protesting three times, and at last [we] not submitting to their threatnings, Dirick Willree the Generall[99] made an offer to remitt the differance to the King of England and their States, which I submitted to and sent all my papers relateing to that differance to the Royall Company and the Company presented them to his Majestie in Councill. William Temple was then goeing into Holland on some other state affaires and his Majestie gave him to understand how ill hee resented the illegall proceedings of their Agents abroad. The Embassadour att his arrivall in Holland made knowne his Majesties pleasure in that particular to the States Generall, whoe immediately commanded the West India Company that they should give orders to their Agents, in noe hostile manner to disturb what interest the English nation was possest of in the time of warr, and from the Royall Company I had express commands not to relinquish a foot of ground that were then possest of, and from that time till this present I never had any dispute therein. In [16]68 from Succondee, Asshume and the Cabosheers sent downe and desired that our nation might settle att that place. I found by severall ships that had been there itt was a place verry considerable for trade and verry good landing, on which I sent Captain Cockram and another Whiteman with some quantity of goods, they stayed 8 or 10 day's, and left some of our black servants in charge of the goods, whoe sold considerable quantityes and were from time to time supplyed with what the trade required. Some of our factors every 10 or 14 dayes were there, and Asshume had the Companys flagg. The Dutch then nor before ever had any settlement or people att that place. Att Dickiscove wee found greate conveniency for corne, wood and water, especially in time of warr with the Dutch, whereupon I made a contract with

---

[98] Alluding to the second Anglo-Dutch War (1665–7). At the beginning of 1665 a Dutch squadron under de Ruyter raided the West African coast, and destroyed or captured all the English factories except Cape Coast Castle.
[99] Director-General of the Dutch West Indies Company at Elmina, 1665–74.

Dick[100] that for every ship that wooded, watered and corn'd att that place hee should have one perpettuanoe and one anchor of brandy, and for demanding the same I gave him a paper under my hand, and sent him a flagg, noe Dutch ever haveing had any pretentions to that place. If anything I have in my ship be serviceable to you pray with all freedome command itt.

The *Eaglet*, Commander John Waugh

[Waugh was reported at Cape Coast on 22 March 1683 (no.437), and took in corn at Anomabu on 17 April 1683 (no.329). He had been intended to go to Whydah,[101] but, as here explained, did not in the event do so.]

636.   John Waugh   St Thoma, 5 June 1683

Haveing this oppertunity thought good for to give you an account of my safe arrivall here to this port for to water, haveing gotten my complement of Negro's upon the Coast of Arda in 12 dayes to windward of Guydah near 15 leagues.[102] Wee have here the bad newes of the coast, for here is 2 ships that were taken by the pyrate and the men of 2 ships more in them, the one Captain Anthony Wilding, an interloper, whoe hath on board the men of a small ship that did attend on Agent Pearson, the other is a Pinke from Rotterdam that hath the men of another interloper of 24 guns belonging to Flushing, whome they all tooke to windward of Cape Trespointas. I have alsoe left neare one third of my cowries and some pautkaes and some long cloaths that came damnified from the Castle and some chercolees, which I would have sent you by this oppertunity but feareing they may miscarry by those pyrates doe resolve to carry them home. This day, God willing, doe intend to saile for Barbado's.

The *Merchants Bonadventure*, Commander John Lowe (second voyage)

[Lowe was at Accra, where he landed goods, on 20 February 1683 (no.391); at Komenda on 27 March (no.104); and at Anomabu, taking in corn, on 20–24 April (nos 331, 333).]

---

[100] i.e. the chief of Dixcove, the latter place being reportedly called 'after the Moorish captain who governs it' (Barbot 1992, ii 344).

[101] Law 1990a, no.8 (Henry Greenhill et al., Cape Coast, 19 April 1683).

[102] i.e. at Keta (cf. no.494).

637.   John Lowe   [Guydah], 10 June 1683

I am sorry I am forct to give you this sad account of our misfortune att this place, for the 16th of May past about 5 in the evening came down 2 pyrates, the one of 28 guns the other of 24, which ship shee tooke on the coast to windward and man'd out of his ship. The admirall clapt our ship aboard and after fireing many broad sides and valleys of small shott supprized our ship, the slaves on the deck 150 and my caske to cleare my hold. Come with the King's jack, ensigne and pennant, wounded 7 of my men, although they made no resistance. Entered 150 men. My mate cutt the cable, upon which hee cutt his and then laid her aboard upon the luff, att which time my people yeilded the ship. Captain Rickards his people cutt their cable and loosed the fore topsaile and put to the shoare, but before shee came ashoare, quited the ship, tooke out the gold and lett the ship and slaves drive ashoare, the which is lost and not one thing saved out of her. Captain Woollifords men quited their ship and left their gold aboard, the which the pyrates found all the next morning and an English woeman and the cooke. Att this action Captain Rickards, Woolliford and my selfe in the country purchaseing our slaves, which Woolliford might have had his slaves long before but much disobliged the blacks, though hee raised the price of booges att least 10 pounds in a slave, and told the Blacks that I was comeing downe which made them keepe their slaves for mee, which I had 150 aboard and 150 ashoare, but not goods ashoare to pay for them, and I was to be dispatcht in 9 dayes more had this not happened, but now my ship is soe much disabled that I feare shall hardly carry her to the Indias, all my low masts shott, soe that all the fishes and provisions I can make will hardly hould, all but 3 shrouds on one mast and 5 on the other gon, my foremast shott; [they have] taken all my sailes, good provisions, cordage, armes and powder with all my cloaths, gold and what was proper for them as they thought of the Company goods, as allejars, chercolees, pintado's, attlases, muzlin; and what booges on my deck and in my boate to goe ashoare, which was 6 caske, [they] throwes overboard. The next day they seized all my officers to the gunnell to shoote to death to confess for more gold, but only shott my gunners mate to death, and the other which was prevented by the English pyrates that was aboard, otherwise all the rest had dyed. Captain Rickards hath used much dilligence in looking after his gold, which was carried by his men and boate to Ofra aboard the Flemings, but broake open and greate part of itt divided amongst them, and on the news to the Flemings two of them weighed and most of his men gon with them. Hee hath gotten part of it againe and 28 marks sent home to the Company per Captain Woolliford, who sailed 2 dayes since. I have now 423 slaves on board on the Companys account and 25 on my mens account, for when the pyrate had quited the ship and had watered his ship out of her, my men desired him to give them something towards their loss, upon which hee gave them my ship, goods and slaves for their owne proper use, and ordered them that if I agreed to itt they should fire 7 gunns, if not att 8 the next morning hee would come aboard and burne her, upon which the next morning they demanded my ship, goods and slaves and to gett her to St Thoma and sell her and divide the money. I answered that itt was not in my power to give nor theirs to receive, but if they would goe about their business and refitt the ship I would find out some way to consider their loss, upon which I told them I would gett creditor for 25 slaves and send for the Factor off, whoe should allow itt and give the Company an account, and that I beleeved 25 slaves would make good all their, loss and desired them to consider whether or noe that was not a safer way, then to be like the pyrates, upon which after many disputes they fired 7 guns, and after the man of warr weighed after haveing been here 4 dayes, soe that I sent for Mr Winder aboard and satisfied him of the thing and hee told them hee would assist them with a letter to the Company to that purpose, upon which they went to worke and in 12 day's time I gott my ship in a pretty good condition and went ashoare againe. In which time Captain Woolliford bought all his slaves but how many I cannot tell. His ship was only taken by 3 prisoners which the pyrate sent aboard and brought the White woeman and the cooke and all the gold aboard. Hee saith hee hath lost greate quantity of goods, but I am sure he hath much abused Mr Winder and pretends all that goods that you sent downe to his factory is lost, and had not Captain Rickards and my brother Woolman left him [= Winder] something could not have supported. Hee hath been verry dilligent in getting part of Captain Rickards gold and my slaves, and now recovered of his sickness very serviceable to the Company. The people of this place are verry kind to him and hee obliges them well, but itt is my opinion that if you doe not send for the time forward as many ships to Ophra as this place the Companys trade will be spoyled, for after our loss when wee brought the remaines of goods ashoare the blacks plundered as well as the pyrates and could gett no satisfaction of them, and the people of Ophra att this time doe promise that if you will send ships there wee shall have a good trade, and I well know there the prizes are settled and 20 per cent less then here, for they grow upon every ship here, soe that if you think convenient to lett Mr Winder goe there and order a seacond or more to that factory and 2 or 3 to this, the two places will strive to outvey the one the other. Your advice to us came 12 houres after our ships was taken, and they stayed by the way att a place called Abrew, some 18 leagues to windward of this place, where Captain Wyborne was getting of slaves for Captain Booth,[103] and that they went on board Captain Booths ship, which gave the pyrate notice that they were a canoe for advice, upon which the pyrate weighed after them and outsailed, otherwise might have had 24 houres notice, for itt was the 17th day of May they came down and your letter of 5 dayes date.

If my brother Thompson and brother Collins be with you pray remember my love to them and tell them I would have them goe home, for their ship and goods is given to the merchant of the greate Fleming the pyrate tooke, and about 2,000

[103] i.e. Little Popo (cf. no.494).

pounds worth of goods more, and that the merchant promis'd mee to goe for Holland and that he would send the ship and her concerns for England to the owners.

[Lowe left Whydah on 19 June (no.494); he was later at Cape Lopes, from which he departed on 23 July 1683 (no.639).]

Unidentified ship, Commander Robert Bell

[Bell was at Sekondi on 11 July 1683 (no.9).]

638. Robert Bell   Commenda, 7 Aug. 1683

Yours of the 7th instant received, and the cargoe of 1905 pounds, 2 shillings and 3 pence is the windward cargoe consigned to mee, wherein the owners are concern'd 560 pounds. I have alsoe an Ardra cargoe on board but noe other. Captain Phenney's cargoe your Worship is satisfied that itt was safe received on board his owne ship, and that was all the cargoes I tooke in and those 3 cargo's I sign'd bills of loading for. I never mett with such dull trade in my life, goods beares noe price. I have on board mee att this time about 120 sayes, and as for our perpetuano's they were verry badly sorted and about two thirds green in each baile besides two redds. I have bought but 7 chests of corne. I intend to come downe with the ship God willing 5 or 6 dayes hence. In our windward cargoe I had 20 barrells of powder and that is all sold.

[Bell passed Accra without stopping in September (no.469), and proceeded to Whydah, from which he departed in October 1683.[104]]

The *Jacob*, Commander Thomas Woolman

[Woolman took in corn at Anomabu on 24 April 1683 (no.333).]

639. Thomas Woolman   On board the Jacob Pink att St Thoma, 25 Aug. 1683

This comes per Captain Smith, a Dutch Ship belonging to the Mina, to informe you of my proceedings. May the first I came downe to Guydah. What has happened since, till the 14th day of June ditto, I referr you to my brother Lowes and Mr Winders letter,[105] which day my brother and I sailed and the 22nd ditto wee come

---

[104] Law 1990a, no.13 (John Winder, Whydah, 21 Oct. 1683).
[105] i.e. nos 494, 637.

to Princes,[106] where wee found Captain Woolliford. The Governour plaid the knave with my brother and I verry much, for hee would not suffer my brother to buy any refreshment untill I had paid a slave custome. The 29th ditto I saild in company with my brother and that night parted with him, and the 8th of July I came into the Gabboone,[107] and the Prince came aboard of mee from a small island[108] and 7 more men, and shewed mee a letter from Captain Anthony Weilden which informed mee that the Prince and the natives were verry civill. I sent a man ashoare while they was aboard, and hee came off and told mee that there was but one man more upon the island. They told mee that the island was the cheifest place of trade, and bid mee fire 2 gunns to give the country people notice. The next day they came aboard and brought a small parcell of teeth and wax with them, which I bought att a reasonable rate, but they told mee I must not expect the trade to be open in less then 2 or 3 dayes. I intended to stay that time there, and then to goe further up the river. I thinking noe harme went ashoare with 3 men more, they treaded mee kindly att the first, but after I had been ashoare about 2 hourse, att my comeing away they panyard mee and all the men and beate and cutt us verry much, wee all looking for nothing but death. After a small time [we asked] why they did soe, they answered that they must have all my slaves and goods,[109] and that an English ship had been there and burnt their towne and kill'd 2 men and carryed off 13 more. I told them that the goods were none of mine and that I could not give them away, but I seeing that here was about a 100 people upon the island that was come over from the maine in a small time, fear'd that they would goe and take the vessell, there being noe more then my mate and one man and a boy aboard. I sent for the slaves and 40 iron barrs and a bunch of beades, but I haveing neither pen nor paper my mate mistooke and sent a chest of beades. After these goods were ashoare, for when they came first aboard I shewed them all my goods, they would have my powder and musketts, kettles, pintado's, booges, soe I sent for 10 kettles, 10 pintado's, 30 musketts, 1 barrell of powder, 3 plaines. After this they would have all the teeth that I bought of them and wax and severall other small things, and after they had kept mee 24 hourse, they lett mee goe. I staid three dayes att the rivers mouth to see if I could gett any Negro's off there, but could not. The 21st ditto I came to an anchor att Cape Lopas, where I found my brother Lowe, Captain Booth and Captain Howe and a Fleming bound for Angola to take in 500 slaves. My brother and Captain Rickards was verry well but has mett with a greate mortallity with his slaves. The 23rd ditto my brother sailed. There is noe trade, for the Negro's sayes that here has been 30

---

[106] Prince's Island (modern Principe).

[107] The River Gabon: for European trade here in the seventeenth century (principally for ivory, but also wax), cf. Patterson 1975, 13–15.

[108] Pongo Island, in the Gabon, which was the most powerful community in the area during the seventeenth century: cf. sources summarized in Patterson 1975, 17–24.

[109] The demand for slaves, as well as goods, is noteworthy; Europeans in the seventeenth century sometimes sold slaves at the Gabon: Patterson 1975, 14.

or 40 saile of ships within this 3 months.[110] They told mee that the privateere were here 6 weeks past with 7 saile in company with him. The 25th ditto there came one Captain Serjant that came out of the Bite, and he inform'd mee that Captain Davis was dead and a greate many of his men, and that hee had but 50 slaves in when hee came away. This Serjant is an interloper and was panyard att the Gabboones 9 dayes before mee, and that they made him pay to the vallue of 150 pounds in teeth and goods, before they lett him goe, upon which Captain How and I agreed to goe downe againe to see if I could recover satisfaction. The 26th wee sailed and mett Captain Clarke, but wee put him to a greate deale of charge, for hee tooke us to be the pyrate. Captain Thompson has tooke his passage upon Captain Howe. The 22nd [sic] ditto I came to an anchor att the rivers mouth and went up the river in Captain Howe. The 30th ditto the Prince and about 30 people more came aboard, and after they had been a small time aboard I came in sight and wee panyard the Prince and 8 men more and killed and wounded 10, and the rest leap'd over board. We kept then 6 dayes and I have gott all my owne slaves and part of my goods, but could not possibly gett all by reason of itt's being distributed up in the country, but I have gott 4 slaves and 160 weight of teeth besides my own teeth for the goods and wee lett the Prince and 2 more goe. The 11th of August I came to an anchor att Cape Lopas againe, where I found Captain Lumley's pink, but hee has been dead this 15 dayes. They have a parcell of verry good slaves and has buried but 2 since they came off the coast. The 13th ditto waid againe and the 17th ditto came unto St Thoma, where Captain How and I was clapt in prison under the pretence of our selling goods and not paying the Kings custome, but I understand better since, for they would force Captain Howe to take his provisions of the Governour and Captain and att what price they would, but I was quickly lett out againe, but Captain Howe they made him come to their price. Since I have been here I understand there has been 2 Portugeeze taken at the Gabboones after the same manner as I was, one had 60 slaves and the other 9 and they tooke all from them both and then lett them goe. I hope to find a better trade att Sherbera[111] to make up my loss time. for neither att the Gabboones nor Cape Lopas is there any trade, soe I hope your honour will not think ill of [me].

[PS] This day I think for to saile.

---

[110] Europeans mainly purchased wood and water at Cape Lopes, but there was also some trade for ivory and wax: cf. Barbot 1992, ii, 717.

[111] Sherbro, in Sierra Leone, where the RAC had a factory (on York Island), mainly for trade in dyewood, though some ivory and wax was also available (Davies 1957, 219–20).

Unidentifed ship, Commander Shilling Terry

[As explained in this letter, this ship arrived in West Africa only by accident, having been driven off course on a voyage to Madagascar.]

640.   Shilling Terry   Cabo Corsoe Roade, 3 Nov. 1683

I was when I came out from England absolutely bound for the Island St Lawrance,[112] but itt pleased God by the time I came into the lattitude of 11 degrees North lattitude I mett with the winds southerly and the raines likewise, which held us from that time per the winds, and them but small and currant that drove us upon this coast about 12 leagues to the westward of the River Cestus on the 17th July last and there lay att anchor till the 7th October, where I lost 21 of my men and all the rest of us have been sick, my selfe hardly yett recovered, but itt pleased God by a small matter of green oranges and plantins wee have, all that are left which is 15 in number, through Gods mercye indifferant well upon our leggs, and now I am come downe heither to crave your assistance, our want being wood and water and some green things from the shoare, as fruitt, cabages or sallating for the further proceeding a through cure for us, and if possible that you could spare by any meanes 4 or 5 men to helpe mee to carry our ship for Barbado's.[113] I came out in company of Captain Robert Bell. Your blackman asked mee if I saw the Companys pink to windward, I have not seene her nor any other ship of the Companys, only your small ship that is gon up for Succondee. I have been sick from the 10th September, neither my selfe nor any one in the ship have ever been here in our lives. If a canoe comes off in the morning, I shall waite on you with all my heart. This being all I can acquaint you for present.

---

[112] An alternative name for Madagascar. At this period, some English traders outside the RAC bought slaves from Madagascar, which was outside the geographical limits of the Company's monopoly: cf. Davies 1957, 100.

[113] Presumably, the ship had been intended to go to the West Indies from Madagascar (to deliver its slaves), but now abandoned its eastern voyage to go home via Barbados.

Concordance

This list gives the provenance within the Rawlinson corpus of all the documents published in this volume. The number in the present volume is given in the leftmost column; the Rawlinson location (including duplicate copies where applicable) in the rightmost.

Letter				Rawlinson C.
1	James Parris	Sekondi	25/03/83	745: 188, 236
2	Mark Bedford Whiting	,,	12/06/83	745: 206, 254
3	,,	,,	20/06/83	745: 206v, 254v
4	,,	,,	26/06/83	745: 213v, 262
5	,,	,,	27/06/83	745: 215v, 264
6	,,	,,	30/06/83	745: 217, 266
7	,,	,,	02/07/83	745: 218, 266v
8	,,	,,	09/07/83	745: 222v, 271v
9	,,	,,	12/07/83	745: 224v, 273v
10	,,	,,	27/07/83	745: 228, 276v
11	,,	,,	06/08/83	745: 231
12	,,	,,	12/08/83	745: 281
13	,,	,,	18/08/83	745: 281v
14	,,	,,	21/08/83	745: 281v
15	,,	,,	27/08/83	745: 285v
16	,,	,,	03/09/83	745: 286v
17	,,	,,	08/09/83	745: 287
18	,,	,,	09/09/83	745: 287
19	,,	,,	15/09/83	745: 288v
20	,,	,,	18/09/83	745: 290
21	,,	,,	22/09/83	745: 291v
22	,,	,,	24/09/83	745: 293
23	,,	,,	28/09/83	745: 294v
24	,,	,,	01/10/83	745: 296
25	,,	,,	03/10/83	745: 297
26	,,	,,	05/10/83	745: 298
27	,,	,,	08/10/83	745: 299v
28	,,	,,	15/10/83	745: 301
29	,,	,,	20/10/83	745: 302v
30	,,	,,	22/10/83	745: 303
31	,,	,,	27/10/83	745: 304v
32	James Nightingale	Komenda	08/11/81	745: 39, 131

33	,,	,,	09/11/81	745: 39v, 131
34	,,	,,	12/11/81	745: 40, 132
35	,,	,,	16/11/81	745: 40v, 132
36	,,	,,	18/11/81	745: 41v, 133
37	,,	,,	22/11/81	745: 42, 133
38	,,	,,	26/11/81	745: 42, 133v
39	,,	,,	29/11/81	745: 43, 134v
40	,,	,,	02/12/81	745: 56(b)v, 137
41	,,	,,	03/12/81	745: 56(b)v, 137v
42	,,	,,	04/12/81	745: 56(b)v, 137v
43	,,	,,	09/12/81	745: 56(b)v, 137v
44	,,	,,	09/12/81	745: 57, 138
45	,,	,,	10/12/81	745: 57, 138
46	,,	,,	20/12/81	745: 58, 139
47	,,	,,	20/12/81	745: 58v, 139
48	John Wender	,,	20/12/81	745: 58v, 139v
49	James Nightingale	,,	22/12/81	745: 59, 139v
50	,,	,,	28/12/81	745: 59v, 140
51	,,	,,	05/01/82	745: 61, 141v
52	,,	,,	24/01/82	745: 69, 152
53	,,	,,	19/01/82	745: 69, 152v
54	,,	,,	21/01/82	745: 70, 153v
55	,,	,,	24/01/82	745: 71v, 154(b)v
56	,,	,,	28/01/82	745: 73, 155v
57	,,	,,	01/02/82	745: 76, 158
58	,,	,,	11/02/82	745: 78v, 160v
59	,,	,,	15/02/82	745: 79, 161
60	,,	,,	20/02/82	745: 80v, 162v
61	,,	,,	23/02/82	745: 81v, 163v
62	,,	,,	03/03/82	746: 143v, 178v
63	,,	,,	03/03/82	746: 144, 179
64	,,	,,	15/03/82	746: 146v, 181v
65	,,	,,	05/04/82	746: 150v, 185v
66	,,	,,	10/04/82	746: 151v, 186v
67	,,	,,	n.d.	746: 155, 190v
68	,,	,,	01/06/82	746: 162, 197
69	,,	,,	09/06/82	746: 163, 198
70	,,	,,	24/06/82	746: 165v, 200v
71	,,	,,	02/07/82	746: 167, 202v
72	,,	,,	03/07/82	746: 167, 202v
73	,,	,,	05/07/82	746: 167v, 203
74	,,	,,	16/07/82	746: 169, 204
75	,,	,,	17/07/82	746: 169, 204v
76	David Harper	,,	02/08/82	746: 170, 206
77	James Nightingale	,,	04/08/82	746: 170, 206
78	,,	,,	14/08/82	746: 173v, 209v
79	,,	,,	17/08/82	746: 174, 210

80	,,	,,	19/08/82	746: 174v, 210v
81	,,	,,	24/08/82	746: 176v, 212v
82	,,	,,	01/09/82	746: 2, 257
83	,,	,,	08/09/82	746: 2v, 257v
84	,,	,,	10/09/82	746: 3, 238
85	David Harper	,,	10/01/83	746: 25, 281v
86	,,	,,	16/01/83	746: 26, 283v
87	,,	,,	19/01/83	746: 27, 285
88	,,	,,	24/01/83	746: 28, 286v
89	,,	,,	26/01/83	746: 28v, 287v
90	,,	,,	28/01/83	746: 29, 288
91	,,	,,	30/01/83	746: 29, 288v
92	,,	,,	08/02/83	746: 30, 290
93	,,	,,	12/02/83	746: 31v, 291
94	,,	,,	16/02/83	746: 32, 291v
95	,,	,,	23/02/83	746: 32v, 292v
96	,,	,,	24/02/83	746: 33, 292v
97	,,	,,	02/03/83	746: 41, 301
98	,,	,,	02/03/83	746: 41v, 301
99	,,	,,	05/03/83	746: 41v, 301v
100	,,	,,	07/03/83	746: 42, 302
101	,,	,,	09/03/83	746: 43, 303
102	,,	,,	11/03/83	746: 43v, 303v
103	,,	,,	18/03/83	746: 44v, 304v
104	,,	,,	27/03/83	746: 46, 306v
105	,,	,,	30/03/83	746: 46v, 306v
106	,,	,,	06/04/83	746: 185, 233
107	,,	,,	12/04/83	746: 186, 234
108	,,	,,	18/04/83	746: 186, 234
109	,,	,,	21/04/83	746: 187v, 235v
110	,,	,,	26/04/83	746: 189, 237
111	,,	,,	05/06/83	746: 192, 240
112	,,	,,	08/06/83	746: 193v, 241v
113	David March	,,	03/10/83	745: 297v
114	,,	,,	11/10/83	745: 301
115	,,	,,	17/10/83	745: 302
116	,,	,,	07/11/83	745: 306
117	Arthur Richards	Anashan	10/02/81	745: 2, 92v
118	,,	,,	20/02/81	745: 5, 95v
119	,,	,,	22/02/81	745: 5v, 96
120	,,	,,	02/03/81	745: 6v, 97v
121	,,	,,	10/03/81	745: 9, 99v
122	,,	,,	12/03/81	745: 9, 99v
123	,,	,,	05/04/81	745: 12v, 104v
124	,,	,,	07/04/81	745: 14, 105
125	,,	,,	16/04/81	745: 14v, 105v
126	,,	,,	22/04/81	745: 15, 106

127	,,	,,	03/05/81	745: 17, 107
128	,,	,,	04/05/81	745: 17, 107
129	,,	,,	10/05/81	745: 18v, 108
130	,,	,,	21/05/81	745: 20v, 109v
131	,,	,,	30/05/81	745: 23, 111v
132	,,	,,	03/06/81	745: 23, 111v
133	,,	,,	07/06/81	745: 23v, 111v
134	,,	,,	08/06/81	745: 23v, 112
135	,,	,,	18/06/81	745: 46v, 173v
136	,,	,,	22/06/81	745: 46v, 173v
137	,,	,,	13/07/81	745: 48v, 175
138	,,	,,	04/08/81	745: 49v, 176
139	,,	,,	06/08/81	745: 49v, 176v
140	,,	,,	13/08/81	745: 50, 177
141	,,	,,	17/08/81	745: 51v, 178v
142	,,	,,	24/08/81	745: 52v, 179v
143	,,	,,	02/09/81	745: 117v
144	,,	,,	03/09/81	745: 118
145	,,	,,	06/09/81	745: 35v, 127
146	,,	,,	07/09/81	745: 25, 118
147	,,	,,	11/09/81	745: 27, 120v
148	,,	,,	12/09/81	745: 27, 120v
149	,,	,,	13/09/81	745: 27v, 121
150	,,	,,	13/09/81	745: 28, 121
151	,,	,,	17/09/81	745: 28, 121v
152	,,	,,	17/09/81	745: 28, 121v
153	,,	,,	20/09/81	745: 28v, 121v
154	,,	,,	25/09/81	745: 29, 122
155	,,	,,	27/09/81	745: 29v, 122v
156	,,	,,	03/10/81	745: 31, 123v
157	,,	,,	15/10/81	745: 35, 127
158	,,	,,	19/10/81	745: 35, 127
159	,,	,,	23/10/81	745: 37, 129
160	,,	,,	07/11/81	745: 39, 130v
161	,,	,,	11/11/81	745: 40, 131v
162	,,	,,	21/11/81	745: 41v, 133
163	,,	,,	23/11/81	745: 42, 133v
164	,,	,,	27/11/81	745: 42v, 134
165	,,	,,	23/12/81	745: 59, 140
166	,,	,,	28/12/81	745: 59v, 140
167	,,	,,	02/01/82	745: 60, 140v
168	,,	,,	04/01/82	745: 60, 141
169	,,	,,	13/01/82	745: 68v, 151v
170	,,	,,	22/01/82	745: 70v, 154
171	,,	,,	01/02/82	745: 75v, 157v
172	,,	,,	02/02/82	745: 77, 159
173	,,	,,	08/02/82	745: 77v, 159v

174	,,	,,	10/02/82	745: 78, 160
175	,,	,,	12/02/82	745: 78v, 160v
176	,,	,,	17/02/82	745: 80v, 162v
177	,,	,,	02/03/82	746: 143, 178
178	,,	,,	10/03/82	746: 145, 180
179	,,	,,	13/03/82	746: 146, 181
180	,,	,,	08/04/82	746: 151, 186
181	,,	,,	09/04/82	746: 151v, 186v
182	,,	,,	05/05/82	746: 154v, 189v
183	,,	,,	20/05/82	746: 159v, 194v
184	,,	,,	01/06/82	746: 161v, 196v
185	,,	,,	20/06/82	746: 164, 199
186	,,	,,	27/06/82	746: 166v, 202
187	,,	,,	14/07/82	746: 168, 203v
188	,,	,,	15/07/82	746: 168, 203v
189	,,	,,	06/08/82	746: 172, 208
190	,,	,,	14/08/82	746: 173v, 209v
191	William Beard	,,	18/08/82	746: 174, 210
192	Richard Thelwall	,,	25/08/82	746: 176v, 212v
193	Arthur Richards	,,	02/09/82	746: 2, 257
194	Benjamin Cantrill	,,	07/09/82	746: 2v, 257v
195	,,	,,	07/09/82	746: 2v, 257v
196	,,	,,	16/09/82	746: 4v, 259v
197	,,	,,	18/09/82	746: 4v, 260
198	,,	,,	22/09/82	746: 5v, 261
199	,,	,,	05/10/82	746: 7v, 263
200	,,	,,	07/10/82	746: 8, 263v
201	,,	,,	11/10/82	746: 8, 263v
202	,,	,,	16/10/82	746: 8v, 264
203	,,	,,	17/10/82	746: 9v, 264v
204	,,	,,	19/10/82	746: 9v, 265
205	,,	,,	24/10/82	746: 10, 265
206	,,	,,	06/11/82	746: 10, 265v
207	David Harper	,,	08/11/82	746: 11, 266
208	Benjamin Cantrill	,,	12/11/82	746: 11, 266v
209	Richard Thelwall	Anomabu	07/02/81	745: 1v, 92
210	,,	,,	11/02/81	745: 2v, 93
211	,,	,,	13/02/81	745: 2v, 93
212	,,	,,	18/02/81	745: 3v, 93v
213	,,	,,	20/02/81	745: 5, 96
214	,,	,,	25/02/81	745: 6, 97
215	,,	,,	28/02/81	745: 6v, 97v
216	,,	,,	04/03/81	745: 7v, 98
217	,,	,,	10/03/81	745: 8v, 99
218	,,	,,	16/03/81	745: 10, 100v
219	,,	,,	25/03/81	745: 12, 104
220	,,	,,	02/04/81	745: 12v, 104

221	,,	,,	06/04/81	745: 13, 104v
222	,,	,,	16/04/81	745: 14v, 105v
223	,,	,,	19/04/81	745: 15, 105v
224	,,	,,	24/04/81	745: 15v, 106
225	,,	,,	12/05/81	745: 20, 108v
226	,,	,,	21/05/81	745: 21, 109v
227	,,	,,	12/06/81	745: 46v, 173
228	,,	,,	22/06/81	745: 46v, 173v
229	,,	,,	09/07/81	745: 47v, 174v
230	,,	,,	15/07/81	745: 48, 175v
231	,,	,,	12/08/81	745: 49v, 176v
232	,,	,,	10/09/81	745: 27, 120
233	,,	,,	12/09/81	745: 27, 120v
234	,,	,,	14/09/81	745: 28, 121
235	,,	,,	17/09/81	745: 28v, 121v
236	,,	,,	22/09/81	745: 28v, 122
237	,,	,,	26/09/81	745: 29, 122
238	,,	,,	27/09/81	745: 29v, 122v
239	,,	,,	30/09/81	745: 30v, 123v
240	,,	,,	30/09/81	745: 30v, 123v
241	,,	,,	13/10/81	745: 34v, 127
242	,,	,,	21/10/81	745: 36v, 128v
243	,,	,,	22/10/81	745: 36v, 128v
244	,,	,,	24/10/81	745: 37v, 129
245	,,	,,	25/10/81	745: 37v, 129v
246	,,	,,	27/10/81	745: 38, 129v
247	,,	,,	29/10/81	745: 38, 130
248	,,	,,	11/11/81	745: 39v, 131v
249	,,	,,	21/11/81	745: 41v, 133
250	,,	,,	23/11/81	745: 42, 133v
251	,,	,,	10/12/81	745: 57v, 138v
252	,,	,,	15/12/81	745: 58, 139
253	,,	,,	28/12/81	745: 59, 140
254	,,	,,	04/01/82	745: 60v, 141
255	,,	,,	12/01/82	745: 68v, 151v
256	,,	,,	13/01/82	745: 68v, 151v
257	,,	,,	16/01/82	745: 69, 152
258	,,	,,	20/01/82	745: 70, 153
259	,,	,,	01/02/82	745: 77, 159
260	,,	,,	16/02/82	745: 80, 162
261	,,	,,	02/03/82	746: 143, 178
262	,,	,,	10/03/82	746: 145, 180
263	,,	,,	13/03/82	746: 145v, 180v
264	,,	,,	14/03/82	746: 146, 181
265	,,	,,	18/03/82	746: 147v, 182v
266	,,	,,	30/03/82	746: 149v, 184v
267	,,	,,	07/04/82	746: 151, 186

268	,,	,,	08/04/82	746: 151v, 186v
269	,,	,,	13/04/82	746: 142v, 187v
270	,,	,,	20/04/82	746: 153v, 188
271	,,	,,	04/05/82	746: 154, 189
272	,,	,,	23/05/82	746: 160, 195
273	,,	,,	27/05/82	746: 160v, 195v
274	[receipts]	,,	28–29/05/82	746: 161, 196
275	Richard Thelwall	,,	03/06/82	746: 162v, 197v
276	,,	,,	20/06/82	746: 164, 199
277	,,	,,	23/06/82	746: 164v, 199v
278	,,	,,	24/06/82	746: 165, 200v
279	,,	,,	27/06/82	746: 166, 201v
280	,,	,,	29/06/82	746: 166v, 202
281	,,	,,	04/07/82	746: 167, 202v
282	,,	,,	06/07/82	746: 167v, 203
283	,,	,,	07/07/82	746: 168, 203v
284	,,	,,	16/07/82	746: 168v, 203v
285	,,	,,	19/07/82	746: 169v, 205
286	,,	,,	n.d.	746: 169v, 205
287	,,	,,	06/08/82	746: 172, 208
288	,,	,,	09/08/82	746: 172v, 208v
289	,,	,,	19/08/82	746: 174v, 210v
290	,,	,,	23/08/82	746: 176, 212
291	,,	,,	23/08/82	746: 175v, 211v
292	,,	,,	30/08/82	746: 177v, 213v
293	,,	,,	13/09/82	746: 3v, 259
294	,,	,,	14/09/82	746: 4, 259
295	[receipt]	,,	16/09/82	746: 4v, 260
296	Richard Thelwall	,,	18/09/82	746: 5, 260
297	Ambrose Meade	,,	18/09/82	746: 5, 260v
298	Richard Thelwall	,,	22/09/82	746: 5v, 260v
299	,,	,,	28/09/82	746: 5v, 261
300	,,	,,	30/09/82	746: 6, 261v
301	,,	,,	04/10/82	746: 7v, 263
302	,,	,,	12/10/82	746: 8, 263v
303	,,	,,	16/10/82	746: 8v, 264
304	[receipts]	,,	15/09–82	
			–19/10/82	746: 10v, 266
305	Richard Thelwall	,,	22/10/82	746: 9v, 265
306	,,	,,	24/10/82	746: 10, 265v
307	,,	,,	08/11/82	746: 10v, 266
308	,,	,,	15/11/82	746: 11, 266v
309	,,	,,	16/11/82	746: 11v, 267
310	,,	,,	22/11/82	746: 12v, 268
311	,,	,,	01/12/82	746: 13, 268v
312	,,	,,	07/12/82	746: 14, 269
313	,,	,,	17/12/82	746: 15, 270v

314	,,	,,	02/01/83	746: 24, 279v
315	,,	,,	04/01/83	746: 24, 280
316	,,	,,	07/01/83	746: 24v, 280
317	,,	,,	17/01/83	746: 27, 284v
318	,,	,,	18/01/83	746: 27, 284v
319	,,	,,	23/01/83	746: 27v, 286
320	,,	,,	08/02/83	746: 30, 289
321	,,	,,	09/02/83	746: 30v, 290v
322	,,	,,	12/02/83	746: 31v, 291v
323	,,	,,	28/02/83	746: 34v, 294
324	,,	,,	10/03/83	746: 43, 303
325	,,	,,	12/03/83	746: 44, 304
326	,,	,,	20/03/83	746: 45, 305
327	,,	,,	22/03/83	746: 45v, 305v
328	,,	,,	31/03/83	746: 47, 307v
329	[receipts]	,,	23/03/83	
			−17/04/83	746: 46, 306
330	Richard Thelwall	,,	19/04/83	745: 186v, 234v
331	,,	,,	20/04/83	745: 187, 235
332	Thomas Burrows	,,	20/04/83	745: 187, 235
333	[receipts]	,,	24/04/83	745: 188, 236
334	Richard Thelwall	,,	01/05/83	745: 189v, 237v
335	Thomas Burrows	,,	03/05/83	745: 190, 238
336	Richard Thelwall	,,	04/05/83	745: 190v, 238v
337	,,	,,	06/05/83	745: 192v, 240v
338	,,	,,	07/05/83	745: 193, 241
339	,,	,,	10/05/83	745: 194v, 242v
340	,,	,,	11/05/83	745: 195, 243
341	,,	,,	11/05/83	745: 195, 243
342	,,	,,	14/05/83	745: 197, 245
343	,,	,,	15/05/83	745: 197v, 245v
344	,,	,,	17/05/83	745: 199v, 247v
345	,,	,,	23/05/83	745: 202v, 250v
346	[receipts]	,,	11/04/83	
			−30/05/83	745: 185v, 233v
347	Richard Thelwall	,,	01/06/83	745: 204, 252
348	,,	,,	07/06/83	745: 204, 252
349	,,	,,	10/06/83	745: 205, 253
350	,,	,,	20/06/83	745: 207, 255
351	,,	,,	29/06/83	745: 216, 264v
352	,,	,,	07/07/83	745: 219v, 268
353	,,	,,	08/07/83	745: 220v, 269v
354	,,	,,	11/07/83	745: 224, 273
355	,,	,,	17/07/83	745: 226, 275
356	,,	,,	18/07/83	745: 226v, 275
357	,,	,,	24/07/83	745: 227v, 276
358	,,	,,	26/07/83	745: 228, 276v

359	,,	,,	29/07/83	745: 229v, 277v
360	,,	,,	03/08/83	745: 230, 278v
361	,,	,,	11/08/83	745: 280v
362	,,	,,	26/08/83	745: 285
363	,,	,,	10/09/83	745: 287v
364	,,	,,	18/09/83	745: 290v
365	,,	,,	20/09/83	745: 290v
366	,,	,,	21/09/83	745: 291
367	,,	,,	22/09/83	745: 292
368	,,	,,	25/09/83	745: 293
369	,,	,,	25/09/83	745: 293v
370	,,	,,	26/03/83	745: 294
371	,,	,,	02/10/83	745: 297
372	,,	,,	05/10/83	745: 299
373	,,	,,	27/10/83	745: 304
374	,,	,,	11/11/83	745: 306
375	Ralph Hassell	Egya	28/01/81	745: 1, 91v
376	Richard Thelwall	,,	06/02/81	745: 1v, 91v
377	Ralph Hassell	,,	13/02/81	745: 3, 93v
378	,,	,,	13/02/81	745: 3, 94
379	,,	,,	19/02/81	745: 3v, 94
380	,,	,,	23/02/81	745: 6, 96v
381	,,	,,	n.d.	745: 7, 97
382	,,	,,	03/03/81	745: 7v, 98
383	James Cunduitt	,,	04/10/81	745: 31, 124
384	Thomas Burrows	,,	08/07/83	745: 219v, 268
385	Hugh Sheares	Winneba	15/08/81	745: 50v, 178
386	,,	,,	18/08/81	745: 51v, 179
387	,,	,,	22/08/81	745: 52, 179
388	,,	,,	28/08/81	745: 53v, 181
389	Arthur Wendover	Accra	27/01/81	745: 1, 91
390	,,	,,	10/02/81	745: 2, 93
391	,,	,,	20/02/81	745: 4, 94v
392	,,	,,	20/02/81	745: 4v, 95
393	,,	,,	14/03/81	745: 10, 100
394	,,	,,	29/03/81	745: 10v, 103
395	,,	,,	25/04/81	745: 15v, 106
396	James Nightingale	,,	25/05/81	745: 22, 110v
397	Francis Franckland	,,	25/05/81	745: 45, 172
398	,,	,,	25/05/81	745: 45, 172
399	,,	,,	06/06/81	745: 46, 173
400	,,	,,	08/07/81	745: 47, 174
401	,,	,,	09/07/81	745: 47v, 175
402	William Pley	,,	14/07/81	745: 48v, 175v
403	,,	,,	18/07/81	745: 49, 176
404	,,	,,	13/08/81	745: 50v, 177v
405	Samuel Stone	,,	17/08/81	745: 51, 178

406	James Nightingale/ George Phipps	„	27/08/81	745: 53, 180v
407	James Nightingale	„	27/07/81	745: 53, 180
408	William Pley	„	08/09/81	745: 25v, 119
409	James Nightingale [inclosure]	„	n.d. 09/09/81	745: 25, 118 745: 117
410	James Nightingale	„	10/09/81	745: 26v, 119v
411	William Pley	„	28/09/81	745: 30, 123
412	Ralph Hassell	„	07/10/81	745: 31v, 124v
413	William Pley	„	07/10/81	745: 34, 126v
414	Ralph Hassell	„	11/10/81	745: 32, 124v
415	„	„	18/10/81	745: 35v, 127v
416	William Pley	„	22/10/81	745: 37, 129
417	Ralph Hassell	„	25/10/81	745: 36, 128
418	„	„	31/10/81	745: 38v, 130
419	William Pley	„	12/11/81	745: 41, 132v
420	Ralph Hassell	„	17/11/81	745: 41, 132v
421	„	„	27/11/81	745: 42v, 134
422	„	„	12/12/81	745: 57v, 138v
423	Ralph Hassell/ William Pley	„	23/01/82	745: 71, 154
424	Ralph Hassell	„	01/02/82	745: 76v, 158v
425	„	„	23/02/82	745: 82v, 164
426	„	„	12/03/82	746: 145v, 180v
427	„	„	18/03/82	746: 147, 182
428	„	„	25/03/82	746: 148v, 183v
429	„	„	03/04/82	746: 150, 185
430	„	„	03/04/82	746: 150, 185
431	„	„	22/04/82	746: 159v, 194v
432	„	„	01/06/82	746: 161v, 197
433	„	„	25/06/82	746: 165v, 201
434	„	„	05/08/82	746: 170v, 206v
435	„	„	09/08/82	746: 173, 209
436	„	„	28/08/82	746: 177, 213
437	„	„	02/10/82	746: 6v, 262
438	„	„	02/10/82	746: 7, 262v
439	„	„	16/10/82	746: 9, 264v
440	„	„	17/11/82	746: 11v, 267
441	„	„	16/12/82	746: 14v, 269v
442	„	„	26/12/82	746: 23, 278
443	„	„	29/12/82	746: 23v, 278v
444	„	„	31/12/82	746: 24, 279
445	„	„	08/01/83	746: 24v, 280v
446	„	„	14/01/83	746: 25v, 282
447	„	„	07/02/83	746: 29v, 289
448	„	„	20/02/83	746: 32v, 292
449	„	„	08/03/83	746: 42, 302

450	,,	,,	09/03/83	746: 42v, 302v
451	,,	,,	14/03/83	746: 44, 304
452	,,	,,	22/03/83	746: 45, 305
453	,,	,,	05/05/83	745: 190v, 238v
454	,,	,,	14/05/83	745: 196, 244
455	,,	,,	22/05/83	745: 200v, 248v
456	,,	,,	12/06/83	745: 205, 253
457	,,	,,	03/07/83	745: 218v, 267
458	,,	,,	09/07/83	745: 221, 269v
459	Robert Young	,,	11/07/83	745: 223v, 272
461	Robert Young/			
	James Nightingale	,,	12/07/83	745: 224v, 273
461	James Nightingale	,,	13/07/83	745: 225, 273v
462	Robert Young/			
	James Nightingale	,,	13/07/83	745: 225v, 274
463	Robert Young	,,	13/07/83	745: 226, 274v
464	,,	,,	22/07/83	745: 226v, 275v
465	,,	,,	02/08/83	745: 229v, 278
466	,,	,,	08/08/83	745: 280
467	,,	,,	24/08/83	745: 282
468	,,	,,	02/09/83	745: 286
469	,,	,,	13/09/83	745: 288
470	,,	,,	23/09/83	745: 292
471	,,	,,	29/09/83	745: 295
472	,,	,,	09/10/83	745: 300
473	,,	,,	22/10/83	745: 303
474	,,	,,	23/10/83	745: 304
475	,,	,,	01/11/83	745: 305
476	John Thorne	Whydah	24/05/81	745: 62, 143v
477	William Cross	Offra	18/08/81	745: 62v, 144
	[inclosure]		18/08/81	745: 66, 149
478	John Thorne	,,	19/08/81	745: 64, 145v
	[inclosure]			745: 66v, 149v
479	John Thorne	,,	04/12/81	745: 64v, 146v
	[inclosure]			745: 66, 149
480	John Thorne	,,	18/12/81	745: 65(b)v, 148
	[inclosure 1]			745: 67v, 150
	[inclosure 2]			745: 66, 149v
481	Petley Wyburne	Whydah	08/01/82	745: 65v, 148v
482	John Thorne	Offra	23/03/82	745: 156, 190v
483	John Winder	,,	23/03/82	745: 156, 191
484	Arthur Wendover	Apa	17/07/82	746: 35, 294v
485	Andrew Crosbie	Whydah	01/09/82	746: 15v, 271
486	,,	,,	01/09/82	746: 16, 272
487	Timothy Armitage	,,	24/10/82	746: 17, 272v
	[inclosure 1]		10/10/82	746: 18, 273
	[inclosure 2]			746: 19v, 274v

	[inclosure 3]		22/10/82	746: 18v, 274
488	Timothy Armitage	,,	28/10/82	746: 17v, 273
	[inclosure]		24/10/82	746: 19. 275v
489	Timothy Armitage	,,	28/10/82	746: 17v, 273v
490	,,	,,	05/12/82	746: 20v, 276
491	Petley Wyburne	,,	08/12/82	746: 22, 277
492	John Thorne	Offra	28/01/83	746: 38v, 298
	[inclosure]		27/06/82	746: 34v, 294
493	John Winder	Whydah	15/03/83	746: 40, 299v
494	,,	,,	24/06/83	746: 210v, 259
495	Petley Wyburne	,,	26/06/83	746: 213, 261v
496	Samuel Starland	*African Merchant*	03/08/81	745: 49, 176
497	,,	,,	06/08/81	745: 49v, 176v
498	,,	,,	28/08/81	745: 52, 179v
499	,,	,,	28/08/81	745: 53, 180v
500	,,	,,	29/08/81	745: 53v, 181
501	,,	Anashan	27/09/81	745: 29v, 122v
502	,,	*African Merchant*	30/09/81	745: 31, 123v
503	,,	,,	02/01/83	745: 59v, 140v
504	,,	,,	05/01/82	745: 60v, 141v
505	,,	,,	11/01/82	745: 61v, 142v
506	,,	Winneba Road	27/03/82	746: 149, 184
507	,,	Mumfort Road	03/04/82	746: 149v, 184v
508	Samuel Starland/ Arthur Richards	Anashan Road	04/05/82	746: 154, 189
509	Samuel Starland	Anashan Road	12/05/82	746: 155, 190
510	,,	*African Merchant*	30/05/82	746: 161, 196
511	,,	,,	11/06/82	746: 163v, 198v
512	,,	,,	23/06/82	746: 164, 199v
513	,,	,,	06/08/82	746: 172v, 208
514	,,	Mouri Road	23/08/82	746: 175v, 211v
515	George Phipps	Anomabu	17/08/81	745: 51, 178
516	James Nightingale	,,	17/08/81	745: 51v, 178v
517	Hugh Shears	Anomabu Road	09/10/81	745: 34v, 126v
518	,,	Alampo	30/10/81	745: 38, 130
519	,,	*John*	02/01/82	745: 60, 140
520	,,	,,	30/01/82	745: 73v, 156
521	,,	Komenda Road	04/04/82	746: 150v, 186v
522	,,	Mouri Road	23/08/82	746: 175, 211
523	Charles Towgood	*Cape Coast*	05/03/82	746: 144, 179
524	,,	Alampo Road	17/03.82	746: 147, 182
525	,,	,,	19/03/82	746: 148, 183
526	,,	,,	24/03/82	746: 148, 183
527	,,	Komenda Road	13/04/82	746: 152, 187
528	,,	,,	15/04/82	746: 153, 188
529	,,	Charles Fort	27/05/82	746: 160v, 195v
530	,,	*Cape Coast*	23/06/82	746: 164v, 200

531	,,	,,	06/08/82	746: 171v, 207v
532	,,	,,	23/08/82	746: 1766, 212
533	Hugh Shears	Alampo	30/09/82	746: 6, 261v
534	,,	Anomabu Road	29/10/82	746: 10, 265v
535	,,	Mina River	28/11/82	746: 12v, 268
536	,,	,,	24/02/83	746: 33v, 293
537	,,	off Anomabu	27/02/83	746: 34, 293v
538	,,	*Cape Coast*	15/05/83	745: 198v, 246v
539	,,	,,	21/05/83	745: 199v, 247v
540	,,	,,	26/05/83	745: 203, 251
541	,,	,,	29/05/83	745: 203v, 251v
542	,,	,,	08/06/83	745: 204v, 252v
543	,,	,,	29/08/83	745: 229, 277v
544	,,	,,	06/08/83	745: 231
545	,,	,,	25/08/83	745: 284v
546	,,	,,	22/09/83	745: 291
547	,,	,,	28/09/83	745: 295
548	,,	,,	10/10/83	745: 300v
549	Charles Towgood	*Ann*	05/12/82	746: 13, 268v
550	,,	,,	07/12/82	746: 14, 269v
551	,,	,,	26/12/82	746: 22v, 278
552	,,	,,	29/12/82	746: 23v, 279
553	,,	,,	09/02/83	746: 31, 290v
554	,,	,,	11/02/83	746: 31, 291
555	,,	,,	24/02/83	746: 33v, 293v
556	,,	,,	12/05/83	745: 195v, 243v
557	,,	,,	15/05/83	745: 197, 245
558	,,	,,	03/07/83	745: 219, 267v
559	,,	,,	11/07/83	745: 223, 272
560	David Harper	*Adventure*	30/06/83	745: 216, 264v
561	John Groome	,,	30/06/83	745: 216v, 265
562	,,	Alampo	09/07/83	745: 221v, 270
563	David Harper	*Adventure*	09/07/83	745: 222, 271
564	,,	,,	05/08/83	745: 230v, 278v
635	John Groome	Anomabu	08/08/83	745: 280
566	,,	Accra	28/08/83	745: 282v
567	,,	Alampo	15/09/83	745: 288v
568	,,	,,	18/09/83	745: 289v
569	,,	*Adventure*	29/09/83	745: 295v
570	Thomas Draper	*Unity*	25/08/83	745: 284v
571	,,	,,	29/08/83	745: 285v
572	,,	Accra	13/09/83	745: 287v
573	,,	*Unity*	16/09/83	745: 289
574	James Nightingale	Anomabu	25/02/81	745: 6v, 97v
575	,,	Winneba	09/03/81	745: 8, 98v
576	James Nightingale/ Robert Hollings	Alampo	25/03/81	745: 11, 101v

577	Robert Hollings	„	25/03/81	745: 11v,102
578	Charles Bowler	*Edgar*	25/03/81	745: 11v,102v
579	James Nightingale	Alampo	06/04/81	745: 13, 104v
580	James Nightingale/			
	Robert Hollings	„	11/04/81	745: 14, 105v
581	Charles Bowler	*Edgar*	20/04/81	745: 15, 106
582	James Nightingale/			
	Robert Hollings	„	25/04/81	745: 16, 106v
583	Charles Bowler	„	25/04/81	745: 16v, 106v
584	James Nightingale/			
	Robert Hollings	Winneba	07/05/81	745: 17v, 107v
585	James Nightingale	„	07/05/81	745: 18, 107v
586	„	„	11/05/81	745: 18v, 108
587	Charles Bowler	*Edgar*	11/05/81	745: 19v, 108v
588	„	Winneba	15/05/81	745: 20, 109
589	James Nightingale	„	15/05/81	745: 20v, 109
590	„	„	20/05/81	745: 21, 109v
591	Robert Hollings	*Edgar*	23/05/81	745: 21v, 110
592	John Lowe/	*Merchant Bonadventure*		
	Thomas Goulding		18/04/81	745: 62, 143
593	Andrew Branfill	[n.p.]	23/05/81	745: 21, 109v
594	William Todd	*Alexander*	02/06/81	745: 46, 172v
595	„	Alampo	13/07/81	745: 48, 175
596	Andrew Branfill	Offra	18/08/81	745: 63v, 145v
597	Samuel Rickard	*Unblessed Blessing*	13/08/81	745: 50, 177
598	„	[n.p.]	20/08/81	745: 52, 179
599	Abraham Wise	[Offra]	14/11/81	745: 64v, 146v
600	Abraham Cooke	*Vine*	19/08/81	745: 51v, 179
601	Giles Lawrence	*Lion*	26/08/81	745: 52v, 180
602	Arthur Wendover	Winneba Road	05/01/82	745: 61v, 142v
603	Edward Hill	Anomabu	25/01/82	745: 72v, 155
604	„	„	26/01/82	745: 73, 155
605	„	*Charles*	31/01/82	745: 74, 156v
606	„	Anomabu	10/02/82	745: 78, 160
607	„	„	03/03/82	746: 143v, 178v
608	„	[n.p.]	25/04/82	746: 153v, 188v
609	John Smith/			
	John Winder	*John Bonadventure*	30/01/82	745: 74, 156
610	„	„	01/02/82	745: 74v, 156v
611	Daniel Gates	*Alapeen*	01/02/82	745: 75, 157
612	„	„	18/02/82	745: 78, 160
613	„	Alampo	06/03/82	746: 144, 179v
614	„	*Alapeen*	17/03/82	746: 146v, 184v
615	Thomas Attwell	*Arcanie Merchant*	15/04/82	746: 152v, 187v
616	„	Anomabu Road	25/04/82	746: 153v, 188v
617	„	„	28/05//82	746: 160v, 195v
618	Richard Shepherd	*St George*	04/06/82	746: 162v, 197v

619	„	„	06/06/82	746: 163, 198
620	„	[Whydah]	05/07/82	746: 15v, 271
621	George Bathurst	Anomabu	16/07/82	746: 168v, 204
622	Richard North	„	05/08/82	746: 170v, 206v
623	Timothy Armitage	„	05/08/82	746: 171, 207
624	Richard North	„	09/08/82	746: 173, 209
625	Robert Ware	„	21/08/82	746: 175, 211
626	Lott Ambrose	[Anomabu]	13/09/82	746: 3v, 258v
627	„	„	15/09/82	746: 4, 259
628	Henry Nurse	*Mary*	01/10/82	746: 6v, 262
629	Andrew Branfill	[n.p.]	n.d.	746: 15v, 271
630	William Maple	Cape Coast	15/01/83	746: 26, 283
631	William Williford	[Guydah]	09/05/83	745: 207, 255
632	„	„	09/06/83	745: 208, 256
633	David Harper	*Hopewell*	15/05/83	745: 198, 246
634	„	„	16/05/83	745: 199, 247
635	Thomas Pearson	*Seven Oaks*	22/05/83	745: 201v, 249v
636	John Waugh	*Eaglet*	05/06/83	745: 207v, 255v
637	John Lowe	[Whydah]	10/06/83	745: 208v, 256v
638	Robert Bell	Komenda	07/08/83	745: 231v
639	Thomas Woolman	*Jacob*	25/08/83	745: 282v
640	Shilling Terry	Cape Coast Road	03/11/83	745: 305v

Bibliography

Akinjogbin, I.A., 1967: *Dahomey and its Neighbours 1708–1818* (Cambridge).

Atkins, John, 1735: *A Voyage to Guinea, Brasil and the West India* (repr. London, 1970).

Barbot, Jean, 1992: *Barbot on Guinea: The writings of Jean Barbot on West Africa 1678–1712*, Ed. P.E.H. Hair, Adam Jones & Robin Law. 2 vols (Hakluyt Society, London).

Bosman, William, 1705: *A New and Accurate Description of the Coast of Guinea* (repr. London, 1967).

Daaku, Kwame Yeboah, 1970: *Trade and Politics on the Gold Coast 1600–1720* (Oxford).

Davies, K.G., 1957: *The Royal African Company* (London).

Debien, G. & Houdaille, J., 1964: 'Les origines des esclaves aux Antilles: sur une sucrérie de la Guyane en 1690', *Bulletin de l'IFAN*, série B, 26: 166–94.

Delbée, 1671: 'Journal du voyage du Sieur Delbée', in J. de Clodoré (ed.): *Relation de ce qui 'est passé dans les Isles er Terre-ferme de l'Amérique, pendant la dernière guerre avec l'Angleterre, et depuis en exécution du Traitté de Breda* (Paris), ii, 347–473.

'Documenta' 1915: 'Documenta ad historiam Missionis Guineae spectantia', *Analecta Ordinis Minorum Cappucinorum*, 21: 327–38, 357–9.

Greene, Sandra E., 1988: 'Social change in eighteenth-century Anlo: the role of technology, markets and military conflict', *Africa*, 58: 70–86.

Groeben, Otto Friedrich von der, 1985: 'Otto Friedrich von der Groeben's account of his voyage to Guinea', in Adam Jones (ed.): *Brandenburg Sources for West African History 168–1700* (Sttuttgart, 1985), 23–57.

Henige, David, 1972a: 'A new source for English activities on the Gold Coast, 1681–99', *Transactions of the Historical Society of Ghana*, 13/2: 257–60.

Henige, David, 1972b: 'A Guide to Rawlinson C.745–747 (Bodleian Library, Oxford): Correspondence from the Outforts to Cape Coast Castle, 1681–1699', typescript (University of Madison-Wisconsin).

Henige, David, 1975: 'Adom/Supome and Jabi/Yarbiw: cases of identity in a period of shifting paramountcies', *Transactions of the Historical Society of Ghana*, 16/1: 29–45.

Inikori, Joseph E., 1992: 'The volume of the British slave trade, 1655–1807', *Cahiers d'Études Africaines*, 32: 643–88.

Jones, Adam (ed.), 1985: *Brandenburg Sources for West African History 1680–1700* (Stuttgart).

Kea, Ray A., 1982: *Settlements, Trade and Polities in the Seventeenth-Century Gold Coast* (Baltimore).

Latham, A.J.H., 1973: *Old Calabar 1600–1891* (Oxford).

Law, Robin, 1977: 'Royal monopoly and private enterprise in the Atlantic trade: the case of Dahomey', *Journal of African History*, 18: 555–77.

Law, Robin, 1983: 'Trade and politics behind the Slave Coast: the lagoon traffic and the rise of Lagos, 1500–1800', *Journal of African History*, 24: 321–48.

Law, Robin, 1989: 'Between the sea and the lagoons: the interaction of maritime and inland navigation on the pre-colonial Slave Coast', *Cahiers d'Études Africaines*, 29: 201–29.

Law, Robin (ed.), 1990a: *Correspondence from the Royal African Company's Factories at Offra and Whydah on the Slave Coast of West Africa in the Public Record Office, London, 1678–93* (Centre of African Studies, University of Edinburgh, Occasional Paper No.24).

Law, Robin, 1990b: 'The gold trade of Whydah in the seventeenth and eighteenth centuries', in David Henige & T.C. McCaskie (eds): *West African Economic and Social History: Studies in memory of Marion Johnson* (African Studies Program, University of Wisconsin-Madison), 105–18.

Law, Robin, 1991a: *The Slave Coast of West Africa 1550–1750: The impact of the Atlantic Slave Trade on an African society* (Oxford).

Law, Robin, 1991b: 'Computing domestic prices in precolonial West Africa: a methodological exercise from the Slave Coast', *History in Africa*, 18: 239–57.

Law, Robin (ed.), 1992: *Further Correspondence of the Royal African Company of England relating to the 'Slave Coast', 1681–1699: Selected documents from Ms Rawlinson C.745–747 in the Bodleian Library, Oxford* (African Studies Program, University of Wisconsin-Madison).

Law, Robin, 1993: 'The Royal African Company of England's West African correspondence, 1681–1699', *History in Africa*, 20: 173–84.

Ly, Abdoulaye, 1958: *La Compagnie du Sénégal* (Paris).

Nørregård, Georg, 1966: *Danish Settlements in West Africa 1658–1850* (Boston).

Patterson, K. David, 1975: *The Northern Gabon Coast to 1875* (Oxford).

Phillips, Thomas, 1732: 'A journal of a voyage made in the Hannibal of London', in Awnsham Churchill & John Churchill: *Collection of Voyages and Travels* (6 vols, London), vi, 187–255.

Ryder, A.F.C., 1969: *Benin and the Europeans 1485–1897* (London).

Tattersfield, Nigel, 1991: *The Forgotten Trade, comprising the Log of the Daniel and Henry of 1700 and accounts of the slave trade from the minor ports of England, 1698–1715* (London).

Thilmans, G. & de Moraes, N.I, 1976: 'Villault de Bellefond sur la Côte occidentale d'Afrique: les deux premières campagnes de l'*Europe* (1666–71)', *Bulletin de l'IFAN*, série B, 38: 257–99.

Tilleman, Erick, 1994: *En Kort og Enfoldig Bretning om det Lanskab Guinea og dets Beskaffenhed (1697)*, trans. & ed. Selena Axelrod Winsnes (African Studies Program, University of Wisconsin-Madison).

Van Dantzig, Albert, 1976: 'Rawlinson C.745–746: A Selection of Letters from Offra and Whydah', typescript (University of Ghana, Legon).

Van Dantzig, Albert (ed.), 1978: *The Dutch and the Guinea Coast 1674–1742: A collection of documents from the General State Archive at The Hague* (Ghana Academy of Arts & Sciences, Accra).

Van Dantzig, Albert, 1980: *Les hollandais sur la Côte de Guinée à l'époque de l'essor de l'Ashanti et de Dahomey 1680–1740* (Paris).

Van Dantzig, Albert, 1984: 'Some late seventeenth century British views on the Slave Coast', in François de Medeiros (ed.): *Peuples du Golfe du Bénin* (Paris), 71–85.

Van Dantzig, Albert, 1990: 'The Akanists: a West African Hansa', in David Henige & T.C. McCaskie (eds): *West African Economic and Social History: Studies in memory of Marion Johnson* (African Studies Program, University of Wisconsin-Madison), 205–16.

Verger, Pierre, 1968: *Flux et reflux de la traite des nègres entre le Golfe de Bénin et Bahia de Todos os Santos* (Paris).

Vogt, John, 1979: *Portuguese Rule on the Gold Coast, 1469–1682* (Athens, Ga.).

Wilks, Ivor, 1959: 'The rise of the Akwamu empire, 1650–1710', *Transactions of the Historical Society of Ghana*, 3/2: 99–136.

Indexes

[NB: Numbers refer to documents, not pages]

Places and Peoples

Persons

Ships
[Commanders, where known, in brackets]

Selected Topics